the cinema of PAOLO SORRENTINO

DIRECTORS' CUTS

Directors' Cuts

Directors' Cuts focus on the work of the most significant contemporary international filmmakers, illuminating the creative dynamics of world cinema.

For a full list of titles, see pages 233–34.

the cinema of
PAOLO SORRENTINO

commitment to style

russell j. a. kilbourn

WALLFLOWER NEW YORK

Wallflower Press is an imprint of Columbia University Press.
Columbia University Press
Publishers Since 1893
New York   Chichester, West Sussex
cup.columbia.edu
Copyright © 2020 Columbia University Press
All rights reserved

Library of Congress Cataloging-in-Publication Data
Names: Kilbourn, Russell J. A. (Russell James Angus), 1964– author.
Title: The cinema of Paolo Sorrentino : commitment to style / Russell J. A. Kilbourn.
Description: New York : Wallflower Press, [2020] | Series: Directors' cuts |
    Includes bibliographical references and index.
Identifiers: LCCN 2019046912 (print) | LCCN 2019046913 (ebook) |
    ISBN 9780231189927 (cloth) | ISBN 9780231189934 (paperback) |
    ISBN 9780231548625 (ebook)
Subjects: LCSH: Sorrentino, Paolo—Criticism and interpretation.
Classification: LCC PN1998.3.S623 K55 2020 (print) | LCC PN1998.3.S623 (ebook) |
    DDC 791.4302/33092—dc23
LC record available at https://lccn.loc.gov/2019046912
LC ebook record available at https://lccn.loc.gov/2019046913

Columbia University Press books are printed on permanent and durable acid-free paper.
Printed in the United States of America

Cover image: Photo 12/Alamy Stock Photo

To my mother

CONTENTS

ACKNOWLEDGMENTS

IN KEEPING WITH the settings of some of Sorrentino's best-known films, this book came into being between Venice, where my wife, Sandra Parmegiani, first suggested it, and Rome, at a 2017 conference at the American University on "Innovations and Tensions: Italian Cinema and Media in a Global World." Not only did I receive invaluable feedback on early versions of certain chapters, I also made the acquaintance of a wonderful group of talented and cosmopolitan people from around the world. I therefore thank my colleagues in the field of Italian film and media studies: Chiara Mariani, Flavia Laviosa, Dana Renga, Catherine O'Rawe, Alan O'Leary, Alex Marlow-Mann, Frank Burke, Marguerite Waller, Danielle Hipkins, and Nicoletta Marini-Maio. Without their individual and collective advice and inspiration, this book would not only lack altogether a chapter on *Loro*, it would simply not exist. If it already also lacks a chapter or two on even newer material, then we can only thank Sorrentino the filmmaker for continuing to be so prolific, provocative, and engaged.

I also thank the editorial team at Columbia University Press, who present a model of professionalism and ongoing support for film studies as a discipline whose insights have a greater urgency today then ever before.

I gratefully acknowledge that the financial support for the research for this book was received from a grant funded by Wilfrid Laurier University's Office of the Dean of Arts and Faculty of Graduate Studies and Research.

INTRODUCTION

Commitment to Style

> Melancholy, nostalgia, and the relationship with solitude. These are the dominant
> themes that traverse all my films.
> —Paolo Sorrentino, interview with Alain Elkann

IT WOULD BE easy to proclaim Italian director Paolo Sorrentino the answer to the
decades-long dearth in Italian cinema of anything resembling a *grande auteur*—a
cinematic authorial presence in the tradition of Fellini, Antonioni, Rossellini, De Sica,
Visconti, Pasolini, Bertolucci, and others, all male.[1] In certain ways Sorrentino
is a throwback to the golden age of Italian auteurist cinema, writing (or cowriting,
with Umberto Contarello) and directing all of his feature films.[2] In 2009 he was
hailed as "one of the most promising young directors of the new millennium,"[3] and
in the same year, after *Il Divo* (2008) won the Jury Prize at Cannes the year before,
Guido Bonsaver remarked that this "confirmed Paolo Sorrentino as the most promising Italian director of his generation."[4] Alex Marlow-Mann describes him as "one
of the most interesting filmmakers to have emerged" in postmillennial Italy, producing work "distinct from anything in contemporary Italian or perhaps, world
cinema,"[5] and yet in a 2013 collection on popular Italian cinema Sorrentino gets
no mention at all.[6] While new books in Italian on Sorrentino's oeuvre (or aspects
thereof) are appearing at an increasing rate, as of this writing there is no comprehensive overview of Sorrentino's film and television work in English.[7] The present book
addresses this lack of attention—more pronounced in the critical literature than in
the popular discourse, and in English rather than in Italian—considering Sorrentino
as both a leading Italian director and as a representative twenty-first-century Euro-
transnational filmmaker. The designation of *transnational*, it must be said, applies
equally to the style and to the diegetic content of his cinema and television work.
In this book therefore I focus as much on the meaning and value of Sorrentino's
allegedly mannered audio-visual style as on the content of his film's diverse stories.
As will be explored at length, these stories, and the distinctive manner of their telling,
are linked in complex ways through the protagonist in each case, representing a
series of variations on what I call the Sorrentinian subject.

By subject or subjectivities here I refer to human types, conventional social roles, performative identity categories, and so forth[8]—as opposed to the subject of Freudian, Lacanian, or feminist psychoanalytic theory that until the 1990s or so was privileged in much contemporary film analysis. The new millennium has brought new paradigms of film theory; for instance the variations on affect theory (and related approaches), which are certainly of relevance to this study. In what seems a necessary recursion to an earlier period in the history of film theory, others have analysed Sorrentino's films from a feminist-psychoanalytic perspective.[9] More broadly (and still in historical perspective), feminist theorists of melodrama in the 1980s and 1990s identified the "over-valuation of masculinity" as a fundamental problem in North American mainstream culture.[10] Therefore I introduce the category of melodrama here for good reason: as will be seen below, and especially in chapter 8 on *The Young Pope* (2016), the ubiquity of melodrama as a (generally gendered) cultural modality has to be seen in a transnational perspective, with Italian neorealism as a significant formative period—witness any of the major films, from *Rome Open City* (1945) to *The Bicycle Thieves* (1948) to *Umberto D.* (1952) to later works, such as Visconti's *Rocco and His Brothers* (1960), whose scenery-chewing boxing coach is a precursor to the verbally abusive soccer coach in *One Man Up*'s (2001) second opening scene. Outside of Italian film, classical Hollywood provides the more famous model for melodrama, in the form of various genres, from weepies to the woman's picture to what eventually becomes the television soap opera. But for our purposes here the most interesting aspect of melodrama as pervasive cultural mode is its adaptability across a variety of national cinemas to masculine narratives: stories of men structured around classic melodramatic tropes.[11]

My approach in this book therefore draws equally from this rich branch of feminist-infused poststructuralist theory and the kind of post-Marxist ideological critique typical of cultural studies. It goes beyond both, however, insofar as the former in its psychoanalytic guise is too prone to reducing every film narrative to an allegory of the Oedipal family romance, and every female body to a cipher for castration anxiety; the latter (cultural studies), for its part, tends to deprivilege film form in favor of story content as the basis of an insufficiently critical view of realism. In film, after all, any so-called unconscious dimension, like everything else, is right on the surface.[12] Throughout film history, even the most intimate moments of subjective interiority, if they are manifested on screen, end up looking (and sounding) much the same as everything else. I use the term *subject* therefore in a philosophical or narratological sense, as ground for identity or self, as concatenation of attributes or traits. But by *subject* I also mean a visual-optical position in space, a mobile point-of-view upon the objective world, upon others, or the other. Historically, in the occidental tradition in which my argument is necessarily based, this subject is silently but inescapably gendered masculine. In a fundamental sense, then, my analysis of Sorrentino's oeuvre is reducible to his contribution, for better or worse, to the ongoing legacy of this subject; to the representation, in short, of masculinity in the film, television, and literary work.[13]

The other aspect of this subject, of course, is the question of identification, which includes everything summed up in Laura Mulvey's psychoanalytic theory of the male gaze, but much more besides.[14] Spectatorial identification with this or that film character may be productively considered in relation to theories of affect—both the affective experience of the viewer and the affects or intensities circulating on-screen and on the soundtrack—as well as with cognitive theory. Identification—what Murray Smith (1995) refers to in terms of "levels of engagement"[15]—is always reducible to some kind of visual-cognitive-emotional structure, which Smith helpfully addresses in the dyad of allegiance vs. alignment. Marlow-Mann makes effective use of Smith's categories in his groundbreaking readings of Sorrentino's first films, connecting their complex manipulation of the viewer's cognitive and/or emotional engagement with this or that character to the director's penchant for recurring character types, or what I refer to as the Sorrentinian subject:

> One of the most immediately obvious characteristics of [Sorrentino's] work is a penchant for ambiguous or downright unsympathetic protagonists, and [his] decision to make a film on such an ambivalent and oft-despised figure as Giulio Andreotti instantiates a tendency that began with his portrayal of the arrogant, self-absorbed, middle-aged pop singer with a predilection for cocaine and casual sex, Tony Pisapia, in his debut, *L'uomo in più*. The extent to which the spectator is, or is not, encouraged to "identify" with such atypical protagonists constitutes one of the most unusual and distinctive elements of Sorrentino's films.[16]

Questions of spectatorial identification or engagement are tied up with the viewer's identity, especially with respect to gender construed in conventional binaristic terms. Therefore, as unfashionable as it may sound, it is necessary to grapple with the question of realism in any critical appraisal of Sorrentino's cinema.[17]

Beyond Realism: Toward a Cinematic Ethics

In *Theory of Film* (1997) Siegfried Kracauer identifies what he calls the two main tendencies in film style from its origins in the late nineteenth century: the realist and the formative, or what we might call illusionism, each of which entails a distinct valuation of cinema's function as audiovisual medium.[18] Considering Sorrentino in relation to this highly artificial but heuristically useful binary illuminates his distance from a neorealist conception of film as a way of forging an ethical relation to a specific social reality, in contrast to his openness to the notion of art as a form of lying—a trick (*un trucco*), as Jep Gambardella would say, only one that discloses a more substantive truth about the fundamental nature of cinema.[19] This binary is complicated by recent reassessments of Andre Bazin's work on Italian neorealism and of cinematic realism generally as an ethical stance toward the world.[20] This is a point Dudley Andrew makes in his foreword to Rosalind Galt and Karl Schoonover's *Global Art Cinema*, where he cites "Bazin's incomparably crucial distinction between realism as a set of conventions and neorealism as a moral attitude toward the alterity of what is nearby."[21] Andrew invokes Visconti's *La terra trema* (1948) as an example of this kind of film that bridges the gap between local vernacular—both the distinctive

Sicilian dialect and the specifics of Italian neorealist style—and a more international approach to film language foundational to the new modernist art cinema: "Modernist cinema arose when new realities . . . in postwar Italy forced filmmakers into concocting ingenious narrative and stylistic strategies to bring them onto the plane of expression."[22] Analogously, every Italian filmmaker since has had to face this double challenge, at once negotiating and balancing the internal legacy of neorealism and the external demands of the global marketplace. Sorrentino is a recent, spectacular, and particularly successful example.

> Galt and Schoonover define the art cinema as congenitally "impure":[23] art cinema has from its beginnings forged a relationship between the aesthetic and the geopolitical or, in other words, between cinema and the world. Thus it is the critical category best placed to engage pressing contemporary questions of globalization, world culture, and how the economics of cinema's transnational flows might intersect with trajectories of film form.[24]

My invocation of the term *art film* or *art cinema* therefore is not indicative of a lack of historical understanding or an attempt to apply an anachronistic term to a contemporary body of work. What Dudley Andrew calls the "third *optique*"—after the first two: "national folk films" and "global entertainment movies"[25]—art cinema remains a useful and, dare I say, necessary category, as long as it is qualified by an adjective such as *global, international*, or, as I favor here, *transnational*. This contemporary brand of art cinema, as exemplified in Sorrentino's films, is not reducible, after all, to what Deleuze in the mid-1980s called the postwar cinema of the "time-image," any more than it corresponds to the logically—if not historically—and stylistically precedent movement-image. Sorrentino's films do not qualify as post-Tarkovskian slow cinema any more than they do as slavish imitations of American commercial genre film. (Nor, needless to say, do they represent an Italian "national folk" cinema, in Andrew's term.) As will be seen in what follows, Sorrentino's films exemplify the contemporary art film's tendency to stylistic hybridity and spectacularity, while adhering to an ethics focalized in the body and the face in medium and close-up shot (what Deleuze calls the affection-image[26]) set over against another person or entity—whether object of desire, friend, or God—both conceptually, within the diegesis, and also visually-structurally, in the complexity of the montage and the sinuosity of the camera work.[27]

The ethical understanding of cinema adumbrated in Bazin mediates between the two extremes of realism and illusionism, which are therefore revealed to be complementary.[28] This is not a question of an unwarranted privileging of the legacy of neorealism, however; the equivalent reading is there in Deleuze's analysis of the emergence of the postwar time image, which for him begins with neorealism. Italian cinema retains a special place in this taxonomy; Deleuze quotes Barthélemy Amengual's description of Fellini's peculiarly hybrid contribution to the time-image: "'The everyday is identified with the spectacular . . . Fellini achieves the deliberate confusion of the real and the spectacle' by denying the heterogeneity of the two worlds, by effacing not only distance, but the distinction between the spectator and the spectacle."[29] It is not hard to recognize here an anticipation of

Sorrentino's spectacular style.[30] The two tendencies of realism and illusionism (really, two extremes on a continuum) are ever-present in Sorrentino, engaged in a stylistic dialectic described by Millicent Marcus as a distinctly Italian "post-realism" in which she sees:

> a self-conscious step beyond [neorealism's] storied precedent, at once challenging its linguistic orthodoxy while reinforcing realism's imperative to monitor the Italian national condition. The "afterness" of post-realism, then, inheres less in the impulse to supersede the earlier moment than to advance it through a process of linguistic remodeling that incorporates contemporary media codes while preserving the moral agenda of the realist tradition.[31]

I invoke Marcus's reading of *Il Divo*'s stylistic tendencies—and the ensuing debate in the pages of *The Italianist*—precisely because it leaves open the possibility for serious political critique where some see at best only postmodern playfulness or at worst self-indulgent masculinist display.[32] One major difference, of course, is that the object of this critique is not necessarily "the Italian national condition." Marcus's reading allows Sorrentino to take his place first of all in a specific ethically charged line of postwar Italian cinema: "Sorrentino's achievement harks back to the *cinema politico* of Francesco Rosi, Elio Petri, and Paolo and Vittorio Taviani in the 1960s, 70s and early 80s whose penchant for spectacle and whose stylistic departure from the naturalism of Neorealist cinematography can be seen as important harbingers" of the postrealist aesthetic for which Sorrentino has been both lauded and criticized.[33] (As will be seen in the ensuing chapters, however, it is every bit as relevant to compare Sorrentino's style to that of Martin Scorsese, Joel and Ethan Coen, David Lynch, Brian De Palma, Quentin Tarantino,[34] and other American filmmakers. This kind of transcultural stylistic appropriation and recontextualization is precisely what grounds Sorrentino's unique contribution to both contemporary Italian and transnational filmmaking.[35]) It must also be allowed, however, that Marcus's description names a stylistic tendency that extends well beyond Sorrentino, contemporary Italian cinema, and any mean-ingful notion of cinematic realism. Also, Sorrentino's affinities with many or most of the abovementioned Italian forebears is mainly on the thematic or diegetic and not the stylistic or formal level. (*Il Divo* and Rosi's *Salvatore Giuliano* [1961], for instance, are—at first blush at least—radically different in form.) Sorrentino's more recent exploits—most notably the television series *The Young Pope*—locate him in the vanguard of a transnational narrative style that transcends both Italian film and cinema per se. From this point of departure it is necessary to formulate a comprehen-sive reading of Sorrentino's oeuvre, beyond such decidedly Italian films as *Il Divo* or *Loro* (2018)—a reading that, in accounting for his feature film and television work, would also (where relevant) take into consideration his literary output, most notably his first novel, *Hanno tutti ragione* (*Everybody's Right*) and his short story collection, *Tony Pagoda e i suoi amici* (*Tony Pagoda and His Friends*), but also, potentially, the experimental novel *Gli aspetti irrilevanti*, as well as the published screenplays, the short films, and his 2005 film for television of the Eduardo De Filippo play *Sabato, domenica e lunedì*. Considerations of space compel me to privilege the films and

TV series, but the fact remains that Sorrentino is nothing if not a thoroughly inter- and intramedial cultural producer.

This book considers Sorrentino's unique contribution to postmillennial trans-national filmmaking: not merely the capturing onscreen of some version of the real nor some extravagant innovation in film form or language but rather the exploration of the relation between these two supposed poles, realism and an often spectacular illusionism, through a recognition of narrative cinema's unique ability to engage ethically with reality while conveying subjective interiority via cinema's irreduc-ible exteriority. Construing *political* in a very particular sense, Rosalind Galt asks: "Why can't we understand Italian cinema as political (or valuable) in and through the image?"[36] This book's reading of Sorrentino is subtended by the equivalent question: Why can't we understand Sorrentino's cinema as ethical, and therefore valuable, in and through the image? For this study I extend this understanding of the ethical potential of cinema within a context determined in part by Italian film history but also by the more general history of the question of cinema's capacity to effect positive social change in the world outside the theatre space. At certain key stages in cinema's history the goal of social change has been bound up with questions of realism in all its permutations; in Italy this has been combined with an insufficiently reflective auteurist paradigm. Before the 1980s, and the impact of cultural studies on film analysis, Italian film scholarship was held back by what Tiziana Ferrero-Regis calls "an equation in which the absence of recognizable grand auteurs indicated the absence of a national cinema altogether."[37] Alongside auteurism, moreover, the other major myth of postwar Italian film scholarship is that the very identity of this national cinema is inextricably bound up with the legacy of neorealism. The challenge presented by a contemporary auteur such as Sorrentino, then, is to clearly distin-guish how realism and film's ethical potential alike can be understood outside of the neorealist paradigm. The one category that links all of these discussions—around auteurism, (neo-) realism, the move beyond the national to a transnational identity, the emergence of a global art cinema modality—is intermediality. As will be touched on in the following chapters, closely related to the centrality of intermediality is the impact of digital technology, from the latest cameras to postproduction techniques, on Sorrentino's filmmaking; to a very meaningful extent, any lingering debates about realism and related questions become moot when one recognizes that the realism-formalism (illusionism) dichotomy dissolves in the face of digital's pervasiveness.[38] By this I mean that, where realism historically may be defined in terms of a film's photographically conveyed diegetic content, and where the self-reflexivity encom-passed by special effects and other techniques may be historically defined in terms of a film's stylistic departure from realism's immersive norms, digital production today means that a typical feature film release is determined by digital technology all down the line, from image capture/construction to visual effects, color grading, distribu-tion, and so forth. This is also why Sorrentino is right in stating that, "his should be viewed as a relatively conservative approach" to digital visual effects.[39] That said, films from *Il Divo* on display what has since the turn of the millennium become the new normal for international art cinema; as Brendan Hennessey explains, even a relatively visually unspectacular film such as *Il Divo* boasts several set-pieces created partly or entirely in the digital intermediate phase.[40] In fact *Youth* (2015) is his first feature shot exclusively in digital, in this case thanks to the Red Epic Dragon camera.[41] Once one enters the digital cinematic universe, questions of mimetic indexicality or "referential reliability"[42] become moot insofar as it is no longer possible to be certain of the provenance of *any* onscreen audio-visual signifier, no matter how banal or unspectacular.[43] Realism therefore, if it retains any critical-analytical currency, becomes purely a question of ideology, of believability, not merely in verisimilitudinous but also in cinematic and intermedial terms. In other words, what is real is what reminds one of something seen or heard before in some other film. What this shift means for Sorrentino's more recent films, not to speak of contemporary Italian cinema more broadly, is what Hennessy calls a "formalist retreat" from the narrative of "the afflicted state of the Italian nation."[44] For the present study, however, this global turn to the digital characteristic of contemporary commercial and arthouse cinema alike is part and parcel of the current instantiation of intensified style, whose crucial aspects for a filmmaker like Sorrentino include both intermediality and the digital interface (cinematography, postproduction, and so forth).[45]

The Sorrentinian Subject

With respect to Sorrentino's films specifically, it is crucial to distinguish between their ethical engagement with social reality and the films' politically problematic relation to gender and gendered identities—problematic because of the seemingly contradictory combination of socially critical ironic reflexivity with a degree of so-to-speak middlebrow indifference toward the social transformations wrought by feminism in occidental society over the past fifty-odd years.[46] The first problem that arises in any attempt to read Sorrentino's films within a meaningfully ethical framework, in other words, is the thoroughly gender-specific identity of the subject privileged here; the abovementioned Sorrentinian subject, embodied in a series of protagonists, all of whom are white, male, heterosexual, mostly (but not always) European, and of a certain age or generation.[47] I therefore examine Sorrentino's films in terms of their evident preoccupation with specific character types and traits, ranging from "the ridiculous man"[48] or "ambivalent anti-hero"[49] of the first three feature films to the postsecular New Man of *The Young Pope*—all men whose identities are defined by their relationships with power. This subject constitutes the main through-line, linking the various chapters together, allowing the other themes and questions—(neo-) realism, national cinema, auteurism, commercial genre film vs. art cinema, and so on—to coalesce around this subjective focus. But I also examine the complement to this constellation: what I refer to for short as the enigmatic figure of "woman"—the "monolithic and transhistorical entity" identified by Molly Haskell in her canonical 1974 text, *Reverence to Rape*.[50] Sorrentino's films are also considered here in terms of their simultaneous critique and perpetuation of specific gender-based, sexist and, for some, misogynistic, stereotypes of femininity. This places Sorrentino into a long line of (mostly but not entirely male) filmmakers for whom the female body is at best a paradox or contradiction and at worst the ultimate reified object of heterosexual-consumerist desire. Sorrentino is hardly the first Italian director to engage in this kind of self-reflexive critique of the male gaze as it tends to manifest in Italian popular culture, a fact which only foregrounds the difficulty of exploiting such images in order to critique them without on some level appearing to participate in the perpetuation of a whole range of negative stereotypes.[51] Sorrentino confronts these questions head-on in his 2012 novel, *Hanno tutti ragione* (*Everybody's Right*), whose highly specific narrative voice—fictional 1970s singer Tony Pagoda (based on Toni Servillo's performance of Tony Pisapia in *One Man Up*) provides the author with a classic opportunity for eating one's cake and having it, too. For instance:

> When the days press in upon us we take off our clothes. And [Beatrice] took off her clothes. Striking dumb my yearning for sex. So vast was my desire that it made me break out in a cold sweat. . . . Because what I was seeing was too much for just one man. And still it was too much even for all the men in the world. However fortunate and privileged I might be, I would have to get used to the idea that a body like that, without adequate adjectives, was giving itself up to me and no one else. But I got used to it.[52]

Two things are worth noting: (1) "without adequate adjectives" leaves the reader in no doubt about the significance of medium specificity when it comes to a verbal description of a character's body. Here it is less about Beatrice's body in itself—where/what is that body?—and much more in the end about how the sight of her body makes *the narrator feel*; it is a description, in the end, of *his* experience of her body. And (2) "a body like that . . . was giving itself up to me . . .": Beatrice is reduced discursively, rhetorically, to a body, and one moreover with its own agency even as the woman in question is denied any more complex subjectivity. In other words, Sorrentino's parody of a certain kind of megalomaniacal male narcissist allows him as author to indulge, ironically, in the worst kind of sexist language. This narrative strategy succeeds, especially if one reads the book in the context of the long line of lecherous egocentric cads that populate the Western literary canon.[53] When it comes to the representation of women in the films, however, it is a necessarily different, rather more complicated, story.

(*The Persistence of*) *The Auteurist Fallacy*

Ultimately, to invoke in any interpretive act the author's gendered identity, coupled with the intentional fallacy underpinning any auteurial approach, risks opening up a critical minefield unless this is balanced with a consideration of as much as possible of the film's surrounding context. That Sorrentino himself might not endorse this critique is a risk that I willingly run, which underscores my final point here: that, for all of its inevitable rhetorical dependency upon a certain long-standing tradition of thinking about film history as the narrative of a series of great directors, this book's arguments are ultimately predicated upon the understanding that the filmmaker as auteur is only the first of many myths of film theory and criticism of the past sixty-odd years. Like many myths, the myth of the auteur must be met with critical skepticism even as it is recognized that an auteurist discourse can be very useful—and is to a certain extent unavoidable—in any such analytical discussion of a single filmmakers' canon. To put it as simply as possible, my approach here locates itself necessarily on a continuum between two seemingly incommensurable extremes: on the one hand, it is my contention that the filmmaker and her/his/their intentions is/are only present in and relevant to the final film in the form of the artistic choices she or he or they made and whose traces end up on the screen or soundtrack. On the other hand, it is virtually impossible in today's critical climate to not take into account at some point the historically and culturally determined, embodied person of the filmmaker as a specific subject with an identity shaped (like anyone else's) along the axes of gender, sexual orientation, ethnicity or race, language, nation, age/generation, and so on. What sounds like a contradiction among incommensurable positions, therefore, is actually a continuum on which the filmmaker and her/his/their story signifies as one intertexual node amongst many others, albeit an often privileged one. In order to mitigate this apparent contradiction as much as possible, then, and to avoid altogether the trap of essentialism lurking at the heart of any unreflective identity politics, alongside the transnational paradigm my approach foregrounds the films' highly intermedial nature: their frequent and complex intertextual engagement with cinematic history, including but not limited to Italian cinema. It goes without saying that intermediality, as a key feature of Sorrentino's formal approach, simultaneously militates against the unreflective privileging of the director as godlike authority presiding over a film's meanings (a phenomenon for which Fellini's slightly outsized reputation is the perfect example). Hence this book's schizoid agenda: to interrogate the contradictions of entrenched habits of filmic interpretation by implicitly critiquing the cult of the director as auteur even while celebrating Sorrentino's already significant contribution to Italian cinema and to world cinema more broadly. The best way to achieve this is to displace authorship and textual authority back onto the films themselves, paying close attention to the often complex relationship of image and soundtrack, to their characteristic intermediality, and to their unapologetic recourse to the beautiful or spectacular image. After all, the best riposte to an uncritically auteurist approach is the poststructuralist axiom that language—in this case cinema—belongs to no one and everyone alike. A film such as *The Great Beauty*, for instance, harkens back to the beautiful *image* of 1980s European and Hollywood cinema, exemplified by the *cinema du look* in France,[54] by films as diverse as *Diva* (Beineix, 1981) and *Wings of Desire* (Wenders, 1987). And, as will be seen below, in the transition from his feature films to the long-form television series, Sorrentino's treatment of gender acquires a politically progressive appearance in which the sheer beauty of the image is tempered or even overpowered by its affective impact within the montage.[55] The thematic shift is occasioned by a modal shift from a transnational art film style toward a hybrid species of postsecular male melodrama. As will be seen, I bring the postsecular and male melodrama together here because of the peculiar confluence in certain contemporary (post-1990s) films and television programs of a perceived crisis of masculinity with a renewed interest in the sacred, an intersection explored within the crucible of melodrama which, in

Linda Williams's terms, provides a space in which masculine bodies may be temporarily feminized in attitudes of radical passivity—a position epitomized by the Passion narrative, the Gospel story of Christ's ordeal on the cross. The etymological confluence of masculine passivity, melodramatic pathos, and Christian passion is at the crux of this investigation.[56]

Running through this book is a critical consideration of the representation of gender, beginning from the marginalization, sexualization, and, needless to say, objectification of the female subject in Sorrentino's films and television work. The aim of this critique is to better understand the significance of woman for the cinematic and mnemic constitution of the Sorrentinian subject.[57] In the process I situate Sorrentino's work in the context of the contemporary transnational art cinema tradition set into dialogue with the current rise of prestige television programming. And, in a shift from the desiring and objectifying intradiegetic gaze to what Rosemarie Garland-Thomson in the context of disability studies calls "the stare," in chapters 3 and 8 I also analyse Sorrentino's fascination with non-normative identities whose onscreen function as locus of a radical alterity remains essentially ambiguous. From film to film to television series the treatment of gender grows increasingly comprehensive, even as it moves in what appears to be a more thematically and generically conservative direction with respect to the nexus of memory and whatever secular or postsecular redemption awaits the protagonist.

Sorrentino's ironically dialectical approach becomes most contentious in the representation of gender, especially images of women. In this respect, I am partaking of what feminist film theory calls "images of women" criticism in the most literal sense but without the attendant assumption (to which this approach was prone) of a direct correlation between such images and real-world women:

> Unfortunately mainstream Italian criticism has only flirted with the basics of this preliminary stage, and certainly never moved towards thinking about "images for women." There is in fact an uncomfortable degree of overlap between the most basic "images of women" criticism and a kind of descriptive criticism that merely celebrates a bevy of female beauties, repeatedly fetishizing female stars without analyzing the complex gendered construction that constitutes a star.[58]

As Danielle Hipkins clearly indicates, such images do not bring the actual experience of real women to the screen in any unmediated sense any more than they address the contradictions of stardom in relation to gender difference.[59] Sorrentino's case is not merely another instance of a male Italian director indulging in the medium's potential for the exploitation of women's bodies.[60] As I argue in the following chapters, Sorrentino creatively exploits all the resources of narrative cinema to engage critically and self-reflexively with questions of identity, power, and representation in a contemporary transnational and—in *The Young Pope*—postsecular context. Hanging over this study, as it does over the director's body of work to date, however, is the question of the cinematic representation of gender difference and what this difference might mean for the status of real women in the world today.

Transnational Intermediality

This book presents a critical overview of Sorrentino's feature films: *One Man Up* (2001), *The Consequences of Love* (2004), *The Family Friend* (2006), *Il Divo* (2008), *This Must Be the Place* (2011), *The Great Beauty* (2013), and *Youth* (2015), as well as the television series *The Young Pope* (2016). I also include a coda on the international version of *Loro* (2018).[61] Where relevant, I also make reference to Sorrentino's short film work and screenplays, as well as his literary output. The general aim of this book is to introduce Sorrentino to a wider audience of nonspecialist film lovers, while underscoring—most obviously by means of the book's chosen language—the fact that Sorrentino has in a relatively short span evolved from a Neapolitan and Italian filmmaker into a cultural producer with transnational appeal. Three of his films to date, as well as *The Young Pope*, were international coproductions, featuring major American and British as well as European actors.[62] Two films in particular—*This Must Be the Place* and *Youth*—tell eclectic transnational stories that unfold in decidedly non-Italian settings. At the same time, Sorrentino's first four films already rank high in the pantheon of contemporary Italian art cinema, while *The Great Beauty*, itself a thoroughly Italian film, with its 2013 Best Foreign Language Film Oscar win, completed the work begun by *Il Divo* and *The Consequences of Love* of bringing contemporary Italian cinema back into the international spotlight.[63]

It is important therefore to recognize Sorrentino's film practice within Italian cinema, including contemporary Neapolitan cinema in particular,[64] if only to illuminate Sorrentino's progressive departure from localized production in the direction of a more expansive and transnational approach to filmmaking. That said, it is equally important not to linger in the context of Italian national cinematic identity when the more recent film and TV work—*This Must Be the Place*, *Youth*, *The Young Pope*—is so clearly transnational in character. The transnational, therefore, alongside the films' characteristic intermediality, constitutes my primary analytical frame. Sorrentino's films are transnational, as opposed to merely European,[65] in more than one sense. As Elizabeth Ezra and Terry Rowden make clear, transnational cinema's inherent hybridity "problematizes the term 'foreign film.' In the United States and the United Kingdom, this term has functioned primarily as a signifier for non-English language films. Practically it has served to relegate those films, and the force of their images of cultural alterity, to the so-called 'art-house circuit' and to the select audiences that frequent them."[66] While some critics dismiss Sorrentino as the "medium talent" purveyor of a mannered, essentially empty style (e.g., Sicinski), many others hold him up as an emergent auteur for the twenty-first century. This book navigates the stormy waters between these extremes, in order to argue for the social-political value of the films and television series on the basis of their formal sophistication but also to critique the institutions of authorship and authority to which much contemporary film criticism is still beholden. In the 1960s American and British critics, such as Andrew Sarris and Peter Wollen, appropriated the notion of the *politique des auteurs* from Francois Truffaut and André Bazin in their mid-century *Cahiers du Cinéma* articles, founding a kind of theology of the film director as ultimate source of meaning in a given film. Sarris is perhaps the most guilty on this score, having famously advanced a schematic of the auteur theory consisting of three concentric rings, with the technique and personal style of the technician and stylist, respectively, standing in for the interior meaning that only the true auteur is capable of conveying in his films. This metaphysical model of directorial intentionality is readily replaced by a pragmatic acknowledgment—such as that recently voiced by David Bordwell[67]—that any commercially and/or critically successful filmmaker can become known by her/his stylistic signature, whether it be a specific formal technique, motif, preferred actor, genre, and so on.[68] Furthermore, while the notion of the auteur "as representative and bearer of national and/or ethnic identity"[69] has been productively complicated by cinema's increasing transnationalization, the myth of the director as god-like author persists today in much popular discourse around film (especially online), while continuing to determine the critical discourse in such respected venues as *Cahiers du Cinéma*.[70] By the late twentieth and early twenty-first centuries both the Hollywood studio and international art film director of stature can function as a name-brand auteur linked to a specific national cinema.[71] "In traditional film historiography," according to Galt and Schoonover, "art cinema has been a way to organize national cinemas via canons of 'great directors,' so that the very international reception of art cinema becomes proof of its national importance."[72] I join these critics in suggesting, however, that "art cinema always carries a comparativist impulse and transnational tenor."[73] This situation is to a large degree the ironic result of capitalism's fostering of a certain kind of global cine-literacy, as a markedly homogeneous popular culture expands exponentially thanks to a highly legible narrative film vernacular and quasi-universally available digital technologies.[74] Transnational cinema, then, "arises in the interstices between the local and the global . . . [where it] is most 'at home,'" reflecting "the hybridized and cosmopolitan identities of so many contemporary filmmakers."[75] Sorrentino is an exemplary twenty-first-century transnational filmmaker, not least in terms of his films' typical production conditions. I invoke the term *transnational* therefore less in its original postcolonial-critical sense and more in terms of a cinema that represents but also critiques a different kind of diasporic experience: that of the global citizen adrift in the nonspaces of twenty-first-century consumer capitalism.[76] Sorrentino's is a decidedly cosmopolitan transnationalism, reflective of a set of values specific to a late modern subjectivity that knows itself to be on the brink of (metaphorical) extinction but does nothing because it is transfixed by the self-reflexive spectacle of watching its own demise as a strange kind of *grande bellezza*.[77] The obverse of this position is what the actor Toni Servillo refers to in an interview as the realization of the "meaninglessness," the "staggering insignificance," of existence.[78]

Finally, one of the most important ways in which the films express their transnational identities is through Sorrentino's eclectic approach to soundtrack music. In a 2009 interview the director admitted that music plays as important a role in his films as in his life, and he has never employed a composer to write the soundtrack music for an entire feature: "A film produces too varied a spectrum of emotions to be interpreted by just one composer."[79] No appraisal of the intermedial or interartistic dimension of his cinematic work would be complete, therefore, without some attention paid to Sorrentino's melomania (from *melos*, melody or music, also the root of melodrama), which puts him into the same camp as such filmmakers as Pier Paolo Pasolini and Rainer Werner Fassbinder—both famous soundtrack mash-up artists avant la lettre.[80] Sorrentino's soundtracks employ musical choices from across the spectrum of genres and styles, ranging from *The Family Friend*'s Italian country-western subculture to David Byrne and a young Irish band called The Pieces of Shit ("exactly the right name for this moment in history") in *This Must Be the Place* to *The Great Beauty*'s eclectic soundtrack, juxtaposing euro-trash EDM to twenty-first-century choral compositions, to the ultrahip resort hotel musicians in *Youth*. Where relevant, therefore, I also discuss specific musical/soundtrack choices and how they complement or contradict the image track in a particular film.

Impegno *and the Political Art Film*

On the level of content—which is to say story, character, or theme, insofar as they can be artificially separated out from the material means of their expression in the film—from his first feature, *One Man Up*, Sorrentino's films have shared a set of consistent preoccupations. In a 2009 interview with the director, Guido Bonsaver claims that his films before *Il Divo* show "no interest in politics."[81] Sorrentino responds that, "a common trait in all my films is the study of relationships of power among individuals."[82] Sorrentino speaks often of his fascination with political power—*il potere*—and the men who wield it, a phenomenon that cuts across cultural and geographical lines: "the psychological mechanisms derived from power are more or less the same in various cultures. In all nations, the dark and crooked paths that a powerful man might follow are very similar. . . . The mechanisms of power are analogous in France, in Italy, and in the U.S."[83] In an article in *Il Foglio*, Andrea Minuz brings together three works as *la trilogia di potere* (the trilogy of power): *potere temporale* (*Il Divo*), *potere spirituale* (*The Young Pope*), *potere mediatico* (*Loro*).[84] While I am not sure that it is necessary to limit the trilogy to just these three works, Minuz's emphasis on different manifestations or qualities of power is certainly instructive, and I will address the temporal, spiritual, and mediatic aspects of power in relation to specific films and their protagonists in the following chapters.

My general approach to the relation between form and content in the films and television series nods to the ongoing relevance for Italian cinema of the notion of *impegno*, best translated as civic engagement or commitment. "Impegno . . . is normally associated with a specific historical period—from the late 1940s to the 1960s—in which cultural and political actors converged on a communal project based on strict ideological premises and tied to emancipatory and potentially revolutionary action."[85] Impegno found its initial cinematic expression in Italian neorealism, which is associated historically with "a strong ethic of civic commitment and a language of filmic signs whose referentiality is never called into question."[86] Impegno remains an important value in Italian film studies, even as the social and political reality with which film is confronted—not to speak of film technology itself—has radically transformed. Musing on the kind of precedent for twenty-first-century Italian cinema set by Matteo Garrone's *Gomorrah* and by his own *Il Divo*, both of which appeared in 2008, Sorrentino states: "I suppose that these precedents can determine a shifting focus on the part of Italian cinema not only toward escapist comedy, but also toward a more serious and committed/engaged authorial cinema."[87] The deeply imbricated relation of political commitment and a hypostatized auteurism is evident in these lines; in other words, as Sorrentino implies: the idea that impegno can manifest in a film is unavoidably predicated on the more deeply entrenched and by now universal notion of the filmmaker as auteur. The latter—the myth of the auteur—is productively mediated through Marcus's reading of Sorrentino's "postmodern *impegno*," in which "the contemporary vogue for stylistic virtuosity—including the use of pastiche, abundant citation, semiotic playfulness, imagistic saturation, decorative exuberance—can coexist with an ethics of political engagement in the arts."[88] Marcus invokes impegno in a contemporary context as indicative of not a single, overarching ideological agenda but of a "diversification" of a generally leftist critical perspective.[89] I would extend this reading to all of Sorrentino's film and television work to date, unyoking Marcus's notion of irony from the realist paradigm that postrealism implies, and connecting it to a notion of impegno as style. In this respect I would go further than Alan O'Leary, who very helpfully argues for a reading of impegno in contemporary Italian cinema as a "discourse."[90] By conceiving of impegno in terms of the formal-material means of its expression, the more or less unconscious privileging of the director as author of and authority over a film's meanings can be short-circuited. As others have noted, this disconnection of impegno from realism is necessary in order to appreciate an ongoing sense of ethical engagement in contemporary Italian film and television work that is *not* beholden to a tradition of cinematic realism understood as a set of photographically based correspondences with an external reality. It is also important to recall, however, the historical connection between the cinematic expression of postwar impegno and the Italian Communist Party founder Antonio Gramsci's notion of the national-popular, implying that the *popular* in this Italian context is always located somewhere between a leftist conception of national identity (epitomized by neorealism) and cinema as commercial, mass-cultural phenomenon.[91]

According to Tim Bergfelder, "despite occasional claims on universality, in the study of transnational cinemas the concept of 'nation' remains the ultimate backbone of identity and cohesion."[92] What does this look like in the Italian context from which Sorrentino has emerged? Although not unrelated to Miriam Hansen's concept of vernacular modernism, my use of the term *vernacular* refers quite literally to the level of language as dialect or local idiom that no single person either invents or completely controls. (I also owe a debt to Homi Bhabha's paradoxical coinage "vernacular cosmopolitanism,"[93] which combines the local and idiomatic with a worldly—and world-weary—open-mindedness.) Historically, the utopian notion of cinema's political potential fed "into post-war neorealist hopes for cinema as a tool for popular emancipation."[94] Such hopes have found a strange kind of renewal in certain contemporary postcolonial theorizations of cinema in a postnational era, in which the universal is replaced by the diasporic and migratory, the national by the transnational. In Bergfelder's view, the more sophisticated instances of contemporary transnational cinema exemplify this double logic, engaging in a critique of the forces of globalization within a text whose very existence depends upon said forces.[95]

In embodying this double bind, Sorrentino's films also engage in a critique, in a self-reflexive redoubling that, for many, does not go far enough to justify the marked perpetuation of sexist stereotypes in the onscreen representation of women.[96]

According to Bayman and Rigoletto, during the 1930s in Italy "cultural industries such as cinema were powerful forces at play within the public arena, where they fostered an increasing awareness for Italian audiences of belonging to a national community."[97] At the same time an anti-Fascist film culture was emerging, which, after Mussolini's downfall and the end of the war, in this period of radical commitment (impegno), became "the embryo of neorealism . . . from a belief that cinema has an ethical purpose granted by its ability to record popular reality"[98]—even if this "popular" is based in a mythic notion of a unified people who were in fact only ever unified or united imaginatively, while at the cinema.[99] "The intersection of class, nation and people in this post-war period of radical engagement (*impegno*) is highly influenced by Gramsci's concept of the 'national-popular' "[100]—a concept at the foundation of the self-understanding of the field of Cultural Studies that emerged first in the U.K. in the 1980s.[101] "The national-popular . . . represents for Gramsci a political project for a kind of culture which the people might recognize as their own, which might make them feel part of one nation and which might lead them to their social and political emancipation."[102] In Bayman and Rigoletto's estimation, "the 'national' part of Gramsci's formulation has often obfuscated the 'popular' within Italian film scholarship."[103]

In Italian, of course, the popular and the people share a common root in *il popolo*.[104] In 1985 film scholar Vittorio Spinazzola made a "distinction between two categories of popular cinema: (1) *films made about the people*, and (2) *films made for the people*."[105] The first category, epitomized by neorealism, is politically "edifying, progressive" popular cinema; the second, epitomized by Fascist-era melodramas, comedies, and genre films, amounts to spectacular, "debasing, de-politicized products for popular consumption."[106] The latter, of course, is more escapist entertainment than realism properly speaking, while neorealism's formal innovations consist mainly in long takes and composition in depth à la Bazin's famous diagnosis of neorealist technique. In 1972, explicitly addressing the possibility of a politically meaningful cinema outside the institutional structures of Hollywood, Jean-Luc Godard stated that, "*the problem is not to make political films but to make films politically*."[107] In Thomas Elsaesser's gloss, "to make films politically" means "to challenge the strategies which contemporary popular culture, especially the cinema, had inherited from the bourgeois novel and theatre."[108] I suspect that there is something of this idea in Sorrentino's stated desire to aspire to a "new approach" to making political cinema in Italy.[109] Not even neorealism qualifies as *this* kind of political cinema, however, whose political engagement, or impegno, is activated on the formal level of audiovisual style—an understanding of political cinema whose radical nature has been helpfully complicated in recent scholarship on Sorrentino and other filmmakers of his generation.[110] In Gary Crowdus's estimation:

> In his call for a "new approach" to political cinema in Italy, Sorrentino seems to be essentially conceding that the days when there was a commercially viable audience for

a cinema of civic conscience, à la Francesco Rosi, are long gone, and that, in a new, highly competitive media and entertainment environment, today's primarily younger moviegoers will have to be enticed to see films dealing with their own political history or contemporary affairs by packaging them in a more compelling, tricked-out visual style, complemented by a generous helping of popular music.[111]

The other kind of popular cinema is only politically useful in the most cynical sense of being useful in the maintenance of hegemony under Fascism or, for that matter, a capitalist democracy.[112] This is where it becomes possible to talk about Sorrentino's films as having an ethico-political valence even when the content seems disengaged from everyday social reality (Italian or otherwise), or lacking in any obvious impegno as traditionally understood. If impegno is conceived in terms of audiovisual style, however, it becomes possible to view *Il Divo*, for instance as only the most obviously political of Sorrentino's films to date. The films partake of a frequently flamboyant visual aesthetic whose self-reflexive tendencies represent a postmodern version of the typical Brechtianisms of a politically modernist postwar art cinema: impegno as film style.

Sorrentino's Intensified Style

This book's argument extends and complicates Marcus's notion of postrealism, as the formal packaging of Sorrentino's stories moves from a new kind of transnational art film to a more conventionally melodramatic modality in *The Young Pope*. At the same time, I would make explicit Marlow-Mann's implicit observation that Sorrentino's films display a particularly stylish species of postclassical cinema, or what David Bordwell in 2002 labeled intensified continuity style: "a mobile camera heavily reliant on dollies and the Steadicam, alternating extremes of long takes and rapid montage, stylized slow motion, a surprising and unconventional choice of pre-existing music, flamboyantly attention-seeking set-pieces, and so on"[113]—what Sicinski reduces to "Sorrentino's hyperactive zoom and crane style."[114] Briefly put, any example of Sorrentino's style offers an illustration of what Bordwell identifies as a new international baseline vernacular, embracing a wide variety of cultural-aesthetic codes: art and avant garde cinema, commercial genre film, advertising, music video, and now, especially, television. "Where the Wenders of *Paris, Texas* . . . would adhere to the basic horizontality of the open road, Sorrentino likes to take a crane (or its digital equivalent) and go quite literally over the top of a scene, vertically swooping over the subject in the landscape, only to edit to another space and then swoop back the other way."[115] Arguably, Sicinski is merely describing Sorrentino's version of what Bordwell captures in his intensified style. The justification for certain more orthodox critics' hostility to Sorrentino-Bigazzi's stylistic approach is often presented as if it were self-evident that a self-conscious style were inherently bad and that a more sober and understated style were somehow intrinsically superior—an old critical canard that is ultimately beholden to an unreflective adherence to what Sicinski unapologetically refers to as "stately master shot realism."[116] Sicinski's critique reveals a reluctance to appreciate a filmic style that dares to combine the self-reflexive and the postrealist in the same shot. More fundamentally, his critique fails to recognize that, in cinema at least, there is no substance without style. Finally, I appropriate Bordwell's model here because, as an understanding of the formal evolution of narrative fiction film, it provides an ideal basis for what I mean by the expression of impegno as style in Sorrentino's works.

This book considers Sorrentino's films in their contribution to a new transnational *cinema politico*—a hybrid phrasing that refers to Sorrentino's specifically Italian cinematic origins while looking ahead to his films' more global, affectively charged ethical commitment, manifested through their innovative yet historically engaged form. I emphasize that my invocation of the term *postrealist* does not necessitate the complementary adoption of realism's alleged stylistic opposite, which Pierpaolo Antonello labels the postmodern.[117] It is necessary to clarify and complicate Sorrentino's status as a *post*modernist filmmaker in the most meaningful sense of one who comes *after* as the knowing heir to a rich cultural tradition—both in relation to cinema's own modernist period and also modernity per se—as well as one who self-consciously attempts to forge something new and meaningful in the face of an ever-expanding mass of (often ephemeral) cultural material. The kind of postmodern stylistic approach to which Antonello refers is more accurately labeled as self-reflexive, metacinematic, and so forth, leaving the postmodern as the name for a cultural or epistemological moment or episteme that manifests diegetically in certain kinds of films. This is what is meant here by the term *postmodern* in reference to Sorrentino's films or to his aesthetic approach more generally as an expression of a specific worldview. Realism vs. postmodernism is a false binary,[118] and if I appropriate postrealism here it is to name precisely a postmodern form of realism, transcending for instance Marcus's more restrictive (because focused on *Il Divo*) sense of a specifically Italian modality of neopolitical cinema. That said, the realism of Sorrentino's post*realism* in *Il Divo* embraces rather than excludes a variety of self-reflexive strategies that together render "obsolete all neorealist imperatives to stylistic transparency," while insisting on a certain level of authentic "historical reference," all the while recruiting the viewer "into an active process of interpretation and critical engagement in remembering and analyzing the workings of the Andreottian regime."[119] Postrealism, then—in an analogy with posthumanist and humanism, or postsecular and secularism—names an expressive modality that appreciates the value of even as it self-reflexively critiques the realist tradition in film.

To identify Sorrentino and Bigazzi's characteristic film style as an evolved species of Bordwellian intensified continuity begs at least two important questions, both of which need addressing at the outset. The first, which is a very common error, is to ask: What does intensified continuity have to do with an Italian or European filmmaker such as Sorrentino? This question is posed by those who labor under the impression that Bordwell identified intensified continuity as a specifically *American* style of film narration. Bordwell never intended to limit his identification of intensified style to American cinema; that was merely the focus of his original article and subsequent elaborations, given his own scholarly proclivities. As he states, the stylistic norms he identifies:

> aren't restricted to North America, having originated in 1970s and '80s European cinema. Werner Herzog (*Aguirre: The Wrath of God*, 1972), Rainer Werner Fassbinder (*Chinese Roulette*, 1976), and *cinéma du look* directors like Jean-Jacques Beineix (*Diva*, 1981) and Léos Carax (*Mauvais Sang*, 1986) elaborated on the intensified continuity devices emerging in Hollywood. The techniques can be found in Luc Besson's *Nikita* (1990), Jane Campion's *Portrait of a Lady* (1996), Tom Tykwer's *Run Lola Run* (1998), and several of Neil Jordan's films. More broadly, intensified continuity has become a touchstone for the popular cinemas of other countries.[120]

The second question is: Assuming that it is accurate to read Sorrentino's films' style in this way, what is their relation to the political impulse running through Italian cinema? How revolutionary are these films in terms of the potential for film form to work in a Brechtian manner to defamiliarize the viewer's received sense of social reality, of the world, of her identity? In Vito Zagarrio's discussion of the possibility of a meaningfully political cinematic form, the presence of anything like a postclassical style, which in the end means an extension—or, in this case, an intensification—of existing entrenched stylistic traits and narrational strategies, means that the film (or body of films) in question can only amount to further expressions of a society's dominant ideological position; i.e., neoliberalist capitalism. "Who said that dolly, establishing shots, master shots, angle- and reverse-angles, and partial coverages are the only grammatical options available, just because such syntax has been historically dominant"?[121] In siding here with form over content, Zagarrio grounds his discussion in Gramsci's remarks about the inherently "revolutionary" quality of a "work of art" (119), reading *art* as "cinema" and *revolutionary* as "political," meaning "the power to influence society, imaginary [*sic*], cultures and consciousness, even *in spite* of its creators and systems of production."[122] In other words, this politically revolutionary type of cinema manifests "the will to express an authorial universe and the desire to transform society."[123]

In nine chronologically ordered chapters, this book analyzes each of Sorrentino's feature films, as well as *The Young Pope* television series, on its own terms, stylistically, narratively, and thematically, and also in relative terms, placing each into the broader context of Sorrentino's still-evolving body of work, whether cinematic, televisual, or literary. This book is focused on Sorrentino as transnational filmmaker; on the films as exemplary instances of a contemporary art cinema laying the ground for the emergence in *The Young Pope* television series of a hybrid genre I call the postsecular male melodrama. The latter foregrounds this book's engagement with the Sorrentinian subject as it evolves across the director's body of work. More than any other feature, though, my readings of the films and other works herein are connected through the films' pronounced intermedial dimension, including intratextual references in more than one media form.[124] As will be seen, this approach reaches a kind of apogee in Sorrentino's 2018 Berlusconi biopic, *Loro*, becoming the basis for the film's stylistically based critique of the Italian televisual landscape in the early twenty-first century.

the cinema of PAOLO SORRENTINO

One Man Up (L'uomo in più)

The Consequences of Coincidence

> I felt powerful. I didn't give a damn about people. I remember everything.
> —Tony Pisapia, *One Man Up*

PAOLO SORRENTINO'S FIRST FEATURE, *One Man Up* (2001),[1] interweaves the stories of two men, both named Antonio Pisapia, living in Naples at the same time in the early 1980s. One is a professional soccer player who, following an injury, is prevented from becoming a coach; the other is a disgraced pop singer who fails to stage a comeback but finds an ironically improbable salvation when his counterpart takes his own life. The latter's suicide, on the face of it a reaction to his frustrated hopes, is equally a fulfillment of the team president's remark that this Antonio will never become a coach because he is a "sad man, and soccer is a game." (With Antonio's profession, Sorrentino inaugurates soccer as a theme in his films, culminating, so far, in Cardinal Voiello's obsession with SSC Napoli, one of several running jokes in *The Young Pope* [2016] emanating from this character.[2]) Tony Pisapia, by contrast, is also a sad man whose ultimate response to life is to laugh at its absurdity while embracing the small moments of beauty.

If Sorrentino hardly registers on the radar of Italian film scholarship—still in thrall to the myth of the auteur—before the mid-2000s, it is likely because he was first classified as an emerging regional Neapolitan filmmaker, not yet perceived as one of the young auteurs who appeared in the new millennium as if to renovate Italian cinema. In contrast to his subsequent work in film and television, Sorrentino's first feature can be seen as an expression of a distinctly Neapolitan cinema. Each of the storylines in *One Man Up* is set in Naples, and the film as a whole contains many regionally specific cultural references.[3] On the other hand, Naples itself hardly features in the film's mise-en-scène, pointing the way to the de-emphasizing of specifically Italian settings in favor of the transnational spaces of existential ennui and depersonalized relations in Sorrentino's subsequent feature, *The Consequences of Love* (2004). Apart from any other factor, however, what distinguishes *One Man Up* from all of his work since is the fact that it is the only one of Sorrentino's films to *not* be shot by director of photography Luca Bigazzi. This, alongside the film's pronounced intermediality, allows for the introduction of another argument against an auteurist recuperation of Sorrentino: the marked difference in form and content between one film and another by the same director occasioned by a change in cinematographer. *One Man Up* was shot by Pasquale Mari,[4] while all of Sorrentino's other features have been shot by Bigazzi, without whom Sorrentino may still have achieved an equivalent level of commercial and critical success but not through the same distinctive cinematographic aesthetic. Therefore, to the extent that such an interpretive template retains any currency, Bigazzi deserves an equal share in the mantle of auteur (just as Emmanuel Lubezki, a cinematographer with whom Bigazzi shares certain distinctive techniques, does for both Alejandro G. Iñárritu's and Terrence Malick's post-2000 films[5]—not to mention the fact that both directors of photography readily embrace digital over film).[6] To clarify: I am not suggesting that Sorrentino only came into his own as a director once he connected with Bigazzi; the films themselves are testament to Sorrentino's talent and imagination as a filmmaker and screenwriter (along with writing partner Umberto Contarello), as well as the manner in which his singular vision is coupled with a deep respect for cinema's past and an occidental humanist legacy more generally.[7] The latter, in fact, may yet prove to be Sorrentino's defining characteristic in terms of the stories he prefers to tell and the individual and collective identities he seeks to explore.

It is a given, moreover, that any director is responsible for a great many things during the preproduction, production, and postproduction of a film, of which the cinematography is only one (albeit crucial) facet. By all accounts, however, Bigazzi's approach to lighting a film is relatively unique among contemporary cinematographers and, apart from the mobility of his camera and his idiosyncratic framing and surprising angles, it should not be forgotten that, even in the digital era, the director of photography is the person responsible for lighting the set. In fact it is a new generation of digital cameras and other technologies, including editing software, that allows for many of the unique lighting and tonal effects one sees in Sorrentino's most recent films.[8] In sum, I would argue that Sorrentino's penchant for a hybrid style combining grand visuals and self-reflexive camerawork with an at times pronounced subjectivity—especially in the dream scenes and flashbacks that pepper the films—finds a highly amenable realization in Bigazzi's approach to cinematography. Like *The Consequences of Love* and *The Family Friend* (2006) (both shot by Bigazzi) however, *One Man Up* is filmed in 35 mm, not digital. This accounts in part for the film's distinctive, generally dark tonalities. It is also shot in 1.85:1, a considerably narrower aspect ratio than Sorrentino's subsequent features, which Bigazzi shot—and continues to shoot—in a wide frame 2.35:1.[9]

With *One Man Up* as the focus then, this chapter introduces what I call the Sorrentinian subject: the recurring figure of a middle-aged (and in the later films, older) man, typically in a creative profession, such as a singer, writer, or filmmaker, who, while often defined by the measure of social or political power he wields, is equally defined by an underlying impotence. Whatever his age, this man, a cinematically realized character, may continue to wield his power over others, in which case the story's thrust is largely to stage the scene of his moral-ethical judgment and downfall (as in *The Family Friend*). On the other hand, if he lacks any tangible power at the outset, the story deals with his redemption, whether through his metaphorical or actual death or through a comparably ambiguous revelatory experience, especially one involving an encounter with memory, mediated through a specific person or event from his past (as in *The Great Beauty* [2013]).[10] Set in Naples in the early 1980s, *One Man Up* is unusual in that it offers a doubled subject: two very different men, both—in an ironic echo of Krzysztof Kieślowski's *The Double Life of Veronique* (1991)[11]—named Antonio Pisapia. The first is a retired soccer player (Andrea Renzi) whose aspiration is to become a coach and who is dismissed by his team's owner as a congenitally "sad man," unsuited to a life in what is ultimately just a game. He is thus the prototype in Sorrentino's canon of the constitutively melancholic masculine subject who either succumbs to his sadness or, for better or worse, transcends it, often through a woman's (unwitting) intervention.[12] The other Pisapia, played by Sorrentino regular Toni Servillo, is a disgraced seafood-loving, cocaine-sniffing pop singer ("il cantante melodico cocainomane")[13] whose story takes precedence by the film's third act. This Pisapia is the cinematic precursor of Tony Pagoda, the protagonist of Sorrentino's first novel, *Everybody's Right* (*Hanno tutti ragione* [2012]), and of his short story collection, *Tony Pagoda and His Friends* (*Tony Pagoda e i suoi amici* [2014]). Ironically, the film's two epigraphs—by Leroi Jones, a.k.a. Amiri Baraka ("What can I say? Is it better to have loved and lost than to put linoleum in your living room?") and Edson Arantes do Nascimento, a.k.a. Pelè ("Tie games don't exist")—might seem closer in spirit to Sorrentino's *Everybody's Right* and the sort of unreconstructed (Neapolitan) masculine identity both celebrated and critiqued therein than to the more literary tonality of the subsequent films, such as *The Great Beauty*, with its epigraph from Céline. I say *might* because, in the end, Sorrentino's novel reads like a kind of twenty-first-century Neapolitan take on the novelistic tradition inaugurated by the French writer decades before.

Sorrentino has disclosed in an interview that "the character of Antonio 'Tony' Pisapia, created thanks to Toni Servillo's performance, inspired him to create the main character of his [novel], the singer Tony Pagoda. For this reason, Sorrentino acknowledges . . . Servillo in the book"[14] as follows: "Toni Servillo. His face, topped by a reddish wig and a pair of blue-tinted Ray-bans, guided the creation of Tony Pagoda."[15] Sorrentino even has Tony Pagoda mention more than once a real song, "Lunghe notti da bar," that Tony Pisapia sings in *One Man Up*, written especially for the film by Toni Servillo and his musician brother, Peppe. The existence of these literary (and musical) texts, also authored by Sorrentino, is testament to the necessity of a term like *subject* to identify the manner in which a central character type links audio-visual and verbal narratives that are otherwise mediatically specific. Tony Pagoda, based on such real-life Italian pop stars as Fred Bongusto, embodies more generally a kind of masculine type possessing several traits that recur in the other protagonists across Sorrentino's canon.[16] In this respect it might be argued that Sorrentino is on the wrong side of the argument around the redefining of masculinity for the twenty-first century, but there are many different ways to mount a critique of such a complex and deeply entrenched identity structure.

As the only one of his features to not be shot by Luca Bigazzi, *One Man Up* is also the least stylistically self-reflexive of Sorrentino's films; although in the second half it does present a quietly sophisticated critique of 1980s Italian television—and, by implication, Berlusconi's Italy—in the form of *Confessioni Pubbliche* (figure 1.1), a relative of reality TV–style programming in which former celebrities confess their past sins on live television.[17] It is while watching this show, on which he too will appear, that Tony Pisapia the washed-up singer faces Antonio Pisapia the washed-up soccer player, looking him in the eye via the television screen, a moment of mutual revelation thoroughly mediated by the televisual apparatus. The despairing Antonio's suicide constitutes a kind of ironically coincidental sacrifice—the "*uomo in più*" of the title[18]—on behalf of his nominal counterpart, who is spurred to action at once vengeful and redemptive. The film's ending, scored anachronistically to Cake's 1996 version of Gloria Gaynor's "I Will Survive," is one of the most ironically upbeat in Sorrentino's oeuvre.

The uncanny relationship between the two Pisapias is finally clarified twenty-five minutes into the film in a scene that cuts back and forth between them in a more explicit manner than heretofore. Antonio the soccer player has just ended his career with a serious knee injury, while Tony the singer has ruined his by having sex with an underage girl. The forces that brought each man to his present circumstances could not be more different, and yet this scene makes it clear that they bear the same name and were both born on the same day, August 15, albeit in different decades. Also, the details of mise-en-scène in each setting—Antonio's hospital room and the police station in Tony's case—makes it clear that they are having these experiences at the same time: each man pauses to look out of a rain-soaked window at a barely visible Naples as he gives his personal data to an official. Indeed, their answers are virtually

FIGURE 1.1 *One Man Up* (Paolo Sorrentino, 2001)

run together on the soundtrack as if they were uncannily connected. Antonio's recurring ballerina dream, which doubles as the title card for the next part of the film, set in 1984—confirms this quasi-metaphysical connection on the level of form: as Antonio throws his miniature soccer men onto his coaches' game board, in a straight cut/match-on-action Tony in effect completes the gesture as he throws a handful of herbs into a steaming panful of fish.

Almost exactly halfway through the film each protagonist makes what appears to be a postdisaster, life-changing decision: Antonio meets Elena, the woman in red, with whom he plans to sail to Capri for an adulterous weekend. Tony, for his part, makes a spur-of-the-moment decision to buy his friend Salvatore's seafood restaurant. The next scene, in which Tony sells his car to make the down payment on the restaurant, is also the moment when Cake's cover of "I Will Survive" kicks in on the soundtrack, providing ironic counterpoint to both men's deluded striving to better their respective lots. What neither realizes—nor is this possible according to the laws of realist narrative underpinning the story—is that his trajectory is predetermined in an even more profound way than usual, in the sense that not only is each man's fate, like any fictional character's, already written; rather, as with the relation between the two young women in Kieślowski's *The Double Life of Veronique*, Tony's specific fate is contingent upon that of Antonio. The former will redress or make good upon the faults or failures of the latter. This is the crux of the film's metaphysics, of which most critics speak with trepidation.

Apart from its subdued lighting and color palette, *One Man Up* does bear some stylistic similarities to the subsequent films shot by Bigazzi, with their sinuously mobile camera and striking visual compositions, often accompanied by idiosyncratic musical choices on the soundtrack.[19] A case in point is the bravura sequence early in the film, soon after the introduction of Tony Pisapia the singer. (The analysis that follows, typical of this book's first two chapters, is intentionally detailed in its noting of shot type and scale, editing patterns, and other aspects of the cinematography and editing, as well as the mise-en-scène and soundtrack. This is done in order to establish early on Sorrentino's/Mari's/Franchini's elaboration of a distinctive postclassical intensified style.[20]) In a single long Steadicam take, Tony and his bandmates enter a nightclub and embark on a late night's revelry. From an overhead angle on the men's heads in the car as it pulls up out front, the camera twists down perpendicular to take in the group in medium shot as they enter the club. The camera moves in behind Tony as he descends the spiral stairs to the club's dance floor. Tony meets and greets well-wishers and random women, only ever pausing long enough to exchange a kiss and a witty word before moving on, the camera following and then shifting around to frame him in medium close-up within the ongoing long take. Losing Tony for a moment, the camera floats through the writhing bodies on the dance floor, past the DJ, to find Tony again as he takes a seat at a table with Titta (Agostino Chiummariello), the band's drummer. The camera swings around in front to a medium shot as they converse over the music. Titta goes to buy drinks and Tony steps onto the floor, dancing to Santa Esmeralda's disco version of "Please Don't Let Me Be Misunderstood," the camera moving away from him as he progresses through the throng of dancers in medium close-up. This particular shot is re-enacted in the opening party

FIGURE 1.2 *One Man Up*

sequence in *The Great Beauty*, Servillo repeating his signature gesture of gripping a cigarette in his teeth. This long sequence shot—like that in Scorsese's *Goodfellas* (1990), which it clearly echoes[21]—dynamizes the protagonist's personality, setting Tony apart from footballer Antonio in the diegesis, showing him off as the center of both the viewer's and the other characters' attention. This sequence therefore also justifies Tony's emergence at the end as the only man left of the two, where Antonio was the superfluous one, *un uomo in più*.

The long tracking shot of Tony entering and moving through the basement night club is a stand-out for its duration and complexity, but it is in fact the norm rather than the exception for this film, in which many scenes play out as single extended takes—albeit, not as protracted as this particular shot. For instance, later in the film Tony returns to the restaurant he wants to buy from his friend only to find that it has already been taken over by local *camorristi* who are already retrofitting it as a café (replacing the aquarium with a pastry counter), the entire scene playing out as a single mobile Steadicam take. The scene opens in medium shot as Tony exits a taxi and crosses the road to the beachside restaurant, tracking him in medium close-up as he saunters alongside the building, only to be brought up short when he catches sight of the sinister-looking men working inside. The camera continues past him, however, taking in the boss out front and his men moving the aquarium in one smoothly swooping shot that then bends back in the reverse angle to Tony, reacting in shocked silence as he leaves. The scene concludes with the camera moving away from the men inside toward a large window, in which Tony is framed, from medium to close-up shot. The camera advances but stops as the window frame disappears at the edge of the image, with Tony, his back to the camera, dragging his overcoat in desultory silence.

From the opening scene in which the credits unspool over muddy shots of two men in scuba gear fishing with spear guns—with one of them coming to a bad end after an encounter with a large octopus—it gradually becomes clear that, of the two

Pisapias, the viewer will in a very meaningful sense get to know Tony the singer better than Antonio the ex-soccer player. This is because of the two, Tony has an inner life to which we gain access via the most conventional and effective of techniques: the dream scene that doubles as a flashback. The opening sequence, as it turns out (over which is heard an instrumental version of what proves to be one of Tony's characteristically melodramatic songs) is an extradiegetic flashback to the moment that determined Tony's adult life, when his brother drowned while hunting octopus. Visually this scene is the darkest in a generally dark film, and it is often difficult to see and therefore difficult to understand exactly what is going on. It opens, for instance, with not two but three divers in the shot, swimming toward the camera, although in all subsequent references to this scene, not to mention the rest of the scene itself, it signifies as an experience Tony shares only with his brother; the identity of the odd man out is never revealed. Critics have pointed out that *The Great Beauty* owes a thematic debt to Rafaelle La Capria's 1961 novel *The Mortal Wound*, but in this detail of plot Sorrentino's first film also references this famous Neapolitan novel, whose protagonist enjoys diving for fish in the Bay of Naples with his younger brother.[22]

The subsequent dream scenes, of which there are three, are framed, lit, and edited in order to signal their status as slices of Tony's oneiric reality and not part of the waking reality of the film's diegesis. (They also contrast sharply with the opening underwater sequence.) Each iteration of Tony's dream conveys more narrative information, or rather the dream adapts to fit with events in Tony's life, providing at once an uncanny commentary upon and motivation for his final actions. This contrasts starkly with Antonio, whose onscreen inner life is limited to the above-mentioned dream sequence involving four white tutu-clad ballerinas performing the "Dance of the Little Swans" from Tchaikovsky's *Swan Lake* against a black background. The sequence culminates in a Busby Berkeley–style overhead crane shot of all the dancers in a circle, the year 1984 appearing in the middle of the formation. Antonio's dream thus does double duty as a title card announcing a four-year jump in story time. Unlike Tony's flashback/dream scenes, Antonio's ballet dream has nothing directly to do with his waking life in the diegesis, apart from giving him something to say when Elena (the woman in red) asks him what kind of theater he enjoys the most. The answer seems to confirm her impression of him as a "non-trivial man . . . full of mystery." What she doesn't realize is that his head is filled only with thoughts of soccer and his heart with his unrequited desire to become a coach. It is also possible that Antonio's balletic dream is a regendered translation of his obsession with the rhombus as a formation in soccer, comprised of 3 + 1 players, the fourth position that of the odd man out (*un uomo in più*). In this light, however, the extra man implied in the film's title (not to mention the octopus sequence) becomes an asset rather than a liability.

The first iteration of Tony Pisapia's dream comes a third of the way through the film, after the four-year jump to 1984, consisting of a single mobile take (figure 1.3). (The dream really wasn't possible before this point in the story, as it is clearly a product of Tony's rapid fall from grace as a result of sleeping with an underage girl he picked up in the nightclub after the opening concert.) Tony and the girl are in the middle of having sex when his wife and mother walk into the bedroom, which belongs to

FIGURE 1.3 *One Man Up*

Tony's daughter. His mother (Angela Goodwin) tells him "you should have [been the one who] died at the bottom of that sea," referring to the film's opening. This scene is followed immediately by another in which Antonio receives his career-ending injury, evidently in retaliation for refusing to participate in the game-fixing scheme that some of his teammates have agreed to in order to earn more money. Tony's dream opens after a straight cut from a completely unrelated scene of Antonio being brushed off again by his team's management in his request for a coaching position. A concluding close-up of Antonio's disappointed face is replaced by a bleached-out shot of waves lapping on a beach. A rapid pan to the left finds Tony from behind in medium shot, dressed in a white suit and overcoat; a rapid push in as a woman in voiceover whispers "Antonio!" while he turns around in close-up to look back toward the off-screen space behind the camera. The final rapid close-up is suddenly replaced in a quasi-jump cut by a new medium shot of Tony once more, facing front again as a black-clad woman moves past him from off-screen left toward the right. The camera completes its leftward arc behind Tony in the foreground, with the woman between him and a figure wearing scuba gear sitting half submerged in the shallows. The camera tracks backward, away from Tony, as the woman walks into the surf toward the diver. The scene ends as she stoops to embrace him, the whole group now framed in a long shot before a cut to Tony lying awake in bed in his apartment.

The second iteration of Tony's dream is again cut straight into the narrative flow, immediately following a scene in which Antonio's wife (uncredited) announces that she is leaving him. The latter scene—with Antonio and his wife—concludes with an unmotivated rightward tracking shot, leaving Antonio in his darkened house, standing looking at his wife in medium shot. A quick cross-fade to the same bleached-out shot of the waves gives way in a second fade; here we see the reverse angle on the first dream's principal shot, Tony in the background in medium, apartment tower in the distance, the black-clad woman in front, moving toward the camera in close-up. The camera tracks backward as she—now visible as Tony's mother—moves forward, her head growing larger in the right side of the frame, with Tony diminishing on the left. There is a cut to the reverse angle, the identical original shot of Tony in the foreground, turned away, looking at his mother as she moves toward the seated diver. Again the dream ends as she reaches him. Immediately after this Tony, awake in bed, discovers a cyst on his temple, then his mother telephones to tell him that his father has died.

The third dream scene continues and concludes the mininarrative that has been unfolding in stages. Following immediately upon the scene of Antonio's suicide on the soccer pitch adjacent to the airport, and preceded also by brief scenes of Tony trying unsuccessfully to reach Antonio on the phone, there is a fade-in to Tony in medium shot, centrally framed with beachfront tower blocks behind (the image has the same bleached-out quality as before). From the start the camera is already pushing in rapidly from a slightly low angle toward Tony's face, bringing him into close-up. Then a quick reverse shot, as if from his point-of-view, again moving rapidly in from a slightly high angle, this time in medium toward his mother and the diver at the surf's edge. The camera pushes into a two-shot close-up, as the diver goes to remove his mask and hood, turning around to reveal Antonio Pisapia looking back over his shoulder at Tony, together with the latter's mother, whose face fills the other half of the frame. This shot almost bleaches out right before cutting to Tony in close-up, looking on, uncomprehending. There is a cut back to the reverse angle on his mother and Antonio, returning his gaze. Cut to Tony again, the camera arcing slowly leftward around his head in close-up, then tracking down his body to stop on his right hand, in which he grasps a deadly looking knife (figure 1.4).[23] This concluding shot, disguised as a moment of oneiric prescience, telegraphs the story's climactic act of vengeful violence, which goes otherwise unshown.

As it turns out, Tony tries to save Antonio before the latter can commit suicide. In the film's most overtly metaphysical sequence, the two Pisapias encounter one another face-to-face for the first and only time—not counting the televisually

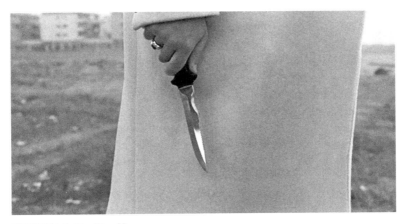

FIGURE 1.4 *One Man Up*

mediated *Confessioni Publicche* encounter, during which Tony states: "I remember a friend, Antonio Pisapia. He was a great soccer player. He wanted to be a coach, but they wouldn't let him be one. And he committed suicide. But I'll never kill myself, because I remember another thing: I've always loved freedom. . . . I'm a free man." They briefly meet in a Naples fish market, where Tony has just bought an octopus for the first time since his brother's death, recounted in the precredit flashback sequence. As noted, Tony even incorporates Antonio into his inner life, giving his, which is to say the actor Andrea Renzi's, face to his brother in his recurring dream about the latter's drowning in a scuba-diving accident. "This sequence multiplies the film's doppelgängers to suggest that Tony's subconscious has substituted Antonio for his brother in order to create the possibility of remedying his actions and alleviating his sense of guilt by avenging Antonio and then fulfilling his disapproving mother's earlier suggestion that he should have been the one to die at the bottom of the sea."[24] This psycho-diegetic sleight-of-hand guarantees that Tony will awake filled with newfound conviction to save himself by having the cyst surgically removed from his temple and then to not save but redeem Antonio, after the fact.[25] (Tony had quite literally tried to save Antonio, having called him on the phone numerous times, but too late.) Tony's dream is the explanation or justification for the uncanny encounter in the fish market—in retrospect, the film's crucial scene—just as the film's opening provides the context for understanding why Tony buys his first octopus right before he and his counterpart exchange an enigmatic glance. Tony will redeem his brother's death by saving Antonio, ironically presaged by the octopus he will take home and consume, overcoming the trauma of his brother's loss and his own superfluity.

Following the murder of the soccer team president, with the French band Air's lilting "Ce matin-là" on the soundtrack, Tony runs from the police, stealing a small boat in order to row out to sea, shouting, "I want to go to Capri!" ("Voglio andare a Capri!"). Antonio, his counterpart, failed to show up for his planned trip to Capri with Elena, embarking instead on his final downward spiral toward suicide. Antonio's despair and suicide are set over against Tony's elation and redemption through making good his own mistakes by avenging Antonio's death.[26] Tony shouts "Voglio andare a Capri!" because Antonio failed to go to Capri with the woman in red, thereby inverting the negativity of Antonio's trajectory into the ironically positive ending of the film's story as a whole. While on *Confessioni Pubbliche*, Tony "insists that . . . he will never commit suicide because he is a free man."[27] The last thing Tony does as a free man, however, is jump into the sea, the camera capturing his descent, white overcoat billowing out around him under the water (figure 1.5). Marlow-Mann reads this as the moment of his death, as if Tony, too, had committed suicide, but in a far more positively assertive sense than was the case with Antonio. Ultimately, to interpret this moment as that of Tony's death, and the subsequent coda as a kind of moment-of-death hallucination, is to overemphasize the significance of the editorial ellipses that structure the entire film: Why wonder (as Marlow-Mann does) how Tony is rescued or arrested just because these actions are not shown? It is also to overlook the quotidian banality of Tony's prison cell and cellmates: the close-ups on the family photos and pornographic centerfolds with which the sequence opens; the men's clothes; the plastic cutlery with which they are constrained to eat the pseudosacramental fish

FIGURE 1.5 *One Man Up*

dinner that Tony prepares (figure 1.6). How does this afterlife differ from the rest of the film's diegetic world?

To ground this counterreading of the film's conclusion, I would return to the analysis above of Tony's dreams, really a single, fragmentary dream that only gradually reveals its meaning to him and to the viewer. These dream scenes invoke a Fellinian style, à la *8 ½* (1963), for instance, that owes as much however to mid-1960s Ingmar Bergman. (These scenes convey a comparable aura of uncanny dream logic, with Tony on the beach physically embodying his own utter lack of comprehension in waking life; compare the opening dream scene in Bergman's *Wild Strawberries* (1957), for instance. For that matter, Antonio's ballet dream similarly nods to Bergman's 1951 *Summer Interlude*, in which ballet dancers also perform Tchaikovsky's "Dance of the Little Swans.") *One Man Up*, for all its regionally specific Neapolitanness (*napoletanità*), can therefore be seen as already aspiring toward something quite different: a kind of hybridized or expanded regional (transregional?) film that clearly anticipates Sorrentino's inexorable movement toward a transnational model of filmmaking. This is already evident in the use of Cake's version of "I Will Survive" in the film's third act, which also connects the two protagonists on an ironically suprarational level. Such a reading goes a ways toward accounting for the film's relation to a 1990s art film like Kieślowski's *The Double Life of Veronique*, with its overtly metaphysical worldview. Sorrentino establishes here a general theme of the significance of the relation to a person that one does not know, as often as not beyond any conventional heteronormative romantic relationship. In *One Man Up*, while Tony never gets to know Antonio in the usual sense of the term, his life takes on renewed meaning as a direct result of the latter's death, and the concluding scene of the quasisacramental fish dinner in the shared prison cell offers one of the most clearly upbeat endings in Sorrentino's canon to date.[28]

Until *The Young Pope*'s miracles, however, this is as metaphysical as Sorrentino will get. Here, in his first feature, the metaphysics are completely different from

FIGURE 1.6 *One Man Up*

those of the later television series: all-too-human, this-worldly, earth-bound. The film's metaphysics only manifest on the level of cinematic form (e.g., when the two Pisapias meet via the TV screen). Sorrentino exploits the uncanny coincidences that impossibly link the two Antonio Pisapias in order to broach what will prove to be a thematic preoccupation until *Youth* at least: what it means to be a man of a certain age, seeking a kind of salvation—in romantic love or some other form of human connection—from the prospect of a death whose only meaning derives from memories of the life one has lived. In the protagonists of the early films we are met with variations on "the enduring appeal of the Italian man who is out of joint."[29] With *This Must Be the Place* this theme opens out to embrace a broader, transnational conception of twenty-first-century masculine subjectivity. And, even though it may seem as though Sorrentino is returning to a similar character type with Jep Gambardella in *The Great Beauty* (also played by Servillo), this is not really the case. With Jep, gone is the Tony Pagoda template, replaced by someone not merely older but more world-weary, whose egocentrism and narcissism lead him to a kind of redemption, not by passing through humiliation but rather through a kind of postmodern revivification of the modernist art film trope of figuring life onscreen as an existential journey to what Céline calls "the end of the night" (au bout de la nuit) but which in *The Great Beauty* (for instance) becomes a navigation of the nothingness at the core of the self. This journey begins, however, in Sorrentino's second feature film.

TWO

The Consequences of Love (Le conseguenze dell'amore)

This Must Be the (Non-) Place

> Last of all comes melancholy, which is a state of grace, and then even that will be gone, because it's inherent in the way things work that even melancholy becomes a distant, unobtainable objective.
>
> —Paolo Sorrentino, *Everybody's Right*

THE CONSEQUENCES OF LOVE (2004) is about a former stockbroker forced by the Cosa Nostra to live in a hotel in Italian Switzerland, receiving and depositing into a local bank suitcases full of large amounts of laundered cash.[1] It is also a film about existential ennui, yearning, and unrequited love that morphs halfway through into a postmodern mafia film, the generic shift seamlessly elided via the film's intensified art cinema style.[2] The highly elliptical narrative allows Sorrentino to maintain tight control over the story, dispensing diegetic information in a judicious manner—in a sense tricking the viewer into believing that they know as much as the protagonist when in fact he holds all the cards and certain key events are only revealed late in the film, when it is narratively auspicious. In this *The Consequences of Love* goes beyond the selective narration of *One Man Up* (2001), where certain key events are revealed to the viewer only at the film's climax.

This chapter analyzes Sorrentino's second feature, the first to receive international distribution,[3] and his first with cinematographer Luca Bigazzi, as an exercise in genre filmmaking whose mode of narration is clearly determined, however, by the director's investment in an international art cinema tradition.[4] Roy Menarini does not go far enough, therefore, in his contention that this film, along with *The Family Friend* (2006)—as well as Matteo Garrone's early-2000s films, most notably *Gomorrah* (2008)—represented a renovation of the *form* of Italian cinema, in terms of both style and genre;[5] *The Consequences of Love* (to speak only of the one film) represented a renovation of cinematic form tout court, introducing a wider international audience to Sorrentino's stylistic vision. The second of his films to star Toni Servillo, the narrative seems to have completely departed from the satirical Italianisms—or even

Neapolitanisms—of *One Man Up* and the Tony Pagoda stories subsequently inspired by one of its two plotlines.[6] On the other hand, *The Consequences of Love* retains the same ambivalence toward the representation of women and their bodies, a trait that will only grow more pronounced, complex, and—for some critics—problematic, in subsequent films. (The character of Sofia—the film's primary object of masculine desire—also represents a kind of living intertextual link with neorealism and postwar Italian cinema through Olivia Magnani, Anna Magnani's granddaughter.)

The one aspect of Sorrentino's ongoing contribution to the contemporary art film exemplified in *The Consequences of Love* is the use of onscreen space—the diegetic space of the film's story-world—to establish mood, but even more so to adumbrate the protagonist's psycho-emotional state in a kind of twenty-first-century echo of Antonioni's modernist use of mise-en-scène as existential—and decidedly gendered—pathetic fallacy. This is consonant with Edward Branigan's claim that subjectivity is "a *production of space attributed to a character*" but in a thoroughly affectively charged sense.[7] According to Anthony Easthope, the postwar European art film is characterized on the formal level with the "erosion of classical cinematic space," which is often connected on the thematic level with the representation of modern (bourgeois) social alienation.[8] A classic example of this kind of film is Michelangelo Antonioni's *L'Avventura* (1960).[9] The first installment in the director's famous trilogy, *L'Avventura* exemplifies Gilles Deleuze's diagnosis of the time-image characteristic of postwar European art cinema, in which:

> a purely optical or sound situation becomes established in what we might call "any-space-whatever" [*l'espace quelconque*], whether disconnected, or emptied. . . . The post-war period has greatly increased the situations which we no longer know how to react to, in spaces which we no longer know how to describe. These were "any spaces whatever," deserted but inhabited . . . waste ground cities in the course of demolition or reconstruction.[10]

Such cinematic spaces are "dehumanized landscapes, or emptied spaces that might be seen as having absorbed characters and actions, retaining only a geophysical description."[11] Deleuze's "any-space-whatever" signifies as both the concrete (albeit empty, banal, or vague) *location* of the action as such and as an allegorical mental space-time of *psychic* action or inaction.[12] In the postwar art film, the primary action, as Deleuze emphasizes, is now that of *looking*—even more overtly, perhaps, than in classical Hollywood. Looking, and waiting: from the real time of postwar neorealism to the dead time (*le temps mort*) of the postwar art film. "The predominance of *temps mort* in the narrative, that is, a representation of a time sequence in the protagonist's life, where nothing happens . . . transitions from one location to another, waiting, having nothing to do."[13] Deleuze's *Cinema 1* is subtitled "the movement-image," and the shift in *Cinema 2* to the "time-image" is very significant in that it represents a shift in cinema practice (and in human life after World War II) from an emphasis on action to contemplation, which equals a very different attitude to or valuation of time, and within which the primary action as such is looking and, secondarily, waiting. Such paradoxically passive actions are exemplified and extended in *The Consequences of Love* by Titta's "insomniac perambulations" through the corridors of his hotel-cum-prison.[14]

In order to understand Titta's place in the narrative it is necessary, however, to consider the role or significance of gender in this understanding of postwar modernist cinema. How is one kind of onscreen space gendered differently from another, thereby projecting an entirely different kind of value to the viewer? Why is a space of domestic drudgery not accorded the same value as the masculinized "any-spaces-whatever" of a ruinous postwar Europe? To what degree, moreover, is the dead time of the art film equated with the existential suffering of the masculine protagonist, while the real time captured on screen in films such as Visconti's *Ossessione* (1943; the exhausted wife surrounded by dirty plates), or De Sica's *Umberto D.* (1952; the pregnant maid making morning coffee) is associated with spaces coded feminine, such as the kitchen?[15] Or, in a related example, what of Chantal Akerman's Jeanne Dielman, who, in the eponymous film, is constrained like Titta to sit and kill time but only when her regular ritualistic domestic routine is interrupted: even the onscreen spectacle of bored lassitude is valued in relation to gender specificity. (In *This Must Be the Place* [2011] Sorrentino offers a kind of answer or antidote to this film's highly gendered use of space in the form of protagonist Cheyenne [Sean Penn], whose androgynous appearance, passive mannerisms, and affected vocal patterns contrast sharply with his wife, Jane [Francis MacDormand], who beats him at handball and works as a firefighter while Cheyenne languishes in indolent retirement.) And, just as the kitchen is exchanged for the anonymous hotel bar, the regional specificity of these neorealist and postwar art cinematic locations is transmutated in Sorrentino's second film into the blandly international setting of Italian Switzerland. Sorrentino admits to being influenced by Marc Augé's analysis of the nonplaces of later twentieth and twenty-first-century global capitalism,[16] a sort of postmodern or late capitalist, anthropologically oriented updating of Deleuze's "any-space-whatever." The nonspace in Augé's sense comes after, chronologically, logically, and epistemologically, the "any-space-whatever" that Deleuze identifies as symptomatic of the mise-en-scène of postwar European art cinema, the cinema of the time-image. Apart from the shift in gender coding and emphasis, by the late 1990s and early 2000s Augé's nonspace denotes a shift from one kind of empty space to another. The one space in *The Consequences of Love* that most closely conforms to Deleuze's "any-space-whatever" is the deserted construction site, in which Titta's (Toni Servillo) final moments are played out. Apart from setting, the editing rhythms and relatively long takes also justify the invocation of Deleuze's time-image. But I would argue (with Franco Vigni) that on the diegetic level we are dealing with a setting more accurately described and evaluated as a nonspace in Augé's terms.[17] The nonspace is characteristic of what Augé calls supermodernity, another name for late or transnational capitalism. "Supermodernity . . . stems simultaneously from the three figures of excess: overabundance of events, spatial overabundance and the individualization of references"; i.e., an excess of *time*, an excess of *space*, and an excess of *self*. Supermodernity therefore "finds its full expression in non-places."[18] In *The Consequences of Love* specific spaces in Lugano—shopping malls, tourist hotels, banks—are used to generate an epistemological as much as an affective atmosphere: the concrete (albeit empty, banal, or vague) *location* of the action as such, as well as an allegorical mental space-time of *psychic* action or inaction.[19] In this film, rather than any straightforward representation of a specific subjectivity, Titta's character emerges out of the onscreen exploration of a set of general existential questions via the mise-en-scène, editing, and so forth. The nonplace is by definition *extraterritorial* as a new kind of universal objective space: the "world-wide space of consumption."[20] At the same time, though, there is what Augé calls the "paradox" of the nonplace: "a foreigner lost in a country he does not know . . . can feel at home there only in the anonymity of motorways, service stations, big stores or hotel chains."[21] If the maid, hostess, or homemaker is too much at home, this kind of man is entirely disconnected from anything positive that home represents in the Western imagination. This is Titta's paradoxical existence; an alienated feeling of at-homeness that he is only able to resolve in the end by courting a death that he believes to be more meaningful than his life.

The story begins in a deceptively simple manner: Titta di Girolamo (Toni Servillo) lives a lonely, regimented, purgatorial life in a high-end hotel in Lugano, in Italian Switzerland. The location is no coincidence, as Titta, unbeknownst to anyone else at the hotel, is a mafia bagman, coerced to fill this role as punishment for a past financial transgression. The film's first half, before his backstory is revealed, observes his ritualistic routine, comprised of weekly heroin doses and periodic trips to the local Swiss bank to deposit the large suitcases full of US dollars that show up without warning in his room (figure 2.1). Taking further the elliptical editing of *One Man Up*, *The Consequences of Love*, while for the most part a quieter story, features a more flamboyant visual style, with varied lens lengths, unusual angles, and more frequent camera movement contrasted with long still takes. In this film, in short, we see the emergence of Sorrentino and Bigazzi's unique approach to an intensified art film style. And, like *One Man Up*, *The Consequences of Love* is filmed in 35 mm film stock, the full shift to digital lying ahead.

FIGURE 2.1 *The Consequences of Love* (Paolo Sorrentino, 2004)

The film's final act, especially, which veers into mafia film territory when the action shifts from Lugano to Naples, is characterized by long mobile takes, a particularly spectacular one from Titta's point of view, and a markedly subjective editing rhythm that exploits an intra-diegetic flashback to cross-cut earlier, heretofore unseen, action with Titta's present-tense predicament. These highly manipulative structural choices bind the narration in the film's final sequence more closely to the main character's subjectivity, amplifying the story's situational ironies while granting him the redemption of a meaningful death—one of the consequences of his having fallen in love with Sofia, the hotel bartender who for ten years he observed and desired but never spoke to.[22] The day he breaks his silence, confessing his love to her is the moment his rigid and sterile routine begins its extended third-act collapse. (Titta to Sofia, immediately after his brother's departure: "Perhaps sitting at this bar is the most dangerous thing I've done in my life.") In this conclusion we see Sorrentino extending the trope of a quasimetaphysically meaningful death from *One Man Up*, betraying a nostalgic affection for generic closure that contradicts the films' general adherence to an art-cinematic ambiguity. He has returned to this trope twice more to date, in *Youth* and then in the final episode of *The Young Pope*.

Complications of the Gaze

The change in director of photography in *The Consequences of Love* is apparent from the opening shot, in which one can see how the cinematography, editing, soundtrack, and mise-en-scène are combined to create a complex, purely cinematic visual: a wide-angle static long take of a uniformed Swiss bank employee standing still on a moving sidewalk as he progresses from back- to foreground on an oblique angle through the space from the left to the right-hand side of the frame, an electronic track, "Scary World Theory" by Lali Puna, playing extradiegetically as the credit sequence unfolds (figure 2.2).[23] The titles are timed to finish just as the young man reaches the end of the walkway, exiting the frame noisily dragging a large suitcase. The very next scene/shot, following a sudden straight cut that interrupts the actor's motion as if to continue it with the camera's, introduces one of Bigazzi's signature camera movements: a relatively rapid, curving push in toward a character/actor, moving subtly from one side of the actor's face to the other. This shot is then typically followed, in a shot-reverse shot sequence, by a mirroring shot that often pushes in on the other character in the exchange, albeit curving in the opposite direction into the close-up. Among other effects, these idiosyncratic shot sequences dynamize relatively static scenes, investing them with movement, adding a layer of ironic meaning that could not be conveyed on the level of the mise-en-scène alone.

This opening sequence is worth analyzing in some detail, following the initial dynamic shot-reverse shot. (As in chapter 1, the object of this detailed analysis is to clearly establish Sorrentino's unique approach to an intensified style, continued and amplified here with the switch in cinematographer.) One of the effects of this seemingly superfluous movement is to subtly but clearly indicate to the viewer that, despite Titta's appearing in all but a few key scenes, the camera is not to be identified

FIGURE 2.2 *The Consequences of Love*

with a specific character/actor within the diegesis in their looking; this becomes clear with the answering shot. After another reverse-angle medium shot on Sofia (Magnani), the hotel bartender, there is a cut to the protagonist, until now unseen. This time the camera pushes straight in from medium to close-up on the impeccably dressed Titta, as he states in the voiceover that will mark this film out from most of Sorrentino's work to date:[24] "The worst thing for a man who spends a lot of time alone is lack of imagination." Another cut and reframing to a central medium shot. "Life, which is already boring and repetitive becomes deadly dull when imagination is missing," intones Titta. These words are spoken over another wider group shot of the ostentatiously dressed man who devours Sofia with his eyes while Titta gazes appraisingly at him. There is a cut back to Sofia in close-up, carrying a tray of cocktails, then the reverse shot of the staring man, while Titta remarks in self-reflexive voiceover, as if confiding in the viewer (the fourth position in the triangle; the odd man out: *un uomo in più*): "Look at this individual with the bow-tie. Many would enjoy speculating about his profession and his relationship with these women." This reference, as if to a storyline in a different film, is followed by a reverse medium close-up of Sofia bending over to serve the drinks while exposing some cleavage, as if for the man's delectation. As she looks up at him there is a cut to Titta in medium close-up looking on from one side, the camera once more curving to the left as it pushes in to a closer framing. "I, on the other hand, see only a frivolous man," he continues in voiceover. As the camera tracks leftward, "I am not a frivolous man. The only frivolous thing I possess is my name, Titta di Girolamo." As Titta turns his head to look left, a cut back to the whole group now shows Sofia still bending and serving the cocktails. As the camera pulls back and up, however, the group around the other man turns as one to look at something off-screen. A cut back to Titta in extreme close-up, as the sound of clopping horses' hoofs is audible. Glancing up, Titta notices the group looking his way. There is a straight cut to an extreme close-up of Sofia's face, still looking off-screen, then a cut to wide group shot, now also including Titta in his

FIGURE 2.3 *The Consequences of Love*

chair in the foreground, the sound of hoofs suddenly foregrounded, as a reflection of a horse and carriage moves across the shot of the group from right to left, signaling to the viewer that the camera is now outside the lobby window looking in (figure 2.3). Titta turns his head to look outside, and a cut to an over-the-shoulder shot reveals what he, too, now sees: a horse-drawn funeral hearse passing by in front of the hotel. Death thus enters the diegesis, announcing itself in a very literal fashion. There is a cut back to the external perspective on Titta in close-up, still looking at the hearse, then back to the reverse angle on Titta from inside, as he writes something in a notebook. (In a subsequent scene in the hotel bar, as Titta glimpses Sofia changing her shirt in the mirror, a close-up on the notebook reveals: "Future plans: Never underestimate the consequences of love.")

Titta's voiceover remarks about this "frivolous man" (*uomo frivolo*) are echoed in a subsequent scene, when his stepbrother (Adriano Giannini, son of Giancarlo) stops by the hotel for an unannounced visit. Titta calls him a "superficial man . . . You're not even a man. You're just a boy." Sorrentino as screenwriter has his protagonist voice a critically nostalgic desire to retain a kind of authentic masculinity, however flawed, in the face of what could already be seen in 2004 as the increasingly infantilized identities offered up by a rapidly globalizing popular culture—a shift that took a unique and especially dispiriting form in Italy from the 1980s on, thanks largely to the influence of Berlusconi's media empire.[25] This may sound like an overreading, but in scanning the corpus of Sorrentino's films and television work one repeatedly finds the comparable emphasis on a masculine subject position which, in various iterations, underpins both the modern postenlightenment humanist tradition and the hypostatized sexist and misogynist attitudes that have in recent years sparked a salutary neofeminist backlash. That said, Titta's own attitude toward not children but childhood (his own) is more complex, while still of a piece with the foregoing analysis. In a subsequent scene, for instance, during a game of cards, his hotel neighbor the Countess (Angela Goodwin) remarks that "we should never break the ties with our childhood," to which Titta responds, a little too loudly, "Never," which he then more quietly qualifies: "Never, we shouldn't." This exchange anticipates Titta's subsequent admission to his stepbrother that he still considers one Dino Giuffré to be his best friend, despite the fact that they have not spoken in twenty years. (As soon as his stepbrother mentions Dino Giuffré, the camera pushes in rapidly on Titta's startled face, sudden strings sobbing melodramatically on the soundtrack. A comparable effect occurs when, in a later scene, Titta, after finally speaking to Sofia after ten years of silence, returns to find a pair of Sicilian hit men comfortably ensconced in his room. As he enters, the nondiegetic violin music on the soundtrack suddenly detunes into a final, sour note, expressing Titta's subjective response.) What becomes clear in these early scenes is Titta's refusal of half-way measures, his absolute way of thinking: "If we were friends once, we're friends for life," he says of Dino Giuffré, recalling the earlier exchange with the Countess about the importance of one's childhood to one's present and future self. By the film's end, this uncompromising attitude will be both Titta's undoing and, for lack of a better word, his salvation.

The first twenty-five minutes of *The Consequences of Love* is a masterful and highly particularized study of existential ennui: Titta's daily routine consists of bouts of idleness between long stretches of boredom, the idleness of waiting manifest onscreen in the stretches of *temps mort* which, thanks to Bigazzi's camera work, Giogiò Franchini's editing, and the film's eclectic soundtrack, is anything but boring for the viewer. Ironically, this style is employed to thematize Titta's unrequited longing masking a core of existential emptiness. The dialogue is also exploited in the service of this theme: "What's going on outside?" the Countess asks after dinner. "Nothing" (*niente*), replies Titta, as the pedestrian crossing signal on the street corner outside silently changes from green to red. Later, when Titta telephones his ex-wife (Gianna Paola Scaffidi) and family, he asks his daughter (Roberta Serretiello) what she is doing, to which she replies "practically nothing." "Good," he responds, I'm doing that too." As the call ends he begins to ask his wife something, but to her query, after an extended pause, answers only, "Nothing." Existential nothingness or negativity in Sorrentino's films represents a thematic vestige of the director's affinities with modernist film[26] but also with late nineteenth- and early twentieth-century European literature. If nothing else, then, this preamble creates a sense of receptivity as much in the viewer as in Titta toward the Baron's (Rafaelle Pisu) repeated insistence that he desires a "spectacular death" to match the kind of life he once lived before losing all his money to gambling debts. As it transpires, Titta may be the only one who takes the Baron at his word. For, as Titta learns too late, the antidote to existential nothingness is not the kind of love he feels for Sofia; the metaphysics of nothingness can only be mitigated by the paradoxical immanence of the ethical relation to a different other, to a friend.

Unlike *One Man Up*, *The Consequences of Love* contains no dream scenes, although it does have at least one quietly hallucinatory episode brought on by Titta's heroin use (his "unconfessable secret"), a bravura sequence-shot in which Bigazzi's camera (with I.S.A.N.'s moodily creepy ambient track "Remegio" in the background) performs a complex recursive arc over Titta's slowly dropping body as the drug kicks in.[27] There is also a single, striking montage sequence, combining extra- and intradiegetic flashback, in which Titta masturbates in bed while picturing various women. The latter contrasts starkly with the fragmentary flashback that is intercut with the climactic scene of Titta's spectacular and self-sacrificial death at the hands of the Cosa Nostra. This early sequence in the hotel is precipitated by one of several interludes in which Titta sits in his favorite window table in the hotel bar, surreptitiously eyeing Sofia as she goes about her work (figure 2.4). At the end of her shift, as she moves behind the bar to change her shirt, the camera temporarily aligns itself with Titta's point of view. This is clear from the fact that Titta, with the viewer, is able to watch her as she removes her shirt, fleetingly revealing her naked back (figure 2.5). This shot is only justified in a realist register if one assumes (retroactively, at least) that Sofia is exposing herself to him deliberately; otherwise, and at the same time, it is an egregious instance of the male gaze as formal principle, which Sorrentino will explore in a more spectacular fashion in *The Great Beauty*, *Youth* and, especially, *Loro*. This is typical of Sorrentino's masculinist style, in which a woman's objectification is subsumed within the male protagonist's desiring gaze, with which the viewer is temporarily aligned. The uncritical, moralistically inclined viewer is left to judge the character rather than the film, just as, in contemporary society, one is always encouraged to judge the individual rather than the system. With Sorrentino's films, as with society, this is generally a mistake as it leaves one without a clear understanding of the bigger picture.

The abovementioned masturbation montage sequence begins with a high angle close-up of Titta's hands and notebook as he writes the words: "Future plans: not to underestimate . . ." Before he can finish there is a cut to an over-Titta's-shoulder shot in which Sofia is visible in blurry outline as she prepares to leave the hotel, then a close-up on Titta looking up only when she is gone. His longing gaze as she greets what turns out to be her driving instructor outside only confirms Titta's state of isolation and unrequited love. A frontal medium close-up of Titta is followed by an unmotivated silent shot of what appears to be his ex-wife in her much-younger guise as a new bride. The camera pushes in as she lifts the veil from her face; a cut to

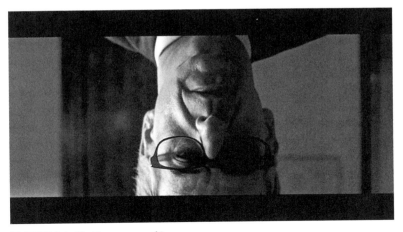

FIGURE 2.4 *The Consequences of Love*

FIGURE 2.5 *The Consequences of Love*

the window frame inside Titta's hotel room at night. The camera drifts leftward to the mini-bar, whose highly polished surface shows Titta in bed. A cut to a frontal, symmetrical medium shot of Titta as he masturbates under the covers.[28] The camera again pushes in slowly, then cuts to another unmotivated shot of his ex-wife in a hospital room, smiling and holding a swaddled baby. At this point it is clear that these inserts are a series of fragmentary flashbacks, marshaled in the service of Titta's meager erotic life. As if to balance the preceding shot, the camera drifts back and away from his ex-wife as she whispers "Ciao." There is a cut back to continue the push in to Titta in bed, then cut to a close-up of his ex-wife, again dressed as a bride, this time frowning pensively beneath her veil. Here the pace of the editing picks up speed: cut to a silent shot of the well-dressed blonde woman from an earlier scene on an escalator at a local upscale mall. She looks directly into the camera, once again briefly optically aligned with Titta's point-of-view; as she pulls her hair from her neck the camera cuts again to Titta, curving in toward him in close-up, this time from the left. Cut to an unknown woman holding a telephone receiver to her ear as the camera as it were continues its trajectory across this montage. This is followed by another quick shot of another mysterious woman seated at his favorite table in the hotel bar, holding a black veil in her hands, as if she were dressed for mourning. There is a cut to push in to close-up on Titta; then a cut to the earlier shot of Sofia visible behind the curtain behind the bar. This time, as she moves off-screen her naked breast is clearly visible, which it wasn't the first time—in "reality." From this a cut to a close-up on Titta in profile, unlit cigarette dangling from his lips as he looks out his window, followed by a cut to what he appears to be looking at: a construction crane in the far distance, framed in silhouette against a Swiss sunset. Cut to a different crane, even farther away, as it rotates; extreme close-up on Titta's tired eyes. If nothing else, it becomes clear from this example that Sorrentino's, which is to say Franchini's, favored transitional device is the straight cut. While this is hardly unusual within a scene, between shots, it acquires more significance as a formal choice in terms of the way in which one scene is linked to the next. The net effect is a dynamically elliptical editing style, compelling the viewer to work harder than is the case in a more classical style of narration, utilizing more overt transitional techniques, such as the fade. Otherwise, the other distinguishing stylistic trait in the films and other works, from *One Man Up* to *The Young Pope*, is the long take combined with a highly mobile camera.

In contrast to this complex masturbation scene, the abovementioned drug-induced hallucination scene barely registers as such, relying as it does on the simplest in-camera effects. This is where Titta, in voiceover, confesses his "unmentionable secret," the fact that he has taken heroin every Wednesday at 10:00 A.M. without fail for twenty-four years. As he explains this, the camera drifts from a close-up of his outstretched arm receiving the needle, to the hotel room window, which rack-focuses into view. Through the window we briefly see Sofia walking to work in the street below. As if in response to her motion, the camera, having completed its outward arc, swings smoothly around to the reverse angle, panning past three seated figures in a painterly composition along the wall next to Titta's bed. The three actors have moved into position in the brief time it took the camera to travel to the window and back; they are two young men and one young woman dressed in white tunics with large crucifixes (figure 2.6). All three are turned to look at Titta, who has in the meantime pulled the bed covers over his head. The camera continues its trajectory, resting briefly on the protagonist, who suddenly sits up, throwing the blankets from his face. As if motivated by this gesture, the camera pans back across the wall, revealing that the seated figures have vanished. As before, in the brief time it took the camera to pause on Titta, the actors have moved out of the shot; the viewer realizes that they were never really there except in Titta's altered perception, but their appearance remains mysterious until the subsequent scene, following that in which the young woman reads a quotation from Céline in the hotel bar. In the scene in question Titta telephones Giulia, his ex-wife. She stands in medium shot, in what appears to be her kitchen, holding the telephone to her ear, as Titta asks if any of his three children are available. Bigazzi's signature slow, drifting push in toward Giulia is superseded by the reverse-angle shot revealing the

FIGURE 2.6 *The Consequences of Love*

same three young people, seated at the kitchen table, having dinner: his daughter and two sons. Only the girl deigns to speak with him. The viewer realizes that, in Titta's heroin-induced vision, his children are dressed as if to attend at their father's funeral, since, as their behavior suggest, he is already dead to them.

The book read by the young woman at the table in the intervening scene is Louis-Ferdinand Céline's first novel from 1932, *Journey to the End of the Night* (also the source of the epigraph to *The Great Beauty*[29]). The quotation, from the novel's third-to-last chapter, is as follows:

> Whatever he wants can happen! A fine mess! That's the advantage of using only one's memories to excite oneself. You can own memories, you can buy even more beautiful ones. But life is more complicated, human life especially so. A frightening, desperate adventure. Compared to this vice of formal perfectionism, cocaine is nothing but a stationmaster's pastime. But let us return to Sophie. . . . We became poetic as we admired her being, beautiful and reckless. The rhythm of her life flowed from different springs than ours. Ours can only creep along, envious. This force of happiness, both exacting and sweet, that animated her from head to toe, disturbed us. It unsettled us enchantingly, but it unsettled us nonetheless.[30]

Titta listens to her reading, as if applying the content of the passage to his own situation, which the viewer is also invited to do. (Sophie, after all, shares her name with Sofia, Titta's love interest.[31]) This scene is followed by a straight cut to Titta's ex-wife in medium shot, standing in what appears to be her kitchen, holding the telephone to her ear, as Titta's abortive conversation with his estranged family commences.

Céline is French literature's modernist misanthrope par excellence and an important noncinematic influence on Sorrentino's filmmaking at the level of story, character, dialogue, and generally ironically misanthropic sensibility.[32] In this sense, at least, Sorrentino reveals himself to be a knowingly and, dare I say, productively retrograde screenwriter, unafraid to delve into subject matter and social issues that many other male cultural producers today would avoid out of fear of controversy and negative publicity. This apparent indifference to anything like a politically correct agenda, for lack of a better word, is most evident in Sorrentino's debut novel, *Everybody's Right*, which owes both a stylistic and thematic debt to Céline's own debut.[33] The novel's protagonist, Tony Pagoda, could be described as one of the great misanthropes of contemporary Italian literature—a description that also applies in a cinematic context to the protagonists of all of Sorrentino's films to date. Céline—or that is to say his antihero, Ferdinand Bardamu—is in this sense revealed as one of the principal spiritual forefathers of the Sorrentinian subject.

A Spectacular Death

The Consequences of Love is not unique in Sorrentino's canon for the significance of literary transmediation to plot, character, and theme. Unlike *The Great Beauty* or *The Young Pope*, however, with their reliance on extradiegetic flashbacks, *Consequences* is unusual in that its flashbacks or dream scenes are integrated into the diegesis, adding texture to the narrative flow, amplifying narrative meaning or explaining character. In this subjective expressivity the film is more akin to *The Family Friend* stylistically than it is to the others. At the same time, its increasingly complex emplotment relies on repressed narrative content that is only revealed very late in the third act. Up to this point the viewer appears to be in possession of the same quantity of knowledge as the protagonist. As it turns out, however, Titta had taken control of events in a completely unforeseen manner unheralded by his character to this point. The narrative's final surprise twist is provided in a key intradiegetic flashback scene that unfolds in fragments—in the mafiosi's car and later while he is being lowered into a vat of liquid concrete—where specific gaps in our knowledge are filled in—gaps of which we were heretofore unaware. This revelation is constructed in such a masterful way that the viewer is barely tempted to balk at the liberties taken by screenwriter and editor alike. For instance: How did Titta get into his parked car and pull the drop sheet back over top? For that matter, why would the hotel manager (and others) display such curiosity about Titta's profession when, as he explains to Sofia, once or twice a week he receives a large suitcase full of money which he then deposits in a nearby Swiss bank but only after striding purposefully through the hotel lobby wearing an especially snappy suit while dragging the suitcase? Even more than his final ride in the mafiosi's car, with its stark ambiguities—When was Pippo D'Antó (Vincenzo Vitagliano) shot? Was there ever a gun lying between the back seats?—these apparent gaps serve to augment the film's portrait of Titta, keeping the narrative tethered to him and his point of view, with the exception of two important sequences. These cutaway shots—like the final image of Dino Giuffré in the Alto Adige—can be read as "fantasy images" or "mental projections" occasioned by Sorrentino's propensity for "hypersubjectivity."[34] The abovementioned scene with the arcing camera over Titta as he shoots up, like the masturbation montage sequence, is emblematic of this tendency.

When the two hit men first impose themselves upon Titta in his room, they are there in Lugano to carry out a job. During this sequence, for the first time in the film, Titta is not part of the action. As Marlow-Mann convincingly explains, the camera work and editing patterns ensure the viewer's alignment—if not allegiance—with the gun-wielding killer as he shoots first an unnamed man in his home and then the man's disabled son, the latter, it seems, merely because he was unlucky enough to be there.[35] Otherwise these characters remain completely peripheral to the main narrative. This scene also ensures that there are no grounds for sympathy with the killers when they are themselves gunned down by Titta in the surprise twist presented in flashback. While the viewer is aligned with the hitman in this sequence, there is no meaningful allegiance established. This is also the first time that the story enters into *poliziesco* territory, foreshadowing the wholesale genre shift by the film's end. Something comparable occurs in the scene of Sofia's car accident, when the viewer is again aligned with another character, this time a more sympathetic one; but again the scene is constructed in a way that precludes identification, not least because it ends with the severely injured Sofia, in medium shot from outside her damaged car, reduced from object of desire (of whom the viewer knows no more than Titta) to a broken mannequin.[36]

The bravura tracking shot that crowns the film's final act lasts nearly seven full minutes without a single cut. This is almost thirty seconds longer than the lengthy tracking shot where Tony enters the nightclub in *One Man Up*, which is just under six-and-a-half minutes. The long sequence shot in the latter film dynamizes the protagonist's personality, showing him off as the center of both the viewer's and the other characters' attention. (As will be seen in chapter 4, the final shot of *Il Divo*, also a lengthy tracking shot, has a comparable but far more ironic effect in relation to the character of Giulio Andreotti.) The long mobile take in *The Consequences of Love*, by contrast, through the equivalent formal means, completely inverts this effect by effectively effacing Titta for most of the long single take journey from the hotel room to the convention hall in which he must explain himself to mafia boss Nitto lo Riccio.[37]

The camera precedes the men out of the room, with mafiosi walking before and after Titta. Moving backwards, down the hall, the camera keeps the group in medium close-up, Titta's face a tight mask of anxiety and fear. As the group rounds a corner in the long hallway, the camera takes up a position behind, the men moving into an elevator. Inside, the camera stays in close on Titta's nervous face; the elevator's facing door opens, allowing the group to proceed out the back, the camera following the lead mafioso past Titta, assuming the latter's point of view as they progress through the hotel. They descend a set of stairs, the man in front turning to look back at the camera, as if at Titta. They move down another hallway; at a corner two men turn to look directly at Titta/the camera. Finally the group turns and enters the convention hall, moving up the center aisle past multiple rows of chairs, toward a banner stretched across the front of the hall that reads "Ipertrofia della Prostata: Xth Corso di Aggiornamento."[38] Mary Wood convincingly glosses this sign as a critique of the fact that the Mafia's "controlling and ordered business practices, which impact in such deleterious ways on humankind, derive from a retrograde and excessive masculinist competitive culture."[39] Partway, the same mafioso turns again to check on Titta, as another man openly watches him, which is to say the camera, pass by. As the camera turns toward the front of the room, Titta walks into his own point of view from the left side, the camera assuming a position again behind the group. Before the table at the front, behind which sit several men, like a kind of tribunal,[40] Titta turns as the camera arcs around to face him. It continues to circle, as he is invited to sit down, ending up behind Nitto Lo Riccio's (Vittorio di Prima) head, as if looking over his shoulder at Titta, who is on the stand, on trial for his life. In fact, we never once see Nitto from the front, a strangely iconophobic courtesy Sorrentino and Bigazzi never extend to another criminal in their films.

The tribunal scene is followed by another lengthy sequence of a completely different nature, when the mafiosi drive Titta overnight to a remote construction site where he will meet his spectacular death, which is really a gratuitous act of self-sacrifice. Like Tony in *L'uomo in più*, he performs a "spectacular action for the sake of a virtual stranger in the name of freedom and in doing so renounces his life."[41] (The ironic application here of *spectacular* to a death as conclusion to a life that was anything but anticipates the even more flagrant use of the term in the subtitle of Sorrentino's fourth feature, *Il Divo: The Spectacular Life of Giulio Andreotti*.) First, though, Sorrentino takes advantage of the long car trip to fill us in on the bits of the story that were heretofore withheld. The scene opens with a point-of-view shot out the front windscreen of the car as it drives through a long highway tunnel. An Italian pop song by Ornella Vanini, "Rossetto e cioccolatto" ("Lipstick and Chocolate"), plays on the car radio as the mafioso (Giorgio Scarpato) in the front passenger seat sings along. From the close-up on the musical gangster the camera cuts to the sleeping Pippo D'Antó in the back, then to Titta himself, framed through the car's open window. As the other man sings about "sensualitá di latina," Titta stares pensively, lost in thought. The camera cuts to an extreme close-up as the audio shifts suddenly from diegetic sound emanating from the car's radio to music playing in Titta's head as he recalls the events in his hotel the day before. The flashback opens with a fast punch in from medium close-up to close-up on Titta reflected in his bathroom mirror, as the two Sicilians leave with the suitcase full of money, the car radio music suddenly interrupted by the zipping sound of the extended suitcase handle. A sudden cut to a rapid, staggered zoom into a close-up on Titta's face, then a brief extreme close-up of Titta's eye in the round shaving mirror, then a cut to the two gangsters in long shot moving down the hotel hallway with the suitcase (figure 2.7). Titta crosses in the foreground, taking the parallel hall in in order to access the controls for the elevator, to which the viewer's attention had been drawn in an earlier scene. Titta shuts off the power, leaving the crooks in medium shot in profile, ineffectually pushing the down buttons.

There is a cut back to a close-up of Titta in the car, "Rossetto e cioccolatto" again playing diegetically. The camera moves from outside the moving car into the space normally occupied by the driver, looking toward the backseat. Titta glances down into the car's interior, and there is a cut to a close-up on a gun with silencer lying between the seats. Pan up to Pippo's apparently sleeping face, followed by a brief shot of the driver's face in the rearview mirror from Titta's perspective, as if to establish that yes, there is in fact someone driving the car despite the camera's impossible

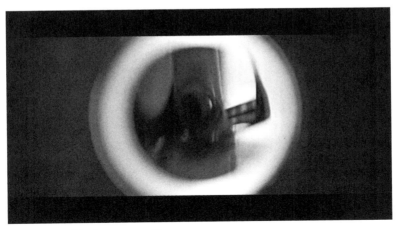

FIGURE 2.7 *The Consequences of Love*

position in the driver's seat a moment before. The camera swings back outside, Titta still in close-up, then a flashback to a close-up of Titta the day before in his room, during the tail-end of his phone conversation with Pippo, as he tells him that he will come to Naples in two days to explain things to Nitto Lo Riccio, the Cosa Nostra boss. A cut to the Sicilians lugging the heavy suitcase down several flights of stairs, then Titta moving quickly to the hallway circuit board, where he restores the elevator power. Another out-of-focus point-of-view shot of the crooks moving slowly down the stairs, then Titta taking the elevator. There is a cut back to Titta in the car, where he notices that the gun is no longer there (was it ever there?), and that Pippo is in fact dead, shot through the heart, for having tried to gain his independence from Nitto. The suggestion is that Pippo was behind the bag heist, having set up Titta to take the fall. The fact the Nitto knew that he was innocent ironically enhances the significance of Titta's self-sacrificial act of not returning the suitcase with the cash, proving once and for all that he is no frivolous man. This long sequence ends with another tracking shot, this time from behind the car in long shot as it speeds along the nocturnal southern Italian highway.[42]

The flashback continues during the next sequence, however, linking the two sections together by means of Titta's subjective narration of the secondary plotline of how things came to this pass. The final scene, in the construction site in the bright southern Italian sun, opens with a wide establishing shot that gives way to a tracking shot across the heavy equipment that eventually finds Titta, bound and suspended by a harness from a construction crane. The camera tracks in toward and arcs around Titta, then pulls away as it sinks to a low-angle long shot, with Titta in the background and the musical mafioso from behind in the foreground, looking up (figure 2.8). A series of cuts back and forth between Titta and the mafiosi establish his passive victimhood, the camera even assuming Titta's point-of-view, looking down from his high-angle point-of-view upon a large rectangular tank of fresh wet cement, with his shoes in the foreground. Then a cut to the Sicilian hit men in the Lugano

FIGURE 2.8 *The Consequences of Love*

FIGURE 2.9 *The Consequences of Love*

hotel parking garage, as Titta's thoughts return to the interrupted flashback, exactly where it left off in the previous scene. A close-up of one crook's hand as he presses the car's remote, the telltale chirp of the lock, then a close-up on the taillight flashing under the drop sheet. As the two men pull this off one of them notices something inside the car; he peers into the tinted window, and there is a cut to the opposite side of the car as the camera sinks below the roofline, matching the crook's movement. The black window conceals a cut to the Sicilian on the opposite side of the car, with one man's face reflected in the glass. A gunshot shatters the pane, killing the first crook, revealing Titta, seated inside holding his gun, with which he then shoots the second (figure 2.9). A high-angle overhead shot of Titta getting out of the car and going around to the bodies. He silences the car alarm, then an elliptical cut to him lifting the last leg into the trunk before he slams it shut and adjusts his tie. A cut to Titta pulling the drop sheet back over the car, and leaving with the suitcase, then a cut to the already familiar scene of Titta waiting in the hotel lobby for Sofia: close-up on the wall clock striking 4:00 P.M., cut to Titta on the sofa in his overcoat. Then the flashback ends with the same shot of the two mafiosi in the bright morning light looking up at Titta, suspended above, off-screen. The crane begins to lower him toward the wet cement, first in long wide-angle shot, then in close-up. Titta looks down at the cement rectangle below. As it moves closer a cut to a black screen conceals a transition to another scene in the Lugano hotel that is not part of Titta's flashback, strictly speaking, but that nonetheless completes the narrative. The camera pans up to reveal the edge of the opened suitcase and the faces of the Baron and his wife standing and looking down in disbelief. There is a cut to the opened case packed full of money, then a cut to a high-angle shot looking up at Titta as he approaches the tank of cement, the camera ascending and passing him as he descends. Another series of cuts back and forth concludes again with the camera aligned with Titta's point of view as he looks down at the cement, now very close. A cut to a close-up on his feet and legs as they enter the grey liquid. The camera pans up to his face as he stares stoically in front of him. Flashback to Sofia in Lugano, as she zips up her winter coat, a look of disdain on her face. The sequence now structurally resembles the earlier masturbating scene, the intervening images an ambiguous hybrid of fantasy and memories. A cut from Titta to a dust cloud in the construction site gives way to a cross-fade of a snowdrift. A cut back to Titta in close-up as his chin nears the cement. Cut to a pattern of parallel power lines as the camera tilts down to reveal an electrical tower in a crepuscular, snowy alpine landscape. There is a cut back to Titta as the top half of his head slips below the surface, a few air bubbles the only trace he was there. A straight cut to an extreme high angle on an orange-clad figure high up the electrical tower, Titta in voiceover, in an impossible temporality (because we just watched him die): "Only one thing's certain. I know it. Every now and then, at the top of an electric pylon, in the midst of a snowy landscape, against a cold, biting wind, Dino Giuffré stops. Sadness [*melanconia*] descends upon him, and he starts to think. And thinks that I, Titta di Girolamo, am his best friend." The present tense suggests that he once spoke these words to himself. More than one critic notes the conclusion's emphasis on "the power of memory."[43] The film concludes with an extreme close-up of Dino Giuffré who turns and gazes out over the snowy landscape. With this concluding shot, it is as if Sorrentino extends the metaphysical conceit of *One Man Up*, transforming the uncanny coincidences that connect two disparate lives into a formal principle for the cinematic expression of one man's self-understanding. For Titta, in the end, love's consequences are manifold and contradictory: where on the one hand his love for Sofia comes to nothing, his irrational devotion to his friend offers him—and, by extension, the viewer—a kind of redemption.

THREE

The Family Friend (L'amico di famiglia)

"Ridiculous Men and Beautiful Women"

Suicide always has an ironic outcome and I can't afford irony.
—Geremia, *The Family Friend*

Redeem yourself, that's my advice.
—Lawyer (to Geremia), *The Family Friend*

THE FAMILY FRIEND (2006) is a film about Geremia di Geremei (Giacomo Rizzo), a sad sack small-time moneylender living in the Pontine region outside Rome. To reduce the film's story to Geremia's particular trajectory, however, is to overlook the impact of the film's complex plot structure and consequently highly selective dispersal of narrative information. As in *One Man Up* and *The Consequences of Love*—but resulting in a very different relationship between viewer and protagonist in each case—*The Family Friend* is edited so as to carefully manage spectatorial knowledge at any given point, ironically pinning the viewer's perspective to Geremia's throughout in a textbook case of alignment over allegiance.[1] Marlow-Mann's analyses of Sorrentino's second and third features from this perspective offer a convincing response to the feminist critique of Sorrentino as misogynist filmmaker. That neither *The Consequences of Love* nor, especially, *The Family Friend* is meaningfully or intentionally misogynist in its representation of women is clear from a close analysis of shot structure, framing, focalization, editing, and other formal factors.[2] That this assessment may not always be applicable to the later films is a question to be explored in this and subsequent chapters. This chapter, then, goes beyond existing readings of *The Family Friend* by considering more closely its presentation of the protagonist as an ironically embodied critique of specific stereotypical anti-Semitic traits, inaugurating a thematic line more explicitly explored in Sorrentino's fifth feature, *This Must Be the Place*. In these films the Sorrentian subject takes the form of a character whose Jewishness, real or imaginary, constitutes a central aspect of his identity. As in chapters 1 and 2, my reading of the third feature places it into the ongoing comparative framework, in which an ethics of human relationships plays out on the level of form.

The Family Friend was filmed in the same central Italian locations as portions of Lina Wertmüller's Fascist era-set *Love and Anarchy* (1973), in particular the town of Sabaudia, built by Mussolini on the reclaimed Pontine Marshes (Agro Pontine), drained in the 1930s by the dictator's orders.[3] (That this history still resonates in contemporary Italy is referenced in the film when a character speaks approvingly of "il nostro Duce's" achievement in draining the marshes and ridding them of malaria-bearing mosquitoes.) As remarked in chapter 2, in his move toward a transnational mode Sorrentino has drawn inspiration from Marc Augé's analysis of the "non places" of later twentieth and twenty-first century global capitalism.[4] The mise-en-scène in *The Family Friend* builds on the comparable use made in *The Consequences of Love* of specific spaces in Lugano—shopping malls, tourist hotels, banks—to generate a specific epistemological and affective atmosphere. In its use of Sabaudia's unique architectural spaces, *The Family Friend* takes Bigazzi's stylistic approach in *The Consequences of Love* even further;[5] in Sorrentino's third feature one sees the idiosyncratic lighting techniques that contributed to *The Great Beauty*'s global success: not only are interiors often shot in chiaroscuro using only available light sources placed within the shot but Bigazzi also goes to the opposite extreme, adding artificial lights and reflectors to the outdoor scenes, granting onscreen bodies a kind of incandescence—e.g., the scene where Geremia, with metal detector, encounters the nearly-naked sunbather; or where, while sitting on a park bench, he reencounters Belana, the Romanian woman he tried to marry at the outset; or the closing credit sequence, where he is on the beach again with his metal detector[6]—an effect that will be exploited to the full in Lenny's flashbacks to his mother in *The Young Pope*.[7]

This chapter considers how *The Family Friend* continues Sorrentino's exploration of powerful but ridiculous men in the (mostly) ridiculous and repugnant figure of Geremia de Geremei, a tailor and small-time loan shark who improbably falls in love with Rosalba (Laura Chiatti), local Agro Pontine beauty contest winner and the woman who will eventually betray his trust the one and only time he grants it to another human being. In a pivotal scene, Geremia seduces Rosalba, or rather she concedes to sex with him on her wedding day, on the condition that he all but forgive her father's outstanding debt, incurred from a loan he arranged in order to stage her large and utterly conventional wedding. In this chapter I read the film in relation not only to Sorrentino's emerging distinctive style but also in relation to how this style serves the narrative's focalization around the protagonist and his many quirks, most notably his radically naïve views on women—a childlike naiveté that is his undoing, in stark contrast to Rosalba's hyperbolically gorgeous youthfulness, which conceals a self-serving cynicism. Her youthful beauty, which she knows is the source of her power over him, introduces the thematic binary of youth vs. old age that Sorrentino will explore in greater depth in the 2015 film *Youth* (*La giovinezza*)—a binary that in his films frequently maps onto that of gender difference. Finally, the price to be paid for being perceived as ridiculous, like Geremia, is to suffer humiliation, where the term is understood not only in respect to enduring mockery but also as the gaining of humility, only too late. The other main theme in *The Family Friend*, therefore, is precisely the negative affective state of humiliation, whether the Shylockian kind to which the protagonist is eventually subjected by his erstwhile friends (to be discussed below) or the ultimately more disturbing form of humiliation experienced by women who must accommodate themselves to a world shaped by and for morally misshapen, consequently ridiculous, men.

The Meaningful Difference of Non-normative Identities, Part 1

The abovementioned scene in which Geremia seduces Rosalba—as in the later scene, preceding the conclusion, in which Rosalba truly seduces him—presents a complex and disturbing example of Sorrentino's (and director of photography Bigazzi's, and editor Franchini's) ability to manipulate spectatorial levels of engagement, controlling alignment, if not allegiance, in Murray Smith's terms, via cinematography, editing, and mise-en-scène. I will only add a few remarks here to Marlow-Mann's masterful analysis of this aspect of the film. The second seduction scene, for instance, complicates any reading of *The Family Friend* as misogynist, even as it substantiates Marlow-Mann's general point about the play of allegiance and alignment across the film. In this late scene, Rosalba appears naked in medium close-up, beautifully lit and framed as if to titillate the heterosexual male viewer, daring this highly specific spectator to identify with Geremia (indeed, Bigazzi's lighting makes Geremia's squalid apartment look comparably attractive as the setting for this most unlikely of trysts) (figure 3.1). When the two actually engage in consensual sex, however, the camera in tight close-ups assumes first Rosalba's then Geremia's optical point of view, shifting the viewer's alignment between the two of them, heightening the disturbingly comic effect, and yet also obviating any possibility of reading the scene (unlike the first, highly elliptical, seduction scene) as representing an act of sexual violence. That Geremia's antimigraine

FIGURE 3.1 *The Family Friend*, (Paolo Sorrentino, 2006)

potato poultice drops onto Rosalba's face during intercourse only bolsters this reading. Furthermore, that Sorrentino has succeeded in bringing the viewer to a state of sufficient alignment (if not allegiance) with Geremia so as to distract her/him from speculating on the likelihood of a woman such as Rosalba being willing to go to bed with a man such as Geremia, even if she stood to gain financially, is testament to the film's masterful manipulation of montage.

Equally as troubling as the visual exploitation of women's bodies, arguably, is the occasional inclusion in Sorrentino's films and the television series of non-normative identities, bodies, and faces. This begins with the critique of masculine power embodied in the grotesque yet oddly sympathetic form of Geremia "heart-of-gold" (*cuore d'oro*), as he calls himself, and continues, in an even more ironically spectacular fashion, in Sorrentino's subsequent film, *Il Divo*, the biopic of Giulio Andreotti (Andreotti, it should be recalled, was famously odd looking, with a hunched back, bat-like ears, and a stiff walk). Looking ahead to *The Young Pope*, however, Sorrentino moves beyond his Fellinian fascination with grotesque and/or hyperbolic human bodies to something more serious, less susceptible to ironic interpretation. This aspect of the television series in particular gives form to a reconsideration of the problem of visual pleasure and spectatorial guilt in the wake of 1970s feminist film theory. Secondary characters such as Melanie (Sonia Gessner), Ballinger's disabled wife in *Youth*; or Girolamo (uncredited), Cardinal Voiello's (Silvio Orlando) disabled charge in *The Young Pope*, graphically, and not unproblematically, demand an analytical model in contrast to a gendered theory of looking. In *Staring: How We Look*, Rosemarie Garland-Thomson elaborates a theory of the stare, otherwise known as the Baroque stare or the colonizing gaze, in the context of disability studies. While Garland-Thomson's examples of the stare are sociological, the visual basis of the stare justifies its application here in aesthetic-ideological rather than sociological terms, with respect to specific filmic examples.[8] Translating Garland-Thomson's stare into the terms of a visual structure helps to illuminate scenes in which an exclusively ideologically based notion of the gaze fails to lead to deeper understanding. In other words, where the feminist-psychoanalytic gaze implies a critique of the process of objectifying another human being, reducing her or him to an object of erotic desire, the stare by contrast reduces the other person to precisely that: an *Other* who is the asexually objectified object of either fascination or disgust or some intermediate but still powerful affective response.[9] Either way, arguably, s/he is reduced to something other than fully human in the process—which in this context is positioned as undesirable. In the grotesque figure of Geremia, once again, *The Family Friend* puts the stare and the (male) gaze into stark opposition, complicating theories of gendered looking that themselves depend on outmoded notions of gendered identities.

As suggested, any mention of the grotesque in Italian cinema leads back, inevitably, to Fellini. Where Antonioni may be the cinematic tutelary deity of *The Consequences of Love*, Fellini has this function for *The Family Friend*:

One assumes that this [Fellinian influence] is not merely because of the grotesques on show but because of the bleak seaside setting and the references to the legacy of fascism. . . . The town is dominated by fascist architecture, soulless, brutalist, grandiose, reeking of fake classicism and false order. More often than not, the streets are deserted and, when people do appear, they stand around in a stylised fashion as if overawed by the buildings around them. There are strong hints of Bertolucci's *The Conformist* here.[10]

Even more than other fascist-era spaces (which, in contrast to their German equivalents, abound in present-day Italy), the Roman *EUR* locations Bertolucci famously exploits in *The Conformist* have gone on to become the favorite setting for any Italian (or non-Italian) filmmaker seeking to represent the existential *anomie* of the postwar European bourgeois masculine intellectual.[11] From Fellini's *La Dolce Vita* to Bertolucci's *The Conformist*, to the 2017 *Suburra* television series,[12] the outsized, rectilinear spaces of *EUR* seem to perform a visual function equivalent to the streets and buildings of Sabaudia in *The Family Friend*.[13]

There is something else going on at the same time, however, that is more distinctively Sorrentinian: whenever Geremia is out and about, Sabaudia is a city populated seemingly exclusively by young, beautiful women, well-lit and provocatively dressed. Such scenes could also be read as an externalization of Geremia's subjective experience and therefore completely different from and far less conventional than his friend Gino's (Fabrizio Bentivoglio) flashbacks. According to French, "as with David Lynch, we're often left wondering whether what we're seeing is real or imaginary, possibly a dream."[14] It is as though in these scenes the city space itself were a projection of the protagonist's desires, desires that he acts upon more than once when the opportunity presents itself. This effect is also indicative of the fact that the story is Geremia's and the viewer's primary alignment is with him, even though their allegiance likely lies elsewhere. I return to this crucial point below.

"My Lady Story"

The Family Friend's four seemingly unrelated opening scenes give the viewer little purchase on the story to follow, suggesting the categorization of art film not only because it appears to conform to no particular genre but also stylistically, with its elliptical editing patterns, long takes, narratively unmotivated camera movement, and so forth. The dynamic opening shot of the nun buried up to her neck in the sand on a beach, while two men in silhouette appear to be waiting for high tide, sets the tone (figure 3.2). This scene is contextualized only later, almost halfway through, when the same shot is repeated in reverse, the camera swinging in towards the head on the beach, only this time the victim is the Bingo Granny (Barbara Valmorin), one of Geremia's clients, a woman seen in subsequent scenes alive and well (albeit with bandaged hands) and, thanks to bingo, with her debt fully paid, suggesting that these images do not represent an actual event that occurred but rather a projection of Geremia's subsequent directive to Gino to "get rid of" her when she initially defaults on her debt. A staticky cut to a bus pulling into the station is comparably disorienting in its complete disconnection from the previous images. This second precredit scene is equally enigmatic, introducing the viewer to a character, Belana (Alina Nedelea), the Romanian immigrant whose main narrative function, as with most of the secondary

FIGURE 3.2 *The Family Friend*

characters, is to cast a revealingly unflattering light upon the protagonist, Geremia di Geremei. Similarly, the third opening scene, in the course of which the credits finally begin (to the mournful tune of Antony and the Johnson's "My Lady Story"), introduces another enigmatic figure, Geremia's friend Gino, who will by contrast play a key role in the story and will prove in the end to be a comparably complex character. (Gino, too, is a ridiculous man; as Geremia asks, in reference to Gino's permanent country-western get up: "Why does a fifty-three-year old man dress like such an idiot?"[15]) Gino is repeatedly framed, lit, and dressed as if he just stepped off the set of a spaghetti western, like some latter-day Lee Van Cleef (figure 3.3).

The fourth of these scenes, continuing the credit sequence, is also incongruous, with a sudden shift to a young women's volleyball game, shot in prurient and fragmentary slow motion (a scene replicated in *The Young Pope*, episode 5—albeit with

FIGURE 3.3 *The Family Friend*

FIGURE 3.4 *The Family Friend*

young nuns in full habits).[16] This scene concludes with an overhead shot of one of the players hitting the ball, sliding to the ground, and rolling over as, in a quasi-post-coital pose, she looks directly into the camera (figure 3.4). The point-of-view here is a kind of ironic colonizing male gaze, simultaneously winking while taking its visual fill of the young and athletic female bodies on display. This scene subtly and indirectly—because the angles and scale are very different—aligns the viewer before the fact with the point-of-view of Geremia who, as we learn in a later scene, enjoys watching the girls play volleyball in the court immediately below his apartment window. This connection is underscored in a subsequent scene in which Geremia brings home an overweight, middle-aged woman who, in her underwear, accessorized with matching head- and wristbands, mimes smacking a series of suspended volleyballs in a grotesque imitation of cinematic slow motion. Here Sorrentino and Bigazzi prove that when they wish to they can produce a beautiful image without the presence of a young woman's nubile form.

Marlow-Mann convincingly argues that this strategy of spectatorial alignment with such a fetishizing masculine gaze does not mean that the film condones the sexual objectification of women. Rather, what one encounters in *The Family Friend* is Sorrentino's relatively complex critique of this very process of fetishistic objectification through the deliberate manipulation of alignment, while eschewing allegiance. To accuse Sorrentino (or rather, his film) of being guilty of this crime is to misread the film in a particular way. "This critical misinterpretation arises from the mistaken assumption that Sorrentino's use of the 'male gaze' inevitably forces the viewer to adopt the character's ethical stance and share his misogyny; in other words, it simplistically conflates the processes of alignment and allegiance."[17] I would go further still and argue that what Marlow-Mann says of Sorrentino here is true of a great many other contemporary filmmakers, whatever their gender. The problem remains, however, of the undeniable onscreen presence of young (and not-so-young) women's bodies, displayed in a visually pleasing fashion that, while it may not correspond ideologically to what Mulvey means by the 'male gaze' in more mainstream genre films, nevertheless suggests that the film in question is exploiting a kind of double standard, in which the means of critique is indistinguishable from because it replicates the image in question.

Philip French notes that, in the four-pronged opening sequence, Geremia is "gradually revealed as the movie's central character"[18] The "greatest risk" Sorrentino takes in the film is "having an antihero so physically and morally despicable that however bravura the performance (and Rizzo is magnificently uningratiating), we won't have any pity for him."[19] From one perspective this aspect of Geremia's character is a red herring for what is going on behind his back, and therefore unbeknownst to the viewer. From this counterfactual perspective it is almost as though his friend Gino were the main character, rather than Geremia; after all, only Gino has an interior life that is made visible on-screen in the form of subjective flashbacks, when his painful (and highly romanticized) memories of his dead wife come back to him, triggered or rather "enabled" by his constant immersion in the country western subculture that appears to have defined their marriage (in Gino's extradiegetic backstory, his wife died in a car accident caused by their being unusually tired after dancing all night at a country-and-western event). By contrast, Geremia's inner life is indicated only by two photos in his possession, neither of which triggers a flashback sequence: one of himself as a boy with his family, including his long-estranged father, and another of his mother as a young, attractive woman. Where Gino's country-inflected identity may appear to be some sort of serious joke, it is easy to overlook the fact that Geremia has exchanged original thinking for factoids out of *Reader's Digest*. What the viewer cannot see on a first viewing, however, is that the grief that Gino appears to be suffering over his wife's death—clearly signaled by the momentary flashback during the country-western bar scene—is in fact his silent struggle with the newly planted idea that he might betray his dead wife by taking up with Rosalba. (The backstory about his wife's death also provides Gino with a justification for tricking Geremia out of his life's savings; as he confesses to the Bingo Granny, all he wants now is to leave Italy and go to Tennessee, "because it is far away." The fact that he ends up protecting Bingo Granny from Geremia and his henchmen, "the twins," also makes him that much more sympathetic to the viewer, so that when Gino's scheme succeeds, the viewer is still discouraged from feeling any allegiance for Geremia.) Moreover, Gino attends the Miss Agro Pontine contest without Geremia, which appears to be the first time he lays eyes on Rosalba (an event that Geremia pointedly refuses to attend because, as he says, "Mother's filthy" and he needs to wash her). During Rosalba's victory dance, she mimics a cowboy on horseback with lasso, as if roping Gino from a distance and pulling him in towards her. A push in to Gino from medium to close-up should tell the viewer everything they need to know about his feelings for her, although at this early stage s/he will be forgiven for not catching this clue. In a later scene when Rosalba goes shopping for wedding *bomboniere* with her parents, her fiancé, Geremia, and Gino, she grants the latter a sly smile when he takes her side in an argument about which gifts to choose. Furthermore, on Rosalba's wedding day, Gino appears at the door to the church looking more like a jilted lover than another friend of the family; but because Geremia is also there, lurking in the background, weeping over the loss of Rosalba, whom he now clearly loves, the viewer's attention

FIGURE 3.5 *The Family Friend*

is distracted from Gino's comparable predicament. Finally, Antony and the Johnson's song "My Lady Story" is reprised over the scene of Geremia as he discovers his dead mother in the film's denouement. The repetition of this song from the extended opening sequence, where it is associated with Gino and his melancholic attachment to his dead wife, does not suggest a link between the two characters as much as it connects the two ends of the film more broadly on the affective level, which is a relatively common way of exploiting specific kinds or styles of music.[20] Ironically, on the lyrical level, "My Lady Story" has absolutely no relation to either character or to the film's story; it is a song about gender reassignment surgery, the "lady" in the title operating not nominally but adjectivally: my *lady* story.

Excessive counterfactual speculation is to be avoided, however. That Gino is not the main character, and that the story is essentially Geremia's, is of course deliberate and entirely necessary to the successful functioning of the plot:

> Sorrentino visibly attempts to align the viewer with Geremia; it is essential to the narrative progression that, like Geremia, the spectator remains unaware of Rosalba's relationship with Gino and thus takes her amorous declarations at face value, however unlikely they may seem. Thus Geremia's discovery of Rosalba's true motivations is also the spectator's, providing a dramatically necessary twist in the final act.[21]

In the end, the tip-of-the-iceberg quality of Gino's character and his relationship with Rosalba serves to strengthen the impact of their betrayal of Geremia, which, after all, is the story's fulcrum.

In Marlow-Mann's phrase, Geremia's relationship with his mother borders on the incestuous.[22] This is clear from several clues scattered across the film. Not only does he wash her hair and engage in what appears to be manual pleasuring, but at one point—in the scene immediately after he first meets Rosalba, in fact—Geremia sits alone on his bed gazing at a photo. There is a cut to a close-up from his point of view on the picture, understood as a photo of his mother—actually the actress

FIGURE 3.6 *The Family Friend*

Clara Bindi, who portrays her—from the 1950s, when she was youthful and attractive (figure 3.5). The juxtaposition of the two scenes suggests an affective connection between the two relationships: Geremia and his mother vs. Geremia and Rosalba, where the seed is already planted for the latter to replace the former in his heart, albeit only long enough for the plot to unfold.

The rich ambiguities of the film's opening sequence are matched by the highly elliptical composition of its ending. On a first viewing, in fact, it is difficult to understand exactly what has transpired. The ending is stylistically distinct from the film's opening, however, in that it is a continuous montage of brief scenes, providing only the barest amount of diegetic information for narrative comprehension, with Laurent Garnier's electronic track "The Man with the Red Face" running overtop. It is easy, for instance, to miss the actual transaction where Geremia hands over the one million euros to Signor Montanaro (Lorenzo Gioelli), the fake bathroom fixture CEO, an event indicated by a single dynamic tracking shot of Geremia and the twins striding into Montanaro's warehouse carrying repurposed detergent boxes full of cash, which he gleefully withdrew from his safety deposit boxes in the preceding scene (figure 3.6). Likewise, his betrayal by Rosalba and Gino is confirmed before his and the viewers' eyes, in a flurry of dynamic shots, Bigazzi's typically restless camera always on the move. This rapid-fire sequence is entirely free of dialogue apart from the single word "Mamma!" shouted by Geremia from his car as he drives to Rome to unsuccessfully confront his estranged father, who (like Jep Gambardella in *The Great Beauty*) lives in a luxurious apartment opposite the Coliseum. Why he embarks on this fruitless errand instead of confronting Gino and Rosalba when he first sees them together in Gino's trailer is not clear; when Geremia does finally return there with the intention of killing them both, they have already absconded, along with his one million euros. The scene in Rome culminates with a narrative coincidence that strains credibility even in this story: while driving past the Coliseum, Geremia happens upon the very same actors who portrayed Signor Montanaro and Atanasio (Marco Giallini), his assistant, who are now wearing gladiator costumes after a late shift working for the Roman tourism industry. As "Montanaro" explains, they helped Gino to fleece Geremia because they are out-of-work actors: "Cinecittá used to be our home." "I was an extra for Fellini, twice," chips in their father, the third gladiator. "Then Italian cinema went into crisis . . ." adds Atanasio. In this brief exchange Sorrentino satirically (and very economically) sums up the story of post-1970s Italian cinema, from Fellini's later films to Berlusconi's television-dominated 1980s and the aesthetic vacuum created thereby, laying the ground for the emergence of new young directors, many from Italy's second capital of cinema, Sorrentino foremost among them.

"The Aesthetics of Repugnancy"

I began this chapter by calling the humiliation that Geremia suffers "Shylockian," in reference of course to the Shakespearean character, a Jewish moneylender in sixteenth-century Venice. The difficulty with this comparison is that, where Geremia—etymologically a Jewish name[23]—is a specific film character embodied by the actor Giacomo Rizzo, who always looks the same no matter how many times you view The Family Friend, Shylock exists only on the page until he is given body, face, and voice by a specific actor in a specific production of The Merchant of Venice (1605).[24] More to the point, this comparison means that, although Geremia is not clearly coded as Jewish, his profession (both legitimate and not, which is to say tailoring and money-lending), physical eccentricities, and general demeanor place him, across a variety of genres and media forms, in what for some time now has been a category of fictional character typified by, if not villains, then by characters who are morally suspect and therefore problematic from the point of view of spectatorial identification or engagement. "If [Sorrentino's] technique of using physiognomic characteristics as shorthand to convey moral judgments on a character is not new, it is usually reserved for villains in films with a simplistic, Manichean moral structure or for secondary characters intended as an object of ridicule in comedies. Few films dare present such a grotesque as Geremia as a protagonist."[25] Even more pointedly than The Merchant of Venice, The Family Friend is willing to put its trust in a protagonist who is not only physically but morally non-normative—and perhaps, as in Shakespeare's play, coded Jewish in his speech and mannerisms. This may translate into specific physical and sartorial attributes, to the point of stereotype; stereotypes, of course, can be very useful for satirical critique—but they can also represent a morally bankrupt point of view on another person, a combination that makes for a very complex experience of engagement on the viewer's part.[26] The implausibility of Rosalba's love for Geremia stems not from his physical ugliness but from his moral failings; this is what makes spectatorial allegiance impossible.[27] In Peter Bradshaw's words,[28] it is his "perverted sentimentality" that makes Geremia simultaneously repugnant and compelling to the viewer. At most one might experience the kind of pity one feels for, say, Macbeth, at the end of Shakespeare's play when he is bear-baited, his manifest guilt tempered by his status as outcast from the rest of humanity. Geremia is here exposed in his self-conscious engagement with "his own status as object of loathing."[29] This sort of affective response is intentional, a function of Sorrentino's ethical approach to his craft:

> In a 2017 *Guardian* interview for the release of *Youth*, Sorrentino insists . . . that his purpose is not to ridicule, or to mock. "I restrain from criticising or judging my characters. I am more inclined to summon up their beauty through their weaknesses and the lack of taste that we all have. I try to transfer the beauty I see in them onto the screen. I never use a morbid or crude approach to showing the naked bodies of older people. That would mean stressing an ugliness I don't see in those bodies.[30]

Indeed, Geremia's/Rizzo's body in *The Family Friend* is treated with something like respect only in the one scene in which he appears completely naked, a beautifully lit medium shot. This occurs immediately after he has returned home to discover his mother lying dead in her bed. Geremia is in his bathrobe, and, as he stands and stumbles backward with the shock, he looks, ironically, like a Roman senator in his toga, holding a bedpan rather than a scroll in his hand. He turns and goes into the other room, the camera following slowly, pausing just long enough to allow Rizzo to drop the bathrobe and be discovered stark naked, his back to the camera, the telephone to his ear (figure 3.7). (Sorrentino repeats this shot in *The Young Pope*'s opening dream scene, the naked male body in question Jude Law's, and the visual impact correspondingly different.) This brief interval of vulnerability—the closest Geremia comes to eliciting audience sympathy—is undercut somewhat in the immediately following shot, which is in fact the next scene, in one of the film's frequent temporal-spatial elisions. As the camera tracks rightward, within his room, the volleyball-playing girls are visible again as if through the window blinds, from Geremia's point of view. This is made clear in the next shot, a profile close-up of Geremia, gazing down out of his window at the game, now dressed in a suit as he awaits his mother's funeral.

FIGURE 3.7 *The Family Friend*

Nevertheless, it seems undeniable that for much of the film, at work in the presentation of Geremia are the visual attributes and clichés of a stereotypical Jewishness, most of them hard to distinguish from anti-Semitic traits and tropes.[31] In *The Jew's Body*, Sander Gilman elaborates the anti-Semitic archetype of the Jewish murderer in early modern Europe:

> The image of the Jew revealed in his sexuality seems to be an accepted manner of labeling the image of the deviant. In this image it is the man . . . who is bestial (read: Jewish). The perversion of the Jew . . . lies in his sexualized relationship to capital. This, of course, echoes the oldest and most basic calumny against the Jew, his avarice, an avarice for the possession of "things," of "money," which signals his inability to understand (and produce) anything of transcendent aesthetic value. The historical background to this is clear. Canon law forbade the taking of interest. The taking of interest, according to Thomas Aquinas, was impossible, for money, not being alive, could not reproduce. Jews, in taking money, treated money as if it were alive, as if it were a sexualized object. The Jew takes money as does the prostitute, as a substitute for higher values, for love and beauty.[32]

In two key montage sequences we witness Geremia at his most unguardedly, deliriously happy, at the bank, at first depositing and later withdrawing the thousands of euros he has amassed in a long career of money-lending at interest. The seemingly facile portrait of avarice conceals the subtle underlying critique of the cultural symbolism of usury. The "Aristotelian or Aquinian argument that usury is a species of unnatural begetting, the selling and buying of nothing,"[33] becomes a grotesque mirroring of Geremia's quasi-incestuous relationship with his mother, a relationship that both sexually and nonsexually produces nothing other than masses of money through the charging of interest, what Antonio in *The Merchant of Venice* dismisses as "a breed for barren metal" (1.3: 126–33). Marlow-Mann asks:

> What is Geremia's misanthropy and amorality if not the ultimate expression of his alienation from his fellow man? His profession as a loan shark provides the perfect metaphor for the commodification of the relationships produced by this alienation and it is only through a financial transaction that he becomes a "family friend."[34]

It is important to note that the equivalent critique takes a different, more complicated, form with respect to Rosalba, who does not prostitute herself in her relationship with Geremia, at least not in the sense Gilman outlines. Rather, while she does as it were allow him to take his pleasure with her in their initial encounter (a disturbing idea in spite of its visually restrained treatment in the film), she does so for her father's sake, for the forgiving of his debt. When she gives herself to Geremia a second time, in an ostensible act of love, on the other hand, she is doing so out of avarice, as a function of her plot with Gino to trick their victim of his fortune. For his part, Geremia has amassed all of his money with the guidance of his bed-ridden Mamma who never lets him forget that he will never be a moneylender of the same stature as his long-estranged father. This also explains why Geremia, after their first sexual encounter, appears happy to learn that Rosalba is pregnant; when he asks if the child might be his, she responds: "I'll find out when its born. If it's a monster, it's yours." To father a child in the time-honored fashion would in Geremia's mind redeem a lifetime spent as a miserly moneylender.

While no other character ever sinks so low as to accuse Geremia of being bestial or animal-like, his humanity is called into question more than once, even by Geremia himself. In addition to Rosalba's comment about his potentially monstrous progeny, for instance, Saverio, Rosalba's father (Gigi Angelillo), remarks to his nameless interlocutor, a chef, discussing Geremia in voiceover as he scurries from safety deposit box to safety deposit box, depositing cash and jewelry and other valuables, culled from his clients: "Is he human?" Chef: "Too human. Short-tempered, stingy, fake, vengeful, talkative. And extremely hideous. He smells foul, he sweats profusely." (This sequence is spatially confusing, insofar as Saverio and his friend appear to be observing Geremia unobserved through a window, although this is impossible, as he is deep inside a bank while they talk.) The point here is not to accuse Sorrentino of indulging in a facile form of anti-Semitic imagery. If this were true, he would have been called out on it upon the film's release. On the contrary, my reading highlights the film's sophisticated critique of the very tropes it exploits, from the risky gamble of Geremia as protagonist to the (more predictable) sexually charged representation of women. As noted above it is the latter area that remains problematic and in which are focused the contradictions of the gaze in Sorrentino's work. And, as will be elaborated in chapter 5, it certainly becomes clear with the appearance of his fifth film, *This Must Be the Place*, that Sorrentino's overt engagement with questions of contemporary Jewish identity are grounded in respect for difference and a genuine desire to explore in a fictional narrative the intersection of humiliation and power. This theme reaches a particular pitch in a completely different, that is to say Catholic, context when Pope Pius XIII, in episode 10 of *The Young Pope*, tells the Vatican Press Secretary, "You have no idea how many objectives can be obtained by humiliating one's fellow man." The theme of humiliation returns one last time in episode 10, when Lenny finally sentences Archbishop Kurtwell, who has confessed to a lifetime of sexually abusing children. As he did once before, with Cardinal Ozolins in episode 2, Lenny directs Kurtwell to the large globe of the world in one corner of the papal office. He asks the archbishop to put his finger on New York City, as a test of his desire to return there. Kurtwell, whose hand shakes violently from a form of Parkinson's disease, plants his finger instead on Ketchikan, Alaska, which is improbably indicated on the globe. The series' representation of this place is as an empty, high Arctic wasteland—more like Igloolik, Nunavut, than the real Ketchikan—where Cardinal Ozolins, during his exile there, would conduct mass out of doors. Rather than any sort of realism, here Sorrentino exploits a real-world location as a sort of running joke: a freezing-cold, purgatorial place, in which errant clergymen are sent to do penance.

It becomes possible to say of Sorrentino's *The Family Friend* what Kenneth Gross observes of Philip Roth's 1993 novel *Operation Shylock: A Confession*, that it "shares with *The Merchant of Venice* an interest in the aesthetics of repugnancy, a willingness to test the limits of the hateful and of hatred, the power of wounded voices—the source of his fascination, Roth acknowledges, with the bluntly, carelessly anti-Semitic writings of Louis-Ferdinand Céline."[35] As noted in chapter 2, Céline's *Journey to the End of the Night*, a novel not lacking in casually racist and anti-Semitic rhetoric, only partially blunted by the author's characteristic cynical irony, is among Sorrentino's favorites.[36] *The Merchant of Venice* is an almost certainly accidental intertext for *The Family Friend*, but then this has always been the beauty of intertextuality as critical tool: authorial intentionality is neither here nor there. This comparison leads, rather, to a more nuanced understanding of how the film works, how it produces its complex meanings. And part of this is recognizing the risks that Sorrentino the screenwriter ran in concocting a loathsome character such as Geremia "heart-of-gold" in the first place. What this discussion points to, therefore, is not some kind of anti-Semitic subtext but rather Sorrentino's abiding interest in what I call the meaningful difference of non-normative identities. This interest extends to his next film, *Il Divo*, where it is expanded into the genre of the biopic and the fictionalized representation of a historical personage. In this case the stakes change considerably, as it is one thing to exploit the ironies inherent in a "grotesque and tragic" figure such as Geremia,[37] and quite another to do so with the figure of Giulio Andreotti, who represents a very different exploration of the grotesque—in Italian political history.

FOUR

"What Will They Remember About You?"

Il Divo *and the Possibility of a Twenty-First-Century Political Film*

> The intellectual courage to speak the truth and the practice of politics are incompatible
> in Italy.
> > —Pier Paolo Pasolini, "What Is This Coup d'État? I Know"

> Is this that world? Are these
> The joys, love, deeds, experience
> We spoke so often of?
> Is this man's fate?
> > —Giacomo Leopardi, "To Silvia"

IL DIVO (2008)[1] is a fictional dramatization of specific events in the life and career of Italian politician Giulio Andreotti, seven times Italy's prime minister (1972–1992).[2] This brief description does not begin to do justice to the film's formal and narrative complexity, however. Where for many critics *Il Divo* is the pivotal film in Sorrentino's career thus far, so is this chapter the pivot of this book, marking the bridge between his earlier, more markedly Italian films and the subsequent works, generally involving a more international production model coupled with a transnational storyline as often as not translated into English for a cast of mostly non-Italians. With the exception of *Loro*—to be discussed in the coda—*Il Divo* can be called the most traditionally Italian of them all, but in a highly specific sense: of all of Sorrentino's films this biopic about Giulio Andreotti (Toni Servillo once again) is the least universal in its address to the non-Italian viewer and her/his globalized cine-literacy, requiring as it does a modicum of historically and culturally specific knowledge in order for its semantic and formal richness to be fully appreciated. That said, *Il Divo* exemplifies what Millicent Marcus calls Sorrentino's "post-realism"—an aesthetic and, in a sense, a philosophical approach to film style whose development is owed in part to Bigazzi's cinematographic innovations, most notably the dynamic camera work and chiaroscuro lighting already evident in *The Family Friend* and *The Consequences of Love*, especially in the frequent interior scenes.[3]

To be precise: the historically and culturally specific knowledge required by the viewer to fully appreciate Sorrentino's achievement in *Il Divo* devolves upon the 1978 kidnapping and murder of Aldo Moro, president of the Christian Democrats. During Italy's Years of Lead (*gli anni di piombo*) from 1969 to 1984, hundreds of people were killed or injured in a series of notorious attacks, attributed to either left- or right-wing terrorism. Where left-wing terrorists engaged in attacks upon what they saw as representatives of a corrupt and unjust state, right-wing terrorism saw itself as facilitating state-inspired authoritarian solutions, even if its actions were not state-sanctioned. The Red Brigades (*Brigate rosse*) were one of several left-wing terrorist organizations that came to embody the Years of Lead. They were ultra-Marxist, the most radical of the radical, and they saw the Communists as enemies. Moro's kidnapping happened as he was on his way to broker what would have been an unprecedented coalition between the Christian Democrats and the Communist Party; his assassination, which closed off one future and determined Italy's current political path, was one of the most collectively traumatic events of this period.[4] "The relevance of the figure of Moro for Italian culture derives from the emblematic force of his assassination. Over the years, Moro has become an icon of martyrdom and has come to encapsulate the anxieties of the Italian public about revolution and violence."[5] In the intervening decades, Moro's kidnapping and murder at the hands of the Red Brigades—and therefore Moro himself in this peculiarly morbid sense—has acquired the status in contemporary Italian society that the Kennedy assassination has for postwar American culture, inspiring a comparable level of paranoid conspiracy alongside more legitimate theorizing.[6] In contrast to a film such as Oliver Stone's *JFK* (1991), which incorporates a variety of different theories and perspectives on this signal event in modern American history and popular culture, *Il Divo* presents Sorrentino's thoroughly researched but highly imaginative take on Andreotti's relation to the Moro affair, among other significant political-criminal assassinations.[7] The screenwriters, aided by the cinematographer, editor, and the soundtrack music, superadd a notable imaginary dimension, dramatizing Andreotti's moral responsibility for these crimes while avoiding any direct accusation. Ever since these events unfolded speculation has swirled around Andreotti as to his relative degree of involvement or guilt in Moro's death. The fact remains that he and the Christian Democratic party did nothing to help Moro be freed; in a sense, the government's official policy of non-negotiation with terrorists allowed Moro to be killed. Why Andreotti and his colleagues took this hard line also remains a matter of speculation.

This complex of social, political, cultural, and affective meanings—the Moro affair—is a key story element in *Il Divo*, even though the film takes place mainly between 1992 and 1996, focusing on Andreotti, who, on the day of Moro's kidnapping was to become Italy's prime minister. With Andreotti recently elected to his seventh term, *Il Divo* opens with a now famous montage of the most infamous political assassinations in modern Italian history. As Cassius's "Toop Toop" plays extradiegetically overtop,[8] the crimes are woven together in the following order,

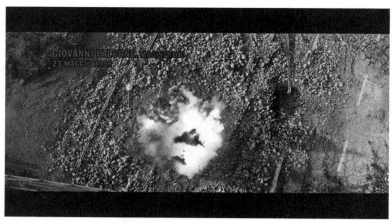

FIGURE 4.1 *Il Divo* (Paolo Sorrentino, 2008)

the relevant information in playfully animated onscreen titles: "Roberto Calvi, Banker, 17 June 1982; Michele Sindona, Banker, 22 March 1986; Mino Pecorelli, Journalist, 20 March 1979; Carlo Alberto Dalla Chiesa, Carabiniere General, 3 Sept. 1982; Giorgio Ambrosoli, Liquidator Privata Italiana Bank, 12 July 1979; Aldo Moro, DC President, 9 May, 1978; Giovanni Falcone, Magistrate, 23 May 1992" (figure 4.1). The only logic to the achronological order of these vignettes I can discern is that they are presented in order of least to most socially and politically significant. (The extradiegetic music also abruptly stops once Moro's assassination is reached.) If this is so, then Falcone's murder is meant to trump Moro's, a reading substantiated in the recurrence of the skateboard as affectively laden symbol in the mise-en-scène.[9] From Andreotti's avowed point of view within the screenplay, however, it is Moro's death that most moved him and which he cannot get over. As prime minister and head of the Christian Democrats, Andreotti was expected by many to do all he could to free Moro. Instead, he consistently refused to bargain with the terrorists, effectively sealing Moro's fate. The impression this gave many was that Moro was deliberately sacrificed to ensure political stability through "strategies of tension."[10]

This opening montage is succeeded by another as part of the introduction of Andreotti's character: the arrival of his political faction, nicknamed "la brutta corrente" which is difficult to translate, as *corrente* is both the word for a faction of this type while still carrying connotations of "current," whether in the air or a body of water: a nasty current. All of these senses are captured in the scene immediately preceding their arrival as Signora Enea, Andreotti's personal secretary, goes to the open window while a strong gust of wind disturbs some papers on her boss's desk: "Presidente, sta arrivando una brutta corrente," translated in the subtitles as "Premier, storm clouds are gathering." According to Marcus:

The arrival of the "brutta corrente" of Giulio's henchmen, including Paolo Pomicino, Vittorio Sbardella, Cardinale Angelini, Giuseppe Ciarrapico, is performed as a series of automobile ads, where gleaming top-of the-line vehicles disgorge important looking men, met by a pair of stunning female associates (in the case of Pomicino), or by a valet who opens the doors, and all recorded by a slow motion camera to give gravitas to the proceedings.[11]

The slow motion lends gravitas to this sequence to the same extent that the same technique lends gravitas to the average hip hop music video.[12] In the same vein, at least one low-angle framing (Vittorio Sbardella, DC MP, alias The Shark) visually echoes the famous low-angle shots of Radio Raheem (Bill Nunn) in Spike Lee's *Do the Right Thing* (1989) (figure 4.2; figure 4.3). In both cases the framing enhances and yet mocks the menace as much as the authority or gravitas of the character in question.

As any number of critics have noted since its release in 2008, *Il Divo*, alongside Mateo Garrone's *Gomorrah* in the same year, "reignited the critical debate on the possible resurgence of an Italian 'political cinema.' "[13] This debate reached an early peak in the 2010 issue of the *Italianist* journal devoted to Sorrentino's film. My analysis of *Il Divo* takes off from this debate, sparked by Marcus's essay, "The Ironist and the Auteur: Post-Realism in Paolo Sorrentino's *Il Divo*." In this chapter and throughout this book I go well beyond this debate in a consideration of the significance of memory for Sorrentino's cinematic practice—whether subjectively, in the form of the classic flashback, or objectively, in terms of the films' engagement with occidental cultural memory as the legacy of humanism, broadly speaking. This means that the shots, scenes, sequences, or set pieces analyzed in detail were chosen as often as not because of their engagement with memory as a theme or because they exemplify the films' representation of subjective memory in action, whether through the flashback or some other device. On the other hand, it should be understood from the start that by *intermediality* I mean precisely the phenomenon that theorists refer to as collective cultural memory in its most common or vernacular form. The focus on memory throughout this book is justified, moreover, in all its various permutations,

FIGURE 4.2 *Il Divo*

FIGURE 4.3 *Do The Right Thing* (Spike Lee, 1989)

by Sorrentino's abiding preoccupation with nostalgia, melancholy, and an ironically elegiac tone.

Marcus's thesis aids in unlocking the formal and diegetic enigmas of the later films in particular, from the ironic elegiac mood that dominates in *The Great Beauty* to *The Young Pope*'s postironic openness to a quasimelodramatic sincerity vis-à-vis the possibility of faith in the twenty-first century. With respect to *Il Divo*, Marcus links the formal level to its politico-ethical contribution, what she calls (echoing Pierpaolo Antonello and Florian Mussgnug) Sorrentino's "postmodern *impegno*," which finds expression in "the contemporary vogue for stylistic virtuosity—including the use of pastiche, abundant citation, semiotic playfulness, imagistic saturation, decorative exuberance"—a tendency that can readily "co-exist with an ethics of political engagement in the arts."[14] In other words, Marcus's essay, and the ensuing *Italianist* debate, broaches an answer to the question: How is *Il Divo* a politically meaningful/ meaningfully political film on the level of *form*?

In his response to Marcus's essay, Alex Marlow-Mann observes that Sorrentino's films display a particularly flamboyant species of postclassical cinema, or what David Bordwell in 2002 labeled "intensified continuity style": "a mobile camera heavily reliant on dollies and the Steadicam, alternating extremes of long takes and rapid montage, stylized slow motion, a surprising and unconventional choice of pre-existing music, flamboyantly attention-seeking set-pieces, and so on."[15] In terms of Sorrentino's subsequent output I would translate this "and so on" in terms of the overt use of digital technology: digital sound recording; a postproduction digital intermediate; nonlinear editing; special effects and visual effects (e.g., the animated documentary-style titles); frequent, overt, and self-reflexive intermediality. Going beyond the *Italianist* debate, then, where Marlow-Mann disavows the link between a kind of political *impegno* and a highly self-reflexive style, I argue that this link is at the basis, paradoxically, of both Sorrentino's stylistic and thematic originality and his alignment with contemporary mainstream visual narrative. In their formal self-reflexivity and occasional forays into art film obscurantism, combined with their postmodern allegiance to popular genres and modes, the films always maintain a clear ethical position vis-à-vis the extracinematic world, to a specific social reality, which is the requisite basis of any meaningfully political text. The potential problem with this for some critics, however, is that the ethics in question are based in a humanist tradition that unconsciously privileges a masculine subject that in the postmillennial period has come under intensified critique from a variety of perspectives, most prominently the latest feminist and black empowerment movements, emanating from the United States and Europe, with strong echoes throughout the developed and developing worlds.

In *Il Divo* Sorrentino takes up his place in a specific politically charged line of postwar Italian cinema: "Sorrentino's achievement harks back to the *cinema politico* of Francesco Rosi, Elio Petri, and Paolo and Vittorio Taviani in the 1960s, 70s and early 80s"—to which list we can add Pasolini, Bertolucci, Bellocchio, Pontecorvo, and, not unproblematically, Wertmüller—"whose penchant for spectacle and whose stylistic departure from the naturalism of Neorealist cinematography can be seen as important harbingers" of the postrealist aesthetic for which Sorrentino has been both lauded and criticized.[16] Sorrentino himself acknowledges his debt in *Il Divo* to the *cinema politico* of Rosi and Petri (especially *Todo modo*) alongside Fellini and the *commedia all'italiana*.[17] As suggested, Sorrentino's cinema fits somewhere in between, as a species of transnational art cinema clearly inflected by the history of a postwar cinematic modernism whose political impact derives from its form as much as its content. This often highly self-reflexive form is typified by a high degree of intermediality, which is instrumental in the production of its meanings. Of obvious significance is the fact, noted by Antonello, that all of *Il Divo*'s major Hollywood cinematic intertexts are either gangster films or films featuring protagonists who are criminal psychopaths: e.g., Tarantino's *Reservoir Dogs* (1992); Scorsese's *Taxi Driver* (1976); De Palma's *The Untouchables* (1987).[18] I return to this dimension of the film below.

Marlow-Mann's critique of Marcus's reading of *Il Divo* turns on the latter's use of the term *realism*: "the attempt to yoke *Il Divo* to an (albeit post-) realist tradition is a troubling one."[19] The "albeit post-" says it all: this is no textbook realism (whatever that means) but something else, something after or beyond, while still in reference to realism but especially, in the Italian context, neorealism. What film scholars refer to in shorthand as Italian neorealism is characterized by a set of pervasive myths that have come to be seen as lapidary truths.[20] Neorealism's so-called documentary-like, authentic and nonprofessional naturalism, it goes without saying, is as constructed as any other mode of realism. Postrealism arises out of an awareness of this constructedness; it is dependent upon the recognition of an irreducible irony at work in a given text—whether operating on a verbal-rhetorical, dramatic-situational, or more global level of the narrative.

Leaving aside Andreotti the historical personage, postrealism thus necessitates a reading of Andreotti the character that is replicated in the film's diegesis. Sorrentino's Andreotti is a man who "lives life at one remove, whose literal existence is a mere facade behind which the hidden operations of power and influence can be wielded";[21] he lives life and wields power ironically, in that his exterior appears to be ever at odds with his interior—although, as we will see below, the latter proves to be a problematic quantity by the film's final scene. Likewise the film's meaning, its truth as such, is at first concealed beneath its spectacular surface. Or at least this is the (ironic) assumption behind the notion of postrealist irony, for rhetorical irony by definition implies at least two levels of sense, one false and the other true, relatively speaking. In an extension of Marcus's reading of *Il Divo*, whether in a fictional narrative or the real world, this model implies a division between those who possess the requisite knowledge to understand what is really going on (knowledge as power) and those who do not. We are reminded of Linda Hutcheon's point "that irony can be used either to reinforce authority or to oppose or subvert it and that this ambivalence should lead us to treat any instance of irony with suspicion."[22] "Irony is the best cure against death," quips Andreotti in *Il Divo*, and "cures against death are always atrocious." Too many well-intentioned critics since the first iteration of identity politics in the early 1990s have rejected irony as a result.[23] This is always a mistake, as irony is one of those logical-rhetorical-textual structures or forces that operates independently of the reader's or the viewer's intentionality or awareness. This, in a sense, is the ultimate, allegorical message of *Il Divo*. On this point therefore I disagree with Marlow-Mann's contention that Sorrentino's "use of cinematic citations . . . unlike Tarantino's, is resolutely unironic."[24] In my view Sorrentino's characteristic referentiality (up to *The Young Pope*), like Tarantino's, is characteristically ironic in both function and tone. (One need only look to Sorrentino's titles to see this: *The Spectacular Life* [*la spettacolare vita*] *of Giulio Andreotti* is only the most obvious example.)[25] The difference between the two filmmakers on this level is that, where Tarantino has proven himself the prototypical postmodern bricoleur, exploiting metacinematic citation more or less for its own sake, epitomizing contemporary popular culture's constitutive autoreferentiality, Sorrentino's frequent cinematic citations gesture outward, beyond the intertextual relation in question to the world outside the film—hence the need for some notion of (politically conscious) realism. Far from being mutually exclusive, Sorrentino's irony is the very substance of his *impegno*.[26] (This is true even—especially?—when *Il Divo* quotes a famous scene from 1992's *Reservoir Dogs*[27]—to be discussed below.) Again, in a further analogy with the extrafilmic world, the kind of ironic structure Marcus identifies in *Il Divo* implies a divided positionality vis-à-vis the work of interpretation, insofar as (on the formal level) an ironic structure always risks being misunderstood, which is to say being read literally rather than receiving the deeper metaphorical or figurative reading the structure demands. I therefore concur with Antonello's observation that Marcus's model of postrealism is another expression of a highly ironic postmodern aesthetic,[28] insofar as it relies upon a particular form of depth-surface binary, not to mention the assumption of transhistorical meaning that this entails. But this has always been the problem with irony; the difficulty in this case lies not with irony itself but with the acceptation of the postmodern as cultural expression of a poststructuralist collapsing of metaphysical depth-surface models. I include this digression here because it does not seem possible to me to discuss Sorrentino's films with any seriousness without first acknowledging the inescapable centrality of a culturally specific irony, not limited to Italian cinema, upon which depends my reading of Sorrentino's films and the relation between the films and *The Young Pope* television series.

Impegno *as Style*

The problem of the political potential of cinema is hardly a new one; nor is it limited to the context of Italian film in its postneorealist phase. In 1972, in a completely different context, Jean-Luc Godard stated that, "the problem is not to make political films but to make films politically."[29] According to Thomas Elsaesser "to make films politically" means "to challenge the strategies which contemporary popular culture, especially the cinema, had inherited from the bourgeois novel and theatre."[30] Not even neorealism qualifies as *this* kind of political cinema, whose political engagement, or impegno, is activated on the formal level of audiovisual style.[31] Sorrentino himself describes *Il Divo* as "less a film about Italian politics than . . . an examination of the meaning of political power."[32] For Marlow-Mann:

> the question remains as to whether the film is politically effective because of Sorrentino's stylistic register or in spite of it. Ultimately *Il Divo* is as much a film about an ambiguous and enigmatic anti-hero and a discourse about political power and corruption as it is an exposé of a real politician which lays any claim to veracity.[33]

Marlow-Mann contributes to the *Il Divo* debate a crucial observation about Sorrentino's exploitation of intermedial linkages for maximum semantic impact. In what follows I disagree, however (as noted above), on the crucial question of irony: Sorrentino's quoting from specific American genre films—including Tarantino's *Reservoir Dogs*—is, like Tarantino's use of citation, resolutely ironic. For instance, in the *brutta corrente* sequence, the visual-structural association established between the members of Andreotti's faction as they enter his Roman palazzo and the members of Joe Cabot's gang as they exit the LA diner could not be more ironic in its impact. Sorrentino's remediation of the *Reservoir Dogs* scene certainly establishes the "unsavoury nature of Andreotti's associates,"[34] but it does so through the explicit contrast between the two groups of men in terms of their line of work (politics vs. bank robbery), the respective settings (a Roman palazzo vs. an LA diner), and the soundtrack music (Teho Teardo's "La corrente" in *Il Divo* vs. George Baker's "Little Green Bag" in *Reservoir Dogs*)[35] set over against the superficial similarities (the fact that they all wear dark suits; the visual resemblance between Mr. White (Harvey Keitel) and Vittorio Sbardella ([Massimo Popolizio], aka the Shark) (figure 4.4; figure 4.5). This ironic contrast makes a rich contribution to *Il Divo*'s complex critique of Italian politics during Andreotti's seventh term as prime minister.

FIGURE 4.4 *Il Divo*

Another ironic intertext is the opening scene of Brian De Palma's *The Untouchables* (1987), where Al Capone (Robert De Niro) is interviewed by reporters while being shaved in an ornate octagonal wood-paneled room. It is true that the main character in each scene, in either case a man of power, is rendered at once "passive and vulnerable."[36] Formally, however, the two scenes could not be more different. *The Untouchables* opens with a wide overhead shot, above the barber chair. After holding this shot for a few seconds, the camera slowly tracks in vertically, toward Capone, bringing him into medium close-up, his face swathed in hot towels. A reporter moves closer to the chair and begins the interview. Apart from three cuts to reverse-angle shots to various onlookers, the camera stays on Capone as he responds to their questions. The comparable scene in *Il Divo* is stylistically completely different: while it is also a scene of the main character being shaved by

FIGURE 4.5 *Reservoir Dogs* (Quentin Tarantino, 1992)

a barber as he holds court with his inner circle, it begins immediately after the final shot in the *la corrente* sequence: a close up on Sbardella (the Shark), with a straight cut to a door opening, as if continuing his action as he moves toward the entrance to Andreotti's apartment. This is a false match-on-action, however, as Bigazzi's camera moves into the space of Andreotti's ornate marble bathroom, over Cardinal Fiorenzo Angelini's (Achille Brugnini) shoulder, who then moves out of the way. "Fiorenzo, sit on the throne," directs the recumbent Andreotti, the cardinal obediently obliging, as Sbardella asks "How's the pope doing?" While being shaved Andreotti recounts an amusing anecdote in which he quotes Pope Pius XI, in accidental anticipation of *The Young Pope* series, still a few years away, in which Jude Law portrays the fictional Pope Pius XIII. Throughout this exchange the cuts are fast, the shot scale always changing, the camera always moving, ranging around the space with little or no regard for the 180-degree rule. Apart from the principal camera, a medium close-up on Andreotti at a high 45-degree angle, the secondary camera ranges around the room, stopping on specific faces but never completely still. Overall the scene is a textbook example of the intensified transnational art film style, so common as to virtually constitute a transnational vernacular, especially in this kind of dialogue-heavy scene.

Il Divo also contains a visual quotation from Scorsese's *Taxi Driver* (1976), a high-angle close-up of a fizzing glass of bicarbonate of soda: "The use of a slow dolly from above onto the effervescence in a glass is used to signal [Travis Bickle's] incipient psychological pathology."[37] In Scorsese's film, the camera moves in for an extreme close-up, as if from Travis's point-of-view, the bubbling surface of the liquid filling the entire visual field, metaphorizing Travis's distracted mental state at this point. Travis's drink, and the headaches it is meant to quell, acquires a meaning wholly other than the equivalent signifiers in *Il Divo*, however. Bigazzi mimics the shot in *Taxi Driver*, filming the glass in close-up from straight above, but rather than pushing in toward the fizzing surface, the camera pulls slowly back and up, followed by a medium close-up of Andreotti drinking the seltzer. A Buñuelean extreme close-up of Andreotti's hand, complete with crawling ants, is followed by the scene of his anxious all-night pacing, Nosferatu-like, in response to the news of this first trial for Mafia collusion.[38] Both scenes are highly economical metaphorical shorthand for psycho-emotional anxiety, but Andreotti's angst is born of a completely different source.

Curiously, each of the two foregoing intertexts features Robert De Niro in the lead: in *Taxi Driver* he plays Travis Bickle, the quintessential 1970s new Hollywood antihero, a mentally unstable Vietnam veteran; and in *The Untouchables* he plays Capone, a psychopathic gangster and antagonist to Kevin Costner's federal agent Elliot Ness. In either case the meanings carried over to the Andreotti character in Sorrentino's film are ambiguous and wholly ironic: after all, like Brando and Pacino, De Niro made his reputation in Hollywood playing Italian-American criminals who also happen to be the heroes (or antiheroes) of the films in which they star. Such intertextual allusions therefore operate on one level not unlike the references in Mateo Garrone's *Gomorrah* (2008) to a seminal gangster film like—once again— De Palma's 1983 remake of *Scarface* with Al Pacino in the lead role. The primary difference is that the young men in *Gomorrah* deliberately refer to *Scarface* in the diegesis as they act out the famous climax from De Palma's movie ("Colombiani dappertutto!"). As a totally different kind of character, Andreotti is obviously not about to behave in a comparable manner, but the references to these scenes—all of them, beginning with the *Reservoir Dogs*/*la corrente* intertext—solidify on the metaphorical level of *Il Divo*'s diegesis Andreotti's indelible association with criminality, with the dark forces of corruption, violence, and political murder and the retention of power at any cost in the name of maintaining social order.

Pierpaolo Antonello concurs with Marcus in arguing that, "Sorrentino's postmodernist style should not be interpreted solely in terms of cinematic bravura, but for its epistemological underpinning. It generates critical reflection (ethical, political, historical) by recruiting the viewer 'into an active process of interpretation and critical engagement in remembering and analysing the working of the Andreottian regime.'"[39] The film's style and its political message are of a piece, in true post-Brechtian fashion. Marcus highlights "Sorrentino's 'inferential strategy,' the 'guilt by montage,' the 'filmic counter-archive' that turns Andreotti's archival strategy against himself and becomes an instrument for 're-cognition' and 're-knowing' on the part of a spectator summoned into 'an interpretative process charged with moral implications'"[40] This sophisticated approach to political filmmaking moreover links up with what Marcus rightly identifies as the film's complex treatment of contemporary Italian collective memory. *Il Divo*'s contribution to this shared cultural database comes via its simultaneous thematization and formal enacting of memory on the individual level of character and situation, as well as on the objective level of contemporary Italian society that stands in the background. This dialectic plays out in the relation between Andreotti's personal archive—his substitute for an imagination—vs. the cultural-political archive that the film constructs and constitutes.

> Whereas the public which has lived through the Andreottian era has experienced these allegations incrementally, scattered over the past several decades, the film reports them as a lump sum, and thus not only reactivates the memory within the collective Italian consciousness, but does so in an aggregate whose sheer volume is incriminating. In other words, the film's allusions to this itemized list of egregious wrongdoing amounts to an archive—the counterpart to the archive which Giulio himself keeps in order to intimidate and silence those who would threaten his hold on power.[41]

Contemporary memory studies recognizes that collective or cultural memory is always already technically mediated. For Astrid Erll, *culture* itself *means* "cultural memory": "whatever we know about the world we know through media and in dependence on media. . . . In this sense, 'the medium is the memory.'"[42] (Several of Fellini's films, for instance, embody this precept.[43]) That the medium is the memory is implicit in the idea of intermediality as another name for cultural memory in material form, ultimately independent of authorial agency. Thus it is a matter not of individual but *social* memory; of not memory's universal character but of its *transsubjective* existence in the form of an intermedially determined cultural sur-round. Cinema specifically has become a kind of global lingua franca: films made according to a loose set of narrative, stylistic, and structural laws travel well and are more or less legible—audiovisually, if not linguistically—for viewers the world over. Cinema's quasi-universality as a language is not a metaphysical hypothesis but a measurable product of its mass reproducibility as medium. This reading of cinema as mode of shared cultural memory is not new; Alison Landsberg, for instance, argues for commercial cinema's potential to function prosthetically in the dissemination and (re-) production of commodified memories derived from the consumption of the same set of films by a diverse array of viewers, who gain an enhanced sense of empathy across wide cultural and ideological divides.[44] Nestor Garcia Canclini iden-tifies the tendency of filmmakers in a transnational cultural landscape "to conform to generic cinematic codes (*cine-mundo*) in order to lure international audiences."[45] Canclini's implicit critique glosses over the very significance of such generic codes, which, in producing an international style consequently form the basis for an artifi-cial collective memory-system—in its broadest sense the matrix within which trans-national identities circulate, undergoing appropriation, recontextualization, and resignification, as a function of the modes of cultural consumption characteristic of the twentieth and now the early twenty-first centuries.

With the example of Sorrentino, I wish to emphasize a different affective dimen-sion of this aspect of cinema's social value, highlighting a non-normative art cine-matic generation of formally innovative memory schemata which then constitute the foundation for subsequent innovation in more mainstream commercial cinema.[46] Hollywood's fascination with returns to the past is evidenced in the ubiquity of the flashback as narrative device throughout its history. The nostalgic and/or bitterly ironic return to the past in postwar modernist cinema has as much in common with a literary as it does with a filmic model of recapturing past time, and it consti-tutes a subgenre of which a handful of films stand as representative. The directors of such films, meanwhile, have come to be associated with this kind of story line (e.g., Bergman's *Wild Strawberries* [1958]; Fellini's *8 ½* [1964]; Tarkovsky's *Mirror* [1974]). In the most interesting films, the line between the documentation of someone's (the screenwriter's, the director's) actual experience of coming of age in a specific place, on the one hand, and the fictional protagonist's dream or memory or fantasy of return, on the other, is blurred, and the mediality of the film comes to take precedence over the categories of memory, dream, or some notion of the past in its authenticity. It is even possible for the mediated and fictionalized memory-representation to com-pletely supplant the actual memory of the past in its authenticity.

The problem with this aspect of *Il Divo*, however, is that it is precisely where the non-Italian viewer, unversed in twentieth-century Italian political history, is left out of the conversation, not being a subject of collective cultural memory in this sense.[47] Instead, the non-Italian viewer is constrained to latch on to the other, subjective level of memory in the film: that of Andreotti's personal struggle with his guilt over the murder of Aldo Moro by the Red Brigades in 1978. This is precisely why Antonello, while acknowledging with Marcus the peculiar political *impegno* of *Il Divo*, also stresses in his conclusion the potential failure of this self-reflexive *impegno* to bring about any real social-political change (in Italy or anywhere else):

> We have entered into a historical phase in which power can absorb any accusation without a wince, while artistic forms of "*denuncia*" have become ineffectual and quixotic, failing to stir widespread collective indignation or awareness. . . . What is left to the viewer/reader is the freedom and responsibility to make a critical judgment that is ethical, even if it cannot be political.[48]

This is precisely why, in the introduction to this study, I already vacillate between the terms political and ethical, where the former's connection to the social collective must be maintained even as we recall the latter's historical basis in theories of individual behavior, even in quasi-theological or postsecular contexts (the fate of the soul). Likewise, a specific modality of memory remains connected to the collective, political level of society, even as individual or personal memory remains the locus of the ethical.

Ultimately, the non-Italian viewer is compelled to rely for understanding not on the elements of a culturally specific Italian narrative, nor on the minimal traces of Andreotti's subjective experience of the present in relation to his own past (e.g., the black-and-white flashback to the Verano cemetery and his courtship of Livia, to be discussed below). Rather, this underprivileged viewer can only fall back on her/his familiarity with a third category of memory: cinema itself, film form as modality of memory not in terms of a specific content but rather in terms of the mechanism or process of recollection.[49]

Public Confessions, Part 2

The foregoing discussion of *Il Divo*'s ironies, its intentional internal contradictions, inspired by the *Italianist* debate, has mainly to do with the text of the film itself. When one considers Andreotti the character, in terms of Sorrentino's characteristically aphoristic dialogue, Servillo's portrayal, and Bigazzi's lighting and framing, the character's ironic demeanor—as his wife, Livia, points out, he is always good for a "wisecrack" (*una batuta*)[50]—things are somewhat different. Where the film's ironies at once conceal and reveal (reveal by concealing) a set of deeper ambiguities, inherent to the film's peculiar treatment of its (ultimately historical, extracinematic) subject, the character of Andreotti proves to have an interior life irreducibly determined by the same mediatized textures from which the film as a whole is constructed. Antonello highlights in this regard Andreotti's highly self-reflexive, spot-lit confession scene: "the intertextual references to *inter alia* Leopardi's *A Silvia*, and to the Catholic 'Atto penitenziale,' the use of bleached pseudo-newsreel footage where a young Andreotti strolls at the Verano cemetery with his future wife" (figure 4.6).[51] (Andreotti's direct address to the camera here anticipates the comparable "breaking of the fourth wall" in *Loro*, which is less blatant but more frequent, becoming—as will be discussed in the coda—an important stylistic motif in Sorrentino's latest film.)

This scene—which both is and is not a "public confession" (shades of *One Man Up*)—is immediately preceded by one in which Andreotti and his wife watch television, Livia channel-surfing to avoid anti-Andreotti content, settling finally on a broadcast of a concert performance of "I migliori anni della nostra vita" ("The Best Years of Our Lives") by Italian singer Renato Zero[52]—a piece of blatantly nostalgic Italian pop music that clearly inspires comparable feelings in Livia, who turns to gaze at her husband in wordless love, the camera, as if ashamed, looking on from over the back of his head. While he doesn't return her gaze, Andreotti does take her hand, as if to acknowledge the song's significance for both of them. "The best years of our lives" resonates ironically with the next scene, Sorrentino's wholly imagined setting of Andreotti confessing in pseudodirect address to, not God, note, but an apostrophized Livia, in which, at a key point, we are actually treated to a flashback to his proposal to her while strolling through the Verano cemetery. As noted, this sequence is presented in a digitally mediated, pseudoarchival footage—with youthful actors playing Andreotti and Livia—signaling a peculiar cinematic pastness that stands in this example paradoxically for a discrete individual memory. While part of the meaning of this might be that even the private reveries of such a public figure are fair game for public consumption, it is also the case that in this sequence Sorrentino is following a time-honored convention of representing the subject's interior life in a radically exteriorized, audiovisual manner. Otherwise, Andreotti's imagined confession is one of the more fantastic, antirealist sequences in the film (figure 4.7).[53] The confession famously ends with Andreotti's line: "God knows it, and I know it too" ("questo Dio lo sa, e lo so anch'io"), which in form and meaning anticipates in a secular political context Pope Pius XIII's demand in episode 5 of *The Young Pope* that his followers display "absolute love and total devotion to God. . . . Blind loyalty to the imperative."[54] In either case, God's will is commensurate with that of the speaker, who embodies the paradoxes of ultimate power. "From this day forth,"

FIGURE 4.6 *Il Divo*

FIGURE 4.7 *Il Divo*

Pius XIII concludes, "that's what the pope wants. That's what the church wants. That's what God wants." The seeds of the TV series' critique of the intermingling of ecclesiastical and state politics are sown in *Il Divo*, manifesting on the individual level of Andreotti's character. In one telling scene, for instance, Andreotti and his faction are gathered for a nocturnal outdoor dinner, arranged around the table in a manner ironically reminiscent of Leonardo Da Vinci's famous *Last Supper* fresco (1495–1498), with Andreotti, unsurprisingly, occupying Christ's central position (figure 4.8). In this example of the film's art-historical intermediality, Sorrentino manages to eat his *formaggio* and have it too as the men compare the giant *burrata* they are about to consume to their colleague, Sbardella, recently defected to another Christian Democrat faction.[55] "Eat Sbardella, Franco, it'll calm you down," intones Andreotti, neatly off-loading the metaphysical implications of the Eucharist,

FIGURE 4.8 *Il Divo*

conflating the theme of Judas's comeuppance for his betrayal with the metaphorical sacrifice implied in the consuming of the bread and wine. As the others raise their wineglasses in a toast to Andreotti, who has agreed to run for president of the republic, he drains his tumbler of bicarbonate of soda.

Il Divo concludes with a dramatization of one of Andreotti's many trials for Mafia collusion. The scene begins with a tracking shot that directly recalls the bravura sequence near the end of *The Consequences of Love*, inaugurating the scene of Titta di Girolamo's trial by the Mafia, in the person of Nitto Lo Riccio, in a directly inverted anticipation of Andreotti's trial here. The tracking shot in *il Divo* replicates the earlier one structurally, as it likewise begins with Servillo framed in medium close-up from behind, as he moves down the courthouse hallway, the Steadicam following at a constant distance. As his bodyguard opens the courtroom doors for him, Andreotti/Servillo deftly moves to the side, as Bigazzi's camera slips in front of the actor, in a repetition of the technique he used in the earlier film during Titta's long walk to face his tribunal. Here the camera assumes Andreotti's optical point-of-view (which it does on one or two other occasions in the film), moving into the courtroom as people turn to look into the camera, as if addressing Andreotti. Eventually (as in *The Consequences of Love*) he moves back into his own point of view as he shakes hands with a row of lawyers. As the same tracking shot continues, the camera swoops away from Andreotti, circling past the judges on the dais as they call the proceedings to order. The camera executes a complete circle before returning to Andreotti, who has by now taken his seat in front. As the presiding judge continues speaking from off-screen, the camera moves in toward Andreotti, from wide to medium close-up, eventually coming to a rest on Andreotti framed frontally. The camera "takes up the position on the judge's bench, looking back at Giulio and thereby adopting a judicial subjectivity which we as spectators are invited to share."[56] The long take continues, however, becoming the final shot of the film. As the dead Aldo Moro (Paolo Graziosi) reads again in voiceover from one of his letters (in the same facsimile of a scratchy analog tape recording heard earlier over the scene of Andreotti's nervous all-night pacing, and also before that, during his 1990 state visit to Gorbachev in Moscow): "What will they remember about you?" asks Moro, rhetorically (figure 4.9). The film concludes with the medium close-up of Andreotti, the courtroom behind him, the color gradually bleeding out of the image, leaving him in bleak greyscale.[57] Moro: "Andreotti remained indifferent, leaden, distant, cocooned in his dark dream of glory. . . . What was the meaning, in the face of all this, of the inconsolable grief of an old spouse, the destruction of a family? What did all this mean for Andreotti, once he'd achieved the power to do evil, just as he'd always done evil in his life? All this meant nothing." The shot continues a few more seconds, wavering slightly, and then the film ends with a cut to black. This final tracking shot clocks in at just over three minutes. As the earlier Moro recording put it (over the all-night pacing scene): "Along with the goodness, flexibility, transparency that undeniably make up the few real Christian Democrats that exist in the world, you'll last a little longer, or a little less, but you'll vanish without a trace." Moro's function in the film is very much like Banquo's ghost in *Macbeth*—or even *il grillo parlante* (the talking cricket) in *Pinocchio*—the highly vocal embodiment of the sort of moral conscience that is the last thing the protagonist wants to heed.[58] In an earlier scene, set in the ministerial bathroom, the dead Moro in fact appears to the obviously guilt-ridden Andreotti, as he does for the viewer in reconstructed "flashbacks" to his time in captivity, much of which he spent writing letters condemning Andreotti's inaction. After Marco Bellocchio's counterfactual resurrection of Moro at the conclusion of 2003's *Buongiorno, notte*, the fantasy sequences featuring the dead Moro "haunting" Andreotti may be the apotheosis of what Alan O'Leary calls "the literalized representation of the haunting of Italy by Aldo Moro's ghost."[59] In Catherine O'Rawe's words, the "fantasy of resurrection" in Andreotti's bathroom presents Moro explicitly as such a figure of conscience, calling him "to account for his behavior."[60] Ironically, as he confesses to his priest, the memory of Moro's murder has traumatically marked Andreotti, the man whose avowed modus operandi is to leave no traces.[61] In an earlier scene, just before Salvo Lima's murder, he remarks: "If one wants to keep a secret, one musn't even confide in oneself. One must never leave traces." Of all the victims of political violence in the Years of Lead, Andreotti admits to his priest, he suffers only for Moro: "Everything always washed over me without leaving a trace, but not Moro. I just can't get him out of my mind. It's like a second migraine, but more agonizing."

An instructive intertextual comparison can also be made between *Il Divo*'s ending and the concluding mirror scene of Mary Harron's 1999 adaptation of Bret Easton Ellis's *American Psycho*, deepening the film's engagement with the theme of emptiness, lack, or nothingness running through Sorrentino's work: the absence of sense or meaning, understood in a psychological or, more precisely, existential sense. As will be seen in chapters 6 and 8, this theme reaches its apogee in *The Great Beauty* and finds its ironic redemption in *The Young Pope*. As András Bálint Kovács convincingly argues, historically this existential theme finds is most

FIGURE 4.9 *Il Divo*

sophisticated articulation in Antonioni's famous trilogy, culminating in *L'eclisse* (1962)—a film that Kovács refers to as "modernist" or "intellectual melodrama,"[62] dramatizing postwar art cinema's flirtation with Sartrean philosophy in contrast to Hollywood's love affair with what Maria LaPlace calls "vulgar Freudianism."[63] In *L'eclisse* lack, emptiness, or nothingness "become ultimate powers, incomparably stronger than the power of the characters' desire for love."[64] In other words, this thematic nothingness is the ultimate and most powerful expression of the trilogy's underlying macrothemes of alienation and the failure of communication.[65] Kovács connects this breakdown directly to the influence of Sartrean philosophy on midcentury intellectual and cultural production, epitomized by Antonioni's films:

> In the final analysis Sartre makes a direct link between the concept of nothingness and fundamental existential experiences of modern man concerning loneliness and disappearance, which makes this concept susceptible to concrete artistic representation. Nothingness in Sartrean philosophy becomes an essential and invisible ingredient in the phenomenological experience of everyday life. It is an invisible but perceptible dimension hiding behind physical reality. And cinema is a particularly appropriate medium to represent the tension between the two. No other medium can represent the physical surface of reality as meticulously as cinema, and no other medium can express the emptiness behind that surface as strongly. . . . Nothingness is the negative power of lost humanistic values.[66]

In *American Psycho* this properly modernist cinematic theme is transformed into its postmodernist counterpart.[67] The postmodern, in this historical understanding, names the moment in which the emptiness beneath the surface of the real is revealed as itself an illusion, leaving nothing but the surface. In the opening scene of Harron's film, Patrick Bateman (Christian Bale) meticulously removes the "herb mint facial masque" that is the focus of the scene, as this voice-over is heard: "There is an idea of a Patrick Bateman, some kind of abstraction, but there is no real me, only an entity, something illusory, and though I can hide my cold gaze and you can shake my hand and feel flesh gripping yours and maybe you can even sense our lifestyles are probably comparable: *I simply am not there*" (figure 4.10). Later, in the film's final scene, Bateman, in response to a colleague's comment about Ronald Reagan's televisual performance, mutters, "Inside doesn't matter." Again in voiceover, as he stares directly into the camera in close-up:

> There are no more barriers to cross. All I have in common with the uncontrollable and the insane, the vicious and the evil, all the mayhem I have caused and my utter indifference toward it, I have now surpassed. My pain is constant and sharp, and I do not hope for a better world for anyone. In fact, I want my pain to be inflicted on others. I want no escape. But even after admitting this, there is no catharsis. My punishment continues to elude me, and I gain no deeper knowledge of myself, no new knowledge can be extracted from my telling. This confession has meant nothing.[68]

The salient difference between this and Andreotti's confession in *Il Divo* is *American Psycho*'s third-act recourse to a richly ambiguous self-reflexivity, in which it is suggested that the protagonist's many heinous crimes may, or may not, be a figment of his imagination, writ large on the screen. In the end, it doesn't matter. Sorrentino's Andreotti, by contrast, as a fictional avatar of a historical figure in what is in effect a postmodern biopic, has no such recourse, which is to say the film can only go so far in the direction of self-reflexive and other ironic techniques before it is confronted by the hypothetical moral-ethical weight of the real politician's actions in the world. Andreotti's personal measure of guilt does matter, even if we may never know it. The lesson for the moment here, however, is that *Il Divo*, unlike *American Psycho*, is a meaningfully political film not because of its subject matter but because of its form. And, where both have been categorized as examples of postmodern cinema, the difference between them on this score also illuminates the difference between Sorrentino's and, say, Tarantino's, postmodern irony (discussed above): where the latter never penetrates the spectacular surface of things, the former demonstrates the degree in which subjective interiority can be revealed via cinema's radical exteriority.

The modern subject remains a metaphysical construct predicated upon an objective reality outside of itself. In the bumpy transition from Romantic to properly modern(ist) to what came after (until recently, for many, the postmodern), the occidental ex-nominatively masculine subject has gone from being predicated upon a certain understanding of God, to an absent God, to the empty space left behind by an absent God, to an empty space, full stop.[69] In the context of a self-consciously critical text such as *American Psycho*—in contrast to more typical commercial or genre films in American mass culture—is the recognition and representation within the artwork of this kind of radical nothingness at the heart of things. This sort of

FIGURE 4.10 *American Psycho* (Mary Harron, 1999)

productively negative or nihilistic outlook is rarely if ever encountered in more mainstream cultural production, which in this case includes Sorrentino's work to date, in particular *The Young Pope*. The conclusion of *Il Divo*, by contrast, is arguably Sorrentino's bleakest and most nihilistic.

For Antonello, "Andreotti's corporeal presence [in *Il Divo*] becomes a cipher, an epitome, of that same [postmodernist] aesthetic, and a corporeal metonym of the kind of ironic detachment seen to be typical of the man (or the myth) himself."[70] The comparison with *American Psycho*, however, allows us to see that, in *Il Divo* at least, Sorrentino's postmodernism does not go as far as Harron's, if only because his historically grounded subject does not allow it, compelling him to stay on the hither side of a satirical deconstruction of Andreotti's character. Despite Moro's condemnatory words—"All this meant nothing"—unlike Patrick Bateman, Andreotti is presented as a man who appears to have an interior life and even, perhaps, a moral conscience. But the two films are meaningfully comparable insofar as they both present a scathingly critical portrait of different avatars of contemporary (later twentieth-century) masculinity. More specifically, *Il Divo* presents a searing critique of "the fundamental emptiness of the neoliberal politician."[71] In the end, only the abovementioned remarkable scene of Andreotti's (fictional) confession, nominally to his wife, Livia, but delivered direct to camera, contains something like an admission of moral-ethical guilt, when he names "the deeds that power must commit to ensure the well-being and development of the country. . . . The monstrous, unavoidable contradiction: perpetrating evil to guarantee good. . . . We must love God greatly, to understand how necessary evil is for good." This is the logic expressed by Saint Ignatius of Loyola: "All means are legitimate (even evil ones) to seek God's will."[72] For Antonello, the highly self-reflexive confession scene represents "the construction of a collective compensatory inferential projection, an imaginative outlet, which corresponds to the desire of an entire nation . . . to hear a confession."[73] It is no coincidence that, of all Andreotti's many nicknames—fox, salamander, hunchback, Molloch, Beelzebub—the film takes its title from "*il divo*," etymologically connected to *divino*, divine or godlike.[74] In this confession scene the film's Andreotti comes closest to either transcending or losing touch with his humanity, in his grotesque figure becoming either much more or considerably less than human.[75]

This comparison between the independent American film (*American Psycho* was distributed by Lionsgate, the Canadian independent) and the Italian coproduction in many ways comes down to the difference between the kind of modernist art cinematic legacy that Harron's film represents, for all its stylistic and thematic postmodernism, and the fact that Sorrentino's films to date always tread a fine line between a latter-day modernist art cinema and something more like commercial genre film. This hybrid identity is not anomalous but typical of much twenty-first-century transnational filmmaking, and, in deeper historical focus, is behind Kovács's identification of the serious and/or playful incorporation of generic tropes and formal and thematic strategies (what Kovács calls forms) in many of the most famous postwar modernist art films.[76] Sorrentino's films represent a particularly rich example of the twenty-first-century transnational manifestation of the kind of art film hybrid Kovács identifies in European modernist cinema from 1960 on. What contemporary filmmakers such as Sorrentino have learned from this tradition is that, in order to capture and retain an audience for a more challenging, noncommercial cinema, it is necessary to adapt recognizable thematic and stylistic forms into new and unusual narrative contexts. His next film, *This Must Be the Place*, provides an outstanding example.

FIVE

This Must Be the Place

From the Ridiculous to the Unspeakable (A Holocaust Road Movie)

> Something's not quite right, here. I'm not sure what exactly. But something.
> —Cheyenne, *This Must Be the Place*

AT THE CONCLUSION of *The Family Friend*, Geremia "heart-of-gold" has experienced humiliation but not humility; unusual for a Sorrentino protagonist, he appears to be more or less the same repugnant yet strangely sympathetic character at the end as at the beginning. It is more likely that the viewer's perception of him has changed instead. Cheyenne (Sean Penn), the protagonist of 2011's *This Must Be the Place*,[1] is another ridiculous man, but one whose encounter with humiliation and transformation takes an utterly different form. Sorrentino's fifth feature tells the story of Cheyenne, a retired American rock star, living in Ireland, who, in returning to the United States for the first time in decades, embarks on a continent-spanning quest to find his Jewish father's wartime tormentor. Any attempt to sum up this multifaceted film in one sentence is doomed to fail, however, for *This Must Be the Place*, of all Sorrentino's films to date, most readily escapes easy description. Diegetically, this film extends and complicates the recurrent theme of humiliation as a significant negative affective dimension of the Sorrentinian subject. Here Sorrentino goes further, positing an experience of humiliation that spans generations—a kind of postmodern prosthetic affective experience, the negative affective equivalent to what in Holocaust and memory studies is called postmemory, coined by Marianne Hirsch to name the experience of survivors' children compelled to remember a traumatic event they did not themselves experience at firsthand, to which they may feel compelled to bear witness despite not being an eye-witness.[2] In Hirsch's formulation, this is an experience of secondhand memory mediated through family photos or other material artifacts. In this respect *This Must Be the Place* dramatizes the questions: Can the son understand and redeem the humiliation that his father experienced firsthand? Can he do so, moreover, without replicating the cycle of violence that produced the desire for revenge or retribution? Can he, in short, expunge the sense of (historical, collective) humiliation? In choosing this theme for his fifth feature, Sorrentino proves definitively what was implicit in *The Family Friend*: that, far from expressing anti-Semitism, he is willing in his films to confront the questions that continue to be raised by the fact of the Holocaust in a manner respectful to contemporary Jewish identity. With regard to the Shylockian motif in *The Family Friend*, moreover, in *This Must Be the Place* we have an actual Jewish (American) protagonist who, while comparably as complex as Geremia di Geremei, in Sean Penn's portrayal is considerably more sympathetic as a character. Here Sorrentino confronts actual anti-Semitism head-on—while also exploring the related themes of victimhood, humiliation, postmemory, and the heritability of an affective burden that is the complement of historical guilt.

One of this book's subsidiary goals is to trace Sorrentino's relationship to realism as it evolves from the satirical postrealism Marcus identifies in *Il Divo* to an arguably even more sophisticated cinematic modality whose ironies are increasingly tempered by melancholy, nostalgia, and other (gender-specific) affectivities.[3] The latter—variations on a kind of ironic elegiac affect—are at least partly the result of Sorrentino's abiding fascination with powerful men of all stripes. With respect to *Il Divo*, despite the fact that (as more than one critic notes) the image of the single all-powerful political figure is a myth, a pop culture cliché, Sorrentino's fascination with power, and with the men who wield it,[4] suits an age that has produced political leaders such as Silvio Berlusconi, Vladimir Putin, and now, preeminently, Donald Trump. These are men who, in the age of social media, appear to hold the lion's share of political and economic power even as the internet's revolutionizing of the mass media allots a microportion of cultural power to anyone with a Wi-Fi connection and a smartphone. In *This Must Be the Place*, however, Sorrentino returns to terrain similar to that explored in *The Family Friend*, with a protagonist who is ridiculous and yet knows himself to be so.[5]

Sorrentino's first English-language film represents a radical break from his earlier work in a number of other ways. *This Must Be the Place* recounts the story of fifty-something millionaire Goth rocker Cheyenne, whose persona is an amalgam of Ozzy Osbourne, the Cure's Robert Smith, and Ian Curtis of Joy Division.[6] In the film's backstory, some twenty years past, two young fans, inspired by his romantically gloomy lyrics, committed suicide, moving Cheyenne to retire to a mansion outside Dublin, Ireland. As in *The Consequences of Love*, the protagonist's eccentric routine is established only to be disrupted by an external force—in this case not love but the death of Cheyenne's orthodox Jewish father, an Auschwitz survivor. Overcoming his many phobias, Cheyenne travels to New York City for the funeral, only to learn there that his father's life-long obsession had been to find the camp guard who tormented and humiliated him. The theme of humiliation was established in *The Family Friend*—in an entirely different, gender-specific context—as the price Rosalba must pay by agreeing to sex with Geremia in exchange for the mitigation of her father's debt. In *This Must Be the Place*, humiliation acquires greater philosophical force, although the ethical cost may be comparable.

The film's title derives from the 1983 Talking Heads' song "This Must Be the Place (Naïve Melody)" that recurs throughout, in various renditions, both intra- and extradiegetically.[7] The song's refrain, "Home, is where I want to be . . ." reflects at first ironically and later more straightforwardly on the protagonist's improvised quest to find his father's persecutor, which in the end—somewhat predictably, perhaps—turns out to be a quest to find himself. The banality of this description is inflected, however, by the film's visual beauty and also by innovations on the level of narrative form and generic convention. The song's refrain also ironically underscores the film's exemplary transnational status, insofar as transnational cinema "arises in the interstices between the local and the global . . . [where it] is most 'at home'," reflecting "the hybridized and cosmopolitan identities" of many contemporary filmmakers.[8]

It becomes clearer with each film that Sorrentino's screenplays combine parodic references to specific film genres or satirical commentary upon some instance of contemporary Italian, European, or in this case American, life, with a seriously ironic meditation upon more fundamental ethical questions. Upon its release *This Must Be the Place* was immediately criticized for daring to mix what is essentially a road movie plotline with a post-Holocaust story. But Sorrentino's gamble succeeds in reinvigorating both genres: Cheyenne's comically pathetic retired rock star grows increasingly sympathetic as he gains self-knowledge and affective maturity, his flamboyant façade of black clothes and fright-wig hair, pancake makeup, eye liner, and red lipstick making him into just one more subcultural oddball on the road across America (figure 5.1). The idiosyncratic storyline also allows Sorrentino to indulge his tendency to incorporate an eclectic mix of other texts (notably Wim Wenders's *Paris, Texas* [1984]), historical events, and cultural references—most outlandishly (speaking of bizarre American subcultures) a quick shot of a Hitler lookalike on a passing flatbed truck, as if on his way to a rally for the so-called alt-right. The latter is only one example of how this film, released in 2011, offers an oblique but prescient commentary upon post-2008 America while anticipating the post-Obama transition to a Trumpian dystopia.

FIGURE 5.1 *This Must Be the Place* (Paolo Sorrentino, 2011)

Where the final scene of *Il Divo* reveals Andreotti's public persona as a mask concealing an inner self that is commensurate with this external one, the opening scene of *This Must Be the Place* shows Cheyenne as yet another man who hides behind a public mask, only in his case the relation of mask and real self beneath—or "face," in Bondanella's terminology[9]—is inverted. Cheyenne literally puts on a mask each morning: a uniform of dyed hair, eyeliner, lipstick, black clothes. At the same time, his name is obviously appropriated from an indigenous nomenclature: a most authentically yet ironically American name.[10] By the film's end he has outgrown this persona, which, he comes gradually to realize, is the outward expression of his life-long failure to become an adult.[11] Nevertheless the subject here remains at bottom the privileged metaphysical subject of modernity, predicated upon not nothing but something; or rather, as with all of Sorrentino's masculine protagonists to date, to one degree or another, this nothing, emptiness, or lack is itself something; as with the nothingness of Sartrean existentialism, being is itself predicated upon nothingness, but this nothingness, invisible in itself, is always already represented by something else, something visible—which is why cinema and memory remain the best analogues for subjective human existence, and finally why the one, memory, folds into the other, cinema.[12] That said, it is not accidental that this film, unlike some of Sorrentino's stories, does not contain a single flashback, whether intra- or extradiegetic. Whereas certain of his works—*One Man Up*, *The Consequences of Love*, *The Great Beauty*, *Il Divo*, and especially *The Young Pope*—rely on the flashback as a key narrative device, his other works rely instead on a less classical, more art film approach to temporal structure, demanding more of the viewer but compensating with greater ambiguity and a richer set of potential meanings.[13] As will be explored below, this is another way in which *This Must Be the Place* resembles a latter-day American art film such as *Paris, Texas* in its general approach to storytelling.

Masculine Identity and the Quest for Self-Knowledge

Early in the film, Mary's (Eve Hewson) mother (Olwen Fouéré) tells Cheyenne: "You never took up smoking because you remained a child." In a later scene, when he is already hunting for former camp guard Aloise Lange (Heinz Lieven), Cheyenne encounters Mordecai Midler (Judd Hirsch), who also criticizes Cheyenne for what he deems to be his immaturity or inadequacy as a man but in the very specific context of his relationship to his Jewish identity. The theme of prolonged childhood or adolescence is important in this film, anticipating the central themes of *Youth*, only from a more specific, Jewish-American, perspective.[14] With respect to its critique of an infantilizing popular culture, *This Must Be the Place* aligns itself with *The Consequences of Love* and *The Great Beauty*, while chiming with the broader leftist critique of contemporary consumer-capitalist culture that manifests in a range of critical texts (e.g., Baudrillard's critique of 1980s American culture,[15] films (e.g., Godard, especially 2000's *Eloge de l'amour*), and literary works (Sorrentino's *Everybody's Right*). Indeed, this theme, in one form or another, is central to Sorrentino's entire output to date, informing its peculiar form of *impegno*.

As already indicated, the idea of a masculine identity constructed out of a perpetual adolescence is in fact crossed here with the postwar international art film trope of an individual—typically male—who is in search of his own identity, whether because he appears to lack one outright or because the one he possesses is revealed to be inauthentic. Historically, this trope is itself the basis for an entire subgenre of postwar art film that András Bálint Kovács has dubbed the wandering, travel, or journey film.[16] The art film's protagonist's journey often turns into a quest for self-knowledge; at one point, this cliché is even invoked as a joke, when Cheyenne's wife, Jane (Frances McDormand), asks him during a transatlantic call if he is trying "to find himself," to which he replies: "I'm not trying to find myself. I'm in New Mexico, not India." In *This Must Be the Place*, the wandering film is crossed with an updating of what Kovács calls the investigation film, where wandering and investigation are the "forms" that are "constitutive of genre."[17] This is an investigation film in both the literal and the existential sense because, in the second act, Cheyenne travels to New York, where he embarks on a quest to find a missing person: his father's tormentor. The modernist investigation film is distinguished from its more mainstream commercial genre film forebear by its emphasis not on the outcome but rather on the process of the investigation. As often as not, there is no clear resolution on hand. The same is true, of course, of the subgenre of the wandering or journey film: as often as not it is the journey itself rather than the goal that is the main focus.[18] Interestingly, the ending of *This Must Be the Place* goes some ways toward undercutting this modernist cinematic truism, complicating the film's relationship to this tradition and inflecting its meanings as much in the direction of a more conventional, middlebrow transnational narrative whose ultimate message, although ambiguous, conveys a positive uplift. As Kovács points out, the hero "in this genre travels around in the world most often with no specific goal. In most cases the motive for wandering is not to arrive somewhere or to find something but to leave a place or to escape."[19] This is clearly the case in *This Must Be the Place*, at least until the end of the first act, when Cheyenne leaves Dublin for New York after neither travelling nor even driving a car for more than twenty years. The film's greatest divergence from its 1970s art film antecedents begins in the film's second act, when the Holocaust is introduced as both theme and real-world historical focus.

The distinctive twist that Sorrentino adds to this type of art film is the fact that, for the entire second act—that is, for the bulk of the film's story—Cheyenne takes on the role of Nazi hunter, which means that not only is the quest or search quite literal, it is also meaningful in an overdetermined way; in fact, Sorrentino runs the risk here of appearing to have appropriated an historical event such as the Holocaust in order to add a moral-ethical weight to his film that it would not otherwise possess. This is, however, an unfair criticism because by incorporating the cultural and historical significance of the Holocaust into the film's story, Sorrentino succeeds in giving form to a unique and quietly scathing critique of contemporary American society on the cusp of drastic or even catastrophic change.

The manner in which the Holocaust is introduced into the film as part of its story is worth examining. After thirty years of rebellion against and estrangement from both his father and his Jewish patrimony, Cheyenne the prodigal son returns

FIGURE 5.2 *This Must Be the Place*

to New York for his father's funeral. There he learns about Mordecai Midler, a famous (fictional) Nazi hunter, modeled on Simon Wiesenthal and others like him.[20] Once he embarks on his cross-country quest to find his father's tormentor, Cheyenne teams up with Midler, who makes a point of filling the gaps in Cheyenne's historical knowledge. "Did you know your father?" "In a general sort of way," replies Cheyenne. "You know about the Holocaust?" asks Midler. Cheyenne: "In a general sort of way."[21] In the following, wordless scene, we see Midler sitting amidst a group of what appear to be high school students, silently staring at a series of slide images projected onto a screen at the front of the classroom (figure 5.2). As will be explored below, the outmoded analog slide technology, while justified diegetically in terms of Midler's age, is also justified in this scene in terms of its intertextual connection to the comparable scene in *Paris, Texas*, in which Travis's (Harry Dean Stanton) memory of his wife, Jane (Nastassja Kinski), is reawakened by his viewing of a Super 8 home movie. In a series of reverse-angle shots Cheyenne comes into focus, at the back of the room, watching in rapt attention. Each slide is on screen for a few seconds, with no commentary from Midler. For the viewer of a certain age the images are all too familiar: the skeletal survivors of liberated Auschwitz and Bergen-Belsen, the heaped piles of naked corpses, child prisoners. After a short while Midler turns and notices that Cheyenne has vanished. It is a strange scene, as on the one hand it reminds us of the extraordinary power of images to bear witness, conveying meanings for which no precise words exist. On the other hand, it reinforces valid fears of the dangers of such decontextualized images: the dangers of losing all specificity of meaning, all historical and cultural groundedness. Who are the people in these photos? Where are they? What happened to them? How can we know, in the absence of an accompanying narrative, the litany of contextual facts that deserve to be remembered as much as these images need to be reproduced and reviewed as precipitants of collective traumatic memory? This brief sequence raises these points even as it takes the story in a wholly new, much more serious, direction. Another question, more specific to the film, emerges: Can this story sustain the moral-ethical weight, the *gravitas*, implied by these images? To confront this question, it will be necessary in what follows to consider the film against a broader-than-usual intermedial canvas.

"Before the Inferno"

Sorrentino as a filmmaker has much in common with New German Cinema cofounder Wim Wenders, not the least of which is a deep investment in the significance of music—all genres, styles, and periods—to their respective creative processes.[22] To say that *This Must Be the Place* intertextualizes a film such as Wenders's *Paris, Texas*, is to overlook the degree in which Sorrentino's film invokes the spirit of this kind of 1970s and early 1980s road movie, characterized as much by certain films of the Hollywood Renaissance (beginning with Dennis Hopper's *Easy Rider* [1969], as well as specific examples of postwar European art cinema, especially in the New German Cinema itself [e.g., Wenders' *Kings of the Road* (1976)]).[23] Ultimately, though, *This Must Be the Place* pays homage to and recontextualizes as it resurrects the kind of prototransnational road movie[24] made famous by New German Cinema works such as Wenders's *Alice in the Cities* (1974) or Werner Herzog's *Stroszek* (1977) (at one point, Cheyenne's pickup truck bursts into flames, ironically recalling the famously surreal and apocalyptic ending of Herzog's film). For reasons to be revealed below, however, it is Wenders's later film, *Paris, Texas*, called "the archetype of the road movie; a journey through America in search of identity,"[25] which I will explore in the most detail. (*This Must Be the Place* features a key cameo by Harry Dean Stanton, who also played the lead in *Paris, Texas*, a canny bit of noncoincidental casting [figure 5.3; figure 5.4].[26]) The aforementioned films are still considered to be prototransnational not only because of their continent-spanning stories but by virtue of their funding structures, which involved complex configurations of capital from various national and international funding bodies.[27] But (for the purposes of my argument) the main thing shared by each of these films is what Silvestra Mariniello and James Cisternos identify as "a European gaze that traverses the emptiness of the American province."[28] *This Must Be the Place* complicates this description by having a hero who is originally American (New York Orthodox Jewish), supplanted to Europe, who then returns to America where the city and landscape are defamiliarized by the perspective provided by time, becoming a peculiarly American extension of what Gilles Deleuze in *Cinema 2* calls "any-space-whatever." As Mariniello and Cisternos imply, the Super 8 home movie that Walter screens for Travis, who was suffering from amnesia, acts as a madeleine-object, a precipitant of memory and then action, rejoining him with Hunter (Hunter Carson), his son, and spurring them both to go in search of Jane, Hunter's mother and Travis's wife (she bears the same name as Cheyenne's wife in Sorrentino's film).[29] The material infrastructure of the Super 8 film technology figures prominently in the transformative process that Travis undergoes in this scene; the grainy, desaturated color image, the absence of sound, the jerky edits, the noise of the projector and of the film strip slapping at the end of the reel—these are the

FIGURE 5.3 *This Must Be the Place*

natural analog traces of a late 1970s cinematically mediated memory. This is also a good example of how a filmic representation of a technically mediated subjective memory comes to signify collectively, through the irreducibly public (social, shared) nature of film as medium.

If, in Wenders's own words, his later film *Wings of Desire* (1987) is a "vertical road movie,"[30] then *This Must Be the Place* could be described as a horizontal descent, or katabasis, into one particular version of hell. As Lee Hill explains, Wenders's first conception of the story for *Paris, Texas* was to create a "modern update" of *The Odyssey*,[31] whose eleventh book contains the prototype of the literary and now cinematic katabasis, a going under or underworld or afterlife journey in search of special knowledge. Arguably, the German director-screenwriter succeeded in transposing or translating specific narrative elements from Homer's epic into the

FIGURE 5.4 *Paris, Texas* (Wim Wenders, 1984)

radically different language and epistemological framework of the feature fiction film. It must be added though, that, insofar as Travis resembles Ulysses, or Jane Penelope, for instance, the resemblance is thoroughly ironic, which is precisely how this intertext contributes to the film's richness of meaning. Likewise, following an intermedial thread, *This Must Be the Place* represents an utterly ironic take on specific elements in *Inferno*, the first book in Dante's fourteenth-century *Commedia*. The film's meanings are thus largely the result of its difference from Dante's source text and the premodern, allegorical Christian worldview that informs it. What is the point of this kind of ironic intermedial adaptation? The answer lies in the mechanism of redemption, already present in pre-Christian form in Homer's *Odyssey*, whose narrative and thematic closure derives from the operation of *nostos*, or homecoming, which drives the story as a whole. As Christian allegory Dante's *Inferno* provides the ideal template for countless modern and contemporary narratives whose outcomes offer endless variations on the literal redemption of the immortal soul that Dante dramatizes. *Inferno*, recounting the first third of the pilgrim's journey, has proven—along with the second book, *Purgatorio*—to hold the most appeal to modernity as the intertextual template for literal and metaphorical katabases, journeys of self-discovery, that conclude with some form of (usually secularized) redemption or its ironic failure. In these modern texts the eschatological dimension so crucial to Dante's narrative is either domesticated, trivialized to the level of self-actualization (e.g., heroic self-sacrifice), or is altogether absent.

In this analogy Cheyenne is to Dante-pilgrim as Mordecai Midler is to Virgil, and Aloise Lange, in his high-altitude snowy desert, is to Satan at the bottom-most level of hell in Dante-poet's eschatological vision (figure 5.5). This reading of the film is justified by the language of Cheyenne's father's journal entries, which are heard in voiceover at intervals in the film's second half, as if from beyond the grave. These journals, with their pencil drawings and notations, constitute the material basis of the film's version of postmemory. The same opening refrain repeats several times:

FIGURE 5.5 *This Must Be the Place*

"Before the inferno . . .," a literal reference to life in Auschwitz but a metaphorical reference as well to the inferno or hell on earth that the camps represented for the inmates. At this point, in fact, the distinction between figurative and literal becomes more or less moot. This phrase is also likely a reference to Primo Levi's *If This Is a Man* (*Se questo è un uomo*, 1958), which already intertextualizes Dantean and classical tropes in the context of an autobiographical account of daily life in Auschwitz.

If This Is a Man signifies even more forcefully than the Dante intertext for the film's second half. More precisely, Dante's *Inferno* signifies in the film through or because of the allusion to Levi's text. This intermedial node in fact conceals a dense and complex web of meanings that resonates across Sorrentino's film as if by default. The fact that the narrative undergoes the shift to an explicitly post-Holocaust storyline and the fact that the screenplay contains the references to "the inferno" makes the association with Levi's text difficult to avoid. That Levi was an Italian Jew, and Cheyenne and his family New York Orthodox Jews, also suggests an underlying connection between European and New World diasporic Jewish identities. Romney points out that "for Cheyenne to subscribe to such a quintessentially gentile cult [as Goth Rock] is surely the ultimate Jewish son's revolt. That said, a few shots of Orthodox Jews in New York suggests that—sartorially at least—Cheyenne hasn't strayed that far from his roots: what is his black garb if not a wild parody of the Hassidic male's uniform?"[32] The theme of diaspora reminds us of the constitutive myth of wandering and homelessness at the core of these identities, this collective diasporic identity, which both Sorrentino and Levi invoke in their respective texts. This myth also stands in contrast to the Christo-Hellenic myth of homecoming, as an end to wandering, whose origins in occidental culture date back to Homer's *Odyssey*.

Insofar as *Paris, Texas* is an ironically condensed reimagining of *The Odyssey*, Wenders's film remediates the theme or myth of homecoming as an end to wandering, updating it by weaving it seamlessly together with the modern Romantic quest for self, for identity, at the heart of the (American) road movie genre. The Levi-Dante intertext in *This Must Be the Place*, by contrast, represents a more complex web of ironically juxtaposed, even contradictory, meanings. I indicated above the central structural contradiction between the horizontal, Jewish but also American direction of the film's plot and the verticality implied by the ironic incorporation of infernal elements, culminating in the possibility of some sort of redemption—still the ultimate Christological narrative trope, even in a putatively secular cultural context. *This Must Be the Place* ends with Cheyenne's literal homecoming, to be sure—anticipated in the various versions of the Talking Heads' song "This Must Be the Place (Naïve Melody)", which opens with the line "Home / Is where I want to be. . . ." (Jane, to Cheyenne, on the phone, from New Mexico: "When are you coming home?"). But on the way to this, before it can come about, Cheyenne must undergo his own ironic katabasis, which involves the special coming-into-knowledge that can only be gained in the confrontation with death. Since its beginnings in myth, after all, katabasis has always entailed "at some level a search for identity. The journey is in some central, irreducible way a journey of self-discovery, a quest for a lost self."[33] Cheyenne is himself a kind of ironic Odysseus in that he travels from Ireland to New York not by airplane but by boat (which is also why he does not get there in time to see his father before he dies). In an otherwise inexplicably hostile discussion of the film, Sicinski accurately captures the ironically Odyssean character of the film's storyline: it "is an interesting lark not just despite itself. Its narrative stall, its odd sense of digression and halted motility, provides a genuinely compelling analog to the depression that grips the film's major characters."[34]

In three separate voiceover readings, the viewer hears two distinct excerpts from Cheyenne's father's notebooks. (This technique recalls the very different use of voiceover in *Il Divo*, in which an actor reads Aldo Moro's letters in the guise of the murdered politician-cum-Andreotti's gulty conscience.) The first occurs over the scene of Cheyenne reading the notebooks soon after his father's funeral: "Before the inferno, I had a light heart." The second voiceover occurs immediately after the subsequent scene in which Cheyenne confesses to musician David Byrne his self-doubt and despair ("That's it, David! That's it!"):

> Before the inferno, I had a light heart. As a child I liked to stare at the Polish sky. The same sky that later I saw from the camp, stained with black stripes, columns of smoke, all that was left of my relatives. Still, that terrible sky didn't stop me from marveling at the beauty of the sky. That's a monstrous thought, like all the thoughts that people trapped in infernos have.

In this passage screenwriters Sorrentino and Contarello very economically broach the theme that Levi explores with subtlety and depth in *If This Is a Man*: what it is to be human (a man, *un uomo*) in the camp. They do this negatively, not by defining the human in this context but by pointing out that every thought that a person has in the camp is monstrous, no matter that person's intentions. In the camp everything and everyone becomes monstrous.[35]

FIGURE 5.6 *This Must Be the Place*

This particular voiceover reading bridges from the New York sequence to Cheyenne some days later, in a rented pickup truck, driving through Michigan (figure 5.6). He sits waiting as some workers raise an enormous artificial bottle of McGinley's whiskey at the side of the road (a visual reference to a scene on a highway outside Milan in Antonioni's *Story of a Love Affair* [1950], in which the giant bottles are vermouth, the vehicle a Maserati). The third voiceover occurs as Cheyenne is leaving Rachel's house in the early morning on his way to Utah to hunt for her grandfather:

> Before the inferno, there was home. I remember sneaking my first kiss in the backyard when I was thirteen. The smell of my mother's cooking, the noise, and everyone talking. And the black clouds. The thrill of approaching thunder. I remember watching the darkening sky from the safety of the corner, near the window. I remember the warm blankets covering me when I was sick with fever, a cool hand on my forehead, blissful boredom, and shivers of joy. At home, you were never really alone. Camp tears you apart from each other. It forces you alone with your thoughts. It creates a new kind of death, a breathing death. There are many ways of dying. The worst of them is to continue living utterly alone.

These words are spoken over a montage of Cheyenne's journey from New Mexico toward Utah, including a shot of Cheyenne staring at the world's largest pistachio, a tourist monument outside Alamogordo, New Mexico, underlining the stark contrast between the content of his father's memories and the kitschily touristic nonspaces of contemporary America through which Cheyenne travels in his quest to find Aloise Lange (figure 5.7). Ironically, perhaps, during the scene where Cheyenne encounters Robert Plath (Stanton) in a restaurant, the subject of tourism comes up in a pejorative light. Learning that Plath revolutionized travel by inventing the wheeled suitcase,[36] Cheyenne (who goes nowhere without his) remarks that he "always thought travellers were a pain in the ass." This anticipates Lenny Belardo's admission to

FIGURE 5.7 *This Must Be the Place*

FIGURE 5.8 *This Must Be the Place*

Cardinal Gutierrez—in episode 1 of *The Young Pope*, as they tour St. Peter's Cathedral after hours to avoid the hordes of foreigners—that he hates tourists "because they're just passing through." In *This Must Be the Place* this sentiment resonates ironically with Cheyenne's accidental rediscovery of his Jewish identity to the extent that he achieves some measure of greater self-knowledge by setting off on a journey whose ostensible goal—to say goodbye to his father—rapidly transmutates into a trans-subjective and teleological journey, not to refind a lost home but to redress a past wrong done to his predecessor. In *The Young Pope* the equivalent sentiment resonates in a very different way, revealing Lenny's misanthropy or rather his disdain for any-one lacking his retrograde brand of spiritual fortitude. This attitude, too, is seen to gradually transform into something more like love as Lenny, likewise, comes into greater self-understanding. Like Cheyenne, this is achieved only at the cost of great self-harrowing.

The above-quoted passage from Cheyenne's father's notebooks juxtaposes the comforts and joys of home, mediated through the nostalgic lens of memory, from "before the inferno," with the horrors of that place from which his father emerged alive but not in the sense he knew before: "There are many ways of dying. The worst of them is to continue living utterly alone." The temporality of the preposition *before* takes precedence over its spatial connotations, as in Kafka's Before the Law parable in *The Trial*, a title that profits from the spatio-temporal ambiguity of *before/ vor* in both English and German. The speaker recalls the time *before* the time in the camp; this is a memory work, implying a time before, during, and after the inferno. In a sense, the most important of the three is the last: the time (and place or position) from which the speaker looks back upon the time during and the time before. The questions are: What of Cheyenne? What are we to make of him in the light of these revelations about his father? Sorrentino dares the viewer to judge Cheyenne harshly, as Mordecai does at first, as a dilettante, a man-child, someone who couldn't possibly understand what it means to really suffer. But then Cheyenne's role in the story of course is not to measure up to his father—after all, the father isn't even a proper character; he is a symbol, a distant relation of the father in Kafka's "Letter to His Father."[37] But the screenplay does not compare Cheyenne's character with his father only; once he begins to contemplate the possibility of committing an act of retributive violence, Cheyenne becomes, ironically, like his prey, like Aloise Lange, the camp guard who humiliated his father. The Nazi hunter risks coming to resemble the one he hunts: the Nazi. This potential of the one acting on behalf of the victim coming to resemble the perpetrator is not often met with in popular treatments of these questions. What is at stake here is underlined when Cheyenne enters a gun shop to buy a weapon. There he meets a strange little man, who tells him: "Believe me, it's an extraordinary thing to kill with impunity. . . . If we're licensed to be monsters we end up having just one desire. To truly be monsters." This scene is followed by one in which Cheyenne, newly purchased gun in a plastic bag, crosses a vast empty mall parking lot. As he gets into his rented pickup truck, a Hitler lookalike standing in a trailer pulled behind a tractor passes in medium close-up, an American flag waving conspicuously in the background (figure 5.8).

"The Canto of Ulysses"

If This Is a Man's eleventh chapter, "The Canto of Ulysses," is named for Inferno canto 26, in which Dante-pilgrim encounters the dead hero of Homer's epic—a work, incidentally, of which Dante knew only at second hand, having no knowledge of the Greek language. In Levi's account, the autobiographical protagonist (Levi himself) is walking with Jean, his fellow prisoner (nicknamed Pikolo) to retrieve the day's ration of soup for their Kommando. As they walk, Levi begins to teach his French friend Italian. For no apparent reason, the Ulysses canto from Inferno comes into his mind, and so he begins to recite it from memory. A gap opens up here between Levi-narrator and Levi-protagonist, commensurate with that between Dante-poet and Dante-pilgrim. Levi seems to overlook that he has already suggested an allegorical understanding of the camps as a uniquely modern version of a classical underworld: at the conclusion of his book's first chapter ("The Journey"), he refers to the German guard travelling in the truck transporting Levi and his fellow prisoners to the gates of Auschwitz as "our Charon,"[38] the name of the ferryman of Hades, who conveys the souls of the dead across the river Styx, which divides the worlds of the living and the dead. And, in the next chapter, "On the Bottom," Levi refers to the camp as "hell."[39] Levi is unable to recall the canto in its entirely, but enough of it comes back to him, a line or two here and there, as they walk through the camp to get the soup for their midday meal. Dante's version of Odysseus's adventures is what in adaptation theory is called an extrapolation, since the events his Ulysses recounts have no counterpart in Homer, offering a sort of alternative ending to the poem that Dante never read. In this version Ulysses's desire to continue his voyage and see the world trumps even his love for his wife, Penelope. "Consider well the seed that gave you birth: / you were not made to live your lives as brutes, / but to be followers of worth and knowledge."[40]

Levi: "Enough, one must go on, these are things that one thinks but does not say."[41] The English translation of Dante in Levi's text is as follows: "Think of your breed; for brutish ignorance / Your mettle was not made; you were made men, / To follow after knowledge and excellence."[42] The Mandelbaum translation, quoted first, is more faithful to Dante's Italian, which in these lines does not include the equivalent noun for "men"; Ulysses is addressing his men but not referring to them as "*uomini*." The gendering of the noun originates in the Italian; the latter translation emphasizes the question implicit in Levi's original title, *If This Is a Man* (*Se questo è un uomo*): What is a *man* in this place, this inferno? What has become of the common humanity *we* formerly shared?

In his fragmentary recitation of the Ulysses canto, Levi emphasizes the humanity of Ulysses and his men, displaying the humanism at the core of his account of survival in Auschwitz. In other words, he does not emphasize his own Jewishness or a shared Jewish identity but rather he espouses a general notion of what it means to be human in the best sense, derived, ironically, from his reading—as any Italian of his generation would understand—of Dante's reimagining of the *Odyssey*, about one Greek hero's return home from the Trojan War. In other words, this is a conception of what it means to be human that is, in its universalism, unreflectively gendered and culturally specific; indeed, it is a conception of the human derived second- or third-hand from a literary construction of an ex-nominative masculine subjectivity. Dante's conceit, of course—picked up in the nineteenth century by Tennyson in his poem "Ulysses"—is that the titular hero doesn't want to stay at home but desires to keep going endlessly until death overtakes him. In Dante, paradoxically, anachronistically (as Levi wants to point out to his friend), this desire is subject to the will of another, which is to say God. But *God* in this context lacks a singular, shared meaning: the first distinction is between a Christian and a Jewish God; the second between a monotheistic deity and what came before, in Homer's time: the gods of classical mythology. In Levi's humanist, dare I say, postsecular, version of Dante's Christian paradigm, the eschatological dimension of the metaphysical structure of the world acquires a particular force.

This sentiment is transmuted in Sorrentino's screenplay into a secular moral schema focusing on a formulation of justice predicated on either revenge or forgiveness. The too-easy analogy here with a Judaic vs. a Christian concept of God as either wrathful or loving, respectively, is mitigated by the ambiguity of the solution Cheyenne achieves. This comes in the quietly climactic scene in which Cheyenne finally confronts Aloise Lange, which begins with the latter in medium shot, speaking to an unseen interlocutor. The camera, as usual with Bigazzi, is in motion from the start, circling slowly leftwards and inwards, toward Lange.[43] As he speaks the camera closes in, then a sudden cut returns the scene to its starting point, Lange embarking on the second part of his discourse; the first began with "imitation," with the example of the Nazi high command, each of whom imitated the one higher up, with Hitler at the top. "Everybody imitated everybody else. Everybody but the Jews. They didn't imitate anyone." But the implied sense, it seems, is that the surviving victim, given time and opportunity, will eventually imitate his persecutor, as Cheyenne's father and Cheyenne himself imitate Lange. The second principle is "humiliation," which refers to the shame suffered by Cheyenne's father the day in winter 1943 when Lange threatened to set his dog on him for a minor infraction during morning roll call. The father wet himself with fear, and Lange laughed, as he recalls. This time the camera moves more slowly in its leftward circuit. "Compared to the horrors of Auschwitz [his humiliation] was nothing," remarks Lange, "but your father never forgot it." As the camera passes his face in close up, Lange speaks of "the unrelenting beauty of revenge. An entire life dedicated to avenging a humiliation." A revenge, however, that his father did not live to realize. The scene sets up the expectation in the viewer: Will Cheyenne take revenge on his father's behalf? Or will be choose a different path? What is the third principle after imitation and humiliation? Might it be retribution or forgiveness? Revenge or redemption? Or something else?

The fact that Cheyenne's father experienced humiliation at the hands of Lange the camp guard means that, at that time, he had not yet become what Levi refers to as a Musselmann, camp slang for:

> a being from whom humiliation, horror, and fear had so taken away all consciousness and all personality as to make him absolutely apathetic (hence the ironical name given to him). . . . He no longer belongs to the world of men in any way; he does not even belong to the threatened and precarious world of the camp inhabitants who have forgotten him from the very beginning. Mute and absolutely alone, he has passed into another world without memory and without grief.[44]

Cheyenne's father did not become such a man—a man who is no longer a man— precisely because he experienced humiliation, which, following the end of the war, the liberation of the camps, and his emigration to New York, transformed into the everlasting desire for revenge. (In translating Agamben, Daniel Heller Roazen is faced with the same dilemma as Stuart Woolf in translating Levi: how to translate "*uomo*" when in certain cases, as here, it refers to an ungendered, quasi-universal human being, despite the fact that the camp in which Levi was incarcerated held no women, just as Dante (not to speak of Homer), in composing *Inferno* canto 26, envisioned a voyage undertaken only by heroes, hence by men.) For the desire for revenge, like humiliation, can only be experienced by someone—some man—who is still on *this* side of the line between being a man, which means being properly human, in a conventional humanist sense, and being something else, something less-than-human, no longer a man.

The continuity of the circling close-up on Lange is interrupted by a cutaway to Midler, waiting in the pickup, then the reverse angle on Lange's high-altitude trailer. A cut back to Lange, the angle now revealing the left side of his face and the side of the room left behind by the camera, revealing Cheyenne, sitting to the rear on the right, impassively listening. Lange's monologue culminates: "On the other side of the barbed wire, we too looked at the snow. And . . . at God. God is like . . . God is . . . God. Never mind. I can't remember any more." The final sentence of the chapter titled "This Side of Good and Evil" in *If This Is a Man* reads as follows: "We now invite the reader to contemplate the possible meaning in the Lager [camp] of the words 'good' and 'evil,' 'just' and unjust'; let everybody judge . . . how much of our ordinary moral world could survive on this side of the barbed wire."[45] In the film's final scene, Cheyenne, newly shorn and free of make-up, returns to Dublin, like an inverse Odysseus, who (with Athene's help) donned a disguise upon arriving back at Ithaca, after twenty years abroad. Cheyenne gazes smiling at Mary's mother, as if in compensation for her son, Tony, whose disappearance is announced at the beginning of the film but who otherwise signifies only as an ambiguously productive absence at the center of the story, which is otherwise not about him at all.[46] Cheyenne's father continues in voiceover (revealing that Lange's first-person plural was in fact a quotation from the father's notebooks or from the letters he sent to Lange): "Then during the inferno, we too from the other side of the barbed wire, we, too, looked at the snow, and at God. That's how God is, an infinite and stupefying form. Beautiful, lazy, and still. With no desire to do anything. Like certain women who, when we were boys, we only dared dream about." Here God signifies not so much the space as the time, outside the barbed wire, before the inferno. God is connected directly to memory in the most painfully nostalgic sense, the source at once of both comfort and suffering. God is here also domesticated and transgendered, conflated with the category of a type of woman who, outside of novels and films, does not exist.

Cheyenne's colloquy with Lange does not end in the latter's death but in something arguably more appropriately punitive, or at least certainly more poetic, in precisely Dante's sense of *contrapasso*: the punishment that matches the crime. A final shot-reverse shot sequence of Midler in the truck, then a shot of what he sees: the trailer in wide shot in the midst of the empty white expanse, then Lange, from a distance, emerging naked from the trailer and beginning to stagger slowly across the snowy ground, his hands held modestly over his genitals (figure 5.9).[47] The resemblance of this shot with Lange's abject naked body to the Holocaust photographs Mordecai showed

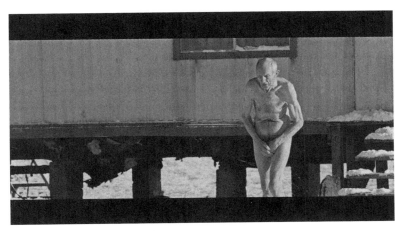

FIGURE 5.9 *This Must Be the Place*

to Cheyenne, is unmistakeable. Rather than killing him, as his father sought to do, Cheyenne instead inflicts on Lange a comparable form of humiliation, a symbolic but no less punitive punishment, making him feel the shame his father felt, reducing him to something less than a man. This is presumably what transpires, as the conclusion of the scene is interrupted in Sorrentino's typically elliptical style.

Throughout Sorrentino's film, Cheyenne is relatively verbose, more than once delivering a heartfelt emotional speech expressing his anxiety and frustration about his life. The sheer number of times that Cheyenne repeats the word *fuck*, for instance, suggests that Sorrentino and Contarello, in seeking to polish the English in the screenplay, looked to cinematic as much as real-world sources, such as the films of Joel and Ethan Coen. The still somewhat stilted quality of some of the dialogue seems to work better in this film than in *Youth*, however, Sorrentino's next English-language outing. This is likely because of the nature of Sean Penn's characterization of Cheyenne as a man who is very uncomfortable in his own skin. With *The Young Pope*, the English dialogue, if not more convincingly idiomatic, is once again more successfully grounded in character.

In general, Cheyenne gets all the best lines; this being a Sorrentino film, moreover, the dialogue is characteristically aphoristic before it is a realistic reflection of how real people actually speak. One senses that this antirealist, aphoristic quality is exacerbated in the transition from Italian to English. The character of Travis in *Paris, Texas*, by contrast, at least in the film's first, more Antonioni-influenced half, is utterly mute, only gradually regaining his voice and then only delivering his one long monologue in the film's culminating scene in the telephonic peep-show.[48] The affective effect of each of these films is therefore very different: *This Must Be the Place* is episodic, punctuated by a series of sharp emotional scenes, leading up to Cheyenne's encounter with Aloise Lange, a scene which as a result is drained somewhat of the emotional punch it might otherwise have had. (If Sorrentino owes a stylistic debt to Antonioni in *This Must Be the Place*, tonally the story is more Felliniesque.) But I suspect that this is deliberate; after all, the film's strongest emotional kick comes in the midsection, between the classroom scene in which Cheyenne learns about the Holocaust and the on-the-road sequence in which Cheyenne, in an anonymous American strip mall parking lot, spies the Hitler lookalike passing by on a flatbed truck. *Paris, Texas*, on the other hand, is a long slow build to the final emotional showdown between Travis and Jane in the peep show. According to Babis Aktsoglou, in *Paris, Texas*, Wenders deals with the themes "that have long fascinated him: memory, lost time, family, the father figure and travel."[49] While the last three items also figure prominently in *This Must Be the Place*, memory, and especially lost time, acquire a very different form and significance in Sorrentino's story. Cheyenne's physical appearance suggests that he lives in the past, stuck in a moment twenty years before, when the two young fans committed suicide to the soundtrack of his songs. (Did he choose to retire in Ireland for the tax breaks on his royalties or because the two fans were buried in Dublin?) Cheyenne's sensitive new age twenty-first-century propensity to give vent to his emotions does not prevent him from failing to face up to the past—whether personally, in the form of his relationship with his father, or objectively, in terms of a knowledge of the Holocaust that he lacks. In specific terms, Sorrentino has yet to return to the kinds of themes he broaches in *This Must Be the Place*, although *The Young Pope* confronts issues of faith and identity head on, albeit from an overtly Catholic perspective. His next film, *The Great Beauty*, furthers the exploration of memory and identity in a return to a decidedly Italian context.

SIX

The Great Beauty (La grande bellezza)

Reflective Nostalgia and the Ironic Elegiac

A line of melancholy is inching across me, after all this time, and it's impossible to miss it. This melancholy is trying to tell me something, though I'm not sure what.
—Paolo Sorrentino, *Everybody's Right*

IN A MASSIVE thematic shift from *This Must Be the Place* (2011), *The Great Beauty* (2013)[1] tells the story of Jep Gambardella (Toni Servillo), a successful arts journalist who, in the aftermath of his sixty-fifth birthday and the death of his first love from forty years before, embarks on an existential journey through the streets of Rome and the spaces of his own memories in an attempt to find the titular beauty in order to give back to his life a meaning he believes it once had. Memory manifests in various ways in this film, most obviously in the flashbacks tied to Jep's subjectivity, introduced through a novel use of digital visual effects. In a more general sense, memory manifests in the mode of nostalgia that pervades the film, particularly in the mise-en-scène, the dialogue, and the soundtrack.

Nostalgia is established as a central theme in the second of two opening scenes, Jep's sixty-fifth birthday party, a tour de force set piece of bacchanalian exhibitionism. At the climax of the scene, in the midst of a group dance (to El Gato DJ's remix of "Mueve la Colita"), Jep steps in slow motion into the space between the lines of dancers, lighting a cigarette as the camera tracks in to a symmetrically framed close-up, as he looks directly into the camera (figure 6.1). (This shot recalls that of Servillo as Tony Pisapia, cigarette dangling from his lips, in the extended nightclub tracking shot in *One Man Up* [2001].) As Jep exhales we hear in voiceover: "To this question, as kids, my friends always gave the same answer: 'pussy.' Whereas I answered, 'the smell of old people's houses.' The question was 'What do you really like most in life?' I was destined to be a sensitive type. I was destined to become a writer." These lines (and their rhetorical complexity) establish the basis of Jep's character, the parameters of his masculine identity, as well as indirectly introducing the theme of nostalgia via the image (if that's the right word) of "the smell of old people's houses" so beloved

FIGURE 6.1 *The Great Beauty* (Paolo Sorrentino, 2013)

of Jep, even as a boy. From the opening scene, this feature of his personality is set at odds with his other defining characteristic, a hedonistic appreciation of the empty and valueless lifestyle of Roman high society in which he has immersed himself for the past forty years. The opening scene emphasizes this defining contradiction, the pensively smoking Jep's thoughts heard in voiceover against the backdrop of a sea of partygoers dancing "La Colita." By the film's conclusion, this other theme, which announces itself in the screenplay through the many repetitions of the word *nothing* (*niente*), becomes the negative obverse of Jep's nostalgically melancholic nature, the ironic counterpart to the metaphysical structure of a more conventionally conceived, unironic, nostalgia.[2]

The Great Beauty treads a fine line between an unironic nostalgia and a more critically complex position. Historically, discussions of the intersection of film and memory have focused on commercial genre films rather than an art cinema tradition.[3] Hollywood's conservative nature, for instance, means that it is far more likely than a more artistically or politically committed transnational art cinema to exploit nostalgia unironically. Nostalgia continues to be invoked in popular discourse in a pejorative sense, a reputation that has influenced popular thinking about memory per se. "Memory is not commonly imagined as a site of possibility for progressive politics," observes Alison Landsberg. "More often, memory, particularly in the form of *nostalgia*, is condemned for its *solipsistic* nature, for its tendency to draw people into the past instead of the present."[4] Nostalgia is recuperated and complicated in Svetlana Boym's distinction between restorative and reflective nostalgia, where the latter allows for a combination of critical irony and affective longing: "Longing might be what we share as human beings, but that doesn't prevent us from telling very different stories of belonging and nonbelonging. . . . Two kinds of nostalgia characterize one's relationship to the past, to the imagined community, to home, to one's self-perception: restorative and reflective."[5] The "two kinds of nostalgia are not absolute types, but rather tendencies, ways of giving shape and meaning to longing. Restorative nostalgia puts emphasis on *nostos* and proposes to rebuild the lost home and patch up the memory gaps. Reflective nostalgia dwells in *algia*, in longing and loss, the imperfect process of remembrance."[6] There is thus to restorative nostalgia an uncritical naiveté that is missing from the reflective kind; the former, restorative, is thereby a constitutive feature of many contemporary popular cultural narratives. Rather than an historical consciousness that might allow for individually and socially progressive political action, therefore, postmodern pop culture gives us collective memory as often as not packaged in nostalgic terms, a tendency in 1980s American cinema critiqued by Frederic Jameson as the "nostalgia film."[7]

The Great Beauty's distance from this kind of nostalgia film is evident in the fact that, while not a historical period piece, it displays a significant historical awareness that is keyed partly to Jep's subjectivity and partly to the film's intertextual or inter-medial dimension. In other words, Jep's personal trajectory, the diegetic core of the film, is inextricably linked to the film's ironic awareness of its own place in (Italian) film history. It is no coincidence, after all, that Jep's formative experience of encoun-tering Elisa (Annaluisa Capasa) on the island off the Amalfi coast is set in 1972, the same period in which Fellini released *Roma* (1972) and *Amarcord* (1973), the two of his films which, with *8 ½* (1963) and *La Dolce Vita* (1960), are the most significant for *The Great Beauty*.[8] But there is at least one other: when Jep's friend Stefania (Galatea Ranzi) accuses him of having spent his youth "loafing around Naples with rich girls," she uses the phrase "fare vitelloni," recalling the 1953 Fellini film with all its thematic relevance for *The Great Beauty*. Also, this reflectively or critically nostalgic theme, or tone, running through the film and focused in the character of Jep, compensates to a degree for what some critics see as the film's—or, to put it in auteurial terms, Sorrentino's—lack of political engagement, or impegno.[9] As his friend Lello (Carlo Buccirosso) remarks (in the same conversation with Stefania): "Jep and civic vocation [*vocazione civile*] never got along. He was lazy, civic vocation

FIGURE 6.2 *The Great Beauty*

was hyperactive." Stefania, by contrast, refers to herself as a "socially engaged writer [romanziere impegnato]." Dadina (Giovanna Vignola) responds: "Are you saying a socially engaged writer gets some sort of free pass compared to a novelist who deals with . . . feelings [sentimenti]?" The latter appears to be an accurate description of Jep, who is moved to tears on more than one occasion; for instance, during the funeral for Viola's schizophrenic son, Andrea, or the time Jep views the installation of an artist's photographic self-portraits, one taken every day of his life (figure 6.2). It seems that, where other contemporary artworks only bring out his ironic cynicism, the latter exhibit moves him because of its content, in which the inexorable process of living and growing older is displayed in a quietly spectacular fashion. As a representation of a contemporary art installation, it is not only surprisingly moving, it is believable. In both respects it contrasts starkly with the film's satirical skewering of pretentious performance art in the Talia Concept sequence. It is also no coincidence, it seems, that the latter is a decidedly feminine, if not a seriously feminist, piece, whereas the former—the display of thousands of the male artist's self-portraits—is an exploration of masculine identity on a monumental scale. The relation between the two fictional artworks is complex, insofar as the Talia Concept scene effectively mocks a tradition of avant garde art literally embodied here by a naked woman with a self-inflicted head wound screaming "I don't love you!" ["non ti amo!"] to her onscreen audience, whereas the self-portrait exhibit, presented in a sincerely positive light, nevertheless inverts received clichés of female vanity, projecting them instead onto the artist as (productively) narcissistic masculine subject (figure 6.3). This reading of the self-portraits tells us as much about Jep, I think, as it does about the photographer-artist, who, as an utterly secondary character, is much less interesting than Talia, despite the fact that his artwork induces in Jep a rare moment of unironic emotional display.

Jep's friend Stefania's remarks about "civic vocation" also signal the film's critique of the Italian political left, the socialist or Communist Other in a state underpinned

FIGURE 6.3 *The Great Beauty*

by center-right capitalist ideology.[10] It is important to recognize that *The Great Beauty* critically analyses both ends of the political spectrum, with Jep representing a position of ironically detached neutrality. As Gary Crowdus argues, for all his sarcasm and irony, Jep never excludes himself from his diatribes against the pretentious behaviour of "Rome's 1 percent."[11] Some would see this a cop-out, an avoiding of one's political obligations, and, even though I believe that *The Great Beauty* in its self-awareness anticipates this reading, it is a charge that Sorrentino, in this film at least, never completely escapes.

"Roma o Morte"

In the conclusion to the monologue in his one-man theatre piece, Jep's friend Romano asks: "What's wrong with feeling nostalgic? It's the only distraction for those who've no faith in the future." Here another important intermedial influence arises: Rafaelle La Capria's 1961 novel *The Mortal Wound*, which shares with *The Great Beauty* what one reader calls an "overarching tone of nostalgic regret," particularly for "the great lost moment . . . a past, fleeting fantasy of love and promise" that haunts the protagonist in either work (Seraillon).[12] For Sorrentino the importance of a "summer love [*l'amore estivo*] that doesn't lead anywhere is, for a young person, left tangled up in their soul."[13] Sorrentino also concedes that La Capria himself was one inspiration for the character of Jep Gambardella. This intertext highlights the complex interrelation between such elegiac affect and the film's primary setting of Rome. *The Great Beauty* famously opens with a literally explosive shot of the Fontanone on the Janiculum Hill: the camera looks straight into the mouth of the cannon as soldiers fire the midday salute from the terrace overlooking the city (figure 6.4).[14] This is followed by a complex sequence in which one sinuous tracking shot is cut into the middle of another; the effect is at once disorienting and dreamlike, and it is utterly typical of Bigazzi's camerawork and Travaglioli's editing at this juncture. Meanwhile an all-female choir sings "I Lie," the haunting David Lang composition, sung in Yiddish. Like a latter-day Song of Songs, the piece "musically and linguistically evokes the longing for the arrival of one's beloved, and therefore that moment of suspension between solitude and the appearance of something that, by the end of the song, has 'gekumen,' that is, has finally arrived."[15] I return to this complex opening scene below, but for the time being it suffices to point out that Lang's lyrical piece introduces at the start the multifaceted theme of loss, longing, and potential redemptive return that characterizes Jep's affective core as protagonist.

As secondary characters, Jep's friends Romano and Ramona play key roles in relation to his trajectory as protagonist. Following his one-man show, Romano bids Jep goodbye after forty disappointing years in Rome, the direct inverse of Moraldo, at the end of *I Vitelloni* (1953), who finally leaves his hometown for the big city. Romano's function is clarified as the principle (masculine) foil to Jep's constitutive melancholic nostalgia, his name likely chosen for its anagrammatical echo of the name of the city in which he failed to find success despite having stuck by his principles, while Jep found success, in spite of having abandoned his. Ramona, for her part, is the

FIGURE 6.4 *The Great Beauty*

feminine foil to Jep's melancholic relation to a beauty that conceals death. Ramona is also another anagram of Roma, as if each of these characters represented a different, gender-specific, personified aspect of the eternal city. In the restaurant where he first takes Ramona,[16] Jep is greeted by Andrea, his friend Viola's schizophrenic son, who quotes Proust and Turgenev on the imminence of death. His words have a visible effect on Ramona, who has not yet revealed to Jep the critical illness for which she needs frequent and expensive treatments. He later exhorts her, in one of the film's most explicit nods to *La Dolce Vita*: "Get up! I'm taking you to see a sea monster today," and in the very next scene she, too, is dead. Death is literally inscribed as a theme from the film's opening on the Janiculum Hill: the inscription on the Fontanone reads "*Roma o Morte*," ("Rome or Death"). The phrase, originally "*O morte o Roma*," dates from the Risorgimento, when the Janiculum (more precisely, Porta Pia, near the site of the Fontanone) was the setting for the annexation of Rome to the recently unified Italy in 1870. The film's opening sequence therefore presents what could be called the primal scene of the birth of the modern Italian nation.[17] Shortly after, a Japanese man wanders away from his bus tour group, takes a photo of the panorama of the Roman cityscape, and drops dead from what appears to be a heart attack brought on by the sheer beauty of the vista.

The interrogation of a particular—and particularly fragile—masculine identity in *This Must Be the Place* gives way in *The Great Beauty* to an exploration of a more familiar masculine subject, as Sorrentino returns to more familiar terrain. The shift from Cheyenne to Jep signals a larger shift from the earlier film's consideration of the quasi-universal issues arising from its treatment of the Holocaust to a much more local, culturally specific story in the later film. It is a shift from the nothingness or radical negativity of the final solution to the fashionable nihilism of Jep's superficial Roman lifestyle. In this sense it is a shift to a far more representative contemporary European identity, embodied by Jep Gambardella, who in his upper-class, late middle-aged, heterosexual masculinity, represents a specifically Italian, postmillennial version of the last gasp of a universal humanist subject whose existential crises provided crucial fodder for the postwar art cinema narrative.

It is important to not forget that there is always another subject, the third term in the triangle, the viewing subject, understood in the dominant film theory of the 1970s and 1980s as the mystified and interpellated subject of ideology: "a position or role that the flesh-and-blood viewer might occupy . . . thought to be positioned as a capitalist subject, lured by textual pleasure and processes of infantile regression into unconscious submission to dominant ideology."[18] Carl Plantinga speaks of this subject as itself a symptom of the history of film theory as it thinks about how films affect or move the viewer—consciously or unconsciously, affectively or intellectually. Ideology, lately dismissed as an outdated term, is understood in either of two senses: insidiously, as false consciousness, or, more neutrally, as a distinct worldview.[19] In this book I deliberately retain the category of ideology in spite of contemporary critical-theoretical trends predicated on the understanding that we live now in a postideological, postrepresentational moment, a moment defined instead by mediation and affectivity.[20] I choose to retain this category for the reason that the ideological effects of certain film texts on certain viewers are as much of a problem as they were in any earlier period in film history. Indeed, in the current era of convergent audiovisual media forms, online and off, the real-world problems emanating from such ideological effects upon the viewer—effects directly linked to the real-world playing out of power relations between and among individuals and/or collectivities, and the moral-ethical valuations imposed thereon—are taking increasingly diverse form even as they tend, paradoxically, to reiterate the same narrow register of meanings. For example, certain general tendencies in the popular cultural representation of women. It is folly, therefore, to abandon subjectivity altogether, including the sort of Cartesian subject-object binary that Derrida, for instance, revealed as one of those hidden hierarchical structures that for centuries underpinned occidental society. This act of deconstruction was certainly necessary, if only to clear the ground for the emergence of other, heretofore unseen and unheard subjectivities. In other words, without this oppositional pair, without some sort of subject vis-à-vis the objective world, how do we do our best to avoid treating another person as precisely that: an object? As the Dude (Jeff Bridges) says of notorious LA pornographer Jackie Treehorn (Ben Gazzara) in the Coen brothers' 1998 film *The Big Lebowski*, "he treats objects like women." Taking the joke at face value, to treat an object as a woman is typically treated in many societies is to treat it as if it were an *image*. Images, of course, give form to ideas, and ideas, for better or worse, are the constitutive elements of ideology. Finally, then, ideology and subjectivity remain salient critical categories here because the ongoing political potential of cinema remains one of this book's abiding concerns, in terms of the specific example of Sorrentino. Politics in this sense always points to the world beyond the film, a place in which real human subjects continue to be affected by power, marshaled—at least initially—in the forms of ideas and images.

Returning to the Italian language and a story set entirely in Italy—principally Rome but also the Amalfi coast—*The Great Beauty* is nevertheless far from a straightforward Italian film. Late in the story "la Santa," Suor Maria (Giusi Merli), the

Mother Teresa-type nun, asks Jep, a lapsed novelist: "Why did you never write another book?" His response: "I was looking for the Great Beauty." What is this great beauty, and how seriously should one read this line? Sorrentino's sixth feature has been described as "one of the greatest films about modern social dissolution,"[21] what Walter Benjamin once called the "desolation of the big-city dweller."[22] In the most obvious sense the great beauty means Rome, which certainly looks very beautiful as lit and shot by Bigazzi; the dynamic camera work and chiaroscuro lighting of *The Family Friend* and *This Must Be the Place* find a kind of apotheosis in Italian cinema's eternal city, just as the earlier films' urban and ex-urban nonspaces are traded for the iconic and ostensibly more authentic spaces of Rome's historical center.[23] But Sorrentino's internationally most successful work to date is also a political film in a manner very different from *Il Divo*.[24] In Bigazzi's estimation, *The Great Beauty*:

> illustrates the result of the last twenty years of Berlusconi, which have ruined the cultural fabric of [Italy]. . . . *La Grande Bellezza* alludes to the objective beauty in the film, but the title is also ironic in terms of the human misery of a population, which has by now gone crazy and out of control. I repeat, the title is ironic.[25]

Assuming that we can take Bigazzi at his word, this irony extends through the film in its entirety, amplifying and complicating the kind of postrealist aesthetic Marcus sees exemplified in *Il Divo* while developing further the intermedial aesthetic of the earlier films. Sorrentino returns to these themes in his 2018 Berlusconi biopic *Loro*.

The Great Beauty's highly intertextual nature is characteristic of Sorrentino's films, especially in terms of its often overt engagement with Italian film history. As has been remarked, Fellini's influence is felt most strongly in both obvious and more covert ways.[26] As noted in chapter 5, according to Bondanella, in Fellini's early films, such as *I Vitelloni*, "masks worn by characters as they act out their socially defined roles are torn off to reveal something of their more intimate personality underneath the mask, that is, their 'face.'"[27] This is equivalent to what Deleuze identifies in *Cinema 1* as the difference between the affection-image, the seat of affect, crystallized in the close-up on the (human) face—the difference between this and the face as mask, once this image of the face is subsumed within the flow of the action unfolding within a clearly determinate and continuous space-time, becoming as a result an expression of mere emotion. "It is only from this point of view that there can be mendacious expression."[28] This "interplay and clash of mask with face" is analogous to the tension in Fellini's films between realist and expressionist stylistic tendencies: "the first explore socially imposed roles, the second the 'psychological depths' of a character."[29] His films' focus upon the clash of outer and inner character marks Fellini as a modernist filmmaker. This begs the questions of *The Great Beauty*: How is Jep Gambardella in this respect *different* from Alberto and the other *vitelloni* in Fellini's film? How is Sorrentino's postrealist irony different from Fellini's modernist irony? At one point Jep asks: "Chi sono? (Who am I?) . . . That's how one of Breton's novels begins." Of the main characters in the film, Carlotta Fonzi Kliemann remarks: "Their social masks are forever glued to their real faces, the cult of the image deforming features, botox and cocaine its faithful allies (in the sequence with the plastic surgeon, his patients from all social classes behave like religious followers)."[30] As Sorrentino clarifies, one of his

> inspirations for this movie was Flaubert's famous statement that he intended to write a novel about nothing. By "nothing" [*niente*] he meant the rumors and gossip, the thousand ways we have of wasting time, the things that irritate us or delight us but that are so short-lived that they make us doubt the meaning of life. That "nothing" makes up many people's entire lives.[31]

This nothing, I might add, is also another version of the titular great beauty. The reference to Flaubert's most famous novel situates the film in relation to the history of realism in the arts as a thoroughly modern issue, where all of "the rumors and gossip" and other trivial or banal details of everyday life are precisely the artistically manipulated raw materials of the new kind of narrative modality which, for theorists from Flaubert to Bakhtin, constituted the novel as the quintessential modern genre. It is precisely in this sense, of course, that the feature-length narrative fiction film came to be seen as in some sense the heir to the novel as a culturally central, formative genre or mode. This is also exactly why the film's thematic exploration of nothing is ultimately more or something other than a mere critique of the empty nothingness at the heart of Roman high society, which has been the prevailing view amongst critics.[32]

Jep's offhand reference to Breton is to the opening line from the French author's 1928 novel *Nadja*. (The book's famous final sentence reads: "Beauty will be CONVULSIVE or will not be at all.") Early on he responds to a stranger who is looking for Jep Gambardella, "*C'est moi*"—an obvious reference to *Madame Bovary* (1857) and Flaubert's famous riposte: "'Madame Bovary'? C'est moi!" "You know that Flaubert wanted to write a book about nothing?"[33] Jep asks on two different occasions. "This is my life," he remarks. "Flaubert wanted to write a book about nothing but failed, so how am I supposed to?" Jep has one book to his credit, a novel titled *L'Apparato Umano* (*The Human Apparatus*), written some forty years before, when he first came to Rome in his late twenties. As another character observes, he must have been "deeply in love" when he wrote it. Now sixty-five, he has long since settled into a life of complacent cynicism, supported by his work as critic for an unnamed major Roman arts magazine.

From Voyeur to Flâneur

As noted in chapter 5, Kovács's identification of the postwar modernist art cinema as a typically hybrid genre is based in the presence in such films of what he calls forms, but which in this contemporary transnational context I would call tropes, motifs, or thematic tendencies, two of which are combined together in the production of meaning in *The Great Beauty*: the first is nothingness, addressed above, the other wandering.[34] Even more than Marcello in *La Dolce Vita*, Jep spends a great deal of time strolling through Rome, flaneur-like, doing nothing except looking, directing the viewer's attention in ways that add nothing to the story but augment tremendously the viewer's appreciation of character, theme, and atmosphere (figure 6.5). The modern city, alongside mass media, such as the cinema, and modes of mass transport, especially the train, originate in the nineteenth century but come into their own in the early twentieth century in their address to a subject as a mobilised citizen-consumer who, as Anne Friedberg makes clear, is also always a *viewer*. Focusing on the "mobilised virtual gaze" conditioned by cinema under late capitalism, Friedberg describes an "increasingly detemporalized" late modern subject, produced at the price of a "diminished capacity to retain the past."[35] Jep, as quintessential Roman flaneur,[36] ambulates daily along the streets of a city that, in its eternal aspect, predates any modern example, even as it obviates this key dimension of Friedberg's updating of Benjamin/Baudelaire's masculine flaneur, whose ambling excursions produce precisely nothing—apart from the set of images the viewer is encouraged to see through Jep's passive gaze. Nothing is produced, not even the negative quantity resulting from the act of consumption, as witnessed by the scene in which Jep buys dresses and shoes for Ramona, as if in ironic homage to the famous scene in Hitchcock's *Vertigo* in which Scotty strives desperately and, to his undoing, successfully, to transform Judy back into Madeleine by clothing her in the same dress, shoes, and above all platinum blonde-dyed hair tied in a tight swirly bun (figure 6.6). (As this scene also duplicates the visual structure of the scene in *The Consequences of Love* in which Titta surreptitiously watches Sofia changing in the hotel bar backroom, so it anticipates the bunga bunga dance sequence in *Loro*, where the camera is positioned behind the male protagonist's head, aligning the viewer with his optical perspective on the woman.) Ramona is no Madeleine, however, and Jep is clearly under no illusions about the possibility of resurrecting Elisa, his first love, by transforming Ramona. The latter dies soon after, while the announcement of Elisa's death kick-starts the narrative, such as it is, eventually moving Jep to what little action he takes, outside of his quotidian, or rather nocturnal, routine.

FIGURE 6.5 *The Great Beauty*

FIGURE 6.6 *The Great Beauty*

Jep's flaneurist tendencies[37] also cast into ironic relief the film's specific engagement with the transnational. As Tim Bergfelder explains, the most prominent of the
"select range of privileged experiences" characteristic of transnational films are:

> instances of (primarily) postcolonial migration and diaspora, which have been champi-
> oned for their emancipatory potential. They overlap to some extent with the condition of
> exile, related to the trauma of loss and displacement, and are more firmly distinguished
> from consumption-led modes of mobility such as tourism.[38]

As twenty-first-century Roman flaneur, Jep embodies the contradictions of a subject
position within a diegesis not grounded in consumerist consumption even as the
film itself represents the highest-quality, award-winning transnational art cinema.
Extending Bergfelder's appropriation of Bhabha's term "vernacular cosmopolitanism,"[39] it is clear that Jep embodies within the diegesis the contradictory identity of
a Euro-transnational cosmopolitanism. At the same time, however, Jep's subjectivity
can also be said to embody the "privileged" Eurocentric perspective of an "Olympian
arbiter of value,"[40] a charge that Sorrentino certainly complicates even as he fails to
evade it completely. He does this by focalizing in the protagonist the film's critically
nostalgic perspective that recognizes the doomed nature of Jep's world even as it
wallows in its beauty. As suggested, this theme intersects with that of nothingness in
several scenes in the film's first act. For instance, following immediately upon the first
flashback scene to Jep's near death-by-motorboat on the Amalfi coast, which ends
with a close-up on the concerned face of the young Elisa, the next, present-tense,
scene begins with a woman's face framed centrally in close-up, addressing the camera
as if it were Jep, asking him if he has seen her daughter. In voiceover he replies to the
negative, and then he appears, aligned with the tracking camera, to follow her into
the depth of the space, toward the Tempietto di Bramante in the Piazza San Pietro,
behind which the woman has vanished. As the camera moves toward the temple

doorway, Jep walks into the interior space in a disorienting shift from optical point-of-view to conventional medium shot, without a cut.[41] As Jep stands in the centre of the room a child asks, from off-screen (using the informal *tu*), "Who are you?" There is a cut to a high-angle shot of Jep looking straight down through a circular hole in the floor. "Who am I?" he repeats. "I am—"; "—You're nobody", the voice replies. The camera drifts slowly away from Jep: "Nobody? But I . . . " He doesn't finish, the camera tracking back and downward, as he stands and walks off screen. The next sequence of shots reveal that the child, the woman's daughter, was standing in the space below the upper room, connected by the circular opening in the floor (figure 6.7). Structurally this short scene is typical of the film's episodic nature, its specific content commenting ironically on the immediately preceding scene through direct juxtaposition, a pattern repeated consistently across the entire film: dramatically serious scene followed by ironically, even comically, juxtaposed scene, often bridged by dialogue. But this scene at the Tempietto is also instructive in our understanding of Jep's character, where he is unable to find an appropriate riposte to the little girl's statement that he is "nobody." This is perhaps the only time in the film where another character, in this case the disembodied voice of a child, tells Jep the truth about who or what he has become. This is the negative obverse of his repeated wish to write a book about nothing. The little girl's words here suggest that Jep has in fact been writing this very novel for the past forty years. Only at the end of the film does he see this clearly, and that even a book about nothing is still about something. More than this, though, the girl's condemnation of Jep draws attention not so much to his ontological irrelevance as to his epistemological blindness: this is no radical postmodern self-reflexive gesture of a character's intuition of his own fictional status (as in Mary Harron's *American Psycho*); rather, this is Jep's dawning awareness of his own lack of self-knowledge. This scene therefore reinforces the film's essentially modernist take on the theme of existential nothingness—a condition that, by the end, Jep presumably transcends.

FIGURE 6.7 *The Great Beauty*

Reading Jep's gaze as more flaneurist than voyeurist mitigates or at least complicates any charges that the film promulgates a straightforwardly sexist, misogynist,
or antifeminist point of view. In one sense, in *The Great Beauty* Sorrentino doesn't
get around this complex of problems as much as he bridges the gap between the
stereotypes of woman-as-saviour vs. woman-as-object of desire. This is achieved
through the recurring shots and set pieces involving nuns, where the nun is the
embodiment of the woman whose life is consecrated to God and whose feminine
figure enshrouded in white embodies the contradictions of a patriarchal construction of womanhood. (This visual motif is also milked heavily in *The Young Pope*, for
reasons that are fairly obvious, given the Vatican setting.) On Jep's frequent walks
around Rome, and even from his apartment patio, he watches these women, often
young and attractive, in ambiguous counterpoint to his voyeuristic but unthreat-
ening gaze, which is generally aligned in these sequences with Bigazzi's drifting,
creeping camera.

In this sense, Jep's flaneurist gaze undermines the " 'cartographic' gaze of the—
often male—cosmopolitan expert or 'connoisseur' . . . one of the key protagonists
in Edward Said's famous attack on western Orientalism," combining this, ironically,
with "the mobile gaze of the—particularly female—mass consumer."[42] For Jep's
position as masculine subject does overlap with the stereotypical female-gendered
consumer-subject in the form of his dandyish investment in his sartorial appearance.[43] As will be discussed in chapter 8, Lenny Belardo, Pope Pius XIII, in *The Young
Pope*, is also presented in a key scene that blatantly exploits the physical beauty of its
lead, Jude Law, as if he were an ironic manifestation of the later twentieth-century
New Man, at once a product of 1980s and 1990s advertising strategies, while also
an expression of the new consumerist habits of metrosexual men in urban centers
throughout the developed world. In hindsight, it is clear that this new masculine type
represents an example of the masculine appropriation of the category of object of the
gaze, which in this instance may or may not be that of a heterosexual male viewer, as
in Mulvey's original conception. That this new man should be invoked in a fictional
portrait of the first American pope is only one of the series' many structuring ironies.
The Great Beauty's presentation of Jep makes clear that his outward appearance—his
mask—is in fact a reliable guide to who he really is, inside. Like Mastroianni's hap-
less director in *8 ½*, Jep's masculinity is tied up with his interiority, which the film
depicts in terms of nostalgically inflected memory. Unlike the elderly male characters
in *Youth*, Jep's memory is intact, a source of both pleasure and melancholy—in a reiteration of the classic modernist revaluation of memory as *pharmakon*, at once poison
and cure, in place since Proust's articulation of involuntary memory in *La Recherche
du temps perdu*. In one of the above-mentioned sequences, for instance, Jep observes
a nun playing with a pair of small children in the convent gardens directly below his
apartment balcony (figure 6.8). A close-up of Jep looking down is succeeded first by
a sequence in the garden in which Bigazzi's camera snakes around, low to the ground,
capturing the *sorella* and her charges as they run, or in close-up as she comforts them.
A cut back to Jep looking is then followed by a high-angle point-of-view shot, as
if from his perspective on the terrace. The sequence ends with Jep again in close-
up, an expression of bittersweet emotion on his face, as if the sight of the nun and

the children recalled something from his own past. Sorrentino refrains from adding a flashback at this juncture, however, leaving the viewer to speculate about the motives for Jep's emotional response. As this scene occurs before Jep learns of Elisa's death, it serves mostly to establish his affective sensitivity, his elegiac melancholia. In this respect *The Great Beauty* is a spectacular apologia for the validity and value of feelings. "Try and write something truly your own, about a feeling, or sorrow," he advises Romano, who is adapting D'Annunzio for the stage. Curiously, the nondiegetic music during the sequence in which he observes the nun is "My Heart's in the Highlands," a Robert Burns poem with a haunting setting by Arvo Pärt. This is the same song that plays again over the scene in which Jep and Ramona exchange stories of their respective first loves. As he prepares to tell her about Elisa forty years before, Jep stands. There is a cut to a close-up, Jep looking pensively into the middle distance as Pärt's song commences. Sorrentino cuts in brief flashes back to the island at night, when he kissed Elisa for the first time. Jep recounts how "she took a step back, and said to me . . . "—but he never finishes the sentence, either because he has momentarily forgotten her words, or, more likely, because he is so lost in his memory that he has forgotten where he is and what he is doing. Visibly uncomfortable, Ramona leaves. The song is heard again in the late scene when Jep encounters the young Elisa of his past—in effect, her ghost—on his first trip in forty years back to the Amalfi coast. At this point the song, despite its cultural and musical specificity, becomes a kind of leitmotif for his character as he re-experiences his most formative experience in flashback-heightened memory.

Repeatedly escaping into mnemic reverie, Jep eventually finds at once renewed inspiration, moral redemption, and a seemingly irony-free manifestation of the great beauty of the title, in a specific memory, staged as a complex, gradually unfolding flashback to a holiday forty years before off the coast of Naples. In this highly subjective sequence, cross-cut with the spectacle of "la Santa" crawling on her knees up the steps of Rome's Scala Sancta di San Giovanni, Jep recalls his last encounter

FIGURE 6.8 *The Great Beauty*

with Elisa, the love of his life, whose off-screen death at the film's start initiates the journey that culminates in this return to his happiest memory. While in the present she is dead, here she still lives, will always be youthful, beautiful, and alive: forever the object of his desire but at this late stage in life even more the source of great, if illusory, consolation.

In this respect *The Great Beauty* exemplifies the degree in which Sorrentino's stylistic approach appears to be commensurate with a masculinist cultural dominant (the director's thirteen minute neo-noir Campari ad, *Killer in Red* [2017], is a case in point). In her classic essay on "Visual Pleasure in Narrative Cinema," Laura Mulvey argues that:

> [Woman's] visual presence tends to work *against* the development of a story line, to freeze the flow of action in moments of erotic contemplation. . . . A woman performs within the narrative, the gaze of the spectator and that of the male characters in the film are neatly combined without breaking narrative verisimilitude. For a moment the sexual impact of the performing woman takes the film into a no-man's-land outside its own time and space.[44]

Although Mulvey's reading of classical Hollywood's hypostatized sexism has since been rethought by others, including herself, the fact remains that in certain films of this type, women's bodies are frequently presented as objects for consumption by a viewer compelled to occupy a specific kind of subject position. And, while resistance has always been possible, Mulvey's basic observations about the intersection of certain psycho-ideological mechanisms and what we used to call the cinematic apparatus will remain relevant as long as this heteronormative and masculinist paradigm holds sway, determining what is still, for many viewers, the ground zero of visual pleasure. Therefore, rather than re-explore this psychic no-man's-land that Mulvey charts,[45] and the attendant questions of alleged narrative disruption, I want to stay as usual on the surface, on the level of the image as visual signifier. In a subsequent essay, for instance, Mary-Anne Doane does just this:

> The woman's beauty, her very desirability, becomes a function of certain practices of *imaging*—framing, lighting, camera movement, angle. She is thus, as . . . Mulvey has pointed out, more closely associated with the *surface* of the image than its illusory depths, its constructed 3-dimensional space which the man is destined to inhabit and hence control.[46]

Like Mulvey, Doane refers primarily to specific ideological effects of classical Hollywood style; nevertheless, she describes a more or less explicit gendering of the image in its Peircian semiotic dimensions that may be useful in our discussion of Sorrentino. In other words, where woman in these films is aligned with the *surface* of the image in its radical exteriority, the masculine protagonist is associated with the visual and metaphorical depths of the image, with the metaphysical depths of memory, and with nostalgia as masculine affect. Thus, where woman in this classical view is coterminous with the image itself in its objecthood, the masculine protagonist is the subject of memory, of melancholy or elegiac remembrance, in which the object of nostalgic desire is, of course, a woman who is as often as not no longer among the living. This woman, however, despite being dead in the present is very much alive in the protagonist's memory, at least insofar as she represents for him—for his narrative trajectory—the eschatological force of his salvation. She is, in short, his saviour—the feminine embodiment or personification of the salvific force of memory. This is the eroto-salvific paradigm so dear to occidental culture; it forms the basis of many famous literary and cinematic narratives, both old and new, from Goethe's *Faust* and Wagner's *The Flying Dutchman* to Hitchcock's *Vertigo* (1958) and Michel Gondry's *Eternal Sunshine of the Spotless Mind* (2004), to name only a few examples.[47] In the cinematic expression of this model, the affective and nonrational dimension of nostalgic or elegiac memory is associated with the masculine; this is the aspect of the image where the illusory force of realism works its magic, occluding the material basis of the image and thus representation itself. On the other hand, the image qua image is aligned with the feminine, the aspect in which the image stops the narrative in its tracks, drawing the viewer's attention away from the content and onto the form of the film, laying bare its formal operations, the potential source of spectatorial emancipation.[48] To read the iconic images of women in Sorrentino's films this way is to resist the more doctrinaire reading traceable to Mulvey, in which the very opposite is seen to occur, the viewer's rational response short-circuited by the overpowering effect of the feminine image in close-up. It is out of the tension between these two perspectives that the richly ambiguous but troubling meanings of the films arise.[49]

The gendered terms of this argument, and the reading of the films on which it is based, are crucial also to this study's understanding of Sorrentino's formal and thematic distance from postwar Italian cinema's neorealist roots. In Rosalind Galt's analysis, for instance, the "prettiness" of the (metaphorically feminine) *cinema carino* that emerged in Italy in the 1980s and 1990s "offered a way out of the 'authoritarian' inheritance of Neorealism."[50] While it would be inaccurate to label Sorrentino's style as either *carino* or, in Galt's word, pretty, its dependence on the aesthetic potentialities of the beautiful, even spectacular, image is testimony to the extent to which his films, too, inscribe a new kind of masculinist authority and moral depth into the twenty-first-century transnational cinematic landscape. This authority and depth are not dependent, thankfully, on the conventional tropes of the action genres but instead are aligned with a modernist humanist tradition, one of whose foundations is the general category of masculine subject explored across the films. This exploration finds an apotheosis of a kind in *The Young Pope*, in the television series' seemingly unironic attention to the structures and institutions of Catholic faith; structures which, for all the series' critical and even satirical edge, end up being reaffirmed by the final episode in a postironic irony characteristic of the contemporary postsecular moment.

"The Fleeting and Sporadic Flashes of Beauty . . ."

With notable Italian cinematic intertexts such as Fellini's *I Vitelloni, La Dolce Vita,*[51] *8 ½*, and *Roma*, as well as Antonioni's *La notte* (*The Night*) (1961) and Ettore Scola's

La terrazza (*The Terrace*) (1980)—*The Great Beauty* positions itself unapologetically in the tradition of filmic explorations of the psycho-emotional life of middle-aged and older heterosexual bourgeois or upper-middle class male intellectuals, epitomized by many of the characters played by Marcello Mastroianni.[52] Protagonist Jep Gambardella represents a significant change in the nature of Italian cinematic masculinity, however, in the transition from postwar to postmillennial. The tone here is generally far more elegiac than in the cinema of the postwar period. His sixty-fifth birthday and the news of her death inspire in Jep a melancholic return to memories of Elisa, his first love, signalled by flashbacks to their time together forty years before off the coast of Naples. Elisa never appears as a character except in flashback,[53] her death at the story's outset the event that precipitates Jep's ultimate epiphany. The concluding scene is structured more conventionally than Jep's earlier flashbacks to his time in southern Italy, which generally begin with him dozing on his bed in Rome, gazing up into the ceiling above, which digitally transmogrifies into the upside-down Tyrrhenian Sea. In Umberto Contarello's words, Jep's "inner sense of time" remains keyed to Naples, even after forty years in Rome.[54]

In this final flashback, present-tense Jep travels by boat to the same coastal area, the act of putting himself into the same place physically and seeing the same lighthouse triggering the mental shift back into his own past (figure 6.9). In a very meaningful sense, therefore, in this final sequence *The Great Beauty* is not merely another contemporary reiteration of the (post-)modernist travel film elaborated by Kovács and exemplified by *This Must Be the Place*; rather, this subgenre is conflated here with its close neighbour, the mental journey film, in which "travel takes place not in the physical world but in [the protagonist's] mind."[55] In this final sequence, both generic tendencies are copresent, combining into an original variation on one of the most time-honored techniques in narrative cinema, also ultimately literary in origin. After all, "the purpose of the mental journey film" is not to explore the visible physical

FIGURE 6.9 *The Great Beauty*

environment but to explore "the 'mental environment' " of a specific character. This kind of film, in other words, exploits the mise-en-scène of the represented reality of the film's world the better to map the protagonist's interiority.[56] Moreover, in such a sequence the past is "evoked not the way it was but the way is it viewed from the perspective of the present."[57] In *The Great Beauty*'s conclusion this is facilitated by the fact that sixty-five-year-old Jep is literally there, on the Amalfi coast, even as he slips back repeatedly into his memories, his older self replacing his younger in his re-enactment or restaging of this formative, primal scene.[58] To quote the film's epigraph from Céline's *Journey to the End of the Night*: "Travel is useful, it exercises the imagination. All the rest is disappointment and fatigue ["delusion and pain" in the DVD subtitles]. Our journey is entirely imaginary. That is its strength."[59]

"This is how it always ends," Jep intones in the voiceover that has proven to be one of Sorrentino's key formal techniques, on the lighthouse steps, in place of his younger self, aligned by eye line match with the youthful Elisa above him. Intercut with this mental journey is Suor Maria, la Santa, crawling on her knees up the Scala Sancta di San Giovanni in Rome, an ascent with Christ as its goal, underlining the irony of this visual and thematic juxtaposition (figure 6.10). In this complex flashback, a consummately cinematic memory, the resurrected Elisa appears on the steps above, baring her breasts and then turning away from the suddenly youthful Jep, the viewer unavoidably sutured into the space between the two lovers via the invisible cut between one shot and the reverse (figure 6.11). The now once-again sixty-five year-old Jep stands watching her retreating, Eurydice-like. It would seem that, although Jep is undoubtedly a sensitive writer, attuned to feelings, what is most important to him is not "the smell of old people's houses," but something considerably more erotic and therefore more banal. In voice-over, he says: "This is how it always ends: in death. But first there was life, hidden beneath the blah blah blah. . . . The fleeting and sporadic flashes of beauty amid the wretched squalor and human misery. . . . Therefore, let this

FIGURE 6.10 *The Great Beauty*

FIGURE 6.11 *The Great Beauty*

novel begin." Protagonist Jep is an exorbitant updating of the morally undeserving late-middle-aged man redeemed by the woman from his past—the age-old trope of gender-specific eroto-salvific redemption, the eschatological framework ironically deconstructed. "What lies beyond lies beyond," he remarks. "That is not my concern." The reference to a new novel beginning indicates that Jep's salvation will take the form of his rebirth as a writer, here, in memory's primal scene, and that this new novel will tell the very story we have just witnessed: his version of Flaubert's book about nothing. And, while Jep's decades-long period of aimless flaneurie is distinct from the nothingness or existential ennui at the centre of Titta Girolamo's life in *The Consequences of Love*, the elegiac nostalgia with which Jep offsets his Flaubertian nothingness anticipates Lenny Belardo's self-abnegating public image in *The Young Pope*—a radically negative identity set into relief by his faith in the fullness of God.

The concluding scene in *The Great Beauty* is saved from falling into cliché[60] by the overall structure of the montage: the intercut shots of la Santa crawling penitently up the stairs toward her symbolic and redundant salvation complicate Jep's elegiac flashback, inflecting its meaning in a richly ambiguous direction, a conclusion underscored by Jep's final line in the film: "it's just a trick" (*è solo un trucco*).[61] In Hipkins's analysis, in *The Great Beauty* "male ageing is a question of redeeming soul and memory, in which the male melodrama of Jep's suffering, as Catherine O'Rawe describes . . . becomes 'the gateway to the sublime.' "[62] In her book on stars and masculinity in contemporary Italian cinema, O'Rawe expands this reading of the scene, highlighting the "importance of nostalgia" in the return "to the past to fill the felt lack of secure masculinity in the present . . . predicated on the *nostos*: the journey home, and the idea of an originary (lost) wholeness" constitutive of such an elegiacally determined masculine subject.[63] I agree with O'Rawe's assessment of *The Great Beauty* as "primarily a male melodrama,"[64] exemplifying the extent to which a species of melodrama pervades even twenty-first-century transnational art cinema. Yet, while it is important to see melodrama's continuities across various national cinemas as a dominant cultural mode, in this study I generally reserve this category for the tonally very different *Young Pope* TV series.

As noted, Ramona's off-screen death, suggested in a highly elliptical montage, along with Romano's decision to leave Rome for good, together precipitate Jep's decision to return to the site of his first encounter with Elisa, on the rocky lighthouse island. These events also seem to be what inspire him, in the end, to finally resume writing after a forty-year hiatus. Romano's decision to return to his home town, for that matter, represents the elegiac inversion of the plotline of Fellini's *I Vitelloni*, which famously ends with Moraldo (Franco Interlenghi) finally leaving his home town, where his friends remain, stuck in their aimless and lazy lives. Romano's departure from Rome is preceded by his one-man theatre performance in which he eulogizes nostalgia as "the last pleasure for those who've given up on the future." There is also an echo here of Fellini's *Roma*, which begins with the director's avatar (Peter Gonzales Falcon) arriving in Rome from the provinces in order, it seems, to make a career. Romano's admission, during his one man show, of his own ordinariness and his unapologetic defense of nostalgia, the desire to return to a place or condition that one associates with home in its most positive valuation, is an ironic response to the Romantic narrative of masculine self-fashioning underpinning Fellini's films. For his part, Jep remains the ultimate *vitellone*, the one, like Fellini himself, who made it, but who nevertheless—more like Marcello in *La Dolce Vita*—gave in to his constitutive laziness, never writing another novel after his initial success. Ultimately, though, it is Suor Maria who inspires Jep to go back to the island in the Bay of Naples by telling him that the reason she eats only roots (*radici*) is because "roots are important." For once the pun is translatable.

SEVEN

Youth (La giovinezza)

Between Horror and Desire (Life's Last Day)

Only now do I understand . . . that all my life I've been waiting, with a scandalous, chaste, yearning, that I've only ever wanted a single thing: to become old.
—Paolo Sorrentino, *Everybody's Right*

It's not paradise. It's youth.
—Rosalba, *The Family Friend*

SORRENTINO'S 2015 FILM *Youth* (*La giovinezza*) tells the story of retired Britten-esque composer Fred Ballinger (Michael Caine) and his old friend filmmaker Mick Boyle (Harvey Keitel),[1] on vacation at a luxury Swiss spa hotel, where they pass the time observing the other guests, discussing prostate problems, and speculating about the vagaries of memory in old age. If *The Great Beauty* is Sorrentino's homage to Fellini's *La Dolce Vita* (1960), *Youth* is his even more oblique homage to *8 ½* (1963). In lieu of blocked film director Guido (Marcello Mastroianni), Sorrentino goes Fellini one better with two stymied creative types: Ballinger, who initially refuses an invitation from the Queen of England to conduct *The Simple Songs*, his most famous composition, at a birthday concert for Prince Philip,[2] and Boyle, who is struggling to finish a screenplay titled *Life's Last Day*, which he hopes will be his cinematic "testament." Ballinger eventually gives in and finds renewed meaning in the work he once pledged to never conduct for anyone but his wife, a former soprano now in the grip of a wasting paralysis and unable to sing. Boyle is met with rejection and failure, his subsequent suicide spurring Ballinger to his eventual redemption. Their relation, with one man's ironically sacrificial death precipitating the other's recuperative action, echoes the conclusion of *One Man Up* (2001), transposed into an almost satirically transnational setting, and without the pseudo-metaphysical overlay. As in Sorrentino's first feature, Ballinger and Boyle echo the two Pisapias as two faces of the congenitally sad man, either giving in to failure or arriving at a kind of redemption that is ironic for its being unearned.

As many critics have pointed out, all of the films since *The Consequences of Love* (2004) (and including *The Young Pope* [2016] series) feature individual shots or whole scenes that may or may not further the narrative but whose sheer beauty arrests the eye. (The latter is largely the result of innovative lighting techniques by director of photography Luca Bigazzi. This is one reason why all of Sorrentino's films after *One Man Up* have a wider color palette and greater tonal contrast than his first feature.) Many of these iconic set pieces feature secondary (or tertiary) female characters in various stages of deshabille. Compare, for instance, the Trevi fountain scene with Mastroianni and Anita Ekberg in *La Dolce Vita*—"perhaps the most famous scene in postwar European cinema"[3]—to the now infamous spa bath scene in *Youth* in which Ballinger and Boyle ogle the stark naked Miss Universe (Madalina Ghenea) (figure 7.1; figure 7.2). From one perspective, the latter represents a far more egregious instance of objectification than its Fellinian antecedent. It is hard to not see Fellini's influence, however, when Sorrentino includes in a film a sequence predicated on the objectification of a woman's body. On the other hand, Fellini himself cannot be blamed for inventing but only for inventively perpetuating this convention. Issues of authorial sexism and misogyny aside, the questions are: Why would a twenty-first-century director like Sorrentino choose to include such a scene? In what ways, if any, do his films succeed in changing the meaning of this kind of generic set piece, inscribing a critique while amplifying the spectacle and exploiting the sheer beauty of the image? It is no exaggeration to say that the scene in the spa pool crystallizes a set of issues raised by Sorrentino's work, up to and including *Loro*, his Berlusconi biopic.

From the perspective offered by Carl Plantinga, by contrast, this scene may also and just as validly be read as disruptive of a conventional scenario in which pleasure derives from voyeurism. According to Plantinga:

FIGURE 7.1 *La Dolce Vita* (Federico Fellini, 1960)

FIGURE 7.2 *Youth* (Paolo Sorrentino, 2015)

While voyeurism may be among the spectator's pleasures, it is characteristic neither of viewing in general nor of pleasure offered by most images and sounds. Although the allure of some films stems from the enticements of sexual pleasure in looking, to describe spectatorship as essentially voyeuristic in this sense oversimplifies the viewing situation. Voyeurism requires two features that confine it to specific situations in specific films: (1) the voyeur derives sexual gratification from observing others, and (2) the voyeur observes others while unobserved, from a secret vantage point.[4]

The latter point is of course essential to the theory of the male gaze inflected by apparatus theory, in which the viewer's scopophilic pleasure derives directly from the fact of his being invisible to the all-too-visible, generally female, object of his gaze. In the spa pool scene, however, Ballinger and Boyle are not only present and visible to the naked Miss Universe; they are themselves (presumably) also naked. That they are never fully displayed in their nakedness does undercut this reading to some degree, but it still seems worth noting. In contrast to the final flashback scene in *The Great Beauty*, the already old men (Caine's Ballinger and Keitel's Boyle) do not appear to be saved or redeemed by the scopophilic vision of a stark naked Miss Universe in the Swiss hotel spa pool. To Ballinger's question, "Who is that?" Boyle sardonically responds, "God"—before correcting himself: "Miss Universe." How different is Marcello's response to Sylvia's trespassing in the *La Dolce Vita* Trevi Fountain scene: "She's right. I've had it all wrong. We've all had it wrong"—whereupon he joins her, both fully clothed, in the fountain.[5] The scene in *Youth* is simultaneously more progressive—the two men, like Miss Universe, are presumably also naked, their elderly bodies hidden underwater—and more retrograde: their fixed intra-diegetic gaze is both a parody and a regrettably unironic example of Mulvey's male gaze. Ballinger doesn't recognize her in the pool—"Who is that?"—because Ghenea, the actress, her body and face, is/are filmed here in a manner completely different from her character's initial appearance in the story. In an earlier scene, when she is introduced to the American actor Jimmy Tree (Paul Dano), she appears to be wearing no makeup, her body hidden under layers of clothing. In the pool scene, by contrast, the mise-en-scène perpetuates the problem of scopophilic objectification in terms of Ghenea's hyperbolically voluptuous body, lit and framed as if for a *Sports Illustrated* photo shoot,[6] the two men looking on in the background, impotent subjects to her youthful and sexually potent object.[7] Sorrentino in effect undoes the ironic impact of the earlier scene by deliberately exploiting Ghenea's/Miss Universe's physical beauty, her evident photogeneity, as if to directly flout her earlier, understated, even dowdy, appearance. In other words, this third and last appearance of Miss Universe effectively restores her to the status of image of woman that she only previously possessed in Ballinger's Venetian dream scene (to be discussed below). Her brief intervening moment of authenticity as a woman is undone. This is one reason why this scene is, for many viewers, the most problematic in the film. In *La Dolce Vita*, by contrast, Sylvia beckons to Marcello, displaying an agency ironically at first granted and then denied her twenty-first-century counterpart in *Youth*. Marcello joins Sylvia in the fountain, their almost-embrace in balanced medium two-shot; the woman remains elusive but with a measure of power over the man, withholding herself at the last minute, a projection perhaps of Marcello's shaky postwar masculinity. In this regard as well the viewer who overidentifies with Marcello will be rewarded with the sophisticated frustration of the postwar art film spectator and spared the phantasmic satisfactions of Mulvey's ideal masculine consumer.

The Image of Woman: The Gendered Gaze, Part 1

This book considers Sorrentino's status as Italian auteur working in a global art cinematic context using the latest digital video technology to produce films that are formally progressive and stylistically cutting-edge.[8] And yet the Italian filmmaker can also be said to indulge to a significant degree in a retrograde point of view on gender difference and the representation of women. He does so in favor of an ironically elegiac meditation upon what it means to be a no longer youthful, late-middle aged, or elderly man in twenty-first-century Europe. In this respect Sorrentino follows in the cinematic footsteps of not only Fellini, a major influence, but also, in terms of the mise-en-scène, the later Stanley Kubrick, with whom the Neapolitan director shares a preoccupation with the female body type exploited visually, for instance, in *Eyes Wide Shut* (1999), particularly in the infamous orgy sequences in the mysterious country manor.[9] In the end, one is left to ponder the significance of the title, *Youth*, with respect to gender difference: *Whose* youth? And what does this mean for politically progressive cinematic representations of subjectivity? Of gender-based—or, for that matter, generational—difference?

From the emasculated male hero of postwar art cinema, we now arrive at the infantilized masculine subject of contemporary consumer culture. Where the first is largely a critical-theoretical construct, the latter is a genuinely problematic product of the current socially mediatized moment. On a more ironically metaphorical level, then, the film's title, *Youth*, foregrounds Sorrentino's abiding concern with a masculinist culture that can never reach adulthood; a generation of perpetually adolescent subjects kept from ethical and axiological maturity through its ongoing interpellation by advertising, trashy television (especially in post-Berlusconi Italy), crass music videos, and, by implication, the internet, especially social media (in this critique Sorrentino echoes the later Godard[10]). Not incidentally, the latter technologies, such as social media, go unrepresented in this and other projects, Sorrentino's stories focusing instead on characters and situations that seem somewhat out of time, if not downright old-fashioned—or just plain old. (Once again Jude Law's young pope presents a complex variation, being at once prematurely old and perpetually immature.[11]) Generational difference emerges in *Youth* as perhaps the most significant determinant of contemporary identity in a culture that is also characterized, in Fredric Jameson's perspicacious critique, by a lack of historical consciousness and a consequent overprivileging of the present—a presentism whose reductio ad absurdum is a perpetual present moment of consumption.[12] This attitude emerges in *Youth* in particular as the unspoken nemesis of any serious person, meaning any *man* of a certain age whose ironic self-understanding in the present is ineluctably tied to his memories of the past. This is not because it is good or necessary to remember specific things, but because in *The Great Beauty* and *The Young Pope* especially remembering per se, even bad or traumatic memories, is prerequisite to the maintenance of a subjectivity determined by an elegiac sensibility that knows itself to be out of date and yet derives an ironically nostalgic pleasure from this critical self-understanding. In an interview from the period after the release of *The Great Beauty*, in the leadup to preparations for preproduction on *Youth*, in answer to the question as to why he is so preoccupied in all his films so far with "characters who are usually male, and well on in years, from middle age on," Sorrentino cites a famous author—"perhaps Tolstoy?"—"who, in response to the question 'what's the driving force behind all your work?,' replied 'I'm seeking the father.' "[13] "Perhaps, in psychoanalytic terms," the director concludes, "I'm searching for a father figure throughout all my films."

Citing an interview in this manner may seem like an unreflective recourse to an auteurial interpretative approach, whereas the fact of fatherhood as theme foregrounds certain long-standing myths of a patriarchal culture that underpin not just this kind of story but any interpretive methodology (such as psychoanalysis) predicated on a mythic or archetypal understanding of family relations. This would include the entire edifice of so-called auteur theory, at least since Andrew Sarris's 1962 "Notes on the Auteur Theory" (2004) as symptomatic manifestation of a stubbornly unreflectively patriarchist and masculinist culture. Therefore I invoke Sorrentino's remark in this interview in a manner that is always already critically and ironically conditioned by an awareness of these systemic biases. In other words, if Sorrentino can on occasion eat his cake and have it too in terms of the representation of women in his films, I, as critic, can invoke the auteurist paradigm as critical-analytical principle the better to deconstruct it, in the process shedding (hopefully) some new light on the films.

Contra Sorrentino's remarks, fathers, fatherhood, and familial relations do not appear to be among the main themes in *The Great Beauty* (to which this interview refers). The other films, in fact, offer much better examples of this concatenation of meanings, at least on the diegetic level. We already saw (in chapter 5) the thematic significance of father-son relations in *This Must Be the Place*. In *One Man Up* we eventually learn that Tony, the elder of the two Pisapias, is a man shaped by his estranged relationship with a father who dies partway through, off screen and unmourned by Tony. In *The Consequences of Love* Titta is himself an absent father to his three children, compelled to confront the godfather figure of the Mafia don in a bid to affirm his crumbling masculine identity. By contrast, *Il Divo*, in Paul Mayersberg's words, "is Sorrentino's *Godfather*, but without the father."[14] As for *The Family Friend*: one couldn't ask for a better (parodic) condensation of the Oepidal drama, played out by Geremia and his mother; this is crystallized in the family photo in Geremia's apartment, showing his father (who left his mother when Geremia was nine to start a new career as a moneylender in Rome) and his new family, in front of the Coliseum. "On the back [the father] wrote: 'Darwin's theory in fast-forward. These are your brothers,' " implying that the boys in the photo are the more evolved version of the species represented by Geremia. (As he recounts this anecdote, Belana, the newly arrived Romanian, is admiring porcelain figurines of the seven dwarfs, arrayed on the same shelf.) "I don't exist for him, and he doesn't exist for me. That's how we get along," explains Geremia.

In retrospect, however, *Youth* thematizes fathers and fatherhood in a manner at once more obvious and more complex while also integral to the story. A late scene, just past the midway point, proves to be pivotal in this respect. While visiting a shop crammed with Swiss clocks and other authentic souvenirs of the Alps, Jimmy Tree (Paul Dano) is confronted by a young girl, who remarks that she once saw him in a film. He assumes at first that she—like Miss Universe—is yet another fan of his most famous performance as a robot in the fictitious *Mister Q.* "No. I saw you in that film where you play a father who never knew his son," she explains, as if paraphrasing a slightly altered version of Wenders's *Paris, Texas.* "He meets him for the first time at a highway diner when the son's already fourteen." There is a cut to Tree and the girl in medium shot, surrounded by cuckoo clocks, Ballinger browsing off to the side. "There's a bit of dialogue I really liked," she continues, over a close-up on Tree, listening intently. "Your son says, 'Why weren't you a father to me?' And you say, 'I didn't think I was up to it.' "

In the very next scene, as he walks along the road through the flower-filled alpine meadow, Tree quotes Novalis: "I'm always going home. Always going to my father's house." Tree's quotation seems to be misremembered from the poet's "Longing for Death" (1800)—or it may just be a question of translation:

Praised be to us the eternal night,
Praised be our eternal sleep.
The day indeed has made us warm
And our cares have made us weak.
Driven no more by a longing to roam,
We want to go back to our father's home.[15]

With Mark Kozelek's "Ceiling Gazing" as musical sound bridge, a transitional montage to the film's third act begins here, including a brief scene with the South

FIGURE 7.3 *Youth*

American Maradona character (Rory Serrano) thinking about *el futuro* as he watches his younger self on an imaginary nocturnal soccer pitch.[16] (The real Maradona played for SSC Napoli, Sorrentino's home team, from 1984 to 1991. He also shows up in archival footage Cardinal Voiello watches on YouTube in episode 3 of *The Young Pope*.[17]) In the course of this sequence, Tree commences his transformation into an impossible, somewhat elderly version of Hitler (on the soundtrack, Kozelek sings: "the last time I saw my father, he was in a box, and they were lowering him into the ground"). This sequence culminates in Tree's approach to the spa hotel, where, in his performance as Hitler, he reveals all the small traits he has borrowed from his new friends or acquaintances at the spa:[18] Ballinger's nose blowing; the South American's cane and limp; and so on[19]—attributes joined in a composite portrait of Hitler as retired despot, vacationing at an exclusive alpine spa (figure 7.3).[20]

Youth's oblique critique of a shallow historical perspective characteristic of the contemporary postmillennial, socially mediatized moment is driven home in a harshly oblique manner when Tree appears in the breakfast room in full Hitler make up and costume—finally revealing to guests and viewer alike the role he has been preparing since the start of the film. Here Sorrentino amplifies the brief Hitler cameo in *This Must Be the Place*, allowing the dictator-revenant to reappear closer to home, picking up, it seems, on the same aspect of the zeitgeist as Timur Vermes's 2012 satirical novel, *Er ist Wieder Da* (*Look Who's Back*), in which Hitler wakes up in present-day Berlin, the same person he was when he supposedly died in May 1945. The questions in either case are ironically analogous to the one faced by the Grand Inquisitor in Dostoevsky's *The Brothers Karamazov*, when Christ reappears in the sixteenth-century Spain of the inquisition: What if Hitler reappeared among us today? How would we respond? Would we pay attention? Would we care? What does it mean to have achieved a sensibility that can conceive of Hitler's return as just one more in a steady stream of mildly shocking events?[21] The film offers no clear answers, however. "Is it a light-hearted role?" asks Ballinger, when they first meet. "That depends on your point of view," responds Tree. It is as though Sorrentino, in writing this scene, were deliberately upping the ante from *This Must Be the Place*. The earlier film's quirky engagement with the morally and philosophically weighty questions raised by the Holocaust is countered here with what appears to be a postmodern invocation of the ultimate perpetrator. Sorrentino chooses to take this in a direction that, while still serious, is considerably lighter in tone, having more to do with individual identity and values rather than world-historical catastrophes.

After the quiet shock of his initial revelation, Tree appears once more in full Hitler attire, in a scene in which he tells Boyle (who is relating an anecdote about his muse, Brenda Morel, who long before expressed an interest in playing Eva Braun, Hitler's mistress) that he has decided to *not* make the film about the dictator after all (figure 7.4). In one of the film's many beautifully lit, nocturnal medium shots, Tree explains what he has learned from his month-long observation of the other hotel guests: that he has gleaned from his masquerade the kind of knowledge Boyle ultimately fails to express in his final screenplay, that in life one must choose between "horror and desire." As a result of his observations of the other, elderly but still lively, guests, he chooses the latter: "You made me see that I should not be wasting my time on the senselessness of horror. . . . I want to tell about your desire, my desire, so pure, so impossible, so immoral, but it doesn't matter because that's what makes us alive." One senses here a hint of an embedded justification for the earlier scene with Miss Universe and the two old men in the pool; i.e., that their desire for her is excused by the fact that it is evidence that they are still alive, that they are not yet dead. That as long as one desires one continues to be—not young, but youthful.

Nevertheless, the Hitler movie will not be made. Ironically, it was necessary for Hitler to make one more appearance here, in Sorrentino's movie, in order for this realization to find expression. Following a final close-up on Boyle's contemplative face, this scene is succeeded by a straight cut to a close-up of the back of the Tibetan

FIGURE 7.4 *Youth*

monk's shaved head, Bigazzi's camera executing one of its signature curving tracks back and down, to a medium shot gradually revealing the monk, levitating, a meter above the ground, against a background of mountains and clouds, triumphant music swelling on the soundtrack, indicating that this image—like Tree's monologue just before—is not to be taken lightly (figure 7.5). This also signals a turning point for Ballinger, who more than once insists that the monk can't actually levitate. The fact that he succeeds means that anything is possible: that Ballinger could go to Venice to visit his sick wife; that he could go to London and conduct his *Simple Songs* without her there to sing them. And, in the end, *Youth* is revealed to be the transnational art cinematic equivalent of Ballinger's middlebrow, popular-serious musical composition.

It is perhaps instructive, however, to consider Tree's brief appearance as Hitler—an event toward which the first half of the film quietly builds and that therefore marks a sort of early climax in the story—in light of the overarching thematization of fathers and fatherhood: What does it say of a society when it chooses a Hitler as collective father figure? Tree's version, moreover, is a composite of traits gleaned from his close observation of his fellow spa guests, mainly middle-aged, elderly, or even disabled men; this is a highly authentic Hitler precisely because of his all-too-human traits from this highly selective sampling of humanity, such as ostentatiously blowing his nose and walking with a limp and cane. The latter are inspired by the South American Maradona character, whose obesity, shortness of breath, and restricted mobility make him into what is in effect a figure of disability, heightening the contrast (clearly intended by Sorrentino) between his present state of "decline and decay"[22] and his past glories as one of the world's greatest soccer players.[23] The aggregate effect in this scene with Tree as Hitler is to represent the latter as domesticated, neutered, no more dangerous than any of the other retired or nearly retired former celebrities, whether footballer, composer-conductor, or filmmaker.

FIGURE 7.5 *Youth*

Finally, it is necessary to consider Tree's performance as Hitler here in light of his own artistic credo, which he articulates in his initial exchange with Ballinger: "You and I have the same problem. . . . We've been misunderstood our whole lives because we allowed ourselves to give in, just once, to a little levity." He goes on to state that he will be "remembered forever" for the single film role of Mr. Q, a robot, whose popularity is proven in a subsequent scene, mentioned above, when Tree is first introduced to Miss Universe. Her confession to him (in a classic shot-reverse shot in close-up) that of all his film roles Mr. Q is her favorite, causes him to respond rudely, as if someone who loves robot movies cannot possibly be very intelligent. "Do you ever watch other kinds of films, other than robot movies?" he asks, without getting up from his chair. She is forced to lean toward him, aggravating the unflattering angle and lighting. "Of course . . . I want to be an actress, and I don't want to just rely on my beauty," she replies. "Do you study, or do you just watch reality TV?" he adds, in one of several exchanges in the film that—whether facetiously or not—pit cinema against its traditional mediatic rival. After an uncomfortable pause (long enough for a wide angle cutaway to a group of alpenhorn players, serenading the assembled hotel clients), Miss Universe responds: "I appreciate irony, but when it is drenched in poison it is drained of its force. . . . I am happy I took part in the Miss Universe pageant. Are you happy you played Mr. Q?" Tree does not respond, merely gesturing that the conversation is over. Her remark zeroes in on Tree's sensitivity about the one role that has come to define him, however, in a genre film apparently very different from the more artistic films he has made with "all the great directors"—much as the American actor Paul Dano has now made *Youth* with Sorrentino. In the end, Miss Universe retains the moral high ground in the face of Tree's unwarranted sexism and misogyny. This conclusion is reinforced by the harsh lighting Bigazzi directs on her blemished, make-up free face, obscured somewhat by her messy, unkempt hair, her body more or less invisible to the viewer.[24] At best, these formal choices serve to emphasize her intelligent response to Tree's petulant sarcasm. But one is left to wonder: Can a woman be both beautiful and brainy in this film's world?

The final third of the film begins after Tree's appearance as Hitler and after the vision of Miss Universe in the spa pool, with the scene of Brenda Morel (Jane Fonda) coming to inform Boyle that she has decided not to star in his latest, and last, film—his testament. In the aftermath of this melodramatic, quietly self-reflexive, scene (at one point they debate the relative virtues of cinema vs. television), Boyle says goodbye to his youthful and idealistic writing team as they depart on a picturesque Swiss mountain train from a tiny wooden alpine train station. As he walks back to the hotel, Boyle is visited by a strange vision of his "more than fifty" former lead actresses, or rather the characters they played in all of his films over the decades, arrayed across the alpine meadow above him (figure 7.6). (Oddly, Brenda Morel, or rather Jane Fonda, is not among them.) "I'm a great woman's director," he tells Tree, after Morel's visit. For his part, after proleptically quoting one of the bits of dialogue from this hallucinatory scene (suggesting that his next great role might be a woman rather than Hitler), Tree responds: "Mr. Boyle, you're not a great woman's director, you're a great director, period." This seemingly straightforward compliment can also be read,

FIGURE 7.6 *Youth*

against the grain of the scene, as a veiled and unconsciously self-reflexive critique of Sorrentino's own directorial prowess, where to be a "great director, period" is to be exempt from having to be overly aware of one's obligation to counteract decades of cinematically justified inequity, sexism, or misogyny. The young sex worker (uncredited) who frequents the hotel's lobby at night, for instance, is one of the stranger secondary character choices in the film. Not only is her presence one of the many flagrantly post-Fellinian, antirealist details in *Youth*'s screenplay; her character, presented in a strongly pathetic affective light, seems to exist for the purpose of going for a chaste walk with Boyle in his last meaningful action before killing himself. Otherwise, the possibility of the prostitute as a woman who has taken some measure of control over her sexual capital, the female flaneuse, equivalent of the masculine flaneur, is nowhere in evidence. As will be seen in chapter 8, in *The Young Pope* Sorrentino persists in presenting the sex worker or prostitute as female type rather than agential subject.

Each woman in Boyle's hypermediated waking nightmare seems to be stuck in a loop, repeating her iconic phrase or bit of dialogue over top of all the others. Several are framed in medium close-up, the tonality and image quality of each shot adjusted in the digital intermediate to approximate the different styles, genres, and periods of Boyle's fifty-year career. This builds to an accusatory cacophony that is the negative affective response to the cowbell symphony conducted by Ballinger in the film's first act. Both sequences—choreographed cows and army of female genre film types—are to be read as waking fantasies, but, where Ballinger's cow chorus is mostly the result of judicious editing, Boyle's fantasy/hallucination stands out for the self-reflexive use of digital postproduction effects. Ballinger's daughter Lina's (Rachel Weisz) hypermediated and hyperkinetically edited music video nightmare of her ex-husband and British pop star Paloma Faith careening down a Swiss alpine road presents an even more spectacular—and spectacularily self-reflexive—example (figure 7.7; figure 7.8). This sequence is not merely a mini masterpiece of pop culture parody; it is also one of Sorrentino's most successful critical inversions of gender stereotypes achieved via the ironic repurposing of a global pop culture's most egregious kind of sexist imagery. As a micronarrative of one formerly powerful man beset by all the women in his life, Boyle's alpine hallucination is also a direct intertextual reference to the famous harem scene in Fellini's *8 ½*, in which Mastroianni's errant film director dreams that he is living in his childhood home with all of the women from his life, although, within the logic of Fellini's diegesis, his are real women—his mother, wife, mistresses, lovers, actresses, and so forth. In his fantasy Boyle imagines that he sees and hears the characters from his movies, as much as the actual women who played them. Diegetically, these are not real women at all but radically fictional characters whose stories were written by him. The distinction between the two scenes, then, comes down to one (Guido) in which the man faces a hostile group of women within his own dream, vs. the other (Boyle) in which the man faces various cinematic avatars of his own imagination. In both cases, therefore, the man is faced with the manifestations of his own psyche, but where one does waken from his nightmare, the other is denied this possibility. This distinction between the two films is further complicated when one remembers that, already in Fellini, there is a clear self-awareness of the stereotypical, constructed nature of each woman's social role; *Youth* self-reflexively questions the ambiguity between real and fictional women by highlighting it, a point that was already made in a considerably subtler fashion in the overt contrast between the two scenes featuring Miss Universe: when she first arrives and when she appears as a divine vision to Ballinger and Boyle in the pool. It should be recalled (as mentioned above) that Miss Universe actually has a third major scene, very early in the film, in a dream sequence when Ballinger nods off during one of the evening performances at the hotel.[25] It is certainly not a coincidence that the one scene in which, as fictional character, she is shown to be a more complex human being comes between two other scenes in which she is represented as unattainable object of desire in a regime of looking determined by an updated version of an all-too-familiar heteronormative male gaze.

FIGURE 7.7 *Youth*

FIGURE 7.8 *Youth*

It should also be noted that Ballinger's nocturnal Venetian dream sequence is clearly marked off as such by his abrupt waking at the end when he appears to drown in the *aqua alta* in Piazza San Marco. The attribution of this dream is initially ambiguous, however, as the scene is immediately preceded by a close-up on the overweight South American gasping for breath with an oxygen mask over his face. By contrast, the other dream sequence, Ballinger's daughter Lina's Paloma Faith music video nightmare, is clearly marked as distinct from anything like waking reality in the film and as attributable to a specific character. The two subsequent scenes, in which first Ballinger (cows) and then Boyle (leading ladies) experience hallucinatory visions in the alpine landscape, are not marked off in any way as being different from the scenes of waking reality that precede and follow them. By contrast, in *The Young Pope* Sorrentino makes clear that the more surreal sequences—topless radical Femen protesting the Pope's stance on abortion; the kangaroo in the Vatican gardens—are not subjective fantasy sequences but direct products of the new pontiff's unorthodox decisions. (The major exception is the interpolated shots of Saint Juana (uncredited) of Guatemala in episodes 7, 8, and 10.) Otherwise, Lenny's recurrent memories of his lost parents are relegated to clearly marked subjectively and affectively freighted sequences—which is to say flashbacks, whether free-standing or within a dream sequence, more than one of which takes place in the same nocturnal Venetian setting as Ballinger's San Marco dream, to which I will return below.

The Meaningful Difference of Non-normative Identities, Part 2

As already shown, *Youth* is not only about men and/as fathers but also women—and sometimes in ways that aren't in the end still about men. Immediately after the spa pool scene, as discussed above, Boyle learns that Brenda Morel, his long-time lead actress (played by Jane Fonda) has quit his latest and final film. Boyle kills himself soon after out of despair at his failed project, his testimony, whereas Ballinger, within the story world, is somehow redeemed, judging by the final scene of his command performance for Queen Elizabeth of his famous, Brittenesque *Simple Songs*, which were written, as he explains at one point, when he "still loved." (In this, he is like the jaded Jep Gambardella, who wrote his one and only novel while young and "deeply in love.") In the immediately preceding scene, Ballinger achieves for himself what appears to be a highly narcissistic form of redemption. Visiting her room in a long-term care facility in Venice for the first time in ten years, he delivers a long monologue ostensibly to his wife, Melanie (Sonia Gessner), who remains silent throughout. The scene is framed so that she is visible in medium shot with her back to the camera as she gazes out the window at Venice, Fred in a chair to one side, facing away, that is, toward the camera. Only at the end of the scene, with Ballinger, after many years of neglect and infidelity,[26] having paid his penance to his wife, do we get the reverse angle from outside the window on Melanie's grotesque, mask-like visage in medium close-up, staring open-mouthed in a frozen rictus, evidently so ill that it is impossible to know if she even heard anything of her husband's confession (figure 7.9). As presented, Melanie is not a proper subject but only a mask, literally a persona, her open mouth a terrible visual mockery of the fact that she was once a gifted soprano for whom Ballinger originally wrote his *Simple Songs*. What is the larger significance of this penultimate image of his incurably ill wife's mask-like face in Venice? What is the significance of the film's title, *Youth*, with respect to gender difference? To ability? After all, Melanie's condition is arguably a kind of disability. What is its significance with respect to age and generational difference? Tacitly broached, these questions are never definitively answered. As will be seen in the coda, Sorrentino revisits the examination of a long-term relationship in its dying days in *Loro*'s dramatization of the demise of Silvio Berlusconi's (Toni Servillo) marriage with his wife, Veronica Lario (Elena

FIGURE 7.9 *Youth*

Sofia Ricci). While the more recent film offers a bitterly convincing portrait of a dysfunctional relationship, it also avoids any further exploration of the kind of delicate territory broached in *Youth*, trading this for another—highly interesting but also problematic—iteration of the by-now familiar trope of masculinist redemption. Also, far more than *Youth*, *Loro* continues down the road of the comparably problematic representation of women that received an arguably more sophisticated treatment in *The Great Beauty*.

The Venetian setting of the hospital scene in *Youth* is explained in the aforementioned dream sequence (or rather the hospital scene provides a retrospective rationale for the dream), in which Ballinger, in his conductor's coat and tails, traverses the raised *passerella* down the center of a beautifully lit, flooded nocturnal Piazza San Marco, where he encounters the oneiric figure of Miss Universe in full beauty pageant regalia (figure 7.10). They pass each other awkwardly on the narrow boardwalk, and, as Miss Universe struts toward the Museo Correr, Ballinger, continuing on toward the Basilica, gradually sinks into the rising *aqua alta*, calling out for his wife: "Melanie!" This opening dream scene thus establishes, albeit obliquely, Ballinger's guilt over his wife's condition and his passive response to it, while at the same time foreshadowing the film's conclusion in which he overcomes his psychological impasse and his sense of guilt by agreeing to conduct his *Simple Songs* once more—with a different singer. The fact that he does this at a special concert commissioned by the Queen of England for her husband, Prince Philip, is not insignificant in this regard: as he remarks to the queen's emissary in the film's opening scene, Ballinger finds the monarchy "endearing . . . because it's so vulnerable. You eliminate one person, and all of a sudden the whole world changes. Like in a marriage."

Youth is unquestionably an excellent example of what we mean by art cinema today when we don't know how else to categorize a film. The fact that it does not abide by stylistic, narrative or structural conventions is significant: *Youth*'s meanings are not produced in the predictable manner of a genre film, like the

FIGURE 7.10 *Youth*

robot movie that Jimmy Tree holds in such disdain. Nor is it comparable to the kind of premillennial commercial programming to which Boyle no doubt refers when, in his final exchange with Brenda Morel, he summarily dismisses all television as "shit." Therefore, the potentially patronizing close-up on Melanie Ballinger in *Youth* demands an analytical model other than a gendered theory of looking. As elaborated in chapter 3, in my discussion of *The Family Friend*, I appropriate here Rosemarie Garland-Thomson's theory of the stare from the context of disability studies. Translating Garland-Thomson's stare into the terms of a visual structure in specific films helps to illuminate scenes in which an exclusively ideologically based notion of the gaze fails to lead to deeper understanding.[27] In other words, even when stripped of its original feminist-psychoanalytic connotations and applied more straightforwardly as a critique of the process of objectifying (reifying) another human being, reducing her/him to an object of erotic desire, the stare by contrast reduces the other person to precisely that: an *Other* who is the object of either fascination or disgust, or some intermediate but still powerful affective response. Either way, arguably s/he is reduced to something other than fully human in the process:

> Cultural othering in all its forms—the male gaze being just one instance—depends upon looking as an act of domination. The ethnographic or the colonizing look operates similarly to the gendered look, subordinating its object by enacting a power dynamic. When persons in a position that grants them authority to stare take up that power, staring functions as a form of domination, marking the *staree* as the exotic, outlaw, alien, or other.[28]

The stare would seem to be clearly at work in *The Great Beauty*, for instance, in those scenes involving Dadina (Giovanna Vignola), Jep's editor, who is in her own words a "dwarf" (*una nana*). Dadina is a fully fleshed out character, however: a successful businesswoman of a certain age with (as implied in the dialogue) an active sex life and a healthily ironic self-image. In showing Dadina as capable of laughing at herself, the film appears open-minded while getting away with exploiting the actor's physical appearance for a melancholically humorous effect (figure 7.11). This unusual casting choice pays off, as Dadina's scenes with Jep emerge as narratively and affectively important because of the light they shed on his character. I return in the following chapter to the question of the stare vs. the gaze as these structures operate in *The Young Pope*.

As will be seen in my discussion of the television series, Sorrentino shifts from the classic secular salvific model of the woman whose death somehow redeems the undeserving artist figure—epitomized in the conclusion of *The Great Beauty*—to an ironic yet openly religious iconographic model of Christ and Mary alike in their redemptive relation to the protagonist. In a sense, both spiritual and erotic salvation are fused in the figure of Sister Mary (Diane Keaton, with Allison Case as the younger version), who also functions as surrogate mother to Lenny Belardo, the "young pope" of the series title—although he seems to be the only character who does not recognize this.[29] It is important to acknowledge the relative complexity of Sorrentino's

FIGURE 7.11 *The Great Beauty*

invocation of these art historical, Christological, and narrative tropes.[30] Arguably as troubling as the exploitation of women's bodies are the occasional inclusion in the films and the television series of non-normative identities, bodies, and faces—although the entrenched normativity of the male body comes in for mild critique in the bodies of the protagonists and other characters, whether melodramatically pathetic (Geremia in *The Family Friend*), pathetically grotesque (the South American in *Youth*), or elegiacally aging (Ballinger and Boyle in *Youth*). Here we see Sorrentino moving beyond his Fellinian fascination with grotesque and/or hyperbolic human bodies to something more serious, less susceptible to ironic interpretation.[31]

EIGHT

Ceci n'est pas un pape

Postsecular Melodrama in The Young Pope

> Nothingness is the negative power of lost humanistic values.
> —András Bálint Kovács, *Screening Modernism: European Art Cinema,*
> *1950–1980*

"TELEVISION IS THE FUTURE, Mick. To tell you the truth, it's also the present," intones Brenda Morel (Jane Fonda), in the pivotal scene in *Youth* in which she tells her long-time friend and director that she has thrown over the lead role in his latest—and last—film in order to work in a television series. As noted in chapter 6, the feature-length narrative fiction film came to be seen in the twentieth century as in some sense the heir to the novel as a culturally central, formative genre or mode. Arguably, though, the feature film has always resembled more the literary short story, whereas the multiepisode television series more closely resembles the novel as long-form narrative. At any rate, the technology of streaming video perfected by companies like Netflix, where entire seasons of a television series are released all at once, has inaugurated a so-called renaissance in television production and consumption. The internet's insatiable appetite for competitive content means that TV series' production budgets are at unprecedented levels, as famous film directors work with generous funding packages and international rosters of today's best acting talent.

This chapter focuses on Sorrentino's first foray into the new generation of prestige television, with his internationally successful ten-part English-language limited series *The Young Pope* (2016), written and directed by Sorrentino, with the help of cowriter Peppe Fiore, as well as his usual cinematographer Bigazzi.[1] In ten one-hour episodes the show tracks the career of Lenny Belardo (Jude Law), who, as Pius XIII, at the age of forty-seven becomes one of the youngest and the first-ever American pope. I consider the series in the context of the director's still-evolving body of work, especially in terms of the stylistic and diegetic modulation from *Il Divo*'s postrealism (so-called) to the ironic elegiac tonality of *The Great Beauty* to this series' openness to a melodramatic affect whose seeds are already present in the earlier films. All of these tendencies contribute to what can be called Sorrentino's postmodern *impegno*, combining a commercially acceptable brand of intensified continuity style with an ethically and politically critical edge.[2] The overall tendency, however, as suggested, is the movement from middlebrow transnational art cinema to postsecular melodrama in the television series. This chapter therefore lays bare an argument implicit in the foregoing chapters in relation to the much larger question of the postsecular nature of contemporary culture. To the extent that *The Young Pope* addresses this condition in part explains the turning away from the satirical postrealist irony of *Il Divo* in favor of the (relatively) serious examination of the masculine protagonist's introspective journey to greater self-awareness seen in every film since *This Must Be the Place*.

Postsecular Transmediality

Because of quantitative differences between feature film and TV series, my argument here is based on a close analysis of a selection of representative scenes from across the series, focusing mainly on the new pope's identity in relation to his revolutionary ideas and the show's engagement with major theological questions against the backdrop of a critique of contemporary postsecular society. To be specific: my focus here is on the series' representation—mainly through flashback and dream sequences, especially those with Venice as setting—of Lenny's interiority, his subjective inner life. *The Young Pope* joins a long list of films that use the city's spaces to give form to the res cogitans, the interior life of the protagonist, her or his memories, dreams, and desires.[3] This will allow for a more economical consideration of the series' exploration of the question of faith in a postsecular era.

The postsecular is defined as a position that is as skeptical toward the global persistence of religious faith in the twenty-first century—including the requisite faith in capitalism as dominant economic system—as it is toward the atheistic interrogation of such faith in the name of an uncritical secularity. The latter, after all, is one of the great founding myths of modernity, and *postsecular*, if nothing else, gives a name to the space opened up by the demystification of this myth.[4] In the introduction to their critical collection on postsecular cinema, John Caruana and Mark Cauchi outline an understanding of the postsecular in terms of specific contemporary (post-millennial) films that "challenge the Enlightenment narrative that has dominated Western thought for the last four centuries."[5] They define the cinematic postsecular along a spectrum of films, such as Terrance Malick's *Tree of Life* (2011), that offer "thoughtful meditations on faith," to those, such as Lars von Trier's *Melancholia* (2011), that give voice to a "non-triumphalist atheism."[6] At first glance, *The Young Pope* would seem to exemplify the first tendency, as its diegetic world seems to allow for the miraculous to be taken seriously. At any rate, like its protagonist (at least at first), the series appears to hedge its bets on the question of the existence of God. For a growing body of theorists, then, there is much to be learned about the current postsecular moment by studying specific examples of certain contemporary films, television series, or other audiovisual narrative forms that are representative of what I see as an emergent postsecular style.

The increasingly secular-seeming Europe of the later twentieth and early twenty-first centuries had its analogue in the borderless art cinema of the postwar period, with films from across the continent comprising a constellation of equivalent existential concerns, narrative subjects, and thematic ambiguities. *The Young Pope*'s place in this history, I argue, is not compromised but complicated by the fact that it is a television series. I invoke this understanding of the postsecular therefore not least because of the series' subject matter, which recounts the fictional story of the first American pope in the Vatican's history, in the process exploring the personal and political behind-the-scenes machinations in the papal palace. The series performs a sophisticated critical analysis of the current state of the Catholic Church, examining the nature and value of religious faith in the twenty-first century. In a final irony it appears to come down on the side of the validity of faith, insofar as the titular pope is seen performing more than one miracle and, in the end, having proven his sainthood (a notion which in *The Great Beauty* was the subject of ironic critique but which here is taken much more seriously), is even granted a vision of what appears to be the redeeming Christ in the clouds above the Piazza San Marco in Venice (figure 8.1).[7] The series' treatment of faith is without doubt the most divisive point in its critical reception. I argue, however, that this feature of *The Young Pope* offers a clear example of Sorrentino's postironic exploitation of recognizable genre conventions whose presence within the diegesis, accompanied by all the other less conventional stylistic techniques, produces an unprecedented analysis of the contradictions of the postsecular moment, and one that is not unsympathetic to the possibility of genuine faith in the twenty-first century.[8] In this light I analyze the series' subtle modulation by its latter episodes into a species of postsecular male melodrama.[9]

My reading of *The Young Pope* begins, however, from the series' transmediation of two, or rather three, twentieth-century texts: Rene Magritte's surrealist painting *The Treachery of Images* (1928–1929; figure 8.2), Thomas Mann's *Death in Venice* (*Der Tod in Venedig*, 1912), and Luchino Visconti's 1971 film adaptation. With respect to the

FIGURE 8.1 *The Young Pope* (Paolo Sorrentino, 2016)

latter two, while *The Young Pope* shares certain themes with both novella and film, it obviously remediates this story material in very different ways, sharing its mediatic basis with Visconti's film, which is already a remediation of Mann's novella. This exploration of the series' transmedial complexity sheds light upon its story world by first illuminating its form. On the one hand, then, is Magritte's radical modernist critique of visual-verbal representation ("Ceci n'est pas une pipe"), clearly referenced in the scene in episode 7 of a man's pipe against the background of the papal coat of arms—the very pipe whose brown bowl Lenny has carried around in his pocket since he was left at the age of seven at Sister Mary's (Diane Keaton) orphanage in upstate New York (figure 8.3). As with Freud's cigar, however, sometimes a Meerschaum pipe is just a Meerschaum pipe. Any psychoanalytic connotations are complicated by the pipe's intermedial links with Magritte, modernist painting, and the history of critical self-reflexivity in the visual arts. As part of the mise-en-scène, the pipe is nevertheless also an object rich in affective-mnemic content. It is a kind of *petit madeleine*, a precipitant of ostensibly authentic memory, or what José van Dijck calls a mediated memory object: a material object cathected with subjective emotional content whose source is extrinsic to the pipe qua pipe.[10] As much as this pipe signifies in the diegesis for Lenny's character personally, however, it is also always an intermedial reference to Magritte's surrealist image and its witty critique of visual representation in a century characterized not by painting but by photography, telegraphy, telephony, radio, cinema, and, in its second half, television. Where the latter in Italy came to be defined in its first analog instantiation by RAI and then Berlusconi's Mediaset empire,[11] by the mid-2000s the current revolution in television had begun, exemplified by this collaboration between HBO and Sky TV.

FIGURE 8.2 *The Treachery of Images* (Rene Magritte, 1928–1929)

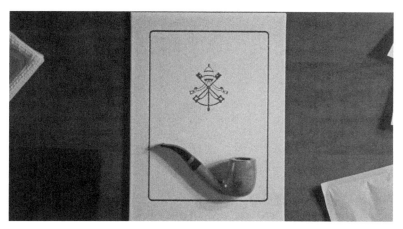

FIGURE 8.3 *The Young Pope*

On the other hand is Mann's, and then Visconti's, narrative exploration of a fin-de-siecle European masculine subject whose inexorable descent into psycho-affective instability and, ultimately, death, can be read as a (modernist) allegory of Nietzsche's thesis in *The Birth of Tragedy*, in which the Dionysian forces of desire and dissolution triumph over the form-giving forces of the Apollonian (figure 8.4). Where the former are utterly and necessarily sublimated in the character of Lenny Belardo, Pope Pius XIII, the latter manifest in the series' (often ironic) visual exploitation of Jude Law's face and body—his much-remarked physical beauty. (As Cardinal Voiello remarks to Lenny in episode 3: "You are as handsome as Jesus, but you are not actually Jesus," to which Lenny responds: "I may actually be more handsome.") This updating of the Tadziu-Aschenbach relationship, in which Lenny is at once both lover and beloved, both subject and object of desire (others desire him even as he so fiercely desires God), is also a twenty-first-century updating of the New Man as identity construct, which first emerged in academic critical discourse in the 1980s in response to a new approach to the representation of masculinity in popular culture, in forms as diverse as Calvin Klein underwear ads and Paul Schrader's 1980 film *American Gigolo* (figure 8.5). (Mary Harron's *American Psycho*, discussed in chapter 4, exploits actor Christian Bale's naked or near-naked body in a manner deliberately reminiscent of Richard Gere in Schrader's film, for instance in the scene where the narcissistic protagonist tries on various outfits before heading out for a night of work. The latter is also a likely inspiration for the scene in episode 5 of *The Young Pope*, to be discussed below, in which Lenny prepares for his first address to the cardinals, trying on a variety of outfits while preening for the camera, as if before a mirror.[12]) In what is now a cultural studies commonplace, the masculine or hyper-masculine is the new beauty alongside representations of women in Western culture, where the male body historically is already the standard for physical beauty:[13] "The implicit heterosexualizing of the Platonic notion of beauty that took place in the Roman and then medieval worlds should not allow us to forget the fact that the

FIGURE 8.4 *Death in Venice* (Luchino Visconti, 1971)

beautiful body of which Socrates spoke was always the young male body, as it was in the Renaissance."[14] As Susan Bordo amply demonstrates, this New Man may be equivalent on the formal level to popular cultural representations of women, but the meanings produced are by no means necessarily equivalent.[15] As a representation, the New Man does nothing to alter the most privileged genre of subjectivity.[16] To further update John Berger's axiom: this man is looked at (by the camera and the viewer) and he looks at himself being looked at, but, like many men, he also just looks (at women, other men, etc.). In this gendered scenario, the objectified looker *as looker* wields the power, as the active wielding of the gaze is the primary cinematic expression of such power, undercutting the fatal passivity historically attributed to the feminized object. As always, the body, or body image, mediates intersubjective social relations.

FIGURE 8.5 *The Young Pope*

As noted above, the most spectacular example of Lenny's narcissism—and of the series' exploitation of Law's physical beauty—occurs in episode 5, in the scene, set to LMFAO's[17] 2011 track "I'm Sexy and I Know it," in which Lenny prepares for his inaugural address to the cardinals. (As will be seen below, this scene is a deeply ironic contradiction of Lenny's intradiegetic insistence, in the meeting with the Vatican marketing chief [Cécile de France] in episode 2, on the effacing of any personal papal identity susceptible to commodification. It is as if the essentially contradictory persona he always insists on—"I am a contradiction. Like God. One in three and three in one"—is being underlined on the level of the series' audiovisual style in terms of the obvious disjuncture between the character's protestations and the series' casting of Jude Law in the role.) In its heavily ironic juxtaposition of the EDM track with shots of Lenny choosing his wardrobe, dressing, or posing shirtless for the camera, this scene recalls as it goes beyond the la corrente scene in *Il Divo*. In the end it may not be the case that Lenny's obvious characterological difference from the men in the LMFAO video trumps the similarities between their bodies and Jude Law's. In short, the superficial visual and physical aspects of the scene trump the subtler diegetic elements, at this point. This is largely due to the music itself. Immediately following one of the series' sweeping aerial shots of the Vatican from the air, there is a cut to a low-angle shot on the papal palace stairwell, the cardinals already descending to gather for the pope's address. A Fellinian cordon of identically dressed cardinals flows past as the song begins: "Girl look at that body / Girl look at that body / I work out." The camera pushes in to a bust of a previous pope, then cuts to a medium shot of a shirtless Lenny walking into frame from left, turning and posing for the camera, to which he nods, as if before a mirror. The sequence proceeds like a music video montage,[18] a relatively rapid series of mostly close-up shots of a po-faced Law, trying on now this surplice, now that one, then an array of papal shoes on a cushion, and so forth. Lenny's self-reflexive narcissism here goes beyond Jep Gambardella's sartorial nihilism in *The Great Beauty*. This papal fashion show, whose only audience is the film's spectator, continues until papal servants wheel in a large crate containing the beehive-like papal tiara, newly returned to the Vatican. There is a cut to a close-up on Lenny's pensive face as he gazes down on the potent symbol of papal power (figure 8.6). The music stops abruptly; a cut to a long shot of the pope in profile in full papal regalia gives way to another of the seated red-clad cardinals, waiting in the Sistine Chapel for his appearance,[19] to the strains of John Tavener's 1993 choral elegy "Song for Athene."[20] Sorrentino's choice of music here is clarified somewhat when the scene of the ceremony is interrupted by a cut from a close-up on Lenny's face, eyes closed, to another flashback to the day of his first arrival at the orphanage. In this classically structured flashback the viewer is granted a vision of Lenny's younger self as he approaches the orphanage gates in upstate New York. He is brought there by his parents, whose textbook hippy appearance might suggest that this flashback is not meant to be taken absolutely literally, as the final truth about his past. While there is no reason to doubt the story of Lenny's being abandoned at the orphanage as a boy, this vision of his parents, like the others scattered across the series, reads like his youthful self's wishful thinking; as if in place of any concrete visual memories, he conjured up these countercultural cliché parents, his father (Colin Smith) with long

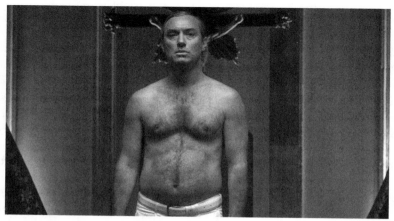

FIGURE 8.6 *The Young Pope*

hair and headband, his mother (Olivia Macklin) with a peasant dress and a pseudo-Botticellian demeanour. As it transpires, however, we are meant to accept that this is what his parents looked like.[21] When the young Lenny, facing the orphanage gates, says to himself "I'm going to turn around, and they'll still be there. I'm going to turn around now and I'll see them: Mom and Dad, waiting for me"—there is no way of knowing if this is an objective representation of the past or if this is the fantasy that Lenny has constructed for himself, whether for consolation or self-flagellation. For, when Lenny does turn around, his parents have magically disappeared, like the giraffe in *The Great Beauty*. The difference, though, is that, in the latter film's story world, there is no doubt that the giraffe was there. In *The Young Pope* it appears that Lenny has embraced God so fervently in an attempt to fill the vacuum created when his parents disappeared from his life.[22]

Outside of his flashbacks and dreams, what we do know of Lenny's parents comes mainly from Sister Mary. In episode 2, for instance, she reveals to him that they left him as a little boy in the orphanage's care because "they had to go to Venice." The next flashback—like some others, more a hallucinatory dream-like sequence—occurs in episode 3, in which the adult Lenny encounters his nine-year old self—dressed in a choirboy's robes. He pursues his youthful hippy parents through the deserted nocturnal *calle*, from San Marco to a vaporetto stop, the camera following, twisting sideways, in a highly expressive sequence that confirms the Venetian setting as the space in which his deepest desires play out as if on stage, as if Venice were not a real place but the land of dream or of the dead.[23] This also partially explains why, when Lenny finally arrives in Venice for real in the final episode, he dies—or at least appears to do so.

The scene of the pope's first address to the cardinals in the Sistine Chapel comes at the end of episode 5 in the structural centre of the ten-part series. Lenny's physical appearance here is also in complete contrast with the immediately preceding scene of his sartorial preparations for the ceremony, discussed above, set to the

FIGURE 8.7 *The Young Pope*

strains of LMFAO's "I'm Sexy and I Know It." In this self-reflexive montage Lenny is at his most parodically sexy, whereas in the following scene, dressed in the heavy studded papal surplice and ornate tiara, seated on a palanquin carried by four servants, he is transformed into a wizened tortoise, glaring out at the assembled cardinals, in a tableau out of the Middle Ages (figure 8.7). That his discourse to the cardinals is also medieval in its worldview is no coincidence. A straight cut from Lenny's flashback to the last time he saw his parents leads to a push-in to a close-up on the pope as he opens his eyes, as if from prayer. "Evangelization? We've already done it. Ecumenicalism? Been there, done that. Tolerance? Doesn't live here anymore." In this juxtaposition of comically ironic postmodern pastiche and seriously ironic neomedieval melodramatics is the contradictory but uncompromising young pope in nuce: "I am the young pope," he declares to Cardinal Voiello in the same episode (5), after the latter fails in his blackmail attempt. "I put no stock in consensus." Pius XIII is a consensus of one.

The Pope Who Wasn't There

Lenny's/Pius XIII's/Jude Law's masculine beauty is commented upon throughout the series, most notably by the pope himself; the power of telegenic celebrity is invoked ironically in that Lenny chooses to *not* exploit this power in an obvious or positive sense. In a doubly ironic structure very different from *Il Divo*'s ironies, there is thus a denial on the diegetic level of what is manifestly emphasized on the level of the film's visual surface. This is one way in which Magritte's painting of the pipe-which-is-not–a-pipe signifies in my reading of the series: *The Young Pope* invokes not so much the letter as the spirit of this inherently paradoxical image, insofar as Lenny/Pius XIII, in refusing to let the Vatican marketing department reproduce his visage on any commercial merchandise, makes a gesture as premodern as it is radically contemporary, and it is in this sort of detail that the series' postsecularity manifests. This contradictory combination is characteristic of the protagonist and the show's story as a whole, as it develops across ten episodes from what appears to be Pius XIII's reactionary and retrograde rewinding of the clock to well before the Second Vatican Council in the early 1960s to Lenny's genuinely revolutionary rebooting of the Catholic Church for the new millennium.

This rebooting is officially announced in Lenny's first address to the cardinals in episode 5. Lenny speaks in close-up, across a series of unmotivated shifts in angle: "Brother cardinals, we need to go back to being prohibited. Inaccessible and mysterious. That's the only way we will once again become desirable. That's the only way great love stories are born. And I . . . want great love stories!" But the seeds of his ideological and theological radicalization of the church are sown in episode 2, during his first meeting with Sofia, the Vatican marketing chief.[24] This scene shows that Lenny's revolutionarily retrograde ideas apply first to himself, that is, to his performance in the role of pope. He lets Sofia deliver her pitch, outlining the urgency of getting an entire line of pope memorabilia into production as soon as possible. These official papal artifacts would include souvenir plates with Pius XIII's image reproduced thereon. Lenny excuses himself, leaving Sofia and Voiello alone in the papal office, the large globe of the world in one corner—a visual nod to Chaplin's *The Great Dictator*. He returns a moment later, taking a position across the room while holding up a blank white porcelain dinner plate (figure 8.8). "This is the sort of merchandise I'm prepared to authorize," he proclaims. "But it doesn't have your image on it," she responds. A slow push-in to Lenny, from medium to medium close-up: "I do not have an image . . . because I am no one. Only Christ exists and I am not worth 45 or even 5 euros. I am worth *nothing*." When Sofia protests that she doesn't understand, Lenny explains that she, as official curator of the papal image, must fire the Vatican's official photographer immediately. "No photographs of the pope are to be issued. . . . Now that I think about it, I've been training my whole life to be an invisible pope. And so for my first address you will see to it that the lighting is so dim no photographer, no TV cameraman, and not even the faithful will see anything of me but a dark shadow, my silhouette. They will not see me because I do not exist." Lenny concludes his discourse to the Vatican marketing chief by rather pedantically testing her knowledge of contemporary cultural figures in various fields of artistic endeavor, all of whom have one thing in common: they never let themselves be photographed. It is not otherwise clarified why J. D. Salinger is the "most important author of the last twenty years" (not least because his one and only important work, *The Catcher in the Rye*, first appeared in 1951), nor why Sorrentino chose Stanley Kubrick over, say, Terrance Mallick, for the "most important film director." Otherwise, his choices for most important contemporary artist—Banksy—and, surprisingly, electronic music group—Daft Punk—are easier to accept.

Going beyond the films (especially *The Consequences of Love*, *The Great Beauty*, and *Il Divo*), the theme of individual nonexistence or nothingness is complicated here, focused in the character of Lenny. In episode 2, a bitter Cardinal Spencer throws Lenny out of his house, telling him that now he is the pope he is "all alone. Just as you've always been. And . . . you're a nothing. Nothing!" On this word Spencer

FIGURE 8.8 *The Young Pope*

closes his door, which then appears to reopen in an inverse match-on-action, as Sister Mary opens her door to admit Lenny, visibly upset at Spencer's words. Later in the same episode, during his first public address in St. Peter's Square, Lenny berates the crowd: "Everyone is alone before God." In this homily Lenny shows himself at his most distant and angry, like the God of the Old Testament, a God not of love but of wrath and retribution, demanding blind obedience. What gradually clarifies as the series progresses is that, for Lenny, the absence of God and the absence of his parents—their abandoning of him as a child—are inextricably connected. Moreover, the question of love, which at this point is absent from Lenny's life and, as a result, from his papacy, also depends on the resolution of the initial, primary absence. Therefore a thematic and diegetic interdependency is established between the banal melodramatics of Lenny's emotional life and the profound theological questions on which the church's existence depends.

Lenny's expressed desire to be the pope by not being the pope—*Ceci n'est pas un pape*—which is to say by not showing himself in public (except in darkened silhouette), by appearing only as a disembodied voice, inflects Magritte's modernist paradox away from aesthetics toward theology and ecclesiastical politics. This also extends the theme of the value of nothing from *The Great Beauty* and from the realm of modernist literature—and Jep's rekindled literary aspirations—to an ironic theology for a postsecular era for which the very idea of something that cannot be represented in the form of an image is inconceivable. In the end, however, it remains a question of how Lenny's auto-iconophobia manifests ironically—and iconophilically—on the series' visual and narrative levels. Finally, as will be explored below, in the section on the series' melodramatic qualities, there is a transition in *The Young Pope* away from the existential, and therefore essentially modernist-humanist, theme of nothingness toward something else. Kovács explains this transition in terms of the difference between modernist and postmodernist tendencies in the European art film: "Nothingness is the only metaphysical category modernism accepts, while mystical or divine parallel worlds belong to the universe of postmodern thinking."[25] In this respect, in contrast to the discussion in chapter 5 of *Il Divo*'s postmodernity in relation to *American Psycho*, we can see how *postsecular* is a more appropriate descriptor for *The Young Pope*'s engagement with the mystical or divine.

The Image of Woman: From Gazing to Staring

Despite its inevitable focus on Lenny as protagonist, a more nuanced understanding of the series can be gained through an examination of the representation of women, both as characters and also as significant aspects of the mise-en-scène. I want to return for the moment to the discussion in chapters 6 and 7 of the (seemingly) gratuitous displays of feminine flesh in *The Great Beauty* and *Youth*. We have compared Miss Universe's pseudotheophany in the alpine spa hotel pool to such an iconic scene as Sylvia and Marcello's nocturnal dip in the Trevi Fountain. It is revealing to also consider here the other iconic scene of Italian postwar cinema: Pina's death in Rossellini's *Roma, città aperta* (1946), a graphic match of the frontal view of Michelangelo's *Pietà* (1499). The famous shot of Don Pietro (Aldo Fabrizi) holding the dead Pina (Anna Magnani) in his arms says as much about Christian iconography as it does about the representation of women in neorealist film (figure 8.9). This comparison transcends postwar Italian cinema, revealing the generic and tropological underpinnings of the Passion narrative as crucial intertext for so much contemporary cultural production. As Lenny remarks to Cardinal Gutierrez (Javiér Camara), in episode 1, as they gaze together upon Michelangelo's statue in St. Peter's Basilica: "It all comes back to this in the end, doesn't it? To the mother." Midway through episode 3, moreover, in a high-angle shot that foreshadows what appears to be his death in the final episode,[26] Lenny faints into the arms of Esther (Ludivine Sagnier), the Swiss guardsman's wife,

FIGURE 8.9 *Roma, città aperta* (Roberto Rossellini, 1946)

FIGURE 8.10 *The Young Pope*

positioned from the series' start as virgin mother (and counterpart to Sister Mary, for all intents and purposes Lenny's foster mother; figure 8.10). Later, in episode 8, Lenny's birth mother is seen in an unattributed hallucinatory vision—and perfect graphic match to the foregoing scene—as virgin mother to the young Dussolier (Jack McQuaid), who, as the adult cardinal (Scott Shepherd), is murdered in Honduras in episode 7. In scenes such as these, the television series complicates and, to a certain extent, transcends the more conventional and troubling representation of women in the films. This reaches a peak in episode 9 when, at the conclusion of a debate on abortion, Lenny remarks to Spencer: "What if, in things of life, everyone is guilty, except for the woman?" Spencer: "Are you talking about your mother?" Lenny: "What else could I be talking about?" That said, just as their debate presents a classically dialectical treatment of a perennially controversial subject, allowing Sorrentino to present well-argued and opposing views on abortion (framed within a Catholic worldview), so the series persists in a pronounced tendency for carefully composed, well-lit static shots of young attractive women (including Lenny's mother) in various stages of undress—especially in the protagonist's fantasies, dreams, and flashback sequences. Once again Sorrentino gets to have it both ways.

As noted in the introduction, the modality of melodrama spans across diverse national cinemas, linking what are otherwise stylistically and thematically disparate films on the generic, structural, and tonal levels. Historically, this is one way in which the Italian and American cinemas are connected—particularly with regard to the close relation in melodramatic narrative between and among gender, a watered-down Christian moral-ethical schema, and what I call a postsecular iconography. A relevant guide to *The Young Pope*'s nexus of passion, pathos, and gender—particularly with respect to the character of Lenny Belardo, Pope Pius XIII—is Linda Williams's 1990s work on the centrality of melodramatic narrative to American popular culture. Among the five characteristics of melodrama, Williams singles out the recurrent type of the "victim-hero," the "recognition of *virtue* involving a dialectic of *pathos* and *action*," in which gender identity (in cinematic and televisual narratives, at least) is revealed as constructed in relation to a power dynamic in which anyone, regardless of biological sex, when in the position of victim, "becomes a woman."[27] This is the moral-affective counterpart to the notion, from 1970s feminist film theory, of the *female* gaze.[28] E. Ann Kaplan builds on Mulvey's earlier psychoanalytic-ideological model, shifting the emphasis from who is doing the looking to the significance of the positions occupied by the "bearer and receiver of the look."[29] According to Kaplan, "the gaze is not necessarily male (literally), but to own and activate the gaze . . . is to be in the masculine position."[30] The gazing subject is coded masculine, while the objectified victim is coded feminine: two distinct subject positions on an ethical-epistemological-axiological continuum in which gender is merely one attribute among several. For Williams, then:

> Recognition of *virtue* orchestrates the moral legibility that is key to melodrama's function. . . . The suffering body caught up in paroxysms of mental or physical pain can be male or female, but suffering itself is a form of powerlessness that is coded *feminine*. Of course the transmutation of bodily suffering into virtue is a *topos* of western culture that goes back to Christian iconography.[31]

Williams amplifies what she calls melodrama's "sentimental politics," which often entails a climax that offers "a feeling for, if not the reality of, justice," in which "the death of a good person offers paroxysms of pathos and recognitions of virtue compensating for individual loss of life"; i.e., "compensation" as *redemption* through self-sacrifice, typically on the part of a woman.[32] The influence of this melodramatically moralistic, complexly gendered representation of victimhood, of suffering-as-virtue, can be detected far beyond the confines of American popular culture. It is no accident that melodrama has transcended its generic status to become one of the characteristic narrative modalities of a visually based contemporary global culture. The connection with Christian iconography, especially Renaissance paintings of the crucifixion, is crucial (pun intended): the spectacle of Christ on the cross, the very moment in the Passion narrative of abject suffering and ecstatic transfiguration. This is also the image par excellence that encapsulates the meaning of divine grace as the promise of forgiveness and redemption at the core of Catholicism. In the twenty-first century, however, it is one thing to be a victim and bear the biological body of a man, while it is another thing altogether to be so in the undeniable, because visually displayed, body of a woman. Each of these signifies in its own way as normative. And there is a third category still: the non-normative body of the disabled person.

Chapter 3 examined the operation of the stare in Sorrentino's *The Family Friend*. An even more glaring example of his exploitation of the stare occurs in *The Young Pope*, episode 2, when Cardinal Voiello (Silvio Orlando) returns at night to his apartment near the Vatican. Sorrentino—or rather his editor, Cristiano Travaglioi— structures the scene as one of thwarted voyeurism: the viewer is aligned with Sister Mary as she spies on Voiello at Lenny's behest. The viewer likewise spies on him, perhaps hoping (with Sister Mary) to catch him out in some unpriestly behaviour in the privacy of his home. This is suggested for instance by the fact that, as he carries a box of pastries into the building, he is followed by an attractive young woman

FIGURE 8.11 *The Young Pope*

in a tight red dress. The framing and mise-en-scène conspire to encourage such a reading, as Sister Mary is able to watch unobserved, à la *Rear Window*, from an adjacent car park, Voiello conveniently visible through the large windows of his lavish apartment. The red dress turns out to be a red herring, though, as from outside we watch Voiello greeting his charge, Girolamo (unnamed in the credits), a young man with a severe physical and perhaps mental disability, played by an actor who is clearly authentically disabled (figure 8.11).

If nothing else Sorrentino's casting choices cannot be accused of cripface: Hollywood's tendency to cast able-bodied actors in treatments of mental and physical disability. There is something to be said for casting genuinely differently abled actors in disabled roles—although it is important to avoid the uncritical conflation of the role and the person playing it. Generally speaking, the difference of disability trumps that of either gender or age—until, that is, all three identities are merged in the same character. *The Young Pope*'s countertendency is announced in the series' opening dream sequence. At one point Lenny says in voiceover over a close-up of a young worshipper with Down syndrome: "God does not leave anyone behind." The fact that this occurs within a dream sequence does not alter the scene's exemplary status as instance of Sorrentino's use of non-normative identities as a spectacular way to underline the series' apparent championing of the meek and powerless, the disenfranchised and disabled, while simultaneously complicating its exploitation of women's bodies and faces—all in the service of adding nuance to our understanding of the principal masculine characters.[33]

Venetian Dreams

The Young Pope opens in bravura style, with one dream nested within another. The first-time viewer may be fooled into thinking that the second dream is waking reality, however, until s/he sees the dreamer awaken for a second time. The dreamer is Lenny Belardo, newly elected pope, the first American, and the youngest on record. The first dream is as audacious as it is mysterious, with a newborn baby crawling atop a mountain of other, apparently sleeping, newborn babies of all races and colors. Then Lenny himself appears, in white papal dress, crawling out from beneath the huge pile of digitally rendered infants, outside the Basilica in Venice's Piazza San Marco, looking across at the Palazzo Correr (figure 8.12). This brief scene thus establishes a visual link with Ballinger's Venetian dream scene in *Youth*, cementing in Sorrentino's canon the status of Italy's most beautiful city as a topos—the locus or focus—of the series' themes of birth, love, loss, death, and redemption, all channelled through the protagonist's personal trajectory as an American orphan who grows up to become the leader of the Catholic Church and God's representative on earth.

This secondary dream ends with a straight cut to an extreme close-up on Lenny's eye, looking upward: an eyeline match and close-up on the crucifix on the wall above his bed. Christ's head and shoulders appear upside down, as if from Lenny's point of view. A cut to a medium shot of the whole sculpture upside-down from a steep low angle confirms this, since in the next centrally framed shot of Lenny sitting up in bed, the sculpture is right side up (figure 8.13). As he moves about the papal apartment, washing and dressing, his bedside radio/alarm clock shifts statickly from classical to atmospheric electronic music—Chris Johnston's "Labradford," which becomes something of a leitmotif for Lenny's character across the series. (As we learn in episode 2, in his first conversation with Sofia, the Vatican marketing chief, if he's not a fan, then he is at least knowledgeable about EDM. This affinity between Lenny and a specific contemporary musical genre also at least partially justifies the choice of LMFAO's "Sexy and I Know It" over the montage, discussed above, of the new pope dressing for his first address to the cardinals. The ultimate justification, however, is the overtly ironic clash between/among who Lenny is as pope, his physical appearance, as portrayed by Law, and the song's lyrical content.)

FIGURE 8.12 *The Young Pope*

FIGURE 8.13 *The Young Pope*

The primary dream then enters into its main phase, its oneiric seams beginning to show. As Lenny moves through the papal palace to begin his address to the crowd gathered in St. Peter's Square, the action shifts into slow motion, lending not gravitas so much as a dreamlike surreality to the scene. An initial medium shot of pope and cardinals proceeding along a corridor lined with Swiss guardsmen recalls the la corrente sequence in *Il Divo* (and its ultimate antecedent in Tarantino's *Reservoir Dogs*), right down to the edit from side-on shot to shallow-depth frontal framing (figure 8.14). As he enters the large chamber giving onto the square, the camera assumes Lenny's optical point of view, weaving around the cardinals and nuns, assembled in the room like chess pieces on a board. As in *Il Divo* and *The Consequences of Love*, the protagonist walks into his own point of view and sits down. There is an audacious cut to a brief flashback to Lenny's young mother, posed nearly naked on an Edenic riverbank in Colorado (figure 8.15).[34] A cut to a young boy in close-up, looking on adoringly: Lenny aged seven, not yet realizing that he will shortly be cast out of this paradise forever. Including a flashback within a dream sequence is not unheard of,[35] but this is an unusual and spectacular instance. (This initial flashback looks ahead, proleptically, to Sister Mary's first speech to Lenny, after her arrival at the Vatican. She reminds him that as pope he must now put aside his painful personal memories in order to lead the church: "The time has come for you to let your sorrows fade. To become irrelevant, distant, memories . . . overpowered by the terrible responsibility that God has given you. From now on you are no longer Lenny Belardo, the fatherless, motherless boy. From now on you are Pope Pius XIII, Father and Mother of the entire Catholic Church." In what is undoubtedly an ironic commentary upon this theological paradox, in more than one episode we see the pope contemplating Jusepe de Ribera's 1631 portrait of Magdalena Ventura, a woman who famously grew a long black beard, and who is portrayed with her husband, her breast bared to suckle her infant son. Depending on the historical viewpoint, she is either a monster or an innovator in gender identity.) At this point, Lenny's dream begins

FIGURE 8.14 *The Young Pope*

to reveal itself as such, even as it calls to mind the papal fashion show sequence in Fellini's *Roma* (1972) (although the ranks of red-clad cardinals in Fellini's film are reduced to empty robes parading on the catwalk). In *The Young Pope*, a made-for-television series, the opening dream sequence is revealed as such once its cinematic intertexts begin to coalesce; the register for a film-dream's authenticity is not waking reality, after all, but its resemblance to filmic dream sequences past. For many of us, arguably, the same is true for waking reality. Even Lenny's transition from inside to outside, to the balcony, is rendered in a cinematically self-conscious way, recalling numerous Spike Lee films in the technique of having the actor in close-up ride on the dolly with the camera as it tracks backward, through the depth of the space. Later, midway through his address, to signal a drastic change in tone, Bigazzi even uses a fast zoom in to a close-up on Lenny, straight out of a 1970s Italian film such as Wertmüller's *The Seduction of Mimi*.[36]

Lenny emerges onto the balcony looking over an obviously digitally enhanced St. Peter's Square; indeed, the address as a whole is clearly not filmed on location.[37] Like Fellini in *La Dolce Vita*, Sorrentino opts for a fabricated St. Peter's, the digital irrealism of the scene retrospectively justified when its oneiric status is revealed. (Like *Youth* before it, *The Young Pope* is filmed with the Red Epic Dragon digital camera. As a made-for-streaming television series, it is only ever a digital object.) This is brought home when Lenny performs the first miracle of the series, when he appears to make the rain clouds disperse and the sun appear: the weather itself is the result of judicious editing, fake rain falling on extras, digitally darkened skies, and clouds cut in from some other location. The speech Lenny finally delivers also comes to resonate in all its ironies when it is compared retroactively to his actual first address, in episode 2. Although the two speeches share much of the same wording—they both begin "What have we forgotten?"—they could not be more different in tone and impact. This difference begins with the meaning of the first person plural in the pope's question: in the dream speech the *we* refers first of all to the church; Lenny is

FIGURE 8.15 *The Young Pope*

invoking its historical failure to address the humanity of its all-too-human followers. In the real speech, by contrast, Lenny's *we* refers to everyone—humankind, or at least the Catholic portion—who has collectively forgotten God. The first, illusory speech is the touchy-feely new age address that everyone hopes the new pope will deliver. The second is the new pope's manifesto for a church founded anew on distance, obedience, and absence. Both are ultimately about love but in diametrically opposed senses. This second, albeit primary, dream ends the same way as the other, with a close-up on the inverted crucifix above Lenny's bed. A cut to a close-up on Lenny muttering a response to Voiello's words in his dream, "You are done with God": "I just got started with God."

Saint Lenny

In many ways, the entire series is structured around a series of dreams—or a single, recurrent dream—of Lenny's, of being in Venice with his parents. Evidently this is an experience that he never actually had. The Venice dreams are visually distinct from the flashbacks to his parents in Colorado or upstate New York, which, unlike his dreams, are not always attributable to Lenny alone. The precredit sequence in episode 5, for instance, opens with Lenny's Venetian dream of his parents leaving in the middle of the night on a 1970s-era vaporetto, as he stands on the quayside, watching them sail off (the stop is San Vio, near the Accademia bridge). In the final travelling shot, taken from the vaporetto as it moves away from the stationary Lenny, Bigazzi uses obvious, large, and very bright halogen spotlights on the quayside, guaranteeing that the pope's white-clad figure remains visible in the depths of the murky Venetian night. There is a straight cut to a shirtless Lenny in medium shot, sitting sideways on his bed, just awoken from this dream. The dark oval frame with the crucifixion (from episode 1) hangs above his head. Lenny lies back; cut to a rear-angle medium close-up as he completes this action, assuming the pose of the crucified Christ: the savior as New Man. This recalls the comparable scene in *The Consequences of Love* in which Sorrentino and Bigazzi approximate visually the effects of heroin on the protagonist. This shot is also echoed in episode 8, when a nearly naked Cardinal Gutierrez wakes up in his New York hotel room, a high angle shot from above the bed showing him with Christ-like arms outstretched. These scenes in which the protagonist is equated, on the iconographic level, ironically or not, with the crucified Christ justify my invocation here of Linda Williams's reading of the prevalence of melodrama in contemporary popular culture, especially in terms of the representation of the male hero as a passive and therefore feminized suffering victim.[38] Lenny gazes into the camera upside down; there is a cut to an upside down shot (as if from his POV) of the nocturnal Venetian scene from a moment before, from the back of the vaporetto on the Canal Grande. The inverted, expressionistic perspective calls to mind the equivalent shot of the upside-down crucifix in episode 1, subliminally cementing the connotations of sacrifice and (recoverable) loss that Lenny comes to associate, as it were unconsciously, with Venice.[39]

In a subsequent scene (episode 5), Lenny is meditating in the Vatican gardens when he is approached by Esther, who has been blackmailed by Cardinal Voiello into seducing him so they can acquire incriminating photos as ammunition for the cardinal's plan to unseat the pope before he ruins the church. She succeeds in having Lenny touch her bared breast as she recites the Hail Mary, while Voiello and his secretary Amatucci (Gianluca Guidi) take pictures with a telephoto lens. "Bingo" says Amatucci, when they get the money shot, as Bigazzi redoubles the already self-reflexively scopophilic array of Voiello-Amatucci spying on Lenny-Esther by capturing both parties within the same long shot. Then Lenny, in a shot-reverse shot sequence with Esther, delivers the following speech, which may be the key to understanding his trajectory across the series, especially in the closing episodes, when he moves toward a more conciliatory position of universal and unconditional love:

> I love God because it's so painful to love human beings. I love a God that never leaves me or that always leaves me. God, the absence of God, always reassuring and definitive. I'm a priest. I've renounced my fellow man, my fellow woman, because I don't want to suffer. Because I'm incapable of withstanding the heartbreak of love. Because I'm unhappy, like all priests. It would be wonderful to love you the way you want to be loved. But I'm not a man. I'm a coward. Like all priests.

Unbeknownst to Lenny, his speech convinces Voiello to abandon his plan to discredit the new pope and have him removed as pontiff. Later in the same episode Voiello speaks the very same words to Sister Mary, in what at first appears to be his attempt to seduce the woman he plainly loves. When she remarks that his words are both "beautiful" and "true," he reveals that they are not his, but the pope's. Voiello does this, he goes on to explain, because he has had a change of heart, a kind of conversion. As he hands Sister Mary the USB key containing the incriminating evidence he collected in order to "destroy" Lenny, he tells her that she was right all along: "Your pope really is a saint."

The next scene opens with an unusual shot straight down the length of the gleaming brass front of a hotel reception desk, the clerk and the front door blurry in the depth of the frame. The camera rack-focuses and Lenny and Dussolier come into view as they enter the hotel lobby, in search of cigarettes (they have gone on the lam from the Vatican, an adventure intercut with a long and unspecifically attributed flashback to the two of them as young boys running away, for a day, from the orphanage). The clerk leaves, and there is a cut to a long shot on the two men, perpendicular to the front desk. High heels clicking on the parquet cause them to look up toward the camera; cut to a medium close-up as they stare, a moment reminiscent of the spa hotel pool scene in *Youth* in which Ballinger and Boyle gape openly at a stark naked Miss Universe. Cut to reverse-angle long shot on Elena (Madalina Bellariu Ion), the woman with the high heels: young, beautiful, in a tight black dress, glancing at them as she crosses the lobby bar, the camera tracking to follow. She invites them to join her at her table. Throughout this initial sequence, Bigazzi's camera is constantly moving, prowling, drifting. Once in the bar the style settles into the shot-reverse shot pattern still characteristic of so much television today, predicated as the medium is upon dialogue-heavy scenes, with more exposition and much less action than in a typical commercial genre film. Elena, a high-end prostitute, in a distinct Eastern European accent, remarks: "did you know I have clients who insist I am proof of the existence of God?" "Interesting theory," remarks Lenny, exchanging glances with Dussolier. "But they are wrong," she continues. "They see me, because they can't see far. Extreme close-up on Lenny's face, as he listens, suddenly interested. "Can you see far?" he asks. "Yes," she replies. "And I have proof of the existence of God." "Show me, I implore you," he begs. She hesitates a moment, then leans toward him, raising her smartphone camera. Cut to the reverse angle on Lenny, her phone in the foreground, his face repeated therein (figure 8.16). She takes the photo, enlarging the area showing his eyes. As the phone drops out of the frame Lenny's real face comes into focus. "Your eyes," she says, consulting her phone's screen. "They are proof of the existence of God." After an uncomfortable pause, the two men get up and leave. Cut to an extreme close-up on Elena's hands holding the phone, whose screen repeats Lenny's eyes in close-up. Why his eyes? As Sister Mary remarks enigmatically to Voiello in episode 2, when he questions Lenny's decision to not show himself in public, "To reveal his eyes, right now, may be too much . . . for the world." Toward the end of the same episode, in a conversation with Lenny, she clarifies her meaning: "I see Christ's reflection in you." As Lenny remarks to Voiello at their first meeting in episode 1: unlike the past, which "is an enormous place, with all sorts of things inside . . . the present is merely a narrow opening, with room for only one pair of eyes. Mine."[40]

Lenny's status as saint develops in indirect relation with his deliberate sowing of doubt around his own faith. In episode 3, he confides self-reflexively to Don Tomasso: "I am the Lord Omnipotent. Lenny, you have illumined yourself. Fuck!" An extreme close-up on his mouth as the scene ends. Two scenes later, however, Lenny is down in his knees in his chambers feverishly apologizing to God for all the things he said in order to fool Don Tomasso into believing in his apostasy. Lenny's sainthood, on the one hand, and his arrogation to himself of God-like power and

FIGURE 8.16 *The Young Pope*

authority—in short, his extraordinary arrogance—on the other, gradually diverge across the series; the latter proves to be a manifestation of his long-term plan to revolutionize the church, driving the plot forward. The former, however—his status as saint—comes to define him in spite of himself, imparting a dimension of affective—or sentimental—seriousness, considerably leavening the ironic tone that defines the early episodes.

The Young Pope *as Middle-Brow Melodrama*

In *The Young Pope* series, as in *The Great Beauty*, memory, even more than dream, is foregrounded as the primary metaphysical framework, whether in the form of the burden of an individual's past or the pressure of history upon the present. The former—subjective memory tied to individual character—manifests in these later works in the form of the flashback in which the highly conventional and artificial cinematic rendering of memory has been naturalized. The flashbacks in the television series function differently than those in *The Great Beauty*, however. The flashbacks to the orphanage in upstate New York are generally tethered either to Lenny's, Sister Mary's, or Dussolier's point of view, casting an often ironic contrapuntal light on the present-tense action. (The flashbacks/dream sequences set in Venice and featuring his parents as young hippies belong to Lenny alone.) This is in part the result of long-form narrative expediency, but it is worth noting that these scenes culminate in a treatment of memory—in general and specifically in terms of the protagonist—that, if not more sophisticated or complex than the films, from the perspective of gender politics appears to be more progressive.

In one telling example, the conclusion of the ninth and penultimate episode of *The Young Pope* represents a thematic and structural inversion of the conclusion of *The Great Beauty*: instead of the dead woman reappearing as her younger self to save the aging and undeserving protagonist, here the pope speaks in voiceover the words of his teenage self to his now middle-aged former beloved, the nameless woman who nevertheless receives the revelation of his love as a gift in the present. But this love letter is read over a montage (with Flume's "Never Be Like You" playing over top) of several other characters from the preceding episodes, each of whom somehow shares in this entirely public confession of love. (This is reminiscent of what has become a stock musical sequence in contemporary American smart film and television, in which several disparate characters, separate in space, are united in a montage by a piece of music played over top.[41] The famous montage in P. T. Anderson's *Magnolia* (1999), in which all the major characters sing the same song while in separate locations, is the self-reflexive ne plus ultra. Sorrentino's employment of a wide variety of musical styles as a principal source of meaning in his films guarantees the frequency of this technique.) Here the voiceover begins with Esther, the Swiss Guardsman's wife, in frame, in what appears to be an answer to the preceding shot of Lenny on the beach near her house in Ostia; his eyeline suggests that he is looking at her, whereas by the time she finds his gift (a photo portrait) he is already flying away in the papal helicopter, like the archangel after the annunciation. This montage sequence clarifies Lenny's character's motivation, at least at this point in the story: having never gotten over the loss of his parents—their abandoning of him at the orphanage—he bears this wound with him ever after, the pain never lessening despite the passing years. In episode 5, in a dinner conversation with Sister Mary, Lenny dismisses the "miracle [he] supposedly performed," emphasizing the "only miracle [he] need[s]. The miracle that doesn't happen and never will: seeing my parents again." Moreover, this loss seems to have rendered him incapable of reciprocating the love of another person, in the individual romantic-erotic sense of love so central to occidental and now global popular culture. That this incapacity is commensurate with his priestly vows of celibacy doesn't diminish the force of this loss for his identity as a heterosexual man. His move into the priesthood can however be read as an escape from this kind of love and a turn toward another, safer, form of love, predicated, ironically, on the absence of God: "reassuring and definitive." Absence, withdrawal, sacrifice, suffering: the story of Lenny's life, a love story. The series' tenth and final episode opens with a radio announcer in voiceover claiming that, "the world has stopped turning. To talk about love." The publication of Lenny's never-posted letters in a fictional *New Yorker* issue has changed the global conversation—especially in the mass and social media outlets—away from "war and terrorism" and evil, toward goodness, unity, and love. As they say in Italian: *magari.*

It is no coincidence that episode 9's voiceover-montage sequence (Lenny's confession to his once-upon-a-time love) is preceded in the same episode by two deathbed scenes, one nested within the other. In the first Cardinal Spencer (James Cromwell) succumbs to cancer, ironically, just as his opportunity to assume the papacy is within sight. In the second scene, another flashback to Lenny's childhood orphanage in upstate New York, the custodian's wife (Ann Carr) lies dying from what also appears to be cancer. (She is first glimpsed in a flashback to his childhood in episode 5; the same one in which we learn how Sister Mary acquired the other half of the Meerschaum pipe that she later uses to try to deceive Lenny into believing that his parents have reappeared.) The two deathbed scenes are ironically juxtaposed as Spencer asks

Lenny to confirm the miracle cure he performed on the sick woman decades before, as evidence of his saintly status. Lenny grants Spencer's dying wish, recounting the event and offering him the comfort of knowing that his faith in God has not been in vain. That Lenny does not perform the same miracle for his expiring former mentor is an irony muted by the series' wholesale descent, if that's the right word, into a hybrid form of postsecular male melodrama. But this is more a description than a criticism, as the affective intensity of the scene is clearly written into the script, with its highly conventional flashback structure guaranteeing the veracity of the miracle for the viewer as much as the other characters who witness and/or hear of it. Thus, the almost kitschily Christological mise-en-scène—a large crucifix (highlighting the passive, because passionate, suffering victimhood of the woman), a statuette of Mary, anti-naturalist lighting effects, actors staring in wide-eyed wonder—contrasts starkly with the final scene in *The Great Beauty*. Again, this scene inverts the one in the film: the man saves the woman who is not dead but dying. The custodian's wife's mask-like visage in this flashback visually echoes Melanie's rigid, open-mouthed expression in *Youth*. It is not the case, however, that the youthful Lenny's (Patrick Mitchell) miraculous curing of his friend Billy's mother, his saving her from death, manages to redeem all those other men in Sorrentino's films. He enacts this miraculous cure by praying to God, in a one-sided conversation (only his contribution is audible), reminiscent of Bess's (Emily Watson) one-sided colloquies with God in Lars Von Trier's *Breaking the Waves* (1996), another contemporary postsecular film that dares to represent a bona fide miracle on screen. This flashback is unusual in the series in that it is explicitly framed as a story recounted by Lenny to Spencer, although it appears in the classic flashback as an intercut scene of past events that in this case also represent a memory shared by Sister Mary, who is there as witness to the miracle in the flashback even as she is there in the background of the present-tense action as witness to Lenny's comforting of his dying mentor.[42]

By comparison to this scene in *The Young Pope*, there is greater artistic sincerity to the elegiac nostalgia of the final flashback in *The Great Beauty*, just as the lack of closure in the latter and in *Youth* is for many viewers paradoxically more satisfying than the television series' melodramatic finale. In this preclimactic climax, the resurrected woman's beatific expression invites the viewer to exchange a stare for an awestruck gaze—whether of sentimental wonder or cynical disbelief, as the case may be. Such a female character, however, no matter how marginalized by age, illness, or gender, is still recoverable, part of the closed masculinist economy of *The Young Pope*'s narrative. She remains in the end a fictional construct, a narrative function. The series' authentically disabled bodies, by contrast, represent identities not susceptible to such melodramatic recuperation, the actors' extradiegetic authenticity translating, paradoxically, but also frustratingly, into a spectacular image of radical unknowability.

Death in Venice

Episode 7 revisits Lenny's dream from the opening of the first episode, with the mountain of newborn babies heaped in front of the Basilica in the Piazza San Marco

FIGURE 8.17 *The Young Pope*

in Venice. The reprised dream scene opens immediately after Lenny reveals to Sister Mary what she already knows: that (so he believes) his long-lost parents have resurfaced because he has received anonymously in the mail a package containing, amongst other things, the stem portion of his father's Meerschaum pipe whose bowl he has been carrying around in his pocket ever since his parents abandoned him at the orphanage forty years before. The dream opens with a long shot on the pile of babies in the nocturnal piazza, from beneath which Lenny's young mother emerges, striding purposefully toward the camera. A cut to a medium profile shot as she joins her young husband in the middle of the square. They progress together, in a scene structurally identical to Ballinger's Venetian dream in *Youth*, in which he encounters Miss Universe in the middle of a flooded nocturnal Piazza San Marco. There is a cut to a point-of-view shot of Lenny in the distance as he moves toward the camera/his parents, arms outstretched (figure 8.17). They walk into their shared point of view as they meet and embrace Lenny, followed by a medium close-up on his face as he weeps with happiness. The frequent flashbacks to his parents, whether in an idyllic rural Colorado or a dreamlike nocturnal Venice, make clear Lenny's obsession with their loss and his desire to see them again. This becomes an all-consuming preoccupation to the point where in episode 7 Cardinal Dussolier asks him "When are you gonna grow up?" "Never," he replies. "A priest never grows up because he can never become a father. He'll always be a son." Ironically, in the series' final episode, Lenny tells Cardinal Guttierez that Sister Mary has "completed her mission" because "the child pope has become a man," and therefore he no longer requires a "motherly presence."

The Young Pope ends as it began, with the pope addressing a huge and adoring crowd, the first episode's oneiric speech in St. Peter's Square in Rome bookended by an actual address to the faithful outside the Basilica in Venice's Piazza San Marco in the final episode. In this concluding scene it becomes clear that his trajectory as pope across ten episodes has been that of the fiery meteorite seen during the credit sequence (with Devlin's instrumental version of "All Along the Watchtower" over top). Thanks to the magic of digital visual effects, the meteorite streaks across the sky, or rather across the skies of a series of famous medieval, Renaissance, baroque, and nineteenth-century paintings, casting an uncanny light, leaving disruption and destruction in its wake,[43] setting alight whatever it touches in its path toward its own inevitable, fiery demise.[44] As if to soften this impression as much as possible, however, the tenth and final episode opens with the pope gazing out of his windows in the Vatican over a magically nocturnal St. Peter's Square, snow falling on a giant Christmas tree. It is midwinter, for Catholic Christians the season of death and incipient rebirth.

The series' final set piece centers on Lenny's second and last pastoral trip, to meet what appears to be his own death in Venice. Venice, as noted, figures throughout the series—as it already did for Ballinger in *Youth*—as the ideal physical backdrop for Lenny's interior life, his quest to be reunited with his parents, which in some uncanny sense is equivalent to his quest to confirm his radically negative relation to God, a relation for which the word *belief* does not do justice. As he remarks to Guttierez in episode 10, "Those who believe in God don't believe in anything." In episode 9, at the end of their colloquy on abortion, Spencer advises Lenny on how he can revivify the church by first exorcising his parents' ghosts: "Go to Venice, and bury two empty coffins." And finally, Don Tomasso (in their last conversation, in episode 10) asks: "And now, where is God?" Lenny: "In Venice." In a way that remains meaningfully obscure, his search for God—in which his faith is sorely tested—and his search for his parents, become the same search, converging in Venice. During Lenny's address in San Marco, the earlier theme of vision returns, focalized (so to speak) in the pope's eyes, captured on the sex worker's smartphone screen in the middle of a sleepless Roman night, as "proof of the existence of God," as Lenny wields the cheap toy telescope ("you can see for more than one hundred metres!"), bought for him by Cardinal Guttierez at the highway Autogrill. He surveys the crowd as if in one last attempt to find his parents—not in the sense of getting them back but to simply see them, from a distance, across the barrier of an absence indistinguishable from death.

Just as the image of the crucifix is juxtaposed across the series with that of the Virgin Mary, in the final, melodramatic, moments it would seem that Lenny, or rather Sorrentino, has achieved a resolution of the feminine principles of forgiveness, tolerance, unconditional love, and sacrificial suffering, with the pope's earlier identification with a masculine God, compounded of vengeful wrath and an inscrutable absence. This hybrid combination resolves or reconciles the paradoxical contradictions of his identity, announced in episode 1, the first of several scenes in which the pope is asked: "Who *are* you, Lenny?" to which he responds, "I am a contradiction. Like God. One in three and three in one. Like Mary, virgin and mother. Like man, good and evil." As the series' conclusion makes clear, however, his theological paradox conceals an epistemological one, as Lenny's dying (?) vision of Christ the Redeemer in the clouds over Venice suggests. Like an optical rebus—is it Jesus or just an oddly shaped cloud? Is it a man's pipe or merely a painting of a pipe?—this digitally enabled cutaway reinscribes at the end the question with which this chapter began, derived from the series' transmediation of Magritte's brain-teasing painting of the pipe-that-is-not-a-pipe. Put into the context of the series as a whole, narratively but also stylistically, formally, this shot stands apart as a rare moment of quasi-self-reflexivity, almost but not quite revealing the means of its own digitally enhanced production. The final effect, however, is that Lenny's journey of self-discovery, his acceptance of his responsibilities, and his decision to give in to love and to reveal himself to the world rather than remain withdrawn, invisible, absent—the final effect is to underline the series' ultimately ambivalent, neohumanist approach to televisual storytelling. Sorrentino's film and television work to date has navigated a fine balance between story and style, content and form—between *impegno* as theme and *impegno* as discourse or style. Sorrentino is unafraid to show that the pipe, or in this case, the pope, is only a representation, an image that, nevertheless, moves the viewer to think, to act, and to feel.

The next and final chapter explores Sorrentino's cinematic critique of early 2000s Italy as refracted through the latter years of Silvio Berlusconi's career, before the full impact of online streaming and television's new golden age would make possible such a sophisticated and politically engaged approach to televisual programming.

Coda

Toward a Post-Political Film: Loro *and the Mediatic Elegiac*

> Truth is a result of our tone of voice and the conviction with which we speak.
> —Silvio Berlusconi, *Loro*

Proviso

This final chapter is the fruit of a close analysis of the international cut of *Loro*, Sorrentino's 2018 biopic of four-time Italian Prime Minister Silvio Berlusconi, released as a single film after its initial Italian theatrical release as a diptych, *Loro 1* and *Loro 2*. While it appears that the two versions of the film do present significantly different manifestations of the same general narrative, at the time of writing I was unable to take account of the original two-part version.[1] In what follows, then, I present a reading of the international release in order to show how the film either elaborates, amplifies, changes, or avoids the themes and formal structures I have traced throughout this book.[2] It should be recalled that, since *Loro*'s initially very limited release in every platform (theatrical, online, DVD/Bluray, or other), Sorrentino has gone on to produce the sequel (if that's the right word) to *The Young Pope* (2016), the Canal+/Sky/HBO television series *The New Pope* (2019), starring Jude Law and John Malkovich. If nothing else, this is evidence of Sorrentino's ongoing productivity and the relative variety of the kind of work he and his team continue to pursue in more than one medium for a transnational audience.

The Mediatic Elegiac

I offer the foregoing proviso in order to put the latest feature film into perspective within Sorrentino's evolving body of work. More than Silvio Berlusconi (Toni Servillo) himself, *Loro*'s first third is concerned with Sergio Morra's (Ricardo Scamarcio) plot to ingratiate himself with his idol by spending his savings to rent a villa in Sardinia overlooking the prime minister's, and stocking it with a bevy of young, attractive, and scantily clad women. This dimension of *Loro*'s story, alongside the film's treatment of Berlusconi's legacy in Italian society, has been dealt with at length by critics and reviewers. The film's flagrant eat-your-cake-and-have-it-too approach to critiquing Berlusconi's notorious womanizing (and other bad behaviors) makes it appear to be Sorrentino's most egregiously misogynist work, although this aspect of the film is interestingly complicated when it is connected to a broader critique of the kind of media culture fostered by the long-term impact of Berlusconi's transformation of television programming and broadcasting regulations in Italy since the 1980s. The power of *Loro*'s critique of this aspect of his career—and the film's claim to a kind of postmodern *impegno*—comes precisely from its being bound up inextricably with the very style of the film itself.[3] This is also why it is problematic for so many viewers. My analysis therefore foregrounds the film's final third, when the narrative makes a palpable shift toward the kind of elegiac tone or affect I have been tracking through Sorrentino's work to date—becoming in *Loro* what I call (adapting Andrea Minuz) the mediatic elegiac.[4]

As noted in chapter 5, one of this book's subsidiary goals is to trace Sorrentino's engagement with realism as it evolves from the satirical postrealism Millicent Marcus identifies to an arguably even more sophisticated post-postrealism whose irony and immersive qualities alike are increasingly tempered by melancholy, nostalgia, and other (gender-specific) affective modes. The latter is at least partly the result of Sorrentino's abiding fascination with powerful men of all stripes. As a fictionalized account of a few years (2006–2010) in Berlusconi's recent career, *Loro* offers what Chiara Gabardi (in reference to the first instalment of the diptych) calls "a complex and sophisticated analysis of what certain men are willing to do to join the upper echelons of power"[5]—a manifestation of power diagnosed by Minuz as "il potere mediatico": mediatic power.[6] Mediatic power is addressed in all its contradictions right from the film's opening epigraph, from Giorgio Manganelli's preface to his book on Pinocchio: "everything is documented, everything is arbitrary."[7] If, as suggested in chapter 4, a parallel with Collodi's famous story is detectable in *Il Divo*'s spectral invocation of Moro as Andreotti's moral conscience, an externalized inner voice, haunting him long after the latter's murder, there is an even more ironic parallel in *Loro*'s portrait of Berlusconi as a kind of postmodern Pinocchio, getting away repeatedly with brazen lies—whether to his long-suffering wife or in the form of political promises to potential voters. Where *Il Divo* depicted a canny politician whose subtle manipulation of the truth kept him in power and out of prison for decades, *Loro*'s Berlusconi is a more contemporary public figure, likely more familiar to non-Italian audiences, whose manipulations of the truth anticipate and set the pattern for the current so-called post-truth era. *Loro* thus presents a revised version of impegno as style embodied in *Il Divo*, for instance. In one early scene in particular, Berlusconi is confronted by his grandson's observation that his *nonno* has just stepped in some "*cacca*," a charge that he immediately and categorically denies. Berlusconi makes clear to his grandson that it doesn't matter if one has in fact stepped in shit; what matters is how convincing you are when you offer a blatantly false version of things: "truth is a result of our tone of voice and the conviction with which we speak," he avers. The scene, set in 2006, is clearly intended to resonate with contemporary post-2017 audiences, and it is one of the moments in the film that speaks directly to a wider non-Italian viewership confronted on a daily basis by officially sanctioned misinformation, conspiracy theories, and so-called fake news.

The Sorrentinian Subject Revisited

Loro represents the apogee, even the apotheosis, of the Sorrentinian subject in the figure of Silvio Berlusconi. In Toni Servillo's portrayal of Italy's former prime minister the viewer is confronted with a masculine protagonist whose final elegiac moments will only inspire in a small percentage of viewers, Italian or otherwise, a feeling of empathy, let alone sympathy, or any other ethically positive emotional response. And yet, as in earlier films, especially *The Family Friend* and *Il Divo*, the viewer is compelled to align herself, if not experience a feeling of allegiance, with Berlusconi. This contradictory effect is achieved through specific formal strategies that are by now recognizable as the stylistic tropes and tics that together comprise the Sorrentinian style. This can be called a postcinematic style insofar as it is also post-televisual—in other words, a style recognizable across various media platforms, where the main visual difference these days between cinema and television is the size of the screen. Narratively speaking, of course, the two media forms can differ more significantly, with prestige television in the era of streaming defined by an emphasis on storytelling while cinema as such remains the bastion of the spectacular image. These are only general distinctions, of course. His masterful use of music to one side, Sorrentino's visual style is comprised of certain signature camera movements and lighting effects, attributable to Luca Bigazzi, combined with the pacing and the editing patterns familiar from the earlier films (*Loro* is edited by Cristiano Travaglioli, who edited all of Sorrentino's film and TV work since 2008's *Il Divo*[8]), as well as the degree of control over mise-en-scène—including the carefully-lit bodies of principals and extras alike—that we have come to expect from the director since teaming up with Bigazzi. *Loro* may present the greatest challenge to the viewer, however, insofar as Berlusconi, like Andreotti a known public figure in Italy, is even better known in the world at large and is consequently even more reviled. Thus when in the later scenes the film leans toward a seemingly sympathetic portrayal, it is necessary to balance the strangely redemptive conclusion with the bulk of the preceding scenes in which Berlusconi's personal reprehensibility is implicitly and explicitly compared to the state of contemporary Italian society as refracted through the lens of the film's style-based critique of post-Berlusconi media culture.[9]

Loro appears to confirm what Sorrentino's harshest critics have asserted since *The Consequences of Love* and *The Family Friend*: that despite their critique of specific visual-ideological structures, the films end up for the most part upholding a retrograde point of view on gender difference and the representation of women. The latter is the—perhaps inevitable—thematic complement to the films' seemingly unironic elegiac meditation upon what it means to be, in this case, an elderly man in twenty-first-century Europe, albeit one who is in denial about certain basic realities of aging even for men of power. *Loro* therefore continues, extends, and complicates—sometimes frustratingly—the main themes and issues from previous films. Among these, the most important for this chapter are the nature and function of a meaningfully political film, where its ethical-political *impegno* is predicated upon, indeed manifested in, an intensified, or in this case spectacularized, transnational style. (Although, by comparison, Bigazzi's and Travaglioli's style in *Loro* is relatively restrained, with far less camera movement overall; the signature technique of cutting one tracking shot into another replaced by a pastiche of other, more overtly self-reflexive techniques, such as slow motion, frontal tableau compositions, etc.) Of all of Sorrentino's films, as a biopic of a major late-twentieth-century Italian politician, *Loro* is the only one other than *Il Divo* to have an explicitly political subject. For reasons to be explored below, however, in comparison to *Il Divo*, *Loro* pushes the viewer into a tighter ethical corner in its final third precisely because of its striking stylistic differences from the Andreotti biopic. In the end, *Loro*'s critical perspective on Berlusconi is complicated by the tonal shift to a visually striking but melancholic meditation on the 2009 L'Aquila earthquake, around which the film's third act is structured. (This shift, it should be noted, is subtly but powerfully abetted by the nonironic use of extradiegetic music; the net effect is at once somber and spectacular.) The other overtly political aspect of the film, it need hardly be pointed out, involves Sorrentino's return to the kinds of images of women that he favored in previous films, especially *The Great Beauty*'s now-famous party sequences. The film thus folds together two very different kinds of politics, one in the form of the Berlusconi biopic and the other in terms of its engagement with the politics of gender and gendered identities and of the representation of women.

The Image of Woman: The Gendered Gaze, Part 2

One of the problems with condemning *Loro* too quickly for its egregious objectification of women's bodies in the #MeToo era is that this dimension of the film's story, as retrograde as it might appear, is intimately bound up with the style-based critique of Berlusconi on offer. Many critics complain that the main character isn't seen (in the original release of *Loro 1*) until well into the film.[10] In the international release version under discussion here, Berlusconi first appears at precisely the forty-minute mark, wearing the costume of an Arabian odalisque out of Disney's *Aladdin* (figure 9.1). As will be argued below, this delay or withholding of the revelation of the real protagonist is necessary insofar as the film's first act serves the purpose of establishing the formal-stylistic parameters of its self-reflexive critique of the Italy produced in the image of the Berlusconian mediascape. It is also much remarked that in the film's opening scene, on board his boat off the coast of Puglia, we are introduced to Sergio Morra as be bribes a local Democratic party member by letting him have sex with a woman, Candida (Carolina Binda), who is in effect a prostitute. Revealed for what he really is, a pimp, Sergio later avails himself of his own wares by taking Candida from behind in the boat's galley (figure 9.2). In a point-of-view (POV) shot we see a close-up of Candida's naked buttocks, Sergio's hands on either side as he thrusts. The medium shot from side-on echoes a scene in Mary Harron's *American Psycho* (1999), where Patrick Bateman (Christian Bale), taking two women from behind at once, preens for the video camera he has set up to record his exploits. With the incongruous sound of a crowd cheering in the background,[11] Sergio likewise postures for the film camera, breaking the fourth wall in a brief anticipation of the subsequent Sardinian poolside party scene.[12] In the POV shot Sergio moves a hand and reveals, smiling up at him/the camera/the viewer, the face of Berlusconi, tattooed at the base of Candida's spine (figure 9.3). (This is the first of two occasions in which Sergio has sex with Berlusconi by proxy or at one remove; the second takes place when Kira [Kasia Smutniak] straddles him as they lie together on her outdoor bed in Rome, while she talks to Berlusconi ["Lui"] on the phone. Their tryst comes to an abrupt halt soon after Sergio's father calls him.) But to say that Candida's tattoo shows Berlusconi's face is only true within the film's fictional universe: it is in fact an accurate rendering of Servillo as Berlusconi, tacitly emphasizing that this is the film's treatment of the politician's life, and that this scene, like the film itself, is a (more or less) complete fabrication. "This film stems from its authors' independent and free imagination," reads the opening disclaimer:

> any reference to real people or events is wholly artistic, and makes no claim to represent an objective truth. The authors took inspiration from news stories to create a narrative that brings together non-existent characters and real people in entirely invented contexts to create an original artistic work. No references to people and/or events except those specifically identified as real is intended or should be inferred.

Il Divo, by contrast, opens with its Glossario italiano, a list of definitions and facts that situate the film's events firmly within historical reality, in spite of the liberties

FIGURE 9.1 *Loro* (Paolo Sorrentino, 2018)

FIGURE 9.2 *Loro*

taken with Andreotti's life and character. The glossary notes that the P2 Lodge (la loggia masonica 'Propaganda due') was an anti-communist Masonic secret society founded during the Cold War, whose "objective was to install an authoritarian government" in Italy. Although the Red Brigades always "maintained that they acted independently," the authorities' search in 1978 for the kidnapped Aldo Moro was "perhaps influenced by the P2 lodge." The glossary also notes at one point that Silvio Berlusconi was a member of P2, thereby establishing retroactively a meaningful link between the two films in their respective fictionalized investigations of two of the most famous and notorious figures in modern Italian politics.

It seems fair to say that *Loro*'s Berlusconi tattoo scene is invented; plotwise, however, the scene is Sergio's eureka moment, when he first conceives the idea that getting close to Berlusconi is the key to his success.[13] That this rather nebulous plan first

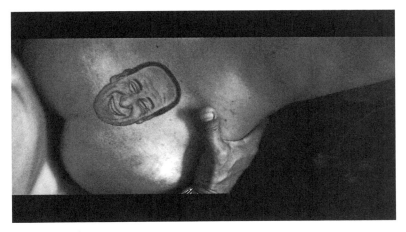

FIGURE 9.3 *Loro*

strikes him as he is having sex with a young, attractive, naked woman in his employ is hardly a coincidence. The bitter irony of this scene, which only becomes apparent toward the end of the film, is that it is Sergio who will be screwed over by Berlusconi. But he is neither the only nor the most unfortunate victim: then, as now, the film's many female characters will be the means for these men to achieve their ends, however ignoble, self-serving, or sordid.

In order to come to grips with the place of women in *Loro* it is necessary to engage with the film's inter- and transmedial dimension, especially as exemplified in the sequences that combine techniques employed in *The Great Beauty*, such as camera work and mise-en-scène, and *Il Divo*: relatively explicit intertextual references to other films and media texts. On the one hand, *Loro* is literally and intensively intermedial, or better transmedial, in that it begins and ends with important scenes featuring television screens broadcasting typical content: in the opening scene, a white lamb wanders into the living room of Berlusconi's villa, encountering a huge television on which the fictional quiz show *Chiedi a Mike* plays soundlessly (figure 9.4).[14] (The same set piece is repeated at the start of the film's second part, with the introduction of Berlusconi dressed in orientalist drag watching the same show from the same spot as the lamb.) Likewise, the film's concluding sequence begins with several different characters in various locations simultaneously watching a live TV broadcast from the ruins of L'Aquila, largely destroyed by an earthquake in 2009. This concluding sequence is the focus of this chapter's final section.

In a different mediatic vein, other critics and commentators have observed that *Loro*'s already notorious party scenes bear a strong resemblance to comparable sequences in such American films as Martin Scorsese's *Wolf of Wall Street* (2013) and Harmony Korine's *Spring Breakers* (2012).[15] More generally, it becomes clearer with each film that Sorrentino's screenplays combine parodic reference to specific film genres or satirical commentary upon some instance of contemporary Italian

FIGURE 9.4 *Loro*

life with a seriously ironic meditation upon much more general ethical questions. Unlike *Il Divo*, whose revelation of Andreotti's interior life comes in the form of a self-reflexive flashback consisting of sepia-toned pseudo-newsreel footage showing the future prime minister courting his future wife, *Loro* resembles more *The Great Beauty* in its single, brief flashback to Berlusconi's wife Veronica (Elena Sofia Ricci) as a young woman cut into a scene right after the midpoint, an interlude in which, presumably, they have sex—the bittersweet preamble to the end of their marriage in the film's third act. The scene begins with a gorgeous symmetrical wide shot of Berlusconi and Veronica framed at opposite ends of the vast expanse of their bedroom's plate glass window. A cut to a medium frontally framed close-up on Berlusconi gazing impassively off-screen gives way to a beautifully lit medium close-up of his naked, fifty-year-old wife reflected in the mirror as she gazes at herself. This fades into the flashback to the twenty-four-year-old Veronica, played by a different actress (Adua del Vesco), centrally framed as she leads the camera into the depth of an empty, beautifully lit city square (figure 9.5). From off-screen Servillo as Berlusconi says "Veronica," whereupon she stops, in medium close-up, turning to face the camera, which she addresses in his place: "Silvio." This shot recalls two scenes in earlier films: the medium close-ups of Elisa on the lighthouse stairs at night in Jep's final flashback in *The Great Beauty* and the nocturnal medium shot of Miss Universe in Ballinger's dream at the beginning of *Youth*, when she struts away from him along the *passerella* in Venice's flooded Piazza San Marco.[16] In *Loro*'s flashback the setting is the Piazza del Duomo in Milan, but the background architecture illuminated by extra-bright halogen lamps is used to the same effect, framing and amplifying the woman's physical appeal. Where visually the scene resembles more the one in *Youth*, tonally or affectively it is closer to *The Great Beauty* flashback. But something happens in *Loro* that is different from either earlier film: here the young Veronica speaks, "Silvio, I've fallen in love with you," addressing the camera directly, as if in

FIGURE 9.5 *Loro*

Berlusconi's place, as he remains heard but unseen in his own memory.[17] The viewer, then, is momentarily optically and aurally aligned with Berlusconi as the remembering subject, an effect that carries over to the next shot of the present-day billionaire, still standing and gazing at his now-older wife (this visual structure harkens back to the Villa Morena party scenes in which, as will be seen below, the viewer is optically aligned with a Berlusconi who has yet to appear in the film). The scene concludes with a complex affective mixture of melancholic regret and erotic longing, setting the scene for the second half in which Berlusconi comes increasingly to view his current career through the lens of elegiac loss. The youthful Veronica's line here also sets up the later scene in which the present-day Veronica tells her husband that she is divorcing him. To his repeated question, "Why did you stay with me all this time if you never thought I had any qualities?" she answers, "Because I was in love. That was your quality. You made me fall in love."

Other than the one flashback, the international release version of *Loro* generally avoids an exploration of Berlusconi's inner life. The film's approach to a critique of his character and his impact on Italian society takes a markedly different form, more overtly self-reflexive than either *The Great Beauty* or even *Il Divo*. It is arguable in fact that *Loro*, of all of Sorrentino's film and television work to date, is the most self-reflexive in terms of its laying bare of the mechanisms of spectatorship, its thematization of the means of its own production, and its delineation of a certain type of spectating subject disturbingly similar to the subject of the narrative, its protagonist, Berlusconi. It is, therefore, the best example in Sorrentino's canon of what I refer to as *impegno* as style. A sequence in the first third, for instance, in which Sergio Morra's character is established, sets the tone in its abrupt deviation from the flirtation with allegory in the film's opening scenes.[18] It begins with a young woman, presumably on television, stepping through a curtain whose colors mimic the Technicolor TV test pattern. "And now girls, it's up to us," she announces. "Youth is fleeting. Let's get busy" (figure 9.6). This is followed by a lengthy montage of smash zooms on the women that will

FIGURE 9.6 *Loro*

FIGURE 9.7 *Loro*

eventually make up Sergio's troupe in the Sardinian villa/honey trap. Each is featured in a different type of commercial advertisement or generic televisual context; several of these shots, impossibly, also feature Sergio, responding in feigned embarrassment, suggesting that this is as much his own fever dream as it is a catalogue of the sirens he will exploit to capture Berlusconi's attention. As in *The Great Beauty*'s flashback scene, but in a far more explicit and humorous manner, the viewer is sutured into the gap between the shots of Sergio looking and those of the women he looks at, occupying the place of a specific type of viewer if only because this sequence is staged as a direct parody of specific televisual set pieces familiar to any Italian of a certain age with a TV. For better or worse, this viewer is focalized in Sergio, an amoral heterosexual thirty-something Italian man whose worldview, and whose ideas about women—including the manner in which these ideas are represented audiovisually onscreen—are largely shaped by the parameters of schlocky Berlusconi-era television programming (figure 9.7).

In the now classic feminist reading, inaugurated by Laura Mulvey and others in the 1970s, "the viewer suspends disbelief in the fictional world of the film, identifies not only with specific characters in the film but more importantly with the film's overall ideology through identification with the film's narrative structure and visual point of view, and puts into play fantasy structures . . . that derive from the viewer's unconscious."[19] In the Italian context this process devolves upon "the *velina* or television showgirl,[20] who is a standard trope" within the *cinepanettone* tradition. As Hipkins (referencing O'Leary) reminds us, the *velina*'s function:

is most often read as debasing to women, as contaminating the genre further through the female actors' origins in the despised medium of television and all its associated particular political problems, and with the women's frequently semi-naked appearance as object of the male gaze. It is worth remembering that for international film audiences, however, this particular vision of women is familiar not so much from Italian television, or the "*cinepanettone*," as from Italy's tradition of art-house cinema, such as the opening scene of

La dolce vita (Fellini, 1960). Such a use of the female body formed, and continues to form, part of the international appeal of Italian cinema, although the growing visual presence of bikini-clad women on Italian television is almost universally deplored.[21]

The quasi-universal critical response heralded by Hipkins is undoubtedly adumbrated in Sorrentino's film, although it can be difficult to recognize. A pattern is established early on in *Loro* of Sergio addressing the camera directly[22]—in the opening scene in his boat with Candida; as he enters the outdoor soirée in Rome (name-checking *La Dolce Vita*); and so on—marking the film as far more self-reflexive than is apparent on a first viewing and setting things up for the big party sequence at the Villa Morena in Sardinia (figure 9.8). It is surprising, therefore, when critics find fault with the party scene's overt self-reflexivity, such as when one of the other male characters addresses the camera directly, breaking the fourth wall to explain the properties of MDMA (otherwise known as ecstasy),[23] while Sergio's progress through the gyrating crowd of blissed out revelers evokes Jordan Belfort in *The Wolf of Wall Street*'s even more debauched party set pieces (figure 9.9). Viewers' surprise at this scene's self-reflexive intermediality is itself surprising if only because it has been anticipated from the beginning when Sergio looks at the camera while taking Candida from behind.

In terms of this intertextual comparison with specific American films, I should note, *Loro* has far more in common with Scorsese's film stylistically than with Harmony Korine's *Spring Breakers*, with which it has also been compared. Stylistically, the latter is an example of indie cinema intensified continuity, which is faster paced, more varied in its editing rhythms, incorporating flashbacks and a more complex use of sound (in the party sequences especially) expressive of a youth-subcultural sensibility. And, as with *The Wolf of Wall Street*, the party scenes are more debauched still. In comparison to these predecessors the scenes of slow-motion, drug-fueled revelry in *Loro* look at once less realistic, more idealized, like many slickly produced

FIGURE 9.8 *Loro*

FIGURE 9.9 *Loro*

hip-hop, soul, or pop music videos, and as a result possibly even more sexist in their representations of women's bodies. I contend that this effect is intentional, which becomes apparent by the film's last third, when Berlusconi is shown walking out on a markedly crass, private bunga bunga dance performance because he has finally been shaken—albeit only temporarily—by intimations of his own mortality and vulnerability.[24] I return to this scene below. For the moment the comparison is telling: the erotic dance and hedonistic party sequences are scenes of staged spectatorship, in which the scantily clad bodies of young women (and some men) are displayed in a spectacular fashion, as if on a stage or on screen for the visual delectation of select viewers—in a sense, one select viewer. In other words, what is happening within the diegetic world of the story is replicated on the level of extradiegetic spectatorship and vice versa: in these moments the filmic and the extrafilmic real world become all but indistinguishable, an effect which I believe Sorrentino hopes the viewer will recognize in order to encourage the opening up of a critical distance between his (or her) ideological position and that of Berlusconi. Ironically, and dangerously, this must happen by virtually putting the viewer into Berlusconi's place—even before he has made his first appearance in the film.

These self-reflexive moments—or entire sequences—in *Loro* connect with the film's critique of Berlusconian Italy through his lasting impact on the nation's television viewing habits.[25] As noted, significant portions of *Loro*'s first half consist of interpolated sequences that transmediate the tone and style of typically crass Berlusconi-era programming: game shows, musical variety shows, advertisements featuring nubile young women in various stages of undress, and so on. Therefore when *Loro* itself replicates these tropes—especially in its egregious exploitation of the bodies of dozens of young attractive extras—it is entirely valid to argue that this is a principle feature of its critique of this very style. The problem is that the film's exploitation of these tropes reaches a point at which the efficacy of the stylistic and cultural critique is all but trumped by the sheer excess of these scenes.[26] The film continues well beyond this point, however, and one begins to suspect that two seemingly contradictory things

FIGURE 9.10 *Loro*

are being accomplished simultaneously: on the one hand, *Loro* perpetuates the visual-ideological structures of what we used to call the male gaze; on the other, the film reinforces its impact—its impegno—by making the sustained male gaze increasingly difficult to bear. The sort of psychoanalytically based reading of visual pleasure inaugurated by Mulvey may be passé, but the extrafilmic ethico-political impact of *Loro's* complex approach is all the more pronounced in the era of #MeToo.

The markedly theatrical spectacle of the ecstasy-fuelled party sequence culminates in a bravura crane shot where the camera tracks in slow motion toward and then over top of the assembled group of partiers, including Kira and Tamara (Euridice Axen). The latter pair stand together, stark naked, on top of the pool's diving board, gazing directly into the camera, as if posing for a soft porn perfume ad (figure 9.10). This is followed by the party's aftermath, consisting of tableau shots of all the partiers in various stages

FIGURE 9.11 *Loro*

of undress, as first Sergio and then Kira remark to no one in particular, "We should all stay like this forever," all the beautiful young people in the villa staring out at the spectacle of the sun setting over the sea, but—as in Fellini—the spectators, and not the sun, are the real spectacle. Early the next morning, while the others sleep off the MDMA, Sergio and Tamara reaffirm their marriage in the middle of the pool, as Stella gyrates alone for the camera, presumably because she is the only one not done in by drugs. There is a cut to a wide shot of the terraced Villa Morena in the early morning sunlight, Stella now a tiny figure as the camera cranes down to reveal a portion of the grounds of Berlusconi's villa in the foreground. An apparently feminine figure in a strange dress and head covering sits in a chair facing the Villa Morena, as if in a sunny Sardinian updating of Plato's Cave, like a solo spectator at a performance meant for her alone, which, in a sense, is exactly what it is (figure 9.11).

He, They, Them: What's in a Pronoun?

The aftermath of the party sequence, culminating in the spatial and narrative transition to the Berlusconi storyline, provides a clue to understanding the film's strange title, whose multivalent significance inheres in the film's tendency to align the viewer with the diegetic Berlusconi's perspective on the action within the film and, by extension, the real-historical Berlusconi's impact upon contemporary Italian society. Initially the focus seems to be straightforward, with Berlusconi, referred to as not merely "lui" but "lui lui" (*him* him), as the other characters' object of desire and fascination. The phrase *lui lui* is first used by Sergio as he and Tamara head to the local Puglia audition for showgirls (*veline*) to appear on Italian television—and, potentially, before Berlusconi himself: "lui lui." It is next heard in the abovementioned scene in which Sergio and Kira first have sex on an outdoor bed in Rome: her cellphone rings as "Lui" displays prominently on the screen. But as the film's second act begins, and the action shifts to Berlusconi's villa, with the man himself first appearing dressed in orientalist drag, the various pronominal attributions implicit in the title begin to unfold, as *Loro*'s exploration of spectatorship intersects with its critique of the ethics of representation, merging in its unique brand of postpolitical cinema.

From "lui" (in the film's first third) there is a subtle shift to "loro" (in the second two-thirds), although the pronominal referent is unstable and clearly shifts again before the end. *Loro*, of course, has more than one meaning, depending on usage and context. *Loro* can indicate the third-person plural *subject* (they), suggesting those who possess and wield power: those who do things; "those who matter."[27] The ambiguity of this pronoun resonates meaningfully across the film. For instance, in a late second-act scene, as they sit astride the carousel on the grounds of Berlusconi's villa, after his rather awkward party, Sergio and Tamara contemplate the failure of their scheme to become members of his inner circle. "Where did we go wrong, Sergio?" she asks. He responds, "When we thought we were smarter than them [*loro*]." Within the story-world, this particular *loro* includes Berlusconi and his ilk, whose rarified circles Sergio erroneously believed he could penetrate by means of the world's second-oldest profession, that of procurer. But in the film's English subtitles this *loro* is necessarily translated as "them," which foregrounds a lexical-semantic ambiguity running through the film. There is a meaningful difference here, in other words, between the conceptual-thematic level of the film's story and the linguistic-grammatical level of the dialogue. Grammatically, of course, *loro* can also indicate the third-person plural *object* (them), which conceptually (if not grammatically) might indicate those who are *subjected to* power: those to whom things are done; those who are insignificant.[28] The latter are exemplified in the film by the displaced inhabitants of L'Aquila, but this subjective-objective pronominal distinction also raises the question as to the audience's position. The typical film-goer would seem to belong to *them*: the collective mass of those who *lack* the power that comes with enormous wealth, the 99 percent in the parlance of a post-2008 political-economic critique. By the same token, *loro* as "they," as the first-person plural *subject*, would seem to *exclude* the typical spectator who is not a member of the 1 percent socio-economic elite; who is not, in short, like Berlusconi. *Loro*, however, can also designate the first-person plural possessive pronoun (their), implying a relationship of acquisition and possession that defines the difference between the two conceptual senses of *loro* just outlined: in the first, the power is theirs, in the second, it is not.[29] On a metafilmic level, however—which I feel it is legitimate to invoke here given *Loro*'s high level of self-awareness as a film—*loro* meaning "they" might also be said to include the film's audience insofar as they belong to the ranks of those who are in the know, or, to be more precise, individual viewers (she/lei and/or he/lui[30]) that have managed to discern the ironic critique structured into the film. On the individual level, this is the spectator that Sergio addresses when in the first third his gaze meets the camera's: the second person addressee (you/lei) that the narrative invites to become part of the general second-person plural (we/noi) who also comprise the third-person *they* from the perspective of the other, alienated viewer who is not in the know, who does not get the joke, as a member of the great unwashed *them*. The latter is the group for whom Sergio speaks in his second-act alienation, and it is no coincidence that he all but disappears from the film at this point. The general popular-journalistic response to the film suggests, in fact, that many viewers would more likely identify with Sergio at this juncture than with the character of Berlusconi, who takes over as protagonist and dominates the narrative until the end. Many reviewers, in other words, were not any smarter than Sergio and his entourage of Berlusconian acolytes, never getting past the film's apparent indulgence in retrograde sexist or misogynist imagery, not realizing that *Loro* is for its duration extending an invitation to the viewer to realize that they (note the pronoun) are smarter than the Berlusconi depicted in the film. *Loro* invites the viewer to become what Jacques Rancière calls an emancipated spectator, but it is up to the spectator as an individual (embodied, gendered, affective, agential) subject to be open to the emancipation that the film offers. Statistics suggest, however, that we are returned instead to what Bayman and Rigoletto—in their account of popular film in the Fascist period—call cinema's "near-mystical powers to induce conformity" in "a mass audience unified in a non-rational public experience."[31] To quote Sergio from the villa party scene: "We should all stay like this forever."

"We Want Jesus Christ Back": The Melodrama of Redemption

In my discussion in chapter 3 of the representation of what in the discourse of disability studies are termed normative and non-normative human bodies and faces, I have applied Garland-Thomson's stare to a visual-ideological structure—cinematic visual pleasure—still understood in the popular conversation in terms of a watered-down version of the male gaze. In my adaptation in chapter 6 of the now classical view inherited from 1970s feminist film theory, *woman* is coterminous with the image itself in its objecthood, while the masculine protagonist is the subject of memory, of melancholic or elegiac remembrance, in which the object of nostalgic desire is a woman who as often as not is no longer among the living. In *The Great Beauty*'s inventive treatment of this trope, this woman—Jep's youthful love Elisa—despite being dead in the present, is very much alive in the protagonist's memory, at least insofar as she represents for him, for his narrative trajectory, the feminine embodiment or personification of the salvific force of memory. In chapter 7 I argued that in *The Great Beauty* and *The Young Pope* especially, remembering per se, even bad or traumatic memories, is prerequisite to the maintenance of a subjectivity determined by an elegiac masculine sensibility that knows itself to be out of date and yet derives an ironically nostalgic pleasure from this critical self-understanding. *Loro*, however, makes it clear that in the case of a protagonist such as Berlusconi this complex subjectivity is only validated if this pleasure and self-knowledge remain grounded in the pursuit and possession of power. At the same time, and as a direct function of the kind of mediatic power that Berlusconi wields, this masculine subject is necessarily blind to the highly tropological nature of its relation to women-as-Other; that is, to the typical onscreen treatment of women's bodies that for many critics reaches a kind of nadir in *Loro*.

It is worth recalling here Jep's makeover of Ramona in *The Great Beauty* (not to mention Titta's of Sofia in *The Consequences of Love*) in comparison to Scotty's obsession with transforming Judy back into Madeleine in Hitchcock's *Vertigo*—the modern cinematic template for this narrative trope: in each case the man's obsession with desire (*eros*) and death (*thanatos*) is crystallized in the figure of the young and beautiful woman who is doomed to die soon, is already dead, or who never existed in the first place. In the end her function in each of these films is to be a kind of sacrifice for the literal or metaphorical redemption of the undeserving or uncomprehending masculine protagonist. In *Loro*, meanwhile, this structure is displaced back onto the postsecular possibility of collective melodramatic redemption, as suggested in the final sequence in L'Aquila. But what is Berlusconi's role in this seemingly sincerely presented redemptive process? The international release of *Loro* seems to position Berlusconi at the end sympathetically or at least uncritically as L'Aquila's savior, as suggested by the rapid completion of the New Town housing project, the set of replacement dentures for the elderly earthquake victim, and the Fellinian reposition of the statue of Christ—all instances of Berlusconi keeping his promises, which is something even he acknowledges he is not known for doing.

Just before the two-hour mark, in a lengthy montage, Morra's *veline* frolic in and around Berlusconi's Sardinian villa, the morning after his less-than-successful party, Sol Rising's ambient track "The Journey" playing extradiegetically. This is inter-cut with Sorrentino's restaging of the *giorno dell'insediamento*, the day of instal-lation of the new government for Berlusconi's fourth term as prime minister of Italy,[32] suggesting the simultaneity of these two events (figure 9.12). As this complex sequence concludes, Berlusconi, after taking the oath of allegiance to his country, looks off-screen, toward the camera, as if in response to the sound of a dog barking. There is a straight cut to a medium close-up of a playground swing set swaying ominously in a preternaturally dark setting. There follows a montage of Sorrentino's digitally generated recreation of the 2009 earthquake in L'Aquila, its buildings fall-ing to pieces—most notably the Cattedrale di San Massimo, whose massive bell is seen to topple into the building's interior.

If *The Young Pope*'s later episodes deliver the redemption of a kind of gendered melodramatic storyline, *Loro* offers instead the melodrama of a redemptive narra-tive—the redemption of yet another undeserving man—where the literal onscreen signifiers of redemption, most notably the statue of the deposed Christ rescued from the ruins of L'Aquila's cathedral, add up to a largely sympathetic portrait of Berlusconi. This effect is strongly abetted by Sorrentino's deviation from his typi-cally ironic or incongruous use of music in relation to the image track; here, as in *The Young Pope*'s later episodes, the music, composed for the film by Lele Marchitelli, matches the action, underscoring rather than disrupting or ironically juxtaposing what appears to be the scene's preferred emotional resonance. As in the scene of the young Belardo's miraculous curing of his friend Billy's mother in episode 9 (as discussed in chapter 8), Sorrentino abandons his trademark irony in favor of a more conventionally dramatic—or melodramatic—stylistic approach.

On the other hand, the generally sympathetic portrayal of Berlusconi with which the film concludes is significantly destabilized by the repetition of a key piece of dia-logue in two separate scenes. In the first Berlusconi randomly cold calls a housewife

FIGURE 9.12 *Loro*

in Verona to sell her a new apartment that exists only in the fantasmatic spaces of his professional salesman's rhetoric. The pitch culminates in his detailed description of the house and its environs: "1,300 square feet, southern exposure, half a mile from your current address . . . ultramodern. The living room? I'm 5 foot 6, so imagine me lying on the floor and multiply by seven and you'll have the length of the room." In the second scene, as Berlusconi finishes his tour of the devastated L'Aquila, he reproduces the earlier speech. Turning away from the elderly survivor, to whom he has promised a new set of dentures to replace those she lost as she fled the devastation, he faces the journalists and photographers: "I'm 5 foot 6. Imagine me lying on the ground and multiply that by four, that's the size of your living room. You will all have new houses, anti-seismic, built in record time. L'Aquila will have a new town. Because I always keep my promises." In the first case, he calls the woman randomly to see if he is able to sell her a nonexistent apartment in order to prove to himself that he is still the consummate salesman of his formative years. Servillo's performance here presents a master class in acting, while the scene also showcases Sorrentino and Contarello's facility with megalomaniacal dialogue. The second scene, by contrast, is positioned structurally for maximum satirical impact: Berlusconi's repetition of his own sales pitch in the context of the immediate aftermath of the L'Aquila earthquake seriously complicates the image of him presented only moments before as a caring, responsible national leader. Note also that the earthquake victims are to have living rooms almost one-quarter smaller in size than the dream home he imagines for the Veronese housewife, which may be because in the second case he actually intends to keep his promise. In response to Berlusconi's concluding remark—"I always keep my promises"—a voice off-screen shouts "Jesus Christ! We want Jesus Christ back!" Berlusconi stands and stares, for once at a loss for words.

The film's most scathing attack on Berlusconi comes in the third act, set in 2009, after his reelection and tour of the L'Aquila earthquake site. This is arguably the crucial final scene in the storyline focusing on Berlusconi's personal life. Having returned from a trip to Naples to attend the eighteenth birthday of Noemi Letizia (Pasqualina Sanna), his (now of legal age) *inamorata*, Berlusconi is confronted by Veronica, who tells him she wants a divorce. In this scene, although he typically tries to take control of the discussion, his wife finally tells him exactly what she thinks of him, her words echoing Stella's considerably gentler put-down in the previous act, when she calls Berlusconi pathetic (*patetico*) for hitting on her, as the smell of his breath reminds her of her grandfather's: "neither sweet nor bad-smelling, merely the breath of an old man," as Berlusconi recounts later. The sequence with Veronica unfolds in a profile two-shot that cuts to conventional shot-reverse shot. To his charge that she is making herself appear ridiculous, she retorts:

You're the one who's ridiculous, Silvio. And pathetic [*patetico*]. You're a sick man, Silvio, not because you like women, but because you had much better things to do, but you didn't. You had an extraordinary opportunity to help the Italians, but you didn't. Because you've never been interested in the Italians, but only yourself. That's why you are sick, Silvio. If there is a God somewhere, he will never forgive you for what you've done. Never! You wanted to be a statesman. You even aspired to become President of the Republic, but you're still nothing but a salesman. When you were young, you sold things. But when you became Prime Minister, you simply sold out. You sold out on Italian culture, people's hopes, and women's dignity!

At the scene's climax, which takes place, tellingly, in the villa's well-equipped kitchen, framed portraits of their numerous household staff on the wall, Veronica puts to him the "question everyone always asks. Where did your fortune come from?" When he offers his stock response that his father lent him 30 million lire, she fires back that it was 130 billion "and no one has ever figured out where it came from." To this Berlusconi says nothing, eventually stating, "I avail myself of the right to remain silent." The line is delivered in a medium two-shot, both figures in profile, facing off over the kitchen range, a gigantic pasta pot like a medieval battlement between them (figure 9.13). The domestic setting, for all its hyperbolic grandeur, is neverthe-less ironic, as the kitchen is the clichéd traditional space of the woman as mother and wife, the private feminine space of the pregnant maid in *Umberto D.*, or of *Ossessione*'s exhausted wife surrounded by mountains of dirty plates. Of course the contrast between this cinematic kitchen and those earlier ones could not be greater, a difference that measures the distance postwar Italian cinema has travelled from its neorealist roots to the present moment—a distance, and a difference, redoubled in the degree of transformation in Italian society between the end of the war and Berlusconi's fourth term as prime minister.

Berlusconi gets the last word, however, responding indirectly to his wife's accusa-tions in a conversation with Mike Bongiorno, the former TV quiz show host (*Chiedi a Mike*) fired by Berlusconi before the film's story began. At intervals throughout the film friends and advisors counsel him to call Bongiorno as a gesture of good will. When his old friend remarks that this is the first time he has ever seen him looking sad, Berlusconi responds (over another slowly paced, medium close up shot-reverse shot sequence):

FIGURE 9.13 *Loro*

The only time I really had fun was when I was selling houses. . . . I went into politics to avoid jail, to salvage what I could, and to control the TV regulations. But I really wanted to do something for my country. I truly love Italy, as I said when I entered politics. But no one believed me, Mike. No one. They say I haven't ever kept a single promise. They say that, after all these scandals, my political career is coming to an end.

"They say": the nameless *loro* who oppose him. Berlusconi attempts to exploit the conversation as an opportunity to affirm his own undiminished youthful vigor, his head full of "plans" rather than old memories, as he says of Bongiorno. But the prime minister protests too much: the scene's affective tonality is not merely sad but melancholic or elegiac, and this remains the dominant register until the end of the film. In *Loro*'s international release the shift arguably occurs at the beginning of the third act, after his failed seduction of Stella, in which she calls him "pathetic." Following this, Berlusconi walks out on Kira's kitschily choreographed group strip-tease performance—one of the film's most awkward moments, yet also one of the scenes in which the film strikes a successful balance between critiquing a soft-porn aesthetic while still exploiting it, undermining the (straight male) viewer's visual pleasure. For this scene's evident sexism is in fact undercut by its complex structure: as the women perform the camera assumes a position directly behind Berlusconi's head in close-up as he sits watching the show before him (figure 9.14). The viewer is therefore once again implicated directly in the scene, interpellated as the voyeuristic spectator closely aligned optically with Berlusconi. Once again the viewer has no choice but to consider what it means to watch this kind of spectacle from this position, a dilemma further complicated by Berlusconi's gesture of refusal as he leaves in recognition of the scene's pathos.

After a lengthy montage of the women lounging around in his villa postparty—notably free of the critical formal strategies marshaled in the preceding sequence—there is a straight cut to Berlusconi and his reconstituted *corrente* at his swearing-in

FIGURE 9.14 *Loro*

ceremony, which concludes with the spatially and temporally incongruous cut to the L'Aquila earthquake. His conversation with Mike Bongiorno, however, is succeeded by a cut to L'Aquila's New Town, promised by Berlusconi in the earlier scene when he toured the devastated city. Not only does this later scene seem to graphically illustrate the prime minister actually keeping one of his many promises—the new houses were in fact constructed in some three months' time, and therefore it makes sense to show the displaced L'Aquilans moving in—but the scene's focus is on the elderly woman who lost her dentures and to whom Berlusconi promised a new set. She enters her new apartment to find a bottle of Prosecco, a signed welcoming note from her prime minister, and the promised false teeth in a gift-wrapped box. There is no trace in the film of controversy around the rapid construction of the nineteen New Towns, making the buildings unsafe ten years after the original quake, mafia-linked contractors exploiting the disaster for financial gain, and the like.

When Berlusconi finally fires off his artificial volcano on the grounds of his Sardinian villa—one of *Loro*'s several running jokes—he does so alone, the resulting explosion an anticlimactic mockery of his own reduced and pathetic erotic, if not political, potency, the mini-Vesuvius in his backyard a bitterly ironic echo of the real natural disaster that constituted the film's third-act focus. As the elderly woman admires her new dentures, her grandson stands watching the new TV in their new, rapidly constructed apartment. The brief volcano scene interrupts this sequence, which we return to in a straight cut to the young man in medium close-up staring up at the television. A slow push in to him and his grandmother is succeeded by the reverse shot, revealing the image of L'Aquila's Cattedrale di San Massimo on the TV screen. An earlier montage of various characters, including the now impoverished Sergio, watching TV in rapt silence, suggests that all of these people are connected in time as they bear witness at one remove to the action with which the film concludes, "Live from L'Aquila" (figure 9.15). The push in to the TV image gives way to a close-up of one of the townspeople on site, looking intently upward, as

FIGURE 9.15 *Loro*

FIGURE 9.16 *Loro*

someone gives instructions in voiceover. The voice is that of the construction fore-
man, guiding his crane operator in the retrieval of the statue of the deposed Christ
from the ruined cathedral. Close-ups and medium shots of the silent and attentive
crowd alternate with shots of the statue being carefully lowered to the ground by
firemen. The sequence concludes with a high-angle shot above the now reposing Christ,
as the firemen remove the ropes, like centurions on Mount Golgotha (figure 9.16). In
the film's closing shot, the camera cranes down, slowly reframing and circling the
statue, gradually descending to a ground-level close-up of Christ's face. They got
their Jesus Christ back—but, as others have pointed out, this is not the first time
he has returned.

Fellini's *La Dolce Vita* famously opens with a statue of Christ the Redeemer flying over Rome, borne aloft by a helicopter (figure 9.17).[33] As Marcello (Marcello
Mastroianni) explains to the women in bikinis on the high-rise rooftop, "They're
taking it to the pope." The presence of the scantily clad women in this scene, along
with workers building Rome's new postwar suburbs, not to speak of the jarring cut
to an Indonesian nightclub dancer with which this sequence ends—all of this militates against any kind of serious reading of the redemptive potential of this particular
image of Christ. According to Peter Bondanella (and despite the director's alleged
Christian humanism), "Fellini wished to show in *La Dolce Vita* a contemporary
world cut adrift from traditional values and symbols, especially those of Christian-
ity, and bereft of any dominant cultural centre."[34] *The Young Pope*, by comparison,
concludes with a different quality of irony: the ambiguous image of the redeeming
Christ in the clouds above Piazza San Marco. Recall that, for Linda Williams:

> Recognition of *virtue* orchestrates the moral legibility that is key to melodrama's func-
> tion. . . . The suffering body caught up in paroxysms of mental or physical pain can be
> male or female, but suffering itself is a form of powerlessness that is coded *feminine*. Of
> course the transmutation of bodily suffering into virtue is a *topos* of western culture that
> goes back to Christian iconography.[35]

Christ's is the "suffering body" par excellence in Western culture, a motif clearly reintroduced in this concluding scene in the ruins of L'Aquila. For this is not Christ resurrected but Christ deposed from the cross, at the lowest point, the nadir of his career, the furthest remove from either his active, embodied, human self or his post-crucifixion persona as redeemer, returned from the grave in order to save humankind. I have offered a reading of the closing scene of the final episode of *The Young Pope* and what the image of the redeeming Christ in the clouds might mean for Lenny's trajectory as pontiff. What do *Loro*'s final scenes set in L'Aquila say about Sorrentino's version of Berlusconi? Williams amplifies what she calls melodrama's "sentimental politics," which often entails a climax that offers "a feeling for, if not the reality of, justice," in which "the death of a good person offers paroxysms of pathos and recognitions of virtue compensating for individual loss of life"; that is, "compensation" as *redemption* through self-sacrifice, typically on the part of a woman.[36] It would be easy to argue that the sacrificial victim in *Loro*'s allegory is the collective, the group represented by the displaced citizens of L'Aquila, or—to generalize further—the betrayed people of Italy (*Italia* is, after all, a feminine noun). But such allegorical-grammatical interpretations present a slippery slope, and we must restrict our interpretation—and our judgment—to what is on the screen (and the soundtrack). After all, it is Berlusconi himself who is pathetic, according to at least two women in the film, and this particular character defect is on a continuum with the *pathos* that determines the passivity and guarantees the virtue of the melodramatic victim. This reading may begin to explain why the opening scene features the accidental sacrifice, by air conditioning and bad television, of an actual lamb, set over against the penultimate scene, just discussed, with a statue of the dead Christ recumbent amidst the ruins of twenty-first-century Italy.[37] The implicit connections between Berlusconi and these rather allegorical figures and any virtue they may embody demand to be read ironically, if only because when he stands in the villa living room in the exact position of the lamb, he is wearing the costume of an odalisque, an orientalist stereotype

FIGURE 9.17 *La Dolce Vita* (Federico Fellini, 1960)

of feminine sexual servitude, while the return of L'Aquila's Savior resonates most powerfully in stark contrast to the ultimately hollow promises he makes as newly installed prime minister.

Loro's final lengthy horizontal tracking shot begins in fact after the film's proper ending, after the screen cuts to black on the face of the statue of the deposed Christ. Fading up out of the darkness, with the title credits over top, in this last long shot— the film's last word on the subject of salvation and sacrifice—the slowly circling camera examines the dirty and exhausted faces of firefighters after a shift in the ruins of L'Aquila, a town in the mountains of Abruzzo, some one hundred kilometers from the nearest coast. Over top can be heard the incongruous sounds of the sea, waves lapping rhythmically on the shore, seabirds calling, continuing even after the long closing shot fades to black.

Conclusion

Style as Commitment

Life goes on, even without all that cinema bullshit.
—Brenda Morel, *Youth*

SINCE THE WORLDWIDE success of *The Great Beauty* (2013), Sorrentino has transcended his status as up-and-coming Italian auteur to emerge as a transnational
superstar, culminating in the (generally) rapturous response to his first foray into English-language prestige television, the HBO series *The Young Pope* (2016). With eight
other feature films to date, six of them Italian-language and the other two in English
with international casts—*This Must Be the Place* (2011) and *Youth* (2015)—Sorrentino
now embodies the contradictions of the contemporary transnational auteur. But he
also provides a focal point for the critical consideration of auteurship as the basis,
in Italian film studies and beyond, for interpreting and judging a body of work.[1]
In Sorrentino's case the transnational intersects with the figure of the auteur in the
films' pronounced intermediality, where the latter (the auteur) is radically qualified
as source or determiner of textual authority or meaning. Auteurism, with neorealism,
stands as one of the two shibboleths of postwar Italian film criticism. Recent critical
revaluations of the artistic and political potentialities of transnational art cinema—
with works by Italian directors at the forefront—have, however, served to open up
new avenues of approach to these persistent national myths. Rethinking *impegno*—
political engagement or commitment—in terms of film style also contributes to the
ongoing deconstruction of the myth of the auteur as guiding rubric for interpretation
and evaluation. As noted in the introduction, there is no substance without style,
meaning: the particular form in which the film appears (the result of a series of specific technical, aesthetic, and budgetary choices on the part of the filmmakers) directly
determines the film's story, characters, themes, mood, and tone. Style inflects generic
categorization by allowing the film to diverge from received genres or compelling it to
hew closely to same. Style determines a film's relationship to the social reality outside
the film and therefore the viewer's relation to onscreen events. Insofar as a given film
can embody or express or enact a kind of political engagement or commitment, it
does so on the level of style: impegno as style, style as impegno.

The notion of the filmmaker as auteur is inherently problematic for many reasons, not the least of which is that it distracts from the truth that without style there is no auteur. The proof of this counterintuitive truth is in the pudding: film critics and reviewers have always worked backwards from their favorite films to create a portrait of the man (and it is usually a man) whose name appears in the credits after "directed by." That said, the auteur is obviously a trope that I have had to rely on throughout this study. Notwithstanding, I have striven throughout to destabilize and productively complicate the idea of the auteur as a critical category by emphasizing the *intra*-textual—or, as in the case of *The Young Pope*, intra-*medial*—patterns running through all of Sorrentino's films as a body of work. The intratextual texture of a filmmaker's oeuvre is the result of all the aforementioned choices made by the director and the various crewmembers in the course of shooting the film—and this is not to mention the many choices already taken by the screenwriter beforehand. The final film, then, is the sum total of the *effects* of all of these choices, the traces left by an intentionality with no other material form. This is the legacy of Roland Barthes's famous proclamation of the death of the author in 1967, which still warrants repeating today. For, like Nietzsche's comparably famous proclamation of the death of God in 1882, neither the author-figure nor God have ever gone away; which is to say: the grounds for invoking either have never been completely eradicated and may today be firmer than ever. The highly inter- and intratexual nature of Sorrentino's films and television work mark them out as transnational, even global, in impact—apart from any other consideration. Sorrentino's films, at least since his second feature, *The Consequences of Love*, are transnational objects precisely because of their formal beauty and legibility, their openness to a popular taste alongside their avoidance of narrative compromise for the sake of accessibility. And it is precisely the transcultural nature of Sorrentino's intermedial influences that marks even the more Italian films as ultimately transnational in their value and meaning.

Through a chronological series of close comparative readings of the feature films and *The Young Pope* television series, I have elaborated an interpretation of Sorrentino as a transnational Italian director in light of the persistence of the myth of the auteur in the popular cultural discourse. This interpretation is predicated on the understanding that every great author is the product of her or his cultural and historical moment. This book's analysis is therefore set over against Sorrentino's emergent status as representative transnational filmmaker, working not only in cinema but in a variety of other media forms, including prestige television, glossy internet advertisements and short films, as well as the novel and the short story. Ultimately this book privileges the centrality to Sorrentino's visual narrative aesthetic of a complex and wide-ranging audiovisual intermediality, coupled with his uniquely hybrid style which, in its combination of a critical realism and playful self-reflexivity, is at the vanguard of twenty-first-century film and television production.

Coming after the end of cinema's first century, well after its modernist moment, Sorrentino's cinema represents a critically postmodern reflection upon these historical impulses. Sorrentino's is an ironically dialectical approach that in certain moments produces a productive contradiction between film form and diegetic content. This allows for a reconciliation of the films' typically self-reflexive style with the ethical commitment of a social and political critique conveyed via a spectacular image. Ultimately, this tendency shifts to a more conventionally melodramatic approach to narration occasioned in part by the change in medium (from cinema to television) and genre or modality (from art film to episodic narrative). That said, this shift toward more straightforwardly melodramatic plotlines and pleasures, in *The Young Pope* especially, could represent a kind of rebalancing of long-standing gender imbalances. This occurs not around the gender makeup of the canon of Italian auteurs—this entire discussion of course only reinscribes Sorrentino's name more deeply into that list—but through the regendering of *genre*. In other words, by appropriating melodramatic tropes in his television series Sorrentino does not masculinize the genre[2] so much as he exploits a traditionally so to speak feminine genre to tell a story about a very particular kind of man. After all, in *The Young Pope*, Belardo's masculinity is so retrograde and unreconstructed at the start that he is able to pass by the end directly to a kind of postmodern, postmasculinist, post- (but not *trans-*) gender subjectivity. It is no accident, however, that he also appears to be dead.

While a certain philosophical-narrative-linguistic subject remains a foundational structure for a shared understanding of individual and collective identity in much global culture today, it is also the case that this subject—still bearing with it the attributes of masculinity, whiteness, heterosexuality, Northern Hemisphericity, etc.—is also itself a product of this culture. As such, the subject remains a problem whose solution may never arrive. And, as long as this subject remains at the center of things, despite, or perhaps paradoxically because of, the now longstanding efforts toward its deconstruction, the films of Paolo Sorrentino will continue to play their essential role of performing a clear-eyed and ironic appraisal. They will do so moreover from a perspective that is increasingly open to an expansive, cosmopolitan, and international worldview, having left behind the filmmaker's origins in the specific cultural context of 1990s Neapolitan cinema. Sorrentino has even transcended any more-or-less delimited understanding of Italian national cinema, having for some time now established himself as a leading transnational filmmaker, producing films and works in other media for a diverse audience of discerning cinephiles.

Sorrentino's approach to form is consistently ironic: surface and substance are juxtaposed in productively complex ways, whether in terms of the films' audiovisual style, in the narrative, or on the level of character. It is necessary to extend this insight more broadly, however, across his entire oeuvre, forging a reading of Sorrentino's work that accounts for his status as transnational filmmaker in the early twenty-first century, in which irony as rhetorical trope is symptomatic of the zeitgeist even as it comes in for renewed attack in a discursive environment (supported mainly but not exclusively by the internet) of proaffective, postironic naiveté. There is also a uniquely Italian aspect to this emphasis on irony, in that, from a traditional leftist perspective, one cannot be both ironic and politically committed: historically speaking, irony and impegno, political commitment, are mutually exclusive impulses. But—as noted with *Il Divo* in chapter 5—Sorrentino's films prove that this is an outmoded distinction; in an analogy with Boym's notion of reflective nostalgia, it is possible to be committed and ironic—and critically reflective—at the same time in the same film.[3]

It is at this point, where the animating human subject behind the text meets the myth of the filmmaker as auteur, that we may soon need to reassess the debunking of the latter insofar as the former—the filmmaker as embodied, gendered, and entirely fallible human being—remains the ground zero for much of the popular reception of films and other audiovisual narratives. In other words: the person behind the work, a real historical personage, culturally embedded, ideologically interpolated, a subject in the now classic poststructuralist sense. For to evaluate a film on the basis of the director's name and reputation is at bottom symptomatic of the (unconscious) desire to engage that other person in moral-ethical debate; to judge them on these grounds in order to see if they measure up or if they fall short of some culturally conditioned set of moral-ethical criteria that for many function as unreflective personal credo. For it is a not unreasonable assumption that behind every text is at least one human person with agency who made certain decisions and choices and that therefore—and here the assumption quickly shades into fallacy—it is ultimately with this individual that one struggles in one's relationship with a given text, for this person is morally and ethically *responsible* for the meanings that are present there. Throughout this book I have striven to argue against such a basis for viewing films and other texts, even while I felt compelled to acknowledge the pervasive and tenacious nature of such habits of thought. But today, in the era of #Metoo and related movements predicated on the politicization of specific identity categories or genres, it is increasingly difficult to argue against all forms of auteurism if it means never taking the individual human producer into account; or, rather, never holding them to account. To repeat a question from an earlier chapter: Why would Sorrentino continue to indulge in his film and television work in such overtly retrograde images of women? In this study I have tried to push this conversation a little further, striving—even when exposing its contradictions—to never lose sight of the films' artistic complexity and genuine cultural-critical value.

Looking beyond the Italian context, then—or rather looking on to the Italian context from an external, transnational, perspective—we live in a new era of postironic irony, and Sorrentino is one of its most accomplished practitioners, bringing it into line with a keen appreciation for the flashback, for instance, as narrative device. In all eight films, as well as *The Young Pope* (although the television series complicates this reading somewhat), irony is the dominant key or modality; an irony tempered not simply by the melancholy of memory, however, but by an elegiac tone that positions the protagonist, if not by extension the viewer, in an ironic-elegiac relation to the past.[4] This elegiac attitude is also the complement, so to speak, to the theme of existential ennui or nothingness that Sorrentino inherits from modernist literature and the postwar art film: an ontological and epistemological problem only for this very subject in its—for the time being—still privileged position, culturally, historically, ideologically, and economically. For—as *The Young Pope* shows—this subject is also the ground for whatever semblance of belief is possible in the twenty-first century. We are confronted, therefore, by Sorrentino's complex engagement with what is now called the postsecular and its expression in the moving image. It remains to be seen in the most recent works—*The New Pope* TV series, to begin with—what will become of the Sorrentinian subject. Will this elegiac tone at some point shade into an epigonal regret; regret either for arriving too late, or for living on, outside of one's proper time? Most of Sorrentino's male protagonists have identities grounded in a problematic, bittersweet relation to the past, and the films, television series, and literary works sustain and are sustained by an ironically critical point of view on their subject matter, on their fictional worlds, and ultimately on the world outside the fiction. Sorrentino's style is as distinctive as it is cosmopolitan, embodying at its best an ethical commitment in a spectacular image.

NOTES

INTRODUCTION: COMMITMENT TO STYLE

Portions of this chapter first appeared in Russell J. A. Kilbourn, "The 'Primal Scene': Memory, Redemption, and 'Woman' in the Films of Paolo Sorrentino," special issue, *Journal of Italian Cinema and Media Studies* 7, no. 3 (2019): 377–94.

The chapter epigraph is from Alain Elkann, "Alain Elkann Interviews Italian Director and Screenwriter Paolo Sorrentino," Alain Elkann Interviews (website), March 5, 2017, http://www .alainelkanninterviews.com/paolo-sorrentino/, 7.

1. This is part of a list supplied by Lanfranco Aceti in William Hope, ed., *Italian Film Directors in the New Millennium* (Newcastle, UK: Cambridge Scholars Press, 2010), 148. Aceti's list is characteristic in that it does not include prominent female Italian directors, such as Lina Wertmüller or Liliana Cavani.

2. By his own account Sorrentino got his start as a screenwriter in Naples. One of his first films was a collaboration with Neapolitan director Antonio Capuana on *Polvere di Napoli* (1998). Guido Bonsaver, "Dall'uomo al Divo: Un'intervista con Paolo Sorrentino," *The Italianist* 29 (2009): 327 and 337n1.

3. Gino Moliterno, *The A to Z of Italian Cinema* (Lanham, MD: Scarecrow Press, 2009), 304.

4. See Guido Bonsaver, "Prince of Darkness" (interview), *Sight and Sound* 19, no. 4 (April 2009): 42. In 2006, with the release of *The Family Friend*, Bonsaver called Sorrentino "one of the most promising Italian directors of his generation." Bonsaver, "*The Family Friend*," *Sight and Sound* 17, no. 4 (2007): 1. See also Marlow-Mann: "[O]f the Italian directors to have emerged this millennium, Paolo Sorrentino has one of the highest international profiles." Alex Marlow-Mann, "Beyond Post-Realism: A Response to Millicent Marcus," *The Italianist* 30 (2010): 161.

5. Marlow-Mann, "Beyond Post-Realism," 171.

6. Louis Bayman and Sergio Rigoletto, "Melodrama as Seriousness," in *Popular Italian Cinema* (New York: Palgrave Macmillan, 2013), 82–97. According to Bonsaver, one of the reasons for Sorrentino's initially restricted impact outside of Italian cinephilic circles was because of the premature death of Kermit Smith, producer of his 2001 debut feature, *L'uomo in più*. Bonsaver, "Prince of Darkness," 43.

7. In addition to Franco Vigni's seminal *La mascherea, il potere, la solitudine: Il cinema di Paolo Sorrentino* (Florence, Italy: Aska Edizioni, 2017)—which, as an overview of all seven of the director's feature films (excluding *Loro*), and also *The Young Pope*, is the closest to the present study in its design—the Italian books on Sorrentino include: Pierpaolo De Santis, Domenica Monetti, and Luca P. Pallanch, *Divi e Antidivi: Il Cinema di Paolo Sorrentino* (Rome: Laboratorio Gutenberg, 2010); Simonetta Salvestroni, *La grande bellezza e il cinema di Paolo Sorrentino* (Bologna, Italy: Archetipo Libri, 2017); Allesandro Tenaglia, "L'aldilà è un soppalco": Uno sguardo teleologico—e

non solo—sull'opera di Paolo Sorrentino fino a *The Young Pope*" (2019). See also Christian Uva, "The New Cinema of Political Engagement," in *Italian Political Cinema: Public Life, Imaginary, and Identity in Contemporary Italian Film*, ed. Giancarlo Lombardi and Christian Uva (Oxford: Peter Lang, 2016), 31–42.

8. In this respect my reading of the films overlaps to a degree with Vigni's notion of the mask worn by each of Sorrentino's protagonists, at least in their initial appearance, before circumstances occur that cause this socially constructed façade to crack. Franco Vigni, *La maschera, il potere, la solitudine: Il cinema di Paolo Sorrentino* (Florence, Italy: Aska Edizioni, 2017), 13–14. My reading diverges from Vigni's in general, however, by its avoidance of psychological tropes in favor of a formalist understanding of character as an emanation of style.

9. Especially *The Great Beauty* (e.g., Annachiara Mariani, "The Empty Heterotopic [Non-] Space of Sorrentino's Female Characters in *The Great Beauty* and *The Consequences of Love*," in *Female Identity and Its Representations in the Arts and Humanities*, ed. Silvia Giovanardi Byer and Fabiana Cecchini [Newcastle, UK: Cambridge Scholars Publishing, 2017], 168–84).

10. Christine Gledhill, "Melodrama and Cinema: The Critical Problem," in *Home Is Where the Heart Is* (London: BFI, 2002), 10. There would appear to be the opposite problem in much contemporary Italian film criticism. Unless it advertises itself as explicitly feminist in approach, the tendency in the scholarship on Sorrentino is to offer what are often highly perceptive readings of the films that completely overlook the significance of gender to his stories and their characters. See e.g., Claudio Bisoni, who offers a nuanced reading of Sorrentino's protagonists (up to and including Jep Gambardella) as "strong subjects," without considering that they are all men. Claudio Bisoni, "Paolo Sorrentino: Between Engagement and *Savoir Faire*," in *Italian Political Cinema: Public Life, Imaginary, and Identity in Contemporary Italian Film*, ed. Giancarlo Lombardi and Christian Uva (Oxford: Peter Lang, 2016), 256. On this score, see also Vigni, *La maschera, il potere, la solitudine*.

11. On the Italian masculine melodrama see e.g., Catherine O'Rawe, "Brothers in Arms: Middlebrow *Impegno* and Homosocial Relations in the Cinema of Petraglia and Rulli," in *Intellectual Communities and Partnerships in Italy and Europe*, ed. Danielle Hipkins (Oxford: Peter Lang, 2012), 149–67; Catherine O'Rawe, *Stars and Masculinities in Contemporary Italian Cinema* (New York: Palgrave Macmillan, 2014); Dana Renga, "*Romanzo criminale* as Male Melodrama: 'It Is in Reality *Always Too Late*,' " in *Italian Political Cinema: Public Life, Imaginary, and Identity in Contemporary Italian Film*, ed. Giancarlo Lombardi and Christian Uva (Oxford: Peter Lang, 2016), 373–88. Regarding the male melodrama outside of Italy see e.g., Philippa Gates, "The Man's Film: Woo and the Pleasure of Male Melodrama," *Journal of Popular Culture* 35, no. 1 (2001): 59–79

12. As Susan Sontag observed, in an essay on Bergman's *Persona*: "it's in the nature of cinema to confer on all events, without indications to the contrary, an equivalent degree of reality: everything shown on the screen is 'there,' present." Susan Sontag, "Bergman's *Persona*," in *Ingmar Bergman's Persona*, ed. L. Michaels (Cambridge: Cambridge University Press, 2000), 67.

13. Sorrentino: "I have a predilection for characters who are usually male and well on in years, from middle age on." "Interview with Antonio Monda," *La grande bellezza*, directed by Paolo Sorrentino (New York: Criterion, 2013), DVD.

14. See Todd McGowan, *The Real Gaze: Film Theory After Lacan* (New York: State University of New York Press, 2007); Carl Plantinga, *Moving Viewers: American Film and the Spectator's Experience* (Berkeley: University of California Press, 2009).

15. Murray Smith, *Engaging Characters: Fiction, Emotion, and the Cinema*. Oxford: Clarendon Press, 1995.

16. Marlow-Mann, "Beyond Post-Realism," 162.

17. For an argument in favor of realism's ongoing relevance and significance for film studies, see e.g., Richard Rushton, *The Reality of Film: Theories of Filmic Reality* (Manchester, UK: Manchester University Press, 2011).

18. Siegfried Kracauer, *Theory of Film: The Redemption of Physical Reality* (Princeton, NJ: Princeton University Press, 1997), 30.

19. See Eugenia Paulicelli, *Italian Style: Fashion and Film from Early Cinema to the Digital Age* (New York: Bloomsbury Academic, 2016), 189; Brendan Hennessey, "Reel Simulations: CGI and Special

Effects in Two Films by Paolo Sorrentino," *The Italianist* 37, no. 3 (2017): 457, https://doi.org/10.1 080/02614340.2017.1409582 2017.

20. See e.g., André Bazin, "Cinematic Realism and the Italian School of the Liberation," in *What Is Cinema?*, trans. Timothy Barnard (Montreal, Canada: Caboose, 2009), 215–50; Burke Hilsabeck, "The 'Is' in What Is Cinema? On André Bazin and Stanley Cavell," *Cinema Journal* 55, no. 2 (2016): 25–42; Daniel Morgan, "Rethinking Bazin: Ontology and Realist Aesthetics," *Critical Inquiry* 32, no. 3 (Spring 2006): 443–81; Philip Rosen, "Belief in Bazin," in *Opening Bazin: Postwar Film Theory and Its Afterlife*, ed. Dudley Andrew with Hervé Joubert-Laurencin (Oxford: Oxford University Press, 2011), 107–18; D. N. Rodowick, *The Virtual Life of Film* (Cambridge, MA: Harvard University Press, 2007); Jeffrey Pence, "Cinema of the Sublime: Theorizing the Ineffable," *Poetics Today* 25, no. 1 (Spring 2004): 29–66.

21. Dudley Andrew, foreword to *Global Art Cinema: New Theories and Histories*, ed. Rosalind Galt and Karl Schoonover (Oxford: Oxford University Press, 2010), viii.

22. Andrew, viii; see also Galt and Schoonover, *Global Art Cinema*, 11.

23. Galt and Schoonover, *Global Art Cinema*, 6.

24. Galt and Schoonover, *Global Art Cinema*, 3.

25. Andrew, foreword to *Global Art Cinema*, x.

26. Gilles Deleuze, *Cinema 1: The Movement Image*, trans. Hugh Tomlinson and Barbara Habberjam (Minneapolis: University of Minnesota Press, 1986), 87.

27. Cinematic ethics is a burgeoning area in the field of film-philosophy. See, e.g., Paul Coates, "The Evidence of Things Not Seen: Sound and the Neighbour in Kieślowski, Haneke, Martel," in *Religion in Contemporary European Cinema: The Postsecular Constellation*, ed. Costica Bradatan and Camil Ungureanu (New York: Routledge, 2014), 91–109; Robert Sinnerbrink, "Postsecular Ethics: The Case of Iñárritu's *Biutiful*," in *Religion in European Cinema: The Postsecular Constellation*, ed. Costica Bradatan and Camil Ungureanu (New York: Routledge, 2014), 166–85; Catherine Wheatley, *Michael Haneke's Cinema: The Ethic of the Image* (New York: Berghahn Books, 2009).

28. See Pence, "Cinema of the Sublime," 29–66.

29. Deleuze, *Cinema 1*, 5.

30. See Mary Wood, "Lipstick and Chocolate: Paolo Sorrentino's the *Consequences of Love*," in *Mafia Movies: A Reader*, 2nd ed., ed. Dana Renga (Toronto: University of Toronto Press, 2019), 277. Wood includes visual spectacle as one of the criteria defining the general style of authorial and art cinema market in the early 2000s when Sorrentino made *The Consequences of Love*.

31. Millicent Marcus, "The Ironist and the Auteur: Post-Realism in Paolo Sorrentino's *Il Divo*," *The Italianist* 30 (2010): 246.

32. Marcus, "Ironist and the Auteur," 246.

33. Marcus, "Ironist and the Auteur," 246.

34. Guido Bonsaver was among the first to identify this aspect of Sorrentino's style, which he terms "una spettacolarità tarantinesca." Bonsaver, "Dall'uomo al Divo," 331.

35. See e.g., Bonsaver's 2009 interview with the director, in which Sorrentino himself points to Scorsese's and Tarantino's influences—alongside that of Rosi, Petri, and of course Fellini—on his work. Bonsaver "Prince of Darkness," 43.

36. Rosalind Galt, "The Prettiness of Italian Cinema," in *Popular Italian Cinema*, ed. Louis Bayman and Sergio Rigoletto (New York: Palgrave Macmillan, 2013), 65.

37. See Tiziana Ferrero-Regis, *Recent Italian Cinema: Spaces, Contexts, Experiences* (Leicester, UK: Troubador, 2009), ix. The persistence and pervasiveness of an auteurist ideology is evident even in Zaccagnini and Spagnoletti's insightful interview with Sorrentino on *Il Divo*, in which both interviewers and subject remark on the inextricability of form and content, filmic style, and political theme—the ever-evolving language of cinema vis-à-vis contemporary Italian politics—framed within an understanding of recent Italian cinema as an ongoing series of masculine auteurs, "*uomini di cinema*." Edoardo Zaccagnini and Giovanni Spagnoletti, "Intervista a Paolo Sorrentino," *Close-up* 23 (2007): 111.

38. Just as any strict distinction between immediacy and hypermediacy inevitably breaks down, in Bolter and Grusin's taxonomy of the double logic of remediation (Hennessey, "Reel Simulations," 456).

39. Hennessy, "Reel Simulations," 455.
40. Hennessy, "Reel Simulations," 455.
41. Neil Matsumoto, "Time and Age," *American Cinematographer* (January 2016): 26.
42. Marlow-Mann, "Beyond Post-Realism," 264.
43. "Filtered through the digital interface in this way, reality is necessarily mediated and thus altered, making digital images different from those of Italian neorealism, lauded by early critics for their total objectivity." Hennesey, "Reel Simulations," 451. By his own admission, Sorrentino is a reluctant latecomer to the digital game. Bonsaver, "Prince of Darkness," 44.
44. Hennessy, "Reel Simulations," 449.
45. Indeed, critics of Sorrentino's "overt formalism" have connected this propensity to the films' reliance on "intertextual quotation" (Hennessey "Reel Simulations," 452), as if this were a bad thing.
46. For discussions of this particularly problematic dimension of Sorrentino's filmmaking, see e.g., Danielle Hipkins, "Why Italian Film Studies Needs a Second Take on Gender," *Italian Studies* 63, no. 2 (2008): http://www.doi.10.1179/007516308X344360; Kilbourn, " 'Primal Scene' "; Alex Marlow-Mann, *The New Neapolitan Cinema* (Edinburgh: Edinburgh University Press, 2011), 164.
47. A feature of the films remarked by many online reviewers and film bloggers; e.g., the film blog *Cinemashame.* Franco Vigni observes that Sorrentino is preoccupied with "characters whose best days are behind them, 'marginalized or living in willful reclusion and locked either into indolence, impotence, or solitude.' " Pasquale Iannone, "Journey to the End of the Night." *Sight and Sound* 23, no. 10 (2013): 38.
48. See Jonathan Romney, "On the Road Again," *Sight and Sound* 22, no. 4 (April 2012). Where Romney is referring to Geremia di Geremei, the protagonist of *The Family Friend,* Sicinski applies the same term to Sorrentino himself. Michael Sicinski, "Paolo Sorrentino: A Medium Talent," *Cinemascope* (2017): 18.
49. Marlow-Mann, "Beyond Post-Realism," 268.
50. Quoted in Hipkins, "Why Italian Film Studies Needs a Second Take on Gender," 215n4.
51. See e.g., the satire of advertising, trashy television, and the objectification of women in Maurizio Nichetti's *Ladri di saponette* (1989), especially via the character of la modella (Heidi Komarek), who, thanks to an act of literalized transmediation, accidentally swims out of a TV commercial into the titular neo-neorealist film.
52. Paolo Sorrentino, *Hanno tutti ragione* (Milan: Feltrinelli, 2012), 49.
53. For just one example see the protagonist of Céline's *Journey to the End of the Night* (1932), which was a major inspiration to Sorrentino the novelist. In the interview with Antonio Monda, Sorrentino admits that his first ambition was to become a writer. Sorrentino, "Interview with Antonio Monda."
54. Kristin Thompson and David Bordwell, *Film History: An Introduction,* 3rd ed. (Boston: McGraw Hill, 2009), 582–84.
55. See Bonsaver, "Prince of Darkness," 43.
56. The notion of a male subject in crisis dates back to the immediate postwar period, at least. Joy Van Fuqua, " 'Can You Feel It, Joe?' Male Melodrama and the Feeling Man," *The Velvet Light Trap* 38 (Fall 1996): 29. According to Fuqua, unlike their 1950s counterparts, the "feeling men" of 1990s male melodrama "have the potential to be recuperated through discourses of suffering and victimage" (29). See also Gates, "The Man's Film"; Danielle Hipkins, "The Showgirl Effect: Ageing Between Great Beauties and 'Veline di turno,' " *Cinepanettone*-Academia: ReadingItaly (website), December 11, 2013, https://wp.me/p2iDSt-bW; O'Rawe, "Brothers in Arms"; Renga, "*Romanzo criminale.*"
57. For Catherine O'Rawe, "the function of women in the economy of the male melodrama [such as *La grande bellezza*] . . . is as structuring absence and loss." O'Rawe, *Stars and Masculinities,* 163.
58. Hipkins, "Why Italian Film Studies Needs a Second Take on Gender," 214–15.
59. The spectacular nature of Sorrentino's images reveal a fictional version of what Jill Godmilow calls "the pornography of the real" in documentary film: "the objectifying of a graphic image, turning it from a subject into an object, so that the thing or person depicted can be commodified, circulated and consumed without regard to its status as a subject." Quoted in Joseph A. Kraemer, "Trauma and Representation in the Animated Documentary," *Journal of Film and Video* 67, no. 3–4 (2015): 65–66.

60. Hipkins, for instance, describes "the much-lauded recent films of Paolo Sorrentino, in which the female is merely a fetish object for the narration of male desire (*The Consequences of Love*, 2004; *The Family Friend*, 2006)." Hipkins, "Why Italian Film Studies Needs a Second Take on Gender," 213.

61. Sorrentino's latest feature was released theatrically in Italy in April 2018 in two parts: *Loro* and *Loro 2*. As of this writing the abbreviated international version had yet to be released in North America.

62. *The Great Beauty*, for instance, was an Italian-French coproduction; *Il Divo*: Italy and France; *This Must Be the Place*: Italy, France, Ireland; *Youth*: Italy, France, UK, Switzerland; *The Young Pope*: Italy, France, Spain, UK, US (IMDb).

63. Sorrentino's films have been winning awards since his first feature, *Un uomo in piú*, took the Venice Film Festival's Silver Ribbon for Best Director and Best Screenplay. Doris Toumarkine, "La Dolce Bellezza," *Film Journal International* 116, no. 12 (2013). Regarding *La grande bellezza*'s tremendous commercial and critical success, see also Marco Cucco, "Che cosa è un film? *La grande bellezza* in una prospettiva di economia e politica dei media," in *La trama dei media. Stato, imprese, pubblico nella società dell'informazione* (Rome: Carocci, 2014), 106.

64. Regarding Sorrentino's place in the "New Neapolitan Cinema" see Alex Marlow-Mann, "Character Engagement and Alienation in the Cinema of Paolo Sorrentino," in *Italian Film Directors in the New Millennium*, ed. William Hope (Newcastle, UK: Cambridge Scholars Press, 2010), 161–74; Marlow-Mann, *New Neapolitan Cinema*, 106–113.

65. For a consideration of the meaning of a distinctively European cinema, inevitably defined over against the Hollywood monolith, see e.g., Stan Jones, "Wenders' *Paris, Texas* and the 'European Way of Seeing,'" in *European Identity in Cinema*, ed. Wendy Everett (Bristol, UK: Intellect, 1996), 51. Jones defines the "European way of seeing" as inherently "ironic" and "self-conscious" (53).

66. Elizabeth Ezra and Terry Rowden, "General Introduction: What Is Transnational Cinema?," in *Transnational Cinema: The Film Reader* (New York: Routledge, 2006), 2–3.

67. Bordwell made this point in his keynote address, "Explanation of Style, Styles of Explanation," delivered at the Classical Hollywood Conference, Wilfrid Laurier University, May 2018.

68. As will be seen later in this chapter, this seemingly self-evident assertion is irreducibly complicated by the recognition that any film's specific style is as much the result of the cinematographer's or director-of-photography's efforts, not to mention the screenwriter, editor, actors, or other technicians.

69. Ezra and Rowden, *Transnational Cinema*, 3.

70. A critical organ chronically opposed to Sorrentino, as it happens.

71. See Galt and Schoonover, "Global Art Cinema," 4. See also Timothy Corrigan, "The Commerce of Auteurism," in *Critical Visions in Film Theory: Classic and Contemporary Readings*, ed. Timothy Corrigan, Patricia White, and Meta Mazaj (Boston: Bedford/St. Martin's, 2011), 416–29, regarding the commercial auteur.

72. Galt and Schoonover, "Global Art Cinema," 7.

73. Galt and Schoonover, "Global Art Cinema," 7.

74. See Ezra and Rowden, *Transnational Cinema*, 3; Dudley Andrew, "The Unauthorized Auteur Today," in *Film Theory: An Anthology*, ed. Robert Stam and Toby Miller (Oxford: Blackwell, 2000), 24; Galt and Schoonover, "Global Art Cinema," 10.

75. Ezra and Rowden, *Transnational Cinema*, 4.

76. Cf. Bisoni, "Paolo Sorrentino," 252; Tim Bergfelder, "Love Beyond the Nation: Cosmopolitanism and Transnational Desire in Cinema," in *Europe and Love in Cinema*, ed. Luisa Passerini, Jo Labanyi, and Karen Diehl (Bristol, UK: Intellect, 2012), 62.

77. Cf. Galt 2013, 64; Bergfelder, "Love Beyond the Nation," 62–63; Miriam Hansen, "The Mass Production of the Senses: Classical Cinema as Vernacular Modernism," *Modernism/Modernity* 6, no. 2 (April 1999): 59–77. As Bergfelder reminds us, cosmopolitanism is also "historically close" to Eurocentrism ("Love Beyond the Nation," 63).

78. In an interview with Antonio Monda for the Criterion DVD of *The Great Beauty*. Sorrentino, "Interview with Antonio Monda."

79. Bonsaver, "Prince of Darkness," 44.

80. See Marcus, "Ironist and the Auteur," 251. Regarding an example of Pasolini's eclectic approach to using pre-existing soundtrack music see *The Gospel According to St. Matthew* (1964), which

juxtaposes works by Bach and Mozart with African American spirituals. Regarding Fassbinder see e.g., *In a Year with 13 Moons*, which goes from Mahler to Connie Francis by way of Roxy Music.

81. Bonsaver, "Prince of Darkness," 43.

82. Bonsaver, "Prince of Darkness," 43.

83. See Zaccagnini and Spagnoletti, "Intervista a Paolo Sorrentino," 115; "[I] meccanismi psicologici derivanti dal potere sono più o meno simili nelle varie culture. Le derive che un uomo di potere può prendere sono molto simili in tutti i paesi. . . . I meccanismi del potere sono analoghi in Francia, in Italia e negli Stati Uniti." Trans. Sandra Parmegiani. Regarding the significance of power as theme in Sorrentino's films, see Vigni, *La maschera, il potere, la solitudine.*

84. Quoted in Nicoletta Marini-Maio, "È solo l'alito di un vecchio," 5.

85. Pierpaolo Antonello and Florian Mussgnug, eds., *Postmodern Impegno: Ethics and Commitment in Contemporary Italian Culture* (Oxford: Peter Lang, 2009), 9.

86. Marcus, "Ironist and the Auteur," 246.

87. "Suppongo che questi precedenti possano mettere in moto un'attenzione, da parte del cinema italiano, non più solo alla commedia di evasione ma anche al cinema d'autore più serio e impegnato." Trans. Sandra Parmegiani. Zaccagnini and Spagnoletti, "Intervista a Paolo Sorrentino," 113. In Geoffrey Nowell-Smith's estimation, the "success in 2008/9 of . . . Sorrentino's *Il Divo* and Matteo Garrone's *Gomorra* is perhaps a sign that Italian cinema is moving to regain the centrality it appeared to have lost." Geoffrey Nowell-Smith, foreword to *Italian Film Directors in the New Millennium*, ed. William Hope (Newcastle, UK: Cambridge Scholars Press, 2010), x.

88. Marcus, "Ironist and the Auteur," 246.

89. Antonello and Mussgnug, *Postmodern Impegno*, 3.

90. O'Leary argues for an understanding of impegno "not as a tag for the political or social concerns of the individual director, but . . . as a discourse, in the sense the term is used in the social sciences." Alan O'Leary, "Marco Tullio Giordana, or The Persistence of Impegno," in *Postmodern Impegno: Ethics and Commitment in Contemporary Italian Culture*, ed. Pierpaolo Antonello and Florian Mussgnug (Oxford: Peter Lang, 2009), 215.

91. Louis Bayman and Sergio Rigoletto, "The Fair and the Museum: Framing the Popular," in *Popular Italian Cinema*, ed. Louis Bayman and Sergio Rigoletto (New York: Palgrave Macmillan, 2013), 7–8.

92. Bergfelder, "Love Beyond the Nation," 62.

93. Bergfelder, "Love Beyond the Nation," 61.

94. Bayman and Rigoletto, "The Fair and the Museum," 5.

95. Bergfelder, "Love Beyond the Nation," 61.

96. E.g., Hennessey, "Reel Simulations," 452.

97. Bayman and Rigoletto, "The Fair and the Museum," 7.

98. Bayman and Rigoletto, "The Fair and the Museum," 7.

99. See Bayman and Rigoletto, who write of cinema's "near-mystical powers to induce conformity" in terms of "the idea of a mass audience unified in a nonrational public experience" ("The Fair and the Museum," 6).

100. Bayman and Rigoletto, "The Fair and the Museum," 6.

101. Eventually giving rise to many local manifestations, including Italian cultural studies; e.g., David D. Forgacs and Robert R. Lumley, eds., *Italian Cultural Studies: An Introduction* (Oxford: Oxford University Press, 1996).

102. Bayman and Rigoletto, "The Fair and the Museum," 8

103. Bayman and Rigoletto, "The Fair and the Museum," 8.

104. Regarding the specificity of the *popular* in Italian cultural history cf. *il popolo*, the *people*, in Gramsci's sense of "workers and peasants" vs. il pubblico, the public, as "passive consumers of entertainment" (Bayman and Rigoletto, "The Fair and the Museum," 12). See also Alan O'Leary, "Political/Popular Cinema," in *Italian Political Cinema: Public Life, Imaginary, and Identity in Contemporary Italian Film*, ed. Giancarlo Lombardi and Christian Uva (Oxford: Peter Lang, 2016), 115–17.

105. Quoted in Bayman and Rigoletto "The Fair and the Museum," 8.

106. Bayman and Rigoletto, "The Fair and the Museum," 8.

107. Quoted in Thomas Elsaesser, "Bertolt Brecht and Contemporary Film," in *Reinterpreting Brecht: His Influence on Contemporary Drama and Film*, ed. Pia Kleber and Colin Visser (Cambridge: Cambridge University Presss, 1990), 175.

108. See Elsaesser, "Bertolt Brecht and Contemporary Film," 175; See also Jean-Luc Godard, *Godard on Godard*, ed. Jean Narboni and Tom Milne (New York: Viking Press, 1972), 31; Steve Neale, "Art Cinema as Institution," *Screen* 22, no. 1 (May 1981), 29.

109. Sorrentino: "I would like to engage viewers in Italian political issues, because there are many strange things in our political life, and it's important for young people to know about them. But to reach that younger audience it's important to develop a different approach to making political films." Quoted in Gary Crowdus, "Exposing the Dark Secrets of Italian Political History: An Interview with Paolo Sorrentino," *Cineaste* (Summer 2009): 34.

110. See e.g., several of the essays in Giancarlo Lombardi and Christian Uva, *Italian Political Cinema: Public Life, Imaginary, and Identity in Contemporary Italian Film*, Oxford: Peter Lang, 2016. Regarding early perceptions of neorealism's politically revolutionary potential see the 1949 Andreotti law, a form of preproduction censorship instituted by the then state undersecretary in charge of entertainment, in order to curtail the number of neorealist films made in Italy at this time. Thompson and Bordwell, *Film History*, 332–33.

111. Crowdus, "Exposing the Dark Secrets," 34.

112. See Bayman and Rigoletto, "The Fair and the Museum," 11.

113. Marlow-Mann, "Beyond Post-Realism," 265.

114. Sicinski, "Paolo Sorrentino," 17.

115. See Sicinski, "Paolo Sorrentino," 19. David Bordwell once remarked that Sorrentino "has never met a crane shot he didn't like." Quoted in Iannone, "Journey to the End of Night," 38).

116. See Sicinski, "Paolo Sorrentino," 20. Hasted quotes Luca Guadagnino, who criticizes Sorrentino for what he calls the essentially televisual style of early 2000's Italian cinema, exemplified by *Il Divo* (2010). From the perspective I am elaborating here, this is exactly what makes a film like *Il Divo* so original and fresh. Nick Hasted, "Maestros and Mobsters," *Sight and Sound* 20, no. 5 (2010).

117. See e.g., Pierpaolo Antonello, "The Ambiguity of Realism and its Posts: A Response to Millicent Marcus," *The Italianist* 30 (2010): 258–62.

118. Precisely the false binary that Sicinski buys into when he remarks that: "*The Great Beauty* is textbook postmodernism" ("Paolo Sorrentino," 20). See also Pierpaolo Antonello, "*Il Divo*: Paolo Sorrentino's Spectacle of Politics," in Lombardi and Uva, 296 for an anticipation of my reading here.

119. Marcus, "Ironist and the Auteur," 253.

120. David Bordwell, *The Way Hollywood Tells It: Story and Style in Modern Movies* (Berkeley: University of California Press, 2006), 140–41.

121. Vito Zagarrio, "The 'Great Beauty,' or Form is Politics," in *Italian Political Cinema: Public Life, Imaginary, and Identity in Contemporary Italian Film*, ed. Giancarlo Lombardi and Christian Uva (Oxford: Peter Lang, 2016), 120.

122. Zagarrio, "The 'Great Beauty,' or Form is Politics," 120.

123. Zagarrio, "The 'Great Beauty,' or Form is Politics," 126.

124. *Intermediality* here means the product(s) of ongoing, omnipresent processes of remediation (see Jay Bolter and Richard Grusin, *Remediation: Understanding New Media* [Cambridge, MA: MIT Press, 1999]) and transmediation. See also Hennessey, "Reel Simulations," 453.

1. *ONE MAN UP (L'UOMO IN PIÚ)*: THE CONSEQUENCES OF COINCIDENCE

1. *L'uomo in Piú (One Man Up)*, Italy: Indigo Film and Key Films, 2001. All quotations from the film included in this chapter are from this source.

2. See Thomas Breuer, "From Maradona to Jude Law: Sport in Paolo Sorrentino's Movies," *Studies in European Cinema* (2018): 11–12, DOI: 10.1080/17411548.2018.1554776.

3. For the definition of a Neapolitan film, see Alex Marlow-Mann, *The New Neapolitan Cinema* (Edinburgh: Edinburgh University Press, 2011), 7.

4. Mari also filmed the Eduardo De Filippo play *Sabato, domenica, e lunedì* for Sorrentino in 2004.

5. For example, Alejandro Iñárritu's *The Revenant* (2015) and Terrence Malick's *The Tree of Life* (2011), respectively.

6. Iannone echoes this observation, connecting Sorrentino's—actually Biggazi's—use of the 2.35:1 aspect ratio in all the features since *The Consequences of Love* to the wide-frame aesthetic of filmmakers as diverse as Wes Anderson and Malick. Pasquale Iannone, "Journey to the End of the Night," *Sight and Sound* 23, no. 10 (2013): 38.

7. See Alex Marlow-Mann, "Character Engagement and Alienation in the Cinema of Paolo Sorrentino," in *Italian Film Directors in the New Millennium*, ed. William Hope (Newcastle, UK: Cambridge Scholars Press, 2010), 172n2 regarding the collaborative nature of Sorrentino's film productions.

8. Alberto Spadafora, ed., The Great Beauty: *Told by Director of Photography Luca Bigazzi* (Self-published, CreateSpace Independent Publishing Platform, 2014), 244.

9. *Loro* (2018) is the exception, shot in 2.39:1.

10. In Antonello's words, Sorrentino as screenwriter "has been consistently interested in representing enigmatic, self-absorbed, lonely, hard-to-read characters, who are followed through a progressive existential decline." Pierpaolo Antonello, "*Il Divo*: Paolo Sorrentino's Spectacle of Politics," in *Italian Political Cinema: Public Life, Imaginary, and Identity in Contemporary Italian Film*, ed. Giancarlo Lombardi and Christian Uva (Oxford: Peter Lang, 2016), 293.

11. See Franco Vigni, *La maschera, il potere, la solitudine: Il cinema di Paolo Sorrentino* (Florence, Italy: Aska Edizioni, 2014) 33; Marlow-Mann, *New Neapolitan Cinema*, 107; Alberto Zanetti, "La doppia vita di Antonio," *Cineforum* 409 (November 2001): 63–65. The Kieślowski connection extends to Sorrentino's use in *The Great Beauty* of Zbigniew Preisner's "Dies Irae," originally composed for the Polish director's *Three Colours* trilogy.

12. In her magisterial 1992 study of melancholia in Renaissance literature, Juliana Schiesari argues that *melancholia* is a historically gendered term used to designate *men's* feelings of loss, which as a result are culturally privileged: "the 'grievous' suffering of the melancholic artist" gives rise to "an eroticized nostalgia that recuperates loss in the name of an imaginary unity and that also gives to the melancholic man . . . a privileged position within literary, philosophical, and artistic canons." Juliana Schiesari, *The Gendering of Melancholia: Feminism, Psychoanalysis, and the Symbolics of Loss in Renaissance Literature* (Ithaca, NY: Cornell University Press, 1992), 11–12. This gendered cultural privileging of melancholia comes at the price of women's suffering, further disempowering women by devaluing their comparably negative affective response as merely depression (Tania Modleski, "Clint Eastwoood and Male Weepies," *American Literary History* 22, no. 1 [November 2009]: 140). Schiesari's reading of masculine melancholia implies therefore that woman's suffering (pathos) is taken on by the man, and therefore the male melodrama's feminization of the male protagonist is also a form of appropriation (Schiesar, *Gendering of Melancholia*, 11–12).

13. Guido Bonsaver, "Dall'uomo al Divo: Un'intervista con Paolo Sorrentino," *The Italianist* 29 (2009): 325.

14. "One Man Up—Trivia" IMDb, accessed December 17, 2019, https://www.imdb.com/title/tt0295671/trivia.

15. *Everybody's Right*, trans. Anthony Shugaar (New York: Europa Editions, 2011), 364.

16. This character type could be said to be the model for Servillo's embodiment of Silvio Berlusconi in *Loro 1* and *Loro 2* (2018), if it weren't for the fact that Berlusconi really did start his career as a cruise ship lounge singer, which makes him the ultimate prototype of this model.

17. An explicit intratextual link with *Everybody's Right* emerges during his *Confessioni Pubblicche* monologue (what we might call his *amarcord* or *mi ricordo* speech), when Tony remarks: "I remember when I sang in New York and Frank Sinatra came to hear me." See Paolo Sorrentino, *Everybody's Right*, trans. Anthony Shugaar (New York: Europa Editions, 2011), 9–10.

18. See Marlow-Mann, *New Neapolitan Cinema*, 112n43.

19. According to Bonsaver, Sorrentino's formal approach here betrays the influence of such diverse stylists as Pedro Almodóvar and Quentin Tarantino. Guido Bonsaver, "Prince of Darkness" (Interview), *Sight and Sound* 19, no. 4 (2009): 43.

20. Giogiò Franchini edited Sorrentino's first three feature films, as well as the TV film *Sabato, domenica e lunedì*.

21. See Marlow-Mann, *New Neapolitan Cinema*, 112n46.

22. See Raffaele La Capria, *Ferito a morte* (1961) (Milano: Oscar Mondadori, 2014).

23. According to Marlow-Mann, this is the same diver's knife seen in the credit sequence/flashback to Tony's brother's death while hunting octopus. Marlow-Mann, *New Neapolitan Cinema*, 108.

24. Marlow-Mann, *New Neapolitan Cinema*, 108.

25. Claudio Bisoni likewise argues that Antonio's status as "victim of fate" is "redeemed and erased by means of the posthumous vendetta by his double, the other Pisapia." Claudio Bisoni, "Paolo Sorrentino: Between Engagement and *Savoir Faire*," in *Italian Political Cinema: Public Life, Imaginary, and Identity in Contemporary Italian Film*, ed. Giancarlo Lombardi and Christian Uva (Oxford: Peter Lang, 2016), 257.

26. Breuer makes the same basic point regarding Tony's redemption as a result of Antonio's suicide. Breuer, "From Maradona to Jude Law," 6.

27. Marlow-Mann, *New Neapolitan Cinema*, 107.

28. In this respect, as well, Sorrentino departs completely from the quiet despair embodied in *The Double Life of Veronique*'s ending, in which the surviving Veronique is confronted by the knowledge of her dead double's impossible sacrifice.

29. Catherine O'Rawe, *Stars and Masculinities in Contemporary Italian Cinema* (New York: Palgrave Macmillan, 2014), 164.

2. THE CONSEQUENCES OF LOVE (LE CONSEGUENZE DELL'AMORE): THIS MUST BE THE (NON-) PLACE

1. *Le Conseguenze dell'Amore* (*The Consequences of Love*), Italy: Fandango, Indigo Film, Medusa Film, 2004. All quotations from the film included in this chapter are from this source.

2. See Renga who reads *Consequences* firmly—and very productively—within the mafia film genre crossed with film noir. Dana Renga, "The Mafia Noir: Paolo Sorrentino's *Le conseguenze dell'amore*," in *Unfinished Business: Screening the Italian Mafia in the New Millenium* (Toronto: University of Toronto Press, 2013), 65–79.

3. Alex Marlow-Mann, "Beyond Post-Realism: A Response to Millicent Marcus," *The Italianist* 30 (2010): 161.

4. Cf. Bondanella, who categorizes this and Sorrentino's next film, *The Family Friend*, as examples of the reinvigorated *poliziesco* in twenty-first century Italian cinema. Peter Bondanella, *The History of Italian Cinema*, 3rd ed. (New York: Continuum, 2009), 491–92. This reading is made explicit in Wood and Renga, for instance, by the designation of *Consequences* as an example of neobaroque Italian film noir. Mary Wood, "Lipstick and Chocolate: Paolo Sorrentino's the *Consequences of Love*," in *Mafia Movies: A Reader*, 2nd ed., ed. Dana Renga (Toronto: University of Toronto Press, 2019), 279; Renga, "The Mafia Noir." In my reading I emphasize instead the manner in which Sorrentino and Bigazzi have exploited certain genre-based techniques (such as those of noir) to forge their own brand of transnational art cinema style. Wood's reading hinges on the degree in which *Consequences* fits the mold of the mafia film genre: "although this film is locally specific in terms of being in the Italian language and without well-known stars, its status as a mafia film meant that international audiences would have an understanding of the sorts of stories, characters and iconography to expect" (Wood, "Lipstick and Chocolate," 277). In my argument throughout this book I dissociate Sorrentino's films from genre-based readings in favor of modalities based in specific creative choices eliciting a distinctive hybrid style that I have characterized as more transnational than Italian. As Wood elsewhere notes: "noir conventions are used so widely that they constitute an intellectual and creative choice, rather than a genre. Noir elements are used to indicate dissatisfaction with official version of events, and/or to evoke a dysfunctional world" (2007, 238).

5. Roy Menarini, "Generi nascosti ed espliciti nel recente cinema italiano," in *Lo spazio del reale nel cinema italiano contemporaneo*, ed. Riccardo Guerrini, Giacomo Tagliani, and Francesca Zucconi (Genoa, Italy: Le Mani, 2009), 42.

6. There is nonetheless a bit of Tony Pagoda in Titta; see e.g., *Everybody's Right*, where Pagoda, also the narrator, notes in passing that he once underwent an extremely expensive "blood-cleansing treatment" in Lausanne, Switzerland. Paolo Sorrentino, *Everybody's Right*, trans. Anthony Shugaar (New York: Europa Editions, 2011), 208. Regarding *Consequences'* new, international appeal, including the choice of a modern Mafia story, see Wood, "Lipstick and Chocolate," 278. In a nutshell, "references to a purely local, Italian situation created problems in targeting audiences because they were less comprehensible and interesting to an international audience" (278).

7. Edward Branigan, *Point of View in the Cinema: A Theory of Narration and Subjectivity in Classical Film* (Berlin, Germany: Mouton Publishers, 1984), 64.

8. Anthony Easthope, "Cinécities in the Sixties," in *The Cinematic City*, ed. David B. Clarke (London: Routledge, 1997), 134.

9. See Easthope, "Cinécities in the Sixties," 134–35; András Bálint Kovács, *Screening Modernism: European Art Cinema, 1950–1980* (Chicago: University of Chicago Press, 2007), 149–56.

10. Gilles Deleuze, *Cinema 1: The Movement Image*, trans. Hugh Tomlinson and Barbara Habberjam (Minneapolis: University of Minnesota Press, 1986), 5–7.

11. Deleuze, *Cinema 1*, 127.

12. Deleuze, *Cinema 1*, 208.

13. See Kovács, *Screening Modernism*, 156; Regarding the relevance to *The Consequences of Love* of Antonioni's use of *temps morts* see Marlow-Mann, "Beyond Post-Realism," 169.

14. Alex Marlow-Mann, *The New Neapolitan Cinema* (Edinburgh, Scotland: Edinburgh University Press, 2011), 167.

15. This general point was made by Cesare Casarino ("Images for Housework: Expression, Representation, and the Time of Domestic Labor in Gilles Deleuze's Study of the Cinema," 2015).

16. See Claudio Bisoni, "Paolo Sorrentino: Between Engagement and *Savoir Faire*," in *Italian Political Cinema: Public Life, Imaginary, and Identity in Contemporary Italian Film*, ed. Giancarlo Lombardi and Christian Uva (Oxford: Peter Lang, 2016), 252.

17. See Franco Vigni, *La maschera, il potere, la solitudine: Il cinema di Paolo Sorrentino* (Florence, Italy: Aska Edizioni, 2014), 68.

18. See Marc Augé, *Non-Places: Introduction to an Anthropology of Supermodernity*, trans. John Howe (London: Verso, 1995), 109; "Supermodernity produces non-places, meaning spaces which are not themselves anthropological places" (78). "Non-places mediate a whole mass of relations, with the self and with others, which are only indirectly connected with their purposes. As anthropological places create the organically social, so non-places create solitary contractuality" (94). Regarding Titta's hotel as a nonplace see Marlow-Mann, "Beyond Post-Realism," 169.

19. See Deleuze, *Cinema 1*, 208. Wood, by contrast, reads the film's use of specific kinds of spaces in Lugano and Sicily in terms of Sorrentino's revisioning of Italian noir style. Wood, "Lipstick and Chocolate," 279.

20. Augé, *Non-Places*, 106.

21. Augé, *Non-Places*, 107.

22. As Renga neatly puts it, while Titta is "redeemed through death, Sofia's erasure from the narrative is without consequences." Renga, "The Mafia Noir," 67.

23. Leotta notes that this long take is a reference to the opening scene of Mike Nichols's *The Graduate* (1967). Alfio Leotta, "Do Not Underestimate *The Consequences of Love*: The Representation of the New Mafia in Contemporary Italian Cinema," *Italica* 88, no. 2 (Summer 2011): 292. Wood describes this opening shot as "stupendous . . . [t]he strongly diagonal orthogonal lines of the composition construct[ing] an asymmetrical composition within the frame and destroy[ing] the spontaneous and complete acceptance of illusion." Wood, "Lipstick and Chocolate," 279. See also Renga, "The Mafia Noir," 68.

24. Curiously, his third film, *The Family Friend*, uses voiceover only in its closing minutes, when Geremia speaks as if to his absent father. Otherwise the film does not rely on this device. In contrast, voiceover is a crucial formal technique in *Il Divo* and *This Must Be the Place*, in which

the musings of dead characters are read aloud by an actor. A similar effect is achieved in episode 9 of *The Young Pope*, for instance, in which Belardo reads the letters, published in a fictional issue of *The New Yorker*, that he never sent to his one and only girlfriend. *The Great Beauty* returns to a more sporadic art cinematic use of the voiceover, in key sequences that are revealing of the protagonist's character.

25. According to Silvio Soldini, "with his television stations, [Berlusconi has] succeeded in changing the people themselves. . . . He's taken everything down to the lowest common denominator. We've all become children." Nick Hasted, "Maestros and Mobsters," *Sight and Sound* 20, no. 5 (2010), 25.

26. One thinks for instance of Fellini's *La Dolce Vita*, with its underlying themes of modern alienation and loss.

27. Marlow-Mann calls this "one of the most remarkable [camera movements] in contemporary Italian cinema." Marlow-Mann, "Beyond Post-Realism," 167. Leotta notes that this scene echoes comparable sequences in Danny Boyle's *Trainspotting* (1996). Leotta, "Do Not Underestimate," 292.

28. For an alternative reading of this sequence see Renga, "The Mafia Noir," 73.

29. "Travel is useful, it exercises the imagination. All the rest is disappointment and fatigue [DVD subtitles: "delusion and pain"]. Our journey is entirely imaginary. That is its strength." Louis-Ferdinand Céline, *Journey to the End of Night* (1932; 1952), trans. Ralph Manheim (New York: New Directions, 2006), epigraph.

30. The foregoing is from the DVD subtitles, translated from the Italian. The original translation (by Ralph Manheim for the 1983 New Directions edition) is notably different: "Think of the saving, getting all your thrills from reminiscences. . . . Reminiscences are something we've got plenty of, one can buy beauties, enough to last us a lifetime. . . . Life is more complicated, especially the life of human forms. . . . A hard adventure. None more desperate. Compared with the addiction to perfect forms, cocaine is a pastime for stationmasters. But let's get back to our Sophie! . . . Every time she performed those simple gestures, we experienced surprise and joy. We made strides in poetry, so to speak, just marveling at her being so beautiful and so much more obviously free than we were. The rhythm of her life sprang from other wellsprings than ours. . . . Our wellsprings were forever slow and slimy. The joyful strength, precise yet gentle, which animated her from her hair to her ankles troubled us, alarmed us in a charming sort of way, but definitely alarmed us, yes, that's the word." Céline, *Journey to the End of Night*, 406.

31. See Leotta, "Do Not Underestimate," 296n4.

32. See Renga, "The Mafia Noir," 68.

33. Of which the author himself remarks in the Preface: "If I weren't under such pressure, such duress, I'd suppress the whole lot . . . especially *Journey*. . . . Of all my books it's the only really vicious one. . . . That's right . . . The heart of my sensibility . . . " (Céline, *Journey to the End of Night*, 1).

34. Marlow-Mann, "Beyond Post-Realism," 167.

35. See Renga, "The Mafia Noir," 65–79, for a detailed reading of this scene.

36. Marlow-Mann, "Beyond Post-Realism," 167.

37. Sorrentino replicates this kind of shot in miniature toward the end of *Loro* in the Noemi Letizia birthday party scene, but with a very different effect.

38. "Hypertrophy of the Prostate. Refresher Course 10."

39. See Wood, "Lipstick and Chocolate," 67.

40. Marlow-Mann's term ("Beyond Post-Realism," 167).

41. See Alex Marlow-Mann, *The New Neapolitan Cinema* (Edinburgh: Edinburgh University Press, 2011), 108. Marlow-Mann takes this in a rather different direction, connecting it to André Gide's idea of an "*acte gratuit*, an unmotivated action performed, in true existentialist fashion, to assert one's liberty in the face of a destiny over which one has no control" (108). See also Marlow-Mann, "Beyond Post-Realism,"169.

42. According to Antonello, this is the same section of highway between Palermo and Capaci on which Judge Giovanni Falcone was assassinated in 1992 and on which Sorrentino recreated this event for *Il Divo*. Pierpaolo Antonello, "*Il Divo*: Paolo Sorrentino's Spectacle of Politics," in *Italian Political Cinema: Public Life, Imaginary, and Identity in Contemporary Italian Film*, ed. Giancarlo Lombardi and Christian Uva (Oxford: Peter Lang, 2016), 300. The setting of the scenes in *The Consequences of*

Love's third act, however, is somewhat ambiguous, as under "filming locations" (apart from Lugano) the IMDb lists only Naples. Also, to the best of my knowledge, there is no Hotel New Europe—where Titta's tribunal scene takes place—adjacent to the airport in Palermo, while there is one in Naples.

43. See e.g. Renga, "The Mafia Noir," 78; Wood, "Lipstick and Chocolate," 278.

3. *THE FAMILY FRIEND (L'AMICO DI FAMIGLIA)*: "RIDICULOUS MEN AND BEAUTIFUL WOMEN"

The phrase is from Jonathan Romney, "Tragedies of Ridiculous Men," *Sight and Sound* 17, no. 4 (April 2007): n.p.

1. Regarding alignment vs. allegiance see Murray Smith, *Engaging Characters: Fiction, Emotion, and the Cinema* (Oxford: Clarendon Press, 1995).

2. Regarding *Consequences* as a misogynistic film, see Dana Renga, "The Mafia Noir: Paolo Sorrentino's *Le conseguenze dell'amore*," in *Unfinished Business: Screening the Italian Mafia in the New Millenium* (Toronto: University of Toronto Press, 2013), 65–79. Renga's interpretation of Sofia as a femme fatale hinges on her reading of the film as an instance of film noir, a frame of reference I do not adopt here (71).

3. Marcus describes Wertmüller's use of Sabaudia as follows: "The harsh, sterile, rectilinear world of Fascist architecture, as typified by the modernist assassination site." Millicent Marcus, *Italian Film In the Light of Neorealism* (Princeton, NJ: Princeton University Press, 1986), 331–32.

4. See Claudio Bisoni, "Paolo Sorrentino: Between Engagement and *Savoir Faire*," in *Italian Political Cinema: Public Life, Imaginary, and Identity in Contemporary Italian Film*, ed. Giancarlo Lombardi and Christian Uva (Oxford: Peter Lang, 2016), 252.

5. Regarding the film's use of the "empty spaces and modernist architecture of the Agro Pontino" as "perfect metonym for alienation," see Alex Marlow-Mann, "Beyond Post-Realism: A Response to Millicent Marcus," *The Italianist* 30 (2010): 170.

6. Like his first two features, *The Family Friend* is shot on 35 mm as opposed to digital.

7. See e.g., Belardo's dream/flashback in episode 1, in which his younger self gazes lovingly upon his mostly naked mother, who reclines in the shade of a tree on a Colorado riverbank, in a composition out of a Pre-Raphaelite painting. Hennessey elaborates the importance of lighting to Bigazzi's, hence Sorrentino's, style and the evocation of a "painterly chiaroscuro" in a digital format. Brendan Hennessey, "Reel Simulations: CGI and Special Effects in Two Films by Paolo Sorrentino," *The Italianist* 37, no. 3 (2017): 449–63, DOI: 10.1080/02614340.2017.1409582 2017. See also Nick Vivarelli, "Paolo Sorrentino on Why Maradona Has a Special Place in His Heart," *Variety*, December 13, 2015, https://variety.com/2015/film/global/paolo-sorrentino-on-making-youth-and -why-maradona-has-a-special-place-in-his-heart-1201660014/.

8. I thank Grace McCarthy for drawing my attention to Garland-Thomson's work and for first suggesting the stare as a cinematic and not merely a sociological structure. According to a 2010 collection of critical essays on disability theory and film, despite formulations of the male, female, and queer gazes, "an examination of the gaze at and of the disabled . . . and its role in perpetuating stereotyping has not yet taken place." Johnson Cheu, "Seeing Blindness On-Screen: The Blind, Female Gaze," in *The Problem Body: Projecting Disability on Film*, ed. Sally Chivers and Nicole Markotić (Columbus: Ohio State University Press, 2010), 68.

9. Rosemarie Garland-Thomson, *Staring: How We Look* (Oxford: Oxford University Press, 2009), 42.

10. Philip French, "*The Family Friend*," *Guardian*, March 18, 2007, https://www.theguardian.com /film/2007/mar/18/worldcinema.thriller.

11. See Angelo Restivo, *The Cinema of Economic Miracles: Visuality and Modernization in the Italian Art Film* (Durham, NC: Duke University Press, 2002), 53 and 118.

12. Not to mention, in a non-Italian example, Luke Monaghan's video for Sam Smith's "Writing's on the Wall," for the 2015 James Bond film *Spectre*, which directly references *The Conformist*'s scene in the fascist police headquarters.

13. See Marlow-Mann, "Beyond Post-Realism," 170.
14. Philip French, "*The Family Friend*."
15. In the film's climactic scene in Rome, Geremia asks the same question of three men dressed as gladiators.
16. Comparisons are inevitable here with the climactic Cardinals' volleyball tournament as they await the missing pope's first address, in Nani Moretti's *Habemus Papam* (2011). Where Sorrentino's Vatican volleyball sequence is also somewhat prurient, Moretti's is highly comic—as is the scene at the beginning of *The Young Pope*'s second episode, when another group of nuns play soccer. Regarding the significance of sport in Sorrentino's film see Thomas Breuer, "From Maradona to Jude Law: Sport in Paolo Sorrentino's Movies," *Studies in European Cinema* (2018), DOI: 10.1080/17411548.2018.1554776.
17. Marlow-Mann, "Beyond Post-Realism," 164–65.
18. French, "*The Family Friend*."
19. French, "*The Family Friend*."
20. Bonsaver reads the integration of image and music in *The Family Friend* somewhat less favorably: "every single shot is so self-conscious and elaborate that it verges on the baroque or, more dangerously, on the style of an MTV music video." Guido Bonsaver, "The Family Friend," *Sight and Sound* 17, no. 4 (2007): 5.
21. Marlow-Mann, "Beyond Post-Realism," 164.
22. Marlow-Mann, "Beyond Post-Realism," 165.
23. Jeremiah is a masculine first name, originating in ancient Hebrew, meaning "God (Yahweh) will raise."
24. To the best of my knowledge, Philip French is the first critic to note the connection between the main characters in Shakespeare's play and Sorrentino's film ("*The Family Friend*." *Guardian*, March 18, 2007. https://www.theguardian.com/film/2007/mar/18/worldcinema.thriller).
25. Marlow-Mann, "Beyond Post-Realism," 165.
26. Stereotypes are inescapable. As Sander Gilman puts it: "I am not speaking here about 'realities' but about their representations and the reflection of these representations in the world of those who stereotype as well as those who are stereotyped." Sander Gilman, *The Jew's Body* (New York: Routledge, 1991), 1. See also Carl Plantinga, *Moving Viewers: American Film and the Spectator's Experience* (Berkeley: University of California Press, 2009), 210–212.
27. Marlow-Mann, "Beyond Post-Realism," 166.
28. Peter Bradshaw, "*The Family Friend*" (rev.), *Guardian Online*, March 16, 2007, https://www.theguardian.com/film/2007/mar/16/worldcinema.drama.
29. Kenneth Gross, *Shylock Is Shakespeare* (Chicago: University of Chicago Press, 2006), 159.
30. Andrew Pulver, "Paolo Sorrentino: 'I Never Use a Crude Approach to Showing the Naked Bodies of Older People,'" *Guardian*, January 15, 2016, https://www.theguardian.com/film/2016/jan/15/paolo-sorrentino-michael-caine-youth-oscar-great-beauty.
31. Regarding the potential reading of Geremia as anti-Semitic stereotype see Marlow Mann: "such a critique demonstrates that the use of unconventional patterns of engagement does not necessarily make a film immune to the kind of ideological criticism often applied to more Manichean structures" ("Beyond Post-Realism," 172n9).
32. Gilman, *The Jew's Body*, 124.
33. Gross, *Shylock Is Shakespeare*, 62.
34. Marlow-Mann, "Beyond Post-Realism," 170.
35. Gross, *Shylock Is Shakespeare*, 171.
36. Alain Elkann, "Alain Elkann Interviews Italian Director and Screenwriter Paolo Sorrentino," Alain Elkann (website), March 5, 2017, http://www.alainelkanninterviews.com/paolo-sorrentino/, 16.
37. The phase is Catherine O'Rawe's, in reference to *Il Divo*'s portrait of Andreotti. Catherine O'Rawe, *Stars and Masculinities in Contemporary Italian Cinema* (New York: Palgrave Macmillan, 2014).

1. *Il Divo*. Italy and France: Indigo Film, Lucky Red, Parco Film, 2008. All quotations from the film included in this chapter are from this source.

2. Italian political terminology can be confusing for non-Italian viewers. For instance, "prime minister," the best translation of *Presidente del Consiglio*, is rendered in the subtitles as "premier." This confusion is exacerbated by the existence of the other, more symbolic, office, *Presidente della Repubblica*, "president of the republic."

3. Marcus, "The Ironist and the Auteur," 246.

4. See Lia Luchetti and Anna Lisa Tota, "The Period of the 'Strategy of Tension' in Italy (1969–1993) and the Piazza Fontana Bombing in Milan," in *Routledge International Handbook of Memory Studies*, ed. Anna Lisa Tota and Tever Hagen (New York: Routledge, 2015), 382.

5. Nicoletta Marini-Maio, "A Spectre Is Haunting Italy: The Double Emplotment of the Moro Affair," in *Terrorism, Italian Style: The Representation of Terrorism and Political Violence in Contemporary Italian Cinema*, ed. Ruth Glynn, Giancarlo Lombardi, and Alan O'Leary (London: IGRS Books, 2012), 158.

6. Regarding the national-cinematic theme of the haunting of Italy by Aldo Moro's ghost, see e.g., Alan O'Leary, "Locations of Moro: The Kidnap in the Cinema," in *Remembering Aldo Moro*, ed. Ruth Glynn and Giancarlo Lombardi (Oxford: Legenda, 2012), 163; Catherine O'Rawe, *Stars and Masculinities in Contemporary Italian Cinema* (New York: Palgrave Macmillan, 2014), 156. See also Antonio Ferrari, "Perché Aldo Moro è il Kennedy italiano," *Corriere della Sera*, March 12, 2018, https://www.corriere.it/extra-per-voi/2018/03/06/perche-aldo-moro-kennedy-italiano-a09644bc-2153-11e8-a661-74ccbd41f00f.shtml.

7. In this respect, despite their marked formal differences, *Il Divo* is similar in spirit to Marco Bellocchio's *Buongiorno, notte* (2003) and Nanni Moretti's *Il Caimano* (2006), which are not biopics so much as imagined alternatives to the real-historical stories of Moro and Silvio Berlusconi, respectively. See O'Rawe, *Stars and Masculinities*, 139–62, for a comparative analysis of all of these films.

8. *The Young Pope* to one side, *Il Divo* has one of the most eclectic soundtracks in Sorrentino's oeuvre, containing more eighteenth-, nineteenth- and early twentieth-century classical and symphonic music than any of his other films. The list includes Vivaldi, Fauré, Sibelius, Saint-Saën, as well as one of the director's strangest audiovisual juxtapositions: a scene in which Toto Riina, Mafia boss of bosses, stops to tend to his tomato plants while Beth Orton's "Conceived" plays extradiegetically on the soundtrack. The song actually bridges this and the previous scene, which concludes with the much-speculated-upon kiss between Riina and Andreotti. Most improbably effective of all is the use, over the film's final scene, of Trio's 1980s hit "Da da da (ich lieb dich nicht du liebst mich nicht)." Marcus highlights what she calls "the incongruous relationship between music and image that drives the entire film." Millicent Marcus, "The Ironist and the Auteur: Post-Realism in Paolo Sorrentino's *Il Divo*," *The Italianist* 30 (2010): 252.

9. An instance of what Marlow-Mann identifies as the film's recurrent "fantapolitica." Alex Marlow-Mann, "Beyond Post-Realism: A Response to Millicent Marcus." *The Italianist* 30 ((2010): 266.

10. Luchetti and Tota, "Period of the 'Strategy of Tension' in Italy," 383.

11. Marcus, "The Ironist and the Auteur," 251.

12. Sorrentino's contention in an interview that he always imagined this sequence in slow motion is entirely unhelpful. Guido Bonsaver, "Prince of Darkness" (Interview), *Sight and Sound* 19, no. 4 (2009): 5.

13. See Christian Uva, "The New Cinema of Political Engagement," in *Italian Political Cinema: Public Life, Imaginary, and Identity in Contemporary Italian Film*, ed. Giancarlo Lombardi and Christian Uva (Oxford: Peter Lang, 2016), 31; See also Riccardo Guerrini, Giacomo Tagliani, and Francesca Zucconi, "Introduzione," in *Lo spazio del reale nel cinema italiano contemporaneo* (Genoa, Italy: Le Mani, 2009), 10; Nick Hasted, "Maestros and Mobsters," *Sight and Sound* 20, no. 5 (2010).

14. Marcus, "The Ironist and the Auteur," 246.

15. Marlow-Mann, "Beyond Post-Realism," 265.

16. See Marcus, "The Ironist and the Auteur," 246; see also Louis Bayman and Sergio Rigoletto, "The Fair and the Museum: Framing the Popular," in *Popular Italian Cinema* (New York: Palgrave Macmillan, 2013), 8. According to Crowdus: "in its hyperbaroque visual stylings, acid-tinged psychobiographical satire, and fantasy-like rendering of controversial political issues, *Il Divo* recalls the cinematic approach of the later films of Elio Petri, such as *Investigation of a Citizen Above Suspicion*, *The Working Class Goes to Heaven*, or *Todo Modo*." Gary Crowdus, "Exposing the Dark Secrets of Italian Political History: An Interview with Paolo Sorrentino," *Cineaste* (Summer 2009): 34.

17. Edoardo Zaccagnini and Giovanni Spagnoletti, "Intervista a Paolo Sorrentino," *Close-up* 23 (2007): 109–116.

18. Pierpaolo Antonello, "*Il Divo*: Paolo Sorrentino's Spectacle of Politics," in *Italian Political Cinema: Public Life, Imaginary, and Identity in Contemporary Italian Film*, ed. Giancarlo Lombardi and Christian Uva (Oxford: Peter Lang, 2016), 301.

19. Marcus, "The Ironist and the Auteur," 264.

20. Peter Bondanella, *The History of Italian Cinema*, 3rd ed. (New York: Continuum, 2009), 48–52.

21. Marcus, "The Ironist and the Auteur," 247.

22. See Alex Marlow-Mann, "Beyond Post-Realism," 265. For a reading of irony as a positive, emancipatory social force, see Richard Rorty, *Contingency, Irony, and Solidarity* (Cambridge: Cambridge University Press 1989), 73–95.

23. An equivalent thing happened in the immediate aftermath of 9/11 when many pundits on both left and right announced the death of irony with the advent of modern global terrorism. See Jeffrey Sconce, "Irony, Nihilism, and the New American 'Smart' Film," *Screen* 43, no. 4 (2002): 353–54.

24. Marlow-Mann, "Beyond Post-Realism," 265.

25. *One Man Up* (or: "one man too many"; *l'uomo in più*) signals the metaphysical redundancy of one of its two main characters; *The Consequences of Love* appears over a black screen following the complete submersion of the protagonist in a large vat of liquid cement; *The Family Friend* follows the misadventures of a repulsive and avaricious man with no friends; *This Must Be the Place* charts the journey of a retired rock star as he tracks down his father's wartime tormentor in the middle of a snowy desert; *The Great Beauty* ends with the protagonist failing to find the titular beauty in his decadent life in one of the world's most beautiful cities; *Youth* is about two old men contemplating their mortality from a position of disappointment; *The Young Pope* is about a newly elected Pope who, while only forty-seven, espouses the values of a premodern Catholic Church.

26. According to Leotta, "Sorrentino proposes a peculiar version of Comedy Italian Style that often relies on irony to denounce social problems." Alfio Leotta, "Do Not Underestimate the Consequences of Love: The Representation of the New Mafia in Contemporary Italian Cinema," *Italica* 88, no. 2 (Summer 2011): 291.

27. Cf. Marlow-Mann, "Beyond Post-Realism," 264. Sorrentino extends this homage to Tarantino's film by casting Harvey Keitel as one of the two leads in *Youth*.

28. Pierpaolo Antonello, "The Ambiguity of Realism and Its Posts: A Response to Millicent Marcus," *The Italianist* 30 (2010): 260.

29. Quoted in Thomas Elsaesser, "Bertolt Brecht and Contemporary Film," in *Reinterpreting Brecht: His Influence on Contemporary Drama and Film*, ed. Pia Kleber and Colin Visser (Cambridge: Cambridge University Press, 1990), 175.

30. See Elsaesser, "Bertolt Brecht and Contemporary Film," 175. See also Jean-Luc Godard, *Godard on Godard*, ed. Jean Narboni and Tom Milne (New York: Viking Press, 1972), 31.

31. Cf. Maurizio Grande: "The political nature of a film reposes on the political theme which inspires it; in the same way, it should inspire its construction and production of meaning, far beyond the representation of a political context; that is to say, the mise-en-scène of the politics." Quoted in Giacomo Tagliani, "Depicting Life, Analyzing the Power: The 'Actuality' of Italian Cinema," *Journal of Italian Cinema and Media Studies* 2, no. 2 (2014): 200.

32. Gary Crowdus, "Exposing the Dark Secrets of Italian Political History," 37.

33. Marlow-Mann, "Beyond Post-Realism," 267.

34. Marlow-Mann, "Beyond Post-Realism," 266.

35. For an insightful interpretation of Teardo's unusual music for this scene, see Pierpaolo Antonello, "*Il Divo*: Paolo Sorrentino's Spectacle of Politics," 295.

36. Marlow-Mann, "Beyond Post-Realism," 266.
37. Marlow-Mann, "Beyond Post-Realism," 264.
38. Regarding Andreotti's resemblance to Max Schreck's vampire in Murnau's 1922 film, see Bonsaver, "Prince of Darkness," 44. The horror film intertexts begin, however, with the opening shot of Andreotti in close-up raising his head to reveal a face full of acupuncture needles, a migraine treatment, the resulting image recalling Pinhead from Clive Barker's *Hellraiser*. See O'Rawe, *Stars and Masculinities*, 154.
39. Antonello, "Ambiguity of Realism," 260.
40. Antonello, "Ambiguity of Realism," 260–61.
41. Marcus, "The Ironist and the Auteur," 254.
42. Astrid Erll, *Memory in Culture*, trans. S. B. Young (New York: Palgrave Macmillan, 2011), 114–15
43. See Marcus, who, in claiming that Fellini's *Amarcord* invokes memory not only in its content but also in its very form, its process, concludes: "[t]he medium is the memory." Millicent Marcus, "Fellini's *Amarcord*: Film as Memory," *Quarterly Review of Film & Video* 2, no. 4 (1977): 424, DOI: 10.1080/10509207709391365.
44. See Alison Landsberg, "Prosthetic Memory: The Ethics and Politics of Memory in an Age of Mass Culture," in *Memory and Popular Film*, ed. Paul Grainge (New York: Manchester University Press, 2003), 148–49. Landsberg emphasizes that, "in contrast to collective memories, which tend to be geographically specific and which serve to reinforce and naturalize a group's identity, prosthetic memories are not the property of a single group" (148–49).
45. Cited in Luisela Alvaray, "National, Regional and Global: New Waves of Latin American Cinema," *Cinema Journal* 47, no. 3 (2008): 62. See also Russell J. A. Kilbourn, *Cinema, Memory, Modernity: The Representation of Memory from the Art Film to Transnational Cinema* (New York: Routledge, 2010).
46. Erll, *Memory in Culture*, 113.
47. See Luchetti and Tota, "Period of the 'Strategy of Tension' in Italy," 384.
48. Marcus, "The Ironist and the Auteur," 261–62.
49. See Kilbourn, *Cinema, Memory, Modernity*, 1–45.
50. In *Loro* Berlusconi is also shown as an inveterate wisecracker and prankster but, unlike *Il Divo*'s depiction of Andreotti, *Loro* suggests that Berlusconi's sense of humour is considerably less sophisticated and ironic.
51. Antonello, "Ambiguity of Realism," 261.
52. The song's title inevitably anticipates that of Marco Tullio Giordana's 2003 film/television series, *The Best of Youth* (*Il meglio gioventù*).
53. O'Rawe, referencing Antonello, "Ambiguity of Realism," calls the confession a "counterfactual" scene offering Italian viewers a phantasmic resolution to a "traumatic past" (*Stars and Masculinities*, 155).
54. It is also like an ironic inversion of the famous title of Pasolini's 1974 *Corriere della Sera* editorial: "What is this coup d'état? I know" ("Cos'è questo golpe? Io so"), in which he states that, although he cannot divulge them for lack of evidence, he knows the names of the politicians responsible for both anticommunist and antifascist actions since 1968: bombings, kidnappings, assassinations, and other atrocities, perpetrated for the purpose of maintaining the political status quo in Italy, with the assistance of the CIA. That Andreotti's would be one of these names is almost certain. See Luchetti and Tota, "Period of the 'Strategy of Tension' in Italy," 385.
55. Regarding the dinner scene as a *Last Supper* set piece, see Marcus, "The Ironist and the Auteur," 251.
56. Marcus, "The Ironist and the Auteur," 255.
57. Although shot in 35 mm, *Il Divo* is the first of Sorrentino's feature films to be put through a digital intermediate for color timing, as well as other post-production processes.
58. "The Cricket . . . makes his first appearance in chapter IV, after Pinocchio's mischief has landed his creator Geppetto in prison, and insists that Pinocchio must either attend school or work, to function properly in the world. When Pinocchio refuses to listen, the Cricket states, 'You are a puppet and what's worse is that you have a head of wood,' whereupon Pinocchio throws a mallet at the cricket, killing him. In chapter XIII, the Cricket appears as a ghost to Pinocchio, telling him to return home rather than keep an appointment with the Fox and the Cat (*Il Gatto e la Volpe*). Pinocchio refuses and in chapter XIV, he is subsequently injured." Wikipedia, s.v. "Pinocchio," last edited on September 25, 2019, 18:09, https://en.wikipedia.org/wiki/Pinocchio.

59. Alan O'Leary, "Locations of Moro," 163; See also Marini-Maio, "A Spectre Is Haunting Italy," 159; O'Rawe, *Stars and Masculinities*, 155–56.

60. See O'Rawe, *Stars and Masculinities*, 156. O'Rawe's reading of this scene differs somewhat in that she sees Sorrentino's Moro as both alive again and yet still dead; as "simultaneously bodiless . . . a phantasmatic presence . . . and as a body that is unkillable"; hence her phrasing of this scene as a "fantasy of resurrection" (156).

61. O'Rawe, *Stars and Masculinities*, 156.

62. András Bálint Kovács, *Screening Modernism: European Art Cinema, 1950–1980* (Chicago: University of Chicago Press, 2007), 96–99.

63. Each of which (Sartrean philosophy and "vulgar Freudianism") is exemplified and parodied in the films of Alfred Hitchcock. According to Antonello, the famous ending of *Psycho* may in fact be referenced in the closing slow track-in to a close-up on Andreotti's mask-like face. Antonello, "*Il Divo*," 301. See LaPlace, "Producing and Consuming the Woman's Film," 153.

64. Kovács, *Screening Modernism*, 99.

65. Kovács, *Screening Modernism*, 96.

66. Kovács, *Screening Modernism*, 95–96.

67. See Russell J. A. Kilbourn, "American Frankenstein: Modernity's Monstrous Progeny," *Mosaic* 38, no. 3 (2005): 167–83.

68. Mary Harron, *American Psycho* (1999). The other, Jewish, pole in this litany of confessions, public and otherwise, occurs in Philip Roth's *Operation Shylock: A Confession* (New York: Vintage, 1993), which tells the highly self-reflexive story of a man, Phillip Roth, forced to impersonate his own double, in order to prevent him from causing a reverse exodus of Jews from Israel to Europe. The book concludes with a "Note to the Reader": "This confession is false" (n.p.).

69. Kovács, *Screening Modernism*, 93.

70. Antonello, "Ambiguity of Realism," 260.

71. See Michael Sicinski, "Paolo Sorrentino: A Medium Talent," *Cinemascope* (2017), 18. Sicinski's analysis of *Il Divo* is dismissive of the formal style yet right about its appropriateness to theme: "Sorrentino's hyperactive zoom and crane style fits *Il Divo* like a power suit, because it swirls round a void" (18).

72. Quoted in Antonello, "*Il Divo*," 297n8. These are Saint Ignatius of Loyola's words, from the *Spiritual Exercises*, the source of Elio Petri's title *Todo Modo* (1976), which examines the Moro scandal, as well as the basis of Andreotti's dialogue in this scene. Antonello also points out that otherwise Andreotti's other confessional scenes are either farcical (with Cossiga, the president of the republic) or deny any responsibility (with his local priest) (302).

73. Antonello, "*Il Divo*: Paolo Sorrentino's Spectacle of Politics," 302.

74. Regarding Andreotti as a god see Tagliani, "Depicting Life, Analyzing the Power," 211.

75. Sorrentino: "My original idea was to make a sort of 'rock opera' about Andreotti. Italian politics has some very grotesque aspects, and I know that some people think *Il Divo* is a grotesque film, but I believe it's actually very realistic" (quoted in Crowdus, "Exposing the Dark Secrets of Italian Political History," 34). See also Bonsaver, "Prince of Darkness," 44, where Sorrentino connects the film's rock opera aspects with its spectacularity. Regarding Sorrentino's style as grotesque see Giovanni Spagnoletti and Roy Menarini, "Istruzioni per l'uso: Forme della politica nel cinema italiano contemporanea," *Close-up* 23 (2007–2008): 3.

76. Kovács, *Screening Modernism*, 99.

5. *THIS MUST BE THE PLACE*: FROM THE RIDICULOUS TO THE UNSPEAKABLE (A HOLOCAUST ROAD MOVIE)

1. *This Must Be the Place*. Italy, France, and Ireland: Indigo Film, Lucky Red, Medusa Film, 2011. All quotations from the film included in this chapter are from this source.

2. Marianne Hirsch, *Family Frames: Photography, Narrative and Postmemory* (Cambridge, MA: Harvard University Press, 1997), 22.

3. As *post-postrealism* is an unwieldy term, however, I will refrain from using it apart from here, to make this point.

4. See Andrea Minuz, "Com'è fosco il potere raccontato dal cinema italiano," *Il Foglio*, February 5, 2018, https://www.ilfoglio.it/cinema/2018/02/05/news/cinema-sono-tornato-sorrentino-fosco-potere-176959/.

5. Even Titta di Girolamo in *The Consequences of Love* isn't immune. As he remarks in voiceover during the scene in the Swiss bank when they discover the missing $100,000: "You've got to be ready to run the risk of looking ridiculous."

6. See Jonathan Romney, "On the Road Again," *Sight and Sound* 22, no. 4 (April 2012): 16–20; Trevor Johnston, "This Must Be the Place," *Sight and Sound* 22, no. 4 (April 2012): 78–79.

7. The Talking Heads featured among three individuals thanked by Sorrentino during his Best Foreign Film Oscar acceptance speech for *The Great Beauty* in 2014. Eugenia Paulicelli, *Italian Style: Fashion and Film from Early Cinema to the Digital Age* (New York: Bloomsbury Academic, 2016), 185. The song "This Must Be the Place (Naïve Melody)" is heard on the soundtrack six times, both diegetically (both David Byrne and Grant Goodman, who plays Rachel's son, Tommy, perform the song) and extradiegetically (Trevor Green, Antonio Andrade, The Old Believers, Gloria). Arcade Fire's cover of the song, while also mentioned, is not featured on the soundtrack.

8. Elizabeth Ezra and Terry Rowden. "General Introduction: What Is Transnational Cinema?," in *Transnational Cinema: The Film Reader* (New York: Routledge, 2006), 4.

9. Peter Bondanella, *The History of Italian Cinema*, 3rd ed. (New York: Continuum, 2009), 139.

10. An act of (ironic) cultural appropriation anticipated by the real-life new wave British rocker Siouxsie Sioux.

11. In Bisoni's words, Cheyenne initially appears to be "paralysed . . . within a perennially post-adolescent condition." Claudio Bisoni, "Paolo Sorrentino: Between Engagement and *Savoir Faire*," in *Italian Political Cinema: Public Life, Imaginary, and Identity in Contemporary Italian Film*, ed. Giancarlo Lombardi and Christian Uva (Oxford: Peter Lang, 2016), 257.

12. See András Bálint Kovács, *Screening Modernism: European Art Cinema, 1950–1980* (Chicago: University of Chicago Press, 2007), 93.

13. See Stan Jones, "Wenders' *Paris, Texas* and the 'European Way of Seeing,' " in *European Identity in Cinema*, ed. Wendy Everett (Bristol, UK: Intellect, 1996), 57.

14. While acknowledging Cheyenne's state of perpetual adolescence, Romney stresses that the retired rock star is also what he calls one of Sorrentino's "Goblin dandies . . . prematurely ancient, pickled in the aspic of his outmoded image." Romney, "On the Road Again," 17.

15. Jean Baudrillard, "Simulation," in *Simulacra and Simulation* (Ann Arbor: University of Michigan Press, 1994), 13–14.

16. Kovács, *Screening Modernism*, 102.

17. Kovács, *Screening Modernism*, 99.

18. Kovács, *Screening Modernism*, 120.

19. Kovács, *Screening Modernism*, 102.

20. Romney, "On the Road Again," 18.

21. Cheyenne's lax historical attitude recalls a scene in Fassbinder's *Ali: Fear Eats the Soul* (1974), in which Ali, a Moroccan *Gastarbeiter*, is asked by his older German wife as they go to eat at Osteria Italiana, the Führer's favorite restaurant in Munich (which was still in the same location as of August 2018): "Hitler, weißt du?" to which Ali blandly replies: "Ja, Hitler."

22. See e.g., Babis Akstoglou's interview with Wenders. Babis Akstoglou, "Wim Wenders, A Filmmaker on the Road," in *Wim Wenders*, ed. Jason Wood and Ian Haydn Smith (London: Wallflower, 2009), 14.

23. On the influence of the American road movie on what he calls the "second period" of European modernist filmmaking in the 1970s, see Kovács, *Screening Modernism*, 102–103. For Romney, "Sorrentino doesn't seem to be exploring the USA so much as revisiting favourite cinematic landscapes." Romney, "On the Road Again," 17.

24. *Proto-* because, while the films' stories are meaningfully transnational, spanning countries and continents, the pre-1989 production conditions predate the emergence of full-blown economic and cultural globalization.

25. Babis Aktsoglou, "Wim Wenders," 38.

26. In Wenders's 1984 film Stanton's character's name, like De Niro's in *Taxi Driver*, is Travis, evidently the go-to name for 1970s and 1980s New Hollywood weirdoes. "Even though Travis seems to have rid himself of his violent obsessions, he—like his namesake in *Taxi Driver*—drives into the night still full of threat in a culture that cultivates and supports men who are possessed by their desire to master women" Kolker and Beicken, quoted in Jones, "Wenders' *Paris, Texas* and the 'European Way of Seeing,'" 52.

27. Regarding *La grande bellezza*'s complex transnational funding structure, see Marco Cucco, "Che cosa è un film? *La grande bellezza* in una prospettiva di economia e politica dei media," in *La trama dei media: Stato, imprese, pubblico nella società dell'informazione* (Rome: Carocci, 2014), 106–108.

28. Silvestra Mariniello and James Cisternos, "Experience and Memory in the Films of Wim Wenders," *SubStance* 34, no. 1 (2005): 166.

29. See also Jones, "Wenders' *Paris, Texas* and the 'European Way of Seeing,'" 54.

30. Coco Fusco, "Angels, History and Poetic Fantasy: An Interview With Wim Wenders," *Cineaste* 16, no. 4 (1988): 16.

31. Lee Hill, "Paris, Texas," *Cinémathèque Annotations on Film* 72 (October 2014), 3.

32. Romney, "On the Road Again," 18.

33. Erling B. Holtsmark, "The *Katabasis* Theme in Modern Cinema," in *Classical Myth and Culture in the Cinema*, ed. Martin M. Winkler (New York: Oxford University Press, 2001), 26. See Russell J. A. Kilbourn, *Cinema, Memory, Modernity: The Representation of Memory from the Art Film to Transnational Cinema* (New York: Routledge, 2010), 30–35.

34. Michael Sicinski, "Paolo Sorrentino: A Medium Talent," *Cinemascope* (2017): 19.

35. On this point see Giorgio Agamben, "The Camp as Biopolitical Paradigm of the Modern," in *Homo Sacer: Sovereign Power and Bare Life*, trans. Daniel Heller Roazen (Stanford, CA: Stanford University Press, 1998), 119–88.

36. Robert Plath and his story of inventing the wheeled suitcase is entirely true.

37. Written in 1919, published 1952.

38. Primo Levi, *If This Is a Man* and *The Truce*, trans. Stuart Woolf (Bungay, Suffolk, UK: Sphere, 1988), 13

39. Levi, *If This Is a Man*, 15.

40. Dante, *Inferno*, trans. Mandelbaum (Toronto: Bantam, 1992), 26:118–20.

41. Levi, *If This Is a Man*, 134.

42. Levi, *If This Is a Man*, 133.

43. "Like *Il Divo*, *This Must Be the Place* underwent a digital intermediate process for color grading, etc. Sorrentino and his team also used a new type of film negative, Vision3 500T 5219, that works particularly well in scenes with lower light levels and more higher dark-light contrasts." "Vision3 500T Colour Negative Film 5219/7219," Kodak Corporation, accessed October 30, 2019, https://www.kodak.com/vn/en/motion/Products/Production/5219/default.htm.

44. Giorgio Agamben, *Homo Sacer: Sovereign Power and Bare Life*, trans. Daniel Heller Roazen (Stanford, CA: Stanford University Press, 1998), 185.

45. Levi, *If This Is a Man*, 98.

46. Romney speculates that the missing son subplot was all but lost in the editing process. Romney, "On the Road Again," 18.

47. In Romney's words (in a nod to Marcel Duchamp), "the oppressor stripped bare like his victims." Romney, "On the Road Again," 20

48. In Aktsoglou's summary, "The film begins with Travis's muteness (the impact of the surroundings in the primitive landscape of the American West is so awesome as to shake the hero's mind, to the point that his loss of speech seems natural) and ends with a shower of words (the peep-show scene)" Aktsoglou, "Wim Wenders," 38.

49. Aktsoglou, "Wim Wenders," 38.

6. THE GREAT BEAUTY (LA GRANDE BELLEZZA): REFLECTIVE NOSTALGIA AND THE IRONIC ELEGIAC

Portions of this chapter first appeared in Russell J. A. Kilbourn, "The 'Primal Scene': Memory, Redemption, and 'Woman' in the Films of Paolo Sorrentino." Special issue, *Journal of Italian Cinema and Media Studies* 7, no. 3 (2019): 377–94.

Paolo Sorrentino, *Everybody's Right*, trans. Anthony Shugaar (New York: Europa Editions, 2011), 210.

1. *La Grande Bellezza* (*The Great Beauty*). Italy and France: Indigo Film and Medusa Film, 2013. All quotations from the film included in this chapter are from this source.
2. Regarding the film's "melancholic resurrection" of times past via the cinematic representation of Rome, see Giuseppina Mecchia, "Birds in the Roman Sky: Shooting for the Sublime in *La grande bellezza*," *Forum Italicum* 50, no. 1 (2016): 184.
3. See e.g., Astrid Erll, *Memory in Culture*, trans. S. B. Young (New York: Palgrave Macmillan, 2011).
4. Alison Landsberg, "Prosthetic Memory: The Ethics and Politics of Memory in an Age of Mass Culture," in *Memory and Popular Film*, ed. Paul Grainge (New York: Manchester University Press, 2003), 144.
5. Svetlana Boym, *The Future of Nostalgia* (New York: Basic Books, 2001), 41.
6. Boym, *Future of Nostalgia*, 41.
7. Frederic Jameson, *Postmodernism, or The Cultural Logic of Late Capitalism* (Durham, NC: Duke University Press, 1999), 287.
8. The two directors have shared the odd actor, as well: e.g., Barbara Steele, who plays Mezzabotta's mistress in *8 ½* (as well as the lead in Mario Bava's *Black Sunday* [1960] and many other films) can be glimpsed briefly behind Jep in the long scene at the contemporary art collector's party, looking on while the little girl creates her giant abstract action painting.
9. Regarding *The Great Beauty* as a "strongly political film" see Andrea Minuz, *Political Fellini: Journey to the End of Italy*, trans. Marcus Perryman (New York: Berghahn, 2015), ix.
10. What Bisoni calls the film's "ironic depiction of middlebrow leftist culture" in postmillennial Italy. ClaudioBisoni, "Paolo Sorrentino: Between Engagement and *Savoir Faire*," in *Italian Political Cinema: Public Life, Imaginary, and Identity in Contemporary Italian Film*, ed. Giancarlo Lombardi and Christian Uva (Oxford: Peter Lang, 2016), 262.
11. Gary Crowdus, "In Search of *The Great Beauty*: An Interview with Paolo Sorrentino," *Cineaste* 39, no. 2 (Spring 2014), 9.
12. See Rafaelle La Capria, *Ferito a Morte* (1961) (Milano: Oscar Mondadori, 2014).
13. "Interview with Antonio Monda," *La Grande Bellezza*, directed by Paolo Sorrentino (New York: Criterion, 2013), DVD.
14. Giuseppina Mecchia, "Birds in the Roman Sky: Shooting for the Sublime in *La grande bellezza*," *Forum Italicum* 50, no. 1 (2016): 188.
15. Mecchia, "Birds in the Roman Sky," 188.
16. During this scene Antonello Venditti's hit "Per sempre" plays on the soundtrack. As Ramona spies Jep spying on her, the quality of the sound shifts suddenly from extradiegetic background to tinny diegetic smartphone music. The song then bridges to the next scene, in a restaurant, where Jep is greeted by Venditti in propria persona. The singer-songwriter is of course beloved of Romans, evidenced by the adoption of his song, "Roma Roma," by A. S. Roma (the Roman soccer team).
17. I thank an anonymous reviewer at Wallflower Press for this observation.
18. Carl Plantinga, *Moving Viewers: American Film and the Spectator's Experience* (Berkeley: University of California Press, 2009), 198.
19. See Plantinga, *Moving Viewers*, 199.
20. See e.g., Richard Grusin, *Premediation: Affect and Mediality After 9/11* (London: Palgrave Macmillan, 2010); Richard Grusin, ed. *The Nonhuman Turn* (Minneapolis: University of Minnesota Press, 2015). See also Ruth Leys, "Trauma and the Turn to Affect," in *Trauma, Memory, and Narrative in the Contemporary South African Novel: Essays*, ed. Ewald Mengel and Michaela Borzaga (Amsterdam: Rodopi, 2012), 9.
21. Atkinson quoted in Carlotta Fonzi Kliemann, "Cultural and Political Exhaustion in Paolo Sorrentino's *The Great Beauty*," *Senses of Cinema* 70 (March 2014): 11, http://sensesofcinema.com/2014/feature-articles/cultural-and-political-exhaustion-in-paolo-sorrentinos-the-great-beauty/.

22. Walter Benjamin, "Paris, the Capital of the 19th Century," *Selected Writings*, vol. 3, *1935–1938*, ed. Howard Eiland and Michael W. Jennings, trans. Edmund Jephcott et al. (Cambridge, MA: Harvard University Press, 2002), 39.

23. Peter Bradshaw, "*La grande bellezza* (*The Great Beauty*)" (rev.), *The Guardian Online*, September 5, 2013, http://www.theguardian.com/film/2013/sep/05/le-grande-bellezza-great-beauty-review.

24. Alberto Spadafora, ed., The Great Beauty: *Told by Director of Photography Luca Bigazzi* (Self-published, CreateSpace Independent Publishing Platform, 2014), 206.

25. Spadafora, *The Great Beauty*, 212–19.

26. Sorrentino: "For me, Fellini is a sort of beacon in the night in the very complex apparatus that is cinema." Sorrentino, "Interview with Antonio Monda."

27. Peter Bondanella, *The Films of Federico Fellini* (Cambridge: Cambridge University Press, 2002), 139.

28. Gilles Deleuze, *Cinema 1: The Movement Image*, trans. Hugh Tomlinson and Barbara Habberjam (Minneapolis: University of Minnesota Press, 1986), 97.

29. Bondanella, *Films of Federico Fellini*, 139.

30. Carlotta Fonzi Kliemann, "Cultural and Political Exhaustion," 8.

31. See Sorentino, "Interview with Antonio Monda." In the same interview, he also said that he wanted to depict "the great thing about life, the fact that you can be surprised by something that you'd decided was vulgar and wretched, and then suddenly what is vulgar and wretched reveals its own entirely unexpected grace."

32. Cf. Mecchia, who argues that, because it lacks a clear political thesis, *The Great Beauty* is "an ethical, not a political denunciation of the corruption and vacuity of Italy's cultural elites." Mecchia, "Birds in the Roman Sky," 191.

33. While Flaubert's unfinished final novel *Bouvard et Pécuchet* (1881), or rather the project the eponymous protagonists never complete, the "Dictionary of Received Ideas," is a more likely candidate than *Madame Bovary*, it would appear that Flaubert never wrote his book about nothing.

34. András Bálint Kovács, *Screening Modernism: European Art Cinema, 1950–1980* (Chicago: University of Chicago Press, 2007), 99.

35. Anne Friedberg, *Window Shopping: Cinema and the Postmodern* (Berkeley: University of California Press, 1994), 4.

36. In an interview for the Criterion DVD, Toni Servillo also describes Jep as a kind of contemporary flaneur.

37. Anticipated in *The Consequences of Love* in the interludic scenes of Titta wandering aimlessly through a high-end shopping mall in Lugano. The only time he is seen actually buying something is when he takes Sofia shopping for expensive shoes, in a scene that has its much more spectacular counterpart in *The Great Beauty*, when Jep takes Ramona shopping for funeral wear.

38. Tim Bergfelder, "Love Beyond the Nation: Cosmopolitanism and Transnational Desire in Cinema," in *Europe and Love in Cinema*, ed. Luisa Passerini, Jo Labanyi, and Karen Diehl (Bristol, UK: Intellect, 2012), 62.

39. Bergfelder, "Love Beyond the Nation," 63.

40. Bergfelder, "Love Beyond the Nation," 63.

41. A similar thing happens in the subsequent scene in the Via Veneto when Jep encounters his old friend Egidio in front of his strip club. Egidio in long-medium shot looks into the camera as it tracks in toward him only to curve to one side so that Jep can step into the frame in profile to greet the other man.

42. Bergfelder, "Love Beyond the Nation," 63.

43. See e.g., Eugenia Paulicelli, *Italian Style: Fashion and Film from Early Cinema to the Digital Age* (New York: Bloomsbury Academic, 2016), 188. Paulicelli also remarks what she calls Jep's "almost-feminine walk" during his early morning sojourns across Rome (191).

44. Laura Mulvey, "Visual Pleasure and Narrative Cinema," in *Film Theory: An Anthology*, ed. Robert Stam and Toby Miller (Oxford: Oxford University Press, 2000), 488.

45. Regarding the latter see e.g., "The viewer suspends disbelief in the fictional world of the film, identifies not only with specific characters in the film but more importantly with the film's overall ideology through identification with the film's narrative structure and visual point of view, and puts

into play fantasy structures . . . that derive from the viewer's unconscious." Marita Sturken and Lisa Cartwright, *Practices of Looking: An Introduction to Visual Culture* (Oxford: Oxford University Press, 2001), 73. For an analysis of these issues within a specifically Italian mediatic context, see Danielle Hipkins, "The Showgirl Effect: Ageing Between Great Beauties and 'Veline di turno,' " *Cinepanettone*-Academia, ReadingItaly, December 11, 2013, https://wp.me/p2iDSt-bW, 1–2.

46. Mary Ann Doane, "Film and the Masquerade: Theorizing the Female Spectator," in *Film Theory: An Anthology*, ed. Robert Stam and Toby Miller (Blackwell: Oxford, 2000), 497.

47. See also Dante's *Paradiso*, where Beatrice guides him toward the final vision of godhead. In what is likely not a coincidence, Tony Pagoda's love interest in Sorrentino's novel *Everybody's Right*—like Dante's, also dead before the story opens—is named Beatrice: " 'That woman doesn't need to eat. She feeds on our torment.' That was the sort of thing everyone said about that woman, suddenly everyone was a poet, no vulgar innuendo, no one ever expressed a thought of sexual greed, as if she were composed of some celestial material, the paradise that everyone dreams of after passing peacefully away." Paolo Sorrentino, *Everybody's Right* trans. Anthony Shugaar (New York: Europa Editions, 2011), 46. See also page 137, where the Dantean connection is made ironically explicit.

48. See Jacques Rancière, *The Emancipated Spectator*, trans. Gregory Elliott (London: Verso Books, 2009); Bertolt Brecht, "A Short Organum for the Theatre" (1948), *Brecht on Theatre*, trans. John Willet (New York: Hill and Wang, 1977), 179–208.

49. The sheer mean-spirited (and inadvertently misogynist) nature of Sicinski's pseudo-feminist critique of *The Great Beauty* is revealed when he remarks parenthetically that, "*The Great Beauty* has little use for women, unless you're an aging stripper, Mother Teresa, or a 'dwarf.' " Michael Sicinski, "Paolo Sorrentino: A Medium Talent." *Cinemascope* (2017): 20.

50. Rosalind Galt, "The Prettiness of Italian Cinema," in *Popular Italian Cinema*, ed. Louis Bayman and Sergio Rigoletto (New York: Palgrave Macmillan, 2013), 59.

51. Regarding *La Dolce Vita*'s influence on *The Great Beauty* see Minuz, *Political Fellini*, viii–ix.

52. As early as 1960 "Pauline Kael called this film genre the 'come-dressed-as-the-sick-soul-of-Europe party.' " For Bradshaw ("*La grande bellezza* [*The Great Beauty*]"), *The Great Beauty* looks like a " 'come-dressed-as-the-fantastically-vigorous-and-unrepentant-soul-of-rich-Europe' party." In Roger Clarke's reading of the film, "this isn't the 1960s bourgeoisie deliquescing into their own emptiness—this is the vaunting pleasure of the modern 'one per cent' reveling in unapologetic wealth" (quoted in Bradshaw, "*La grande bellezza*"). See also Sorrentino, "Interview with Antonio Monda," regarding Jep's resemblance to the character played by Mastroianni in *La Dolce Vita*.

53. Strangely, it appears that Elisa also lived for the past forty years in Rome, with her husband Alfredo, who informs Jep of her death.

54. In an interview for the Criterion DVD.

55. Kovács, *Screening Modernism*, 103.

56. Kovács, *Screening Modernism*, 103.

57. Kovács, *Screening Modernism*, 103.

58. See Kilbourn, "The 'Primal Scene,' " 383.

59. Louis-Ferdinand Céline, *Journey to the End of Night* (1932; 1952), trans. Ralph Manheim (New York: New Directions, 2006), n.p.

60. For a complementary reading of this scene as a "parody of men's obsession with female beauty," see Eszter Simor and D. David Sorfa, "Irony, Sexism and Magic in Paolo Sorrentino's Films," *Studies in European Cinema* 14, no. 3 (2017): 11. DOI: 10.1080/17411548.2017.1386368.

61. Jep is quoting his friend, Arturo, the magician, who in an earlier scene makes a giraffe disappear before Jep's eyes. "È solo un trucco," he explains. Like the scene in *This Must Be the Place* when Cheyenne meets a bison face to face or the sequences with the kangaroo in the papal gardens in *The Young Pope*, this moment of encountering a giraffe when he least expects it signals a turning point for Jep in his journey toward some kind of clarity or understanding of his own life and identity (see also Sorrentino, "Interview with Antonio Monda").

62. See Danielle Hipkins, "The Showgirl Effect"; Hipkins's reading of the film echoes the terms of my argument but with a different valuation of the film's investment in a masculinist nostalgia: "Hailed as part of the 're-birth' of Italian cinema, Sorrentino's intense evocation of Fellini's Rome expresses

nostalgia for and an attempted re-instantiation of the same gender dynamic. The female character is, once again, made to carry the burden of corporeal ageing, like the (feminized) body of Rome itself, whilst male ageing is a question of redeeming soul and memory, in which the male melodrama of Jep's suffering, as Catherine O'Rawe describes . . . becomes 'the gateway to the sublime.' "

63. Catherine O'Rawe, *Stars and Masculinities in Contemporary Italian Cinema* (New York: Palgrave Macmillan, 2014), 163.

64. O'Rawe, *Stars and Masculinities*, 163.

7. *YOUTH* (*LA GIOVINEZZA*): BETWEEN HORROR AND DESIRE (*LIFE'S LAST DAY*)

Portions of this chapter first appeared in Russell J. A. Kilbourn, "The 'Primal Scene': Memory, Redemption, and 'Woman' in the Films of Paolo Sorrentino," *Journal of Italian Cinema and Media Studies* 7, no. 3 (2019): 377–94.

1. "According to Paolo Sorrentino, the character of filmmaker Mick (Harvey Keitel) . . . far from being an autobiographical creation . . . is a fairly non-specific filmmaker, 'a little bit of Roger Corman, a bit of Sidney Lumet, a bit of William Friedkin' " ("*Youth*").

2. "The final scene's look, in which Fred Ballinger (Sir Michael Caine) conducts his piece, is heavily reminiscent of Federico Fellini's *Orchestra Rehearsal*" ("*Youth*").

3. Peter Bondanella, *The History of Italian Cinema*, 3rd ed. (New York: Continuum, 2009), 289.

4. Carl Plantinga, *Moving Viewers: American Film and the Spectator's Experience* (Berkeley: University of California Press, 2009), 23.

5. Fellini famously based this scene on a real incident in which Pierluigi Praturlon, one of the original paparazzi, photographed Ekberg wading in the Trevi fountain. Shawn Levy, *Dolce Vita Confidential: Fellini, Loren, Pucci, Paparazzi and the Swinging High Life of 1950s Rome* (New York: Norton, 2016), 281–82. "Set within a complex series of images and visual ideas . . . this banal, tabloid 'photo opportunity' was transformed by the power of Fellini's fantasy into a symbol for feminine purity and innocence juxtaposed against a world of corruption and decadence, which has quite rightly been called the symbolic image of postwar cinema." Bondanella, *History of Italian* Cinema, 209.

6. Sorrentino's description of Miss Universe in the San Marco dream scene, from the prose text version of the film, provides an even more apt comparison to the world of advertising: "Seen from behind, Miss Universe goes off swinging her hips under the full moon, surrounded by the mass of water as if in some dubious dream-like advert for Dolce & Gabbana." Paulo Sorrentino, *Youth*, trans. N. S. Thompson (London: MacLehose Press, 2015, 14.

7. See Simor and Sorfa's reading of this scene's "excessive style" and parodic "representation of female beauty." Eszter Simor and D. David Sorfa, "Irony, Sexism and Magic in Paolo Sorrentino's Films," *Studies in European Cinema* 14, no. 3 (2017): 11. DOI: 10.1080/17411548.2017.1386368.

8. *Youth* is the first of Sorrentino's features to be shot entirely digitally, with the (in 2015) relatively new Red Epic Dragon digital camera. This means that the master format was itself digital, which was then printed in 35 mm for projection, following the digital intermediate.

9. See also the beautifully lit—but otherwise discomfiting—medium shot of the Countess Meraviglia (Monica Cetti) in *The Young Pope*, episode 7, when she unsuccessfully attempts to seduce Dussolier.

10. See e.g., *Éloge de l'amour* (2001).

11. As Belardo remarks to Cardinal Caltanissetta in episode 3, "I'm an orphan, and orphans are never young." To which Caltanissetta responds: "As an orphan grows older, he may discover a fresh youth within."

12. Fredric Jameson, *Postmodernism, or The Cultural Logic of Late Capitalism* (Durham, NC: Duke University Press, 1999), ix.

13. "Interview with Antonio Monda," *La grande bellezza*, directed by Paolo Sorrentino (New York: Criterion, 2013), DVD.

14. Paul Mayersberg, "Naked Masks," *Sight and Sound* 22, no. 4 (April 2012), 21.

15. Novalis, "Longing for Death," in *Hymns to the Night*, trans. Justin E. H. Smith, Justin E. H. Smith (website), accessed October 31 2019, http://www.jehsmith.com/1/2013/09/novalis-longing-for-death.html.

16. Thomas Breuer connects Sorrentino's obsession with soccer specifically to his films' recurrent nostalgia. Thomas Breuer, "From Maradona to Jude Law: Sport in Paolo Sorrentino's Movies," *Studies in European Cinema* (2018): 2, DOI: 10.1080/17411548.2018.1554776.

17. Sorrentino famously thanked Maradona (along with Fellini, Scorsese, and the Talking Heads) in his acceptance speech for the 2014 Best Picture Oscar for *The Great Beauty*. Regarding the significance of Maradona for Sorrentino, see Breuer, "From Maradona to Jude Law," 8.

18. Just as Brenda Morel, according to Boyle, was such a good actress because of her ability to steal from others, incorporating this material into her characterizations.

19. The prose text version of *Youth* also emphasizes Tree's borrowing of Boyle's habit of brushing the hair back from his forehead, a gesture that does not make it into the film.

20. According to Odile Tremblay, "Les revanches de Sorrentino," *Le Devoir*, December 15, 2015, https://www.ledevoir.com/culture/cinema/458180/les-revanches-de-sorrentino, in choosing this setting Sorrentino was *not* intentionally echoing "the Swiss alpine hotel" that inspired Thomas Mann's 1924 novel, *The Magic Mountain*. The Berghotel Schatzalp, near Davos, was used for many of the exterior scenes. There is no reason, however, to not consider in relation to Sorrentino's film *The Magic Mountain*'s setting in the period leading up to World War I, written as it was during the interwar period, leading up to World War II. In this sense, Mann's novel is one of the key literary texts—alongside their cinematic counterparts—that shed an uncannily prescient light upon the advent of Hitler and the rise of National Socialism in Germany. Mann's *Death in Venice* also has a place, albeit a more tangential one, in this canon. See chapter 8 for a discussion of the significance of this work for *The Young Pope*.

21. The same kinds of questions are broached in Karl Ove Knausgaard's six-volume autofictional novel, *My Struggle* (2009–2011), whose original Norwegian title, *Min Kamp*, is a direct translation of that of Hitler's infamous book. Knausgaard confronts this link directly only in the sixth and final volume.

22. Sorrentino, "Interview with Antonio Monda,"

23. The South American's distended belly, its size often exaggerated in wide angle, is another example, like Geremia di Geremei, of Sorrentino's Fellinian fascination with the grotesque. See Catherine O'Rawe, "Brothers in Arms: Middlebrow *Impegno* and Homosocial Relations in the Cinema of Petraglia and Rulli," in *Intellectual Communities and Partnerships in Italy and Europe*, ed. Danielle Hipkins (Oxford: Peter Lang, 2012), 149–67.

24. From the prose text version: "Miss Universe is an outright disappointment. She is wearing a cheap, baggy jumpsuit that distorts her figure, making her seem overweight. She has bad skin, tired and unwashed hair and, although it's dark, is wearing purple-tinted sunglasses in vulgar frames that appear too large for her face. In addition, she has a grating voice when she shakes Jimmy's hand." Sorrentino, *Youth*.

25. The dream follows without preamble on a scene in which the South American, lying on a pool chair, is given oxygen. On first viewing it is therefore easy to attribute the dream to him.

26. Boyle's projected new screenplay seems to echo Ballinger's situation. As he and his team struggle to write the final deathbed scene in their film, Mick's idea is to have Brenda Morel's character say to her dying husband: "I lost so much time because of you, Michael. I lost the best years of my life."

27. E.g. Fassbinder's *Ali: Fear Eats the Soul* (1974), whose characteristic set piece is a highly formalized, artificial scene in which one or more characters stare blatantly at another marked as their ethno-cultural or racial Other. In Fassbinder's film this strategy adds a clearly Brechtian resonance to the film's meanings.

28. Rosemarie Garland-Thomson, *Staring: How We Look* (Oxford: Oxford University Press, 2009), 42.

29. One of the series' many religiously themed jokes appears when Sister Mary answers her door in the middle of the night wearing a long t-shirt bearing the phrase "I'm a Virgin. This is an old T-shirt."

30. In her Tesi di Laurea on the visual arts in Sorrentino's cinematographic image, Silvia Dotto (2016) offers detailed readings of the series' incorporation of artworks from across history, with a particular focus on the credit sequence. Silvia Dotto, "Paolo Sorrentino: L'arte nell'immagine cinematografica" (Tesi di Laurea [Bachelor's thesis], Università Ca' Foscari, Venezia, 2016).

31. Regarding Sorrentino's penchant for the Fellinian grotesque see O'Rawe, "Brothers in Arms and *Stars and Masculinities in Contemporary Italian Cinema* (New York: Palgrave Macmillan, 2014), 153–57. See Danielle Hipkins, "The Showgirl Effect: Ageing Between Great Beauties and 'Veline di turno,' " *Cinepanettone*-Academia: ReadingItaly, December 11, 2013, https://wp.me/p2iDSt-bW regarding Sorrentino's transition from the onscreen objectification of women to the broader exploitation of non-normative bodies and faces, especially but not exclusively those of women. See especially Lorena (Serena Grandi), the aging former *velina* in *The Great Beauty*'s opening party scene vs. her antecedent in Marcello's harem dream in *8 ½* (2).

8. *CECI N'EST PAS UN PAPE*: POSTSECULAR MELODRAMA IN *THE YOUNG POPE*

1. Umberto Contarello, Sorrentino's frequent cowriter, contributed to two of the episodes, as did Tony Grisoni and Stefano Rulli.
2. In this respect *The Young Pope* can be seen to contrast sharply with the more dominant televisual aesthetic seen in Italian crime dramas such as *Suburra* or *Gomorra* (based on the 2006 Garrone film, in turn adapted from the Roberto Saviano novel of the same title). These shows represent the grittier, handheld extreme of what Bordwell means by "intensified continuity" as new transnational baseline vernacular style.
3. Linda Hutcheon, *A Theory of Adaptation*, 2nd ed. (New York: Routledge, 2012), 14.
4. For a comprehensive discussion of the meaning of the postsecular in a cinematic context, see John Caruana and Mark Cauchi, eds., *Immanent Frames: Postsecular Cinema between* The Tree of Life *and* Melancholia (Albany: State University of New York Press, 2018). See also Costica Bradatan and Camil Ungureanu, eds. *Religion in European Cinema: The Postsecular Constellation* (New York: Routledge, 2014..
5. Caruana and Cauchi, *Immanent Frames*, 1.
6. Caruana and Cauchi, *Immanent Frames*, 1.
7. See Spencer Kornhaber, "What *The Young Pope* Preached About Love," *The Atlantic*, February 14, 2017, https://www.theatlantic.com/entertainment/archive/2017/02/the-young-pope-season-one -finale-hbo/516600/, regarding the ambiguous identity of the apparition in the clouds above San Marco: "The very final moments of the season posed one more mystery as Lenny declared his faith to the audience and then doubled over in pain. As cardinals attended to him and his eyelids flickered, an image of the Virgin Mary appeared in the clouds" (4). I thank Chiara Mariani for this insight regarding Belardo's final vision, and for drawing my attention to its potential implications for my reading of the series.
8. Cf. Louis Bayman and Sergio Rigoletto, "The Fair and the Museum: Framing the Popular," in *Popular Italian Cinema*, ed. Louis Bayman and Sergio Rigoletto (New York: Palgrave Macmillan, 2013), 82.
9. Regarding male melodrama see Dana Renga, "*Romanzo criminale* as Male Melodrama: 'It Is in Reality *Always* Too Late,' " in *Italian Political Cinema: Public Life, Imaginary, and Identity in Contemporary Italian Film*, ed. Giancarlo Lombardi and Christian Uva (Oxford: Peter Lang, 2016), 373–86; Catherine O'Rawe, "Brothers in Arms: Middlebrow *Impegno* and Homosocial Relations in the Cinema of Petraglia and Rulli," in *Intellectual Communities and Partnerships in Italy and Europe*, ed. Danielle Hipkins (Oxford: Peter Lang, 2012), 155.
10. Belardo's father smokes the pipe only once, in episode 8, in a flashback to an idyllic outing on the banks of a river in Colorado.
11. See Geoffrey Nowell-Smith, foreword to *Italian Film Directors in the New Millennium*, ed. William Hope (Newcastle, UK: Cambridge Scholars Press, 2010), ix.
12. In a subsequent scene in episode 6, also echoing Gere's workout sequence in *American Gigolo*, Belardo exercises in the papal chambers, using a baroquely elaborate machine on which he is strapped, as if upon some sort of medieval torture instrument.

13. Susan Bordo, "Beauty (Re) Discovers the Male Body," in *Beauty Matters*, ed. Peggy Brand (Bloomington: Indiana University Press, 2000), 122–29.

14. Linda Hutcheon and Michael Hutcheon, *Bodily Charm: Living Opera* (Lincoln: University of Nebraska Press, 2000), 47.

15. Bordo, "Beauty (Re) Discovers the Male Body," 129–43.

16. See Sean Nixon, "Exhibiting Masculinity," in *Representation: Cultural Representations and Signifying Practices*, ed. Stuart Hall (London: Sage, 1997), 293–95; Susan Bordo, "Beauty (Re) Discovers the Male Body," 112.

17. 'LMFAO' stands for "laughing my fucking ass off."

18. As noted in the previous chapter, Sorrentino had already satirized the form in Lena's Paloma Faith nightmare sequence in *Youth*.

19. Actually a scale replica, built at Cinecittà especially for these scenes. Patricia Thomson, "A New Pope," *American Cinematographer* (May 2017): 24.

20. A curious musical choice, originally inspired by the funeral of one young woman, which was then played at the funeral of another, Princess Diana ("Song for Athene").

21. This is to leave aside the question: Why would these apparently leftist, counterculture-embracing people choose to leave their son to be raised in a conservative Catholic orphanage?

22. In Spencer Kornhaber's words, Lenny "wanted to make the people of the world feel like orphans so that they would ache for God as he ached for his parents." "What *The Young Pope* Preached About Love," *Atlantic*, February 14, 2017, https://www.theatlantic.com/entertainment/archive/2017/02/the-young-pope-season-one-finale-hbo/516600/.

23. See Russell J. A. Kilbourn, "Adapting Venice: Intermedial Relations in Visconti, Sebald, and Kafka," "lifedeath": *Mosaic* special issue 48, no. 3 (Sept. 2015) 57–74.

24. Also known as the head of the Vatican press office.

25. András Bálint Kovács, *Screening Modernism: European Art Cinema, 1950–1980*, (Chicago: University of Chicago Press, 2007) 394.

26. According to Sorrentino in a "making of" promotional video, Belardo does not die at the end of the final episode but goes into a coma. Silvia Fumarola, " 'The New Pope': John Malkovich entra nel cast accanto al 'giovane' Jude Law," *Repubblica*, July 2, 2018, http://www.repubblica.it/spettacoli/tv-radio/2018/07/02/news/_the_new_pope_-200628620/?ref=search&refresh_ce. Because this information will not be officially ratified until the appearance of the next series, *The New Pope*, which premieres in winter 2020, and because the first series' ending made it look as though Belardo was indeed literally dead, I have chosen to adhere to this reading of the finale. Treating the series as a discrete whole, then, it makes no difference to my argument—and to the *Death in Venice* intertext—if he is only metaphorically and not literally dead.

27. Linda Williams, "The American Melodramatic Mode," in *Playing the Race Card: Melodramas of Black and White from Uncle Tom's Cabin to O.J. Simpson* (Princeton, NJ: Princeton University Press, 2001), 28.

28. Cf. Mary Anne Doane: "The cinematic apparatus inherits a theory of the image which is *not* conceived outside of sexual specifications. And historically, there has always been a certain imbrication of the cinematic image and the representation of the woman. . . . For the female spectator there is a certain *over-presence* of the image—she *is* the image." Mary Ann Doane, "Film and the Masquerade: Theorizing the Female Spectator," in *Film Theory: An Anthology*, ed. Robert Stam and Toby Miller (Oxford: Blackwell, 2000), 497–99.

29. Johnson Cheu, "Seeing Blindness On-Screen: The Blind, Female Gaze," in *The Problem Body: Projecting Disability on Film*, ed. Sally Chivers and Nicole Markotić (Columbus: Ohio State University Press, 2010), 69.

30. E. Ann Kaplan, "Is the Gaze Male?," in *Feminism and Film* (Oxford: Oxford University Press, 2000), 130.

31. Williams, "American Melodramatic Mode," 29.

32. Williams, "American Melodramatic Mode," 31.

33. Many critics refused to recognize the complex and problematic significance of such casting choices, reading everything instead in terms of the main character; e.g.: "Tight shots on the imperfect faces

in the rabble gathered in Vatican Square—the plain nun with a prominent mustache, the child with small eyes lidded by deep epicanthic folds—make Law's movie-star features take on a preternatural quality. Melanie McFarland, "HBO's 'The Young Pope' makes high art for TV, but the result is less than divine," Salon.com, January 14, 2017, 3.

34. In episode 8 we learn that this is Belardo's memory of an idyllic holiday in Colorado with his parents before they left him at the orphanage in upstate New York.

35. A famous instance is Isak Borg's (Viktor Sjöström) flashback to his wife's infidelity in the middle of the long dream sequence in Bergman's *Wild Strawberries* (1957).

36. In Wertmüller's film, each time a new villain appears the camera zooms in to the same large mole on each man's face, emphasizing his connection to the others, as the story unfolds. One could also list here the frequent smash-zooms of 1970s horror films, such as Nicholas Roeg's *Don't Look Now* (1973) or Kubrick's *The Shining* (1980), as well as other genres, such as the spaghetti western or the *giallo* (Italian horror).

37. See e.g., Thomson, "A New Pope."

38. Williams, "The American Melodramatic Mode," 29.

39. See Kilbourn, Adapting Venice."

40. This narrow opening anticipates the tiny golden door that the pope displays to the assembled cardinals in episode 5: the portal through which all must pass to enter the church.

41. Regarding the smart film see Jeffrey Sconce, "Irony, Nihilism, and the New American 'Smart' Film," *Screen* 43, no. 4 (2002): 349–69.

42. Spencer's dying words, oddly, are a direct quote from the original *Blade Runner* (1982), in the climactic scene where Roy Batty (Rutger Hauer) the replicant rebel leader, reaches the end of his four-year life-span: "Time to die." Arguably, such ironic intertextual echoes amplify rather than diminish the series' emotional impact.

43. The meteorite finishes by smashing into a statue of Pope John Paul II, resulting in a replica of "The Ninth Hour," a 1999 statue by Maurizio Cattelan, of Pope John Paul II knocked over by a meteorite.

44. For useful glosses on each of the paintings, and their relevance to the series' narrative, see Zusanna Stanska, "*The Young Pope*: All 10 Paintings From the Opening Explained," *Daily Art Magazine*, December 5, 2016, http://www.dailyartmagazine.com/young-pope-paintings-opening-explained/.

CODA: TOWARD A POST-POLITICAL FILM: *LORO* AND THE MEDIATIC ELEGIAC

1. In the absence of the original, I have had to rely on Italian-language reviews and descriptions of the *Loro* diptych.

2. My reading of *Loro* in this chapter is inspired in part by Nicoletta Marini-Maio's paper on the film, presented at the JICMS conference in Rome in June 2019. As I was completing the final edits on this chapter, Dr. Marini-Maio kindly made available to me her contribution to the forthcoming special issue on Sorrentino in the journal *L'Avventura*. In her close reading of *Loro 1* and *2*, which is an expansion of her original conference paper, Marini-Maio privileges "la cifra autoriale di Paolo Sorrentino, che descrive in chiave allegorica le interazioni simboliche del regime dello scambio tra sesso e potere del berlusconismo, concentrandosi sulla catastrofe della vecchiaia e dell'impotenza di fronte al capitale erotico del femminile." (2018, n.p.).

3. Marini-Maio offers a similar reading, explicitly labeling the "narrativizzazione autoreflessiva" as a strategy typical of the film's "impegno postmoderno," connecting the film's visual style to its exploration of sexual and political power. Marini-Maio, "*Loro* (2018)," n.p.n14.

4. Andrea Minuz, "Com'è fosco il potere raccontato dal cinema italiano," *Il Foglio*, February 5, 2018, 5. https://www.ilfoglio.it/cinema/2018/02/05/news/cinema-sono-tornato-sorrentino-fosco-potere-176959/.

5. Chiara Isabella Spagnoli Gabardi, "*Loro* is Sorrentino's New Cinematic Diptych," *Gainsayer*, May 1, 2018, http://www.gainsayer.me/loro-is-sorrentinos-new-cinematic-diptych/.

6. See Gabardi, "*Loro* is Sorrentino's New Cinematic Diptych"; See also Marini-Maio, "*Loro* (2018)," n.p. Mediatic power is from Andrea Minuz, "Com'è fosco il potere raccontato dal cinema italiano," *Il Foglio*, February 5, 2018, 5.

7. Giorgio Manganelli, *Pinocchio: Un libro parallelo* (Milan, Italy: Adelphi, 2002), 1.

8. From *One Man Up* to *The Family Friend* Sorrentino's editor was Giogiò Franchini.

9. For Sorrentino, "Berlusconi è un archetipo dell'italianità e attraverso di lui puoi raccontare gli italiani." Quoted in Andrea Minuz, "Com'è fosco il potere raccontato dal cinema italiano," *Il Foglio*, February 5, 2018, https://www.ilfoglio.it/cinema/2018/02/05/news/cinema-sono-tornato-sorrentino-fosco-potere-176959/. See also Angela Giuffrida, "Berlusconi Biopic *Loro* Is 'a Tender Look at the Weaknesses of an Old Man,'" *Guardian*, May 3, 2018, 1. For a comprehensive analysis of Berlusconi's cinematic treatment in Italian films up to 2015, see Nicoletta Marini-Maio, *A Very Seductive Body Politic: Silvio Berlusconi in the Cinema* (Milan, Italy: Mimesis International, 2015).

10. Jay Weissberg, "Film Review: Paolo Sorrenino's *Loro 1*," *Variety*, May 8, 2018, 3.

11. Which segues into "Down On the Street" by the Stooges, bridging to the next scene, with Sergio's wife, Tamara (Euridice Axen) at home with their three children. Tamara snorts cocaine and downs a martini in the thirty seconds it takes to microwave the kids' snack. In the scene immediately following, when Sergio pulls up to Fabrizio Sala's audition on his motorcycle, the same sound of a crown cheering is again briefly audible.

12. See Marini-Maio, who makes a similar point about this shot ("*Loro* [2018]," n.p.).

13. Weissberg, "Film Review," 2.

14. This scene, set in 2006, also makes anachronistic reference to the media story from April 2017, when Berlusconi adopted five lambs, ostensibly to save them from slaughter for Easter weekend—as a result angering the Italian meat industry—but more likely to garner votes for the Forza Italia party, some of whose MPs are animal rights activists and vegetarians. Berlusconi was photographed hugging, kissing, and feeding the lambs with a baby bottle. "Berlusconi Cuddles Lambs in Vegetarian Easter Campaign," *Guardian*, April 10, 2017, https://www.theguardian.com/world/2017/apr/10/silvio-berlusconi-vegetarian-easter-lambs-italian.

15. See Gabardi, "*Loro* Is Sorrentino's New Cinematic Diptych," 3; Marini-Maio, "*Loro* (2018)," n.p.; Christopher Llewellyn Reed, "Loro: Bad Behaviour," *Hammer to Nail*, October 22, 2018, www.hammertonail.com/film-festivals/loro-review/; Giovanni Robertini, "*Loro 1*, Sorrentino ci prende tutti per il culo," *Rolling Stone Italia*, April 23, 2018, https://www.rollingstone.it/cinema/news-cinema/loro-1-sorrentino-ci-prende-tutti-per-il-culo/409529/.

16. The shot also replicates those in Lenny's Venetian dreams in *The Young Pope*, often featuring his lost parents.

17. This audiovisual structure is replicated in the Tempietto di Bramante scene in *The Great Beauty*, when an anonymous woman asks Jep if he has seen her daughter. In this case, however, it is daytime and he is awake.

18. Regarding Loro's allegorical dimension see Marini-Maio, "*Loro* (2018)," n.p.

19. Marita Sturken and Lisa Cartwright, "Spectatorship, Power, and Knowledge," in *Practices of Looking: An Introduction to Visual Culture* (Oxford: Oxford University Press, 2001), 73.

20. The term *velina* is closely associated with the showgirls on the Canale 5 program *Striscia la notizia*, a political commentary/satire, beginning in the 1980s, that came to exemplify the objectification of women in the era of Berlusconian TV. The word *velina*, originating in Fascist Italy, is still widely used in Italian journalism to indicate a press release coming to the newsroom from an external source. *Velina* literally refers to the carbon-copy paper (*carta velina*) used to type the press release. For decades the young, attractive, scantily clad women who delivered the news on *Striscia la notizia*, often on roller skates, have been known as *veline*, and the metonym is now a synonym for a TV showgirl.

21. See Danielle Hipkins, "The Showgirl Effect: Ageing Between Great Beauties and 'Veline di turno,'" *Cinepanettone*-Academia: Reading Italy,' December 11, 2013, https://wp.me/p2iDSt-bW. On the perpetuation of sexist gender stereotypes in Italian film and television, see also Weissberg, "Film Review," 2.

22. Other characters also address the camera directly; e.g., Paolo Spagnola in the desinfestazione scene at Berlusconi's villa after he chops the head off a snake.

23. The shot of the exploding Roman garbage truck and the subsequent digitally enhanced slo-mo shot of debris sailing through the air lead directly into this scene. This visually echoes the famous montage of super slo-mo shots of objects raining from the sky after the explosions that conclude Antonioni's *Zabriskie Point* (1970).
24. Regarding the term "bunga bunga" in application to this scene see e.g., Marini-Maio, "*Loro* (2018)," n.p.
25. See Marini-Maio, "*Loro* (2018)," n.p.n14. For a feminist critique of the gratuitous exploitation and objectification of women in Italian television, see Lorella Zanardo's 2009 documentary *Il corpo delle donne*, which appeared at the very time of the events of *Loro*'s final third.
26. See Weissberg, "Film Review," 1.
27. Weissberg, "Film Review," 2.
28. Interestingly, the French release of the film is titled *Silvio et les autres* (*Silvio and the others*), "un titolo che mette in risalto la centralità di Berlusconi e al tempo stesso proietta un'ombra di disprezzo sugli 'altri.' " Marini-Maio, "*Loro* (2018)," n.p.n7.
29. *Loro* may also be read as a pun on *l'oro*, gold—a connotation not without relevance for the film's treatment of Berlusconi. For an elaboration of this interpretation of the title see Annachiara Mariani, "Megalomaniac: The Obsession with Power in Sorrentino's Diptych *Loro*" (JICMS Second International Conference: Global Intersections and Artistic Connections: Italian Cinema and Media Across Times and Spaces, American University of Rome, June 2019).
30. This list might also include *they*, but only in an Anglophone context. The twenty-first-century opening up of individual pronominal identification to the historically plural third-person pronoun has yet to happen in Italy. One reason for this, apart from cultural resistance and/or indifference, is linguistic-grammatical: the much older habit of substituting *they* for *he* or *she* in English sentences as a gender-neutral singular pronoun (e.g., "every student should do the best they can") is not possible in Italian, a typical Latinate language in which every noun is gendered. When a universal pronoun is required in Italian, either the masculine pronoun is used or the referent is pluralized; i.e., 'ogni studente dovrebbe fare del suo meglio'; or 'tutti gli student dovrebbero fare del loro meglio.'
31. Louis Bayman and Sergio Rigoletto, "The Fair and the Museum: Framing the Popular," in *Popular Italian Cinema* (New York: Palgrave Macmillan, 2013), 6.
32. The wide shot of Berlusconi and his cabinet posing for a group photo, from the perspective of the photographer, replicates the equivalent scene in *Il Divo* when Andreotti wins his seventh term.
33. See Chiara Isabella Spagnoli Gabardi, "*Loro Part 2*: Sorrentino Finishes Off Silvio Berlusconi." *Gainsayer*, May 4, 2018, http://www.gainsayer.me/loro-part-2-paolo-sorrentino-finishes-off-silvio -berlusconi/.
34. Peter Bondanella, *The History of Italian Cinema*, 3rd ed. (New York: Continuum, 2009), 291.
35. Linda Williams, "The American Melodramatic Mode," in *Playing the Race Card: Melodramas of Black and White from Uncle Tom's Cabin to O.J. Simpson* (Princeton, NJ: Princeton University Press, 2001), 29.
36. Williams, "American Melodramatic Mode," 31.
37. See Marini-Maio, who reads the trinity of lamb, the deposed Christ, and Dio (a character excised from the international release) as "tre copri sacrificali" in "una allegoria sorrentiniana." "*Loro* (2018)," n.p. My sense is that the figures that bookend the film—the lamb as *agnus Dei* (n.p.) and the statue of Christ—have lost a dimension of meaning as a result of the reduction of the diptych to a single feature.

CONCLUSION: STYLE AS COMMITMENT

1. See e.g., Catherine O'Rawe: "The auteurist approach seems deeply entrenched within Italian film studies. . . . There is a need," moreover, "for a scholarship which challenges dominant and resistant auteurist accounts of an Italian 'national cinema,' a cinema that had the function of reflecting and defining the Italian nation" (" 'I Padri e maestri': Genre, Auteurs, and Absences in Italian Film Studies," *Italian Studies* 63, no. 2 [Autumn 2008]: 178–82).

2. See e.g., Catherine O'Rawe, "Brothers in Arms: Middlebrow *Impegno* and Homosocial Relations in the Cinema of Petraglia and Rulli," in *Intellectual Communities and Partnerships in Italy and Europe*, ed. Danielle Hipkins (Oxford: Peter Lang, 2012), 149–67, regarding male melodrama and middlebrow impegno in Italian cinema. The history of this subgenre is of course much older, originating outside Italian film; see e.g., Joy Van Fuqua, " 'Can You Feel It, Joe?' Male Melodrama and the Feeling Man," *The Velvet Light Trap* 38 (Fall 1996): 28–38; Philippa Gates, "The Man's Film: Woo and the Pleasure of Male Melodrama," *Journal of Popular Culture* 35, no. 1 (2001): 59–79; Tania Modleski, "Clint Eastwoood and Male Weepies," *American Literary History* 22, no. 1 (November 2009): 136–58.

3. Moreover, according to Antonio Tricomi, "irony resonates deeply with the Italian national character." Quoted in Pierpaolo Antonello, "*Il Divo*: Paolo Sorrentino's Spectacle of Politics," in *Italian Political Cinema: Public Life, Imaginary, and Identity in Contemporary Italian Film*, ed. Giancarlo Lombardi and Christian Uva (Oxford: Peter Lang, 2016), 299.

4. Hennessey takes this further, equating the older male protagonists of Sorrentino's film's with celluloid film itself, both "destined to meet an eventual end, replaced by the perpetual youth of a digital beginning." Brendan Hennessey, "Reel Simulations: CGI and Special Effects in Two Films by Paolo Sorrentino," *The Italianist* 37, no. 3 (2017): 460, DOI: 10.1080/02614340.2017.1409582 2017.

BIBLIOGRAPHY

FILMS

Akerman, Chantal. *Jeanne Dielman, 23, Quai du Commerce, 1080 Bruxelles*. Belgium and France: Paradise Films and Unité Trois, 1975.

Anderson, Paul Thomas. *Magnolia*. United States: Ghoulardi Film Company and New Line Cinema, 1999.

Antonioni, Michelangelo. *L'avventura*. Italy and France: Cino del Duca. Italy: 1960.

——. *L'eclisse*. Italy and France: Cineriz, 1962.

——. *La notte*. Italy and France: Nepi Film, 1961.

——. *Story of a Love Affair*. Italy: Villani Film, 1950.

——. *Zabriskie Point*. United States. Metro-Goldwyn-Mayer, 1970.

Barker, Clive. *Hellraiser*. United Kingdom: Cinemarque Entertainment BV, Film Futures, Rivdel Films, 1987.

Bava, Mario. *Black Sunday*. Italy: Galatea Film and Jolly Film, 1960.

Beineix, Jean-Jaques. *Diva*, France: Les Films Galaxie, 1981.

Bellocchio, Marco. *Buongiorno, notte*. Italy: Film Albatross, Rai Cinema. Sky, MiBAC: 2003.

Bergman, Ingmar. *Summer Interlude*. Sweden: Svensk Filmindustri, 1951.

——. *Wild Strawberries*. Sweden: Svensk Filmindustri, 1957.

Bertolucci, Bernardo. *The Conformist*. Italy, France, and West Germany: Mars Film, 1970.

Boyle, Danny. *Trainspotting*. United Kingdom: Channel Four Films and Figment Films, 1996.

Capuana, Antonio. *Polvere di Napoli*. Italy: AMA film, GMF, RAI, 1998.

Chaplin, Charlie. *The Great Dictator*. United States: Charles Chaplin Productions, 1941.

Coen, Joel, and Ethan Coen. *The Big Lebowski*. United States and United Kingdom: Polygram Filmed Entertainment, 1998.

De Palma, Brian. *Scarface*. United States: Universal Pictures, 1983.

——. *The Untouchables*. United States: Paramount Pictures, 1987.

De Sica, Vittorio. *The Bicycle Thieves*. Italy: Produzioni De Sica, 1948.

——. *Umberto D.* Italy: Rizzoli Film, 1952.

Fassbinder, Rainer Werner. *Ali: Fear Eats the Soul*. West Germany: Filmverlag der Autoren, 1974.

——. *In a Year with 13 Moons*. West Germany: Filmverlag der Autoren, Pro-jekt Filmproduktion, Tango Film, 1978.

Fellini, Federico. *Amarcord*. Italy and France: F.C. Produzioni, 1973.

——. *8 ½*. Italy and France: Cineriz and Francinex, 1963.

——. *I vitelloni*. Italy and France: Cité Films and Peg-Films, 1953.

——. *La Dolce Vita*. Italy and France: Riama, Cinecittà, Pathé Consortium Cinéma, 1960.

———. *Roma*. Italy and France: Ultra Film and Les Productiones Artistes Associés, 1973.

Garrone, Mateo. *Gomorrah*. Italy: Fandango, Rai Cinema and Sky, 2008.

Giordana, Marco Tullio. *The Best of Youth*. Italy: BiBi Film, 2003.

Godard, Jean-Luc. *Eloge de l'amour*. France and Switzerland: Avventura Films, 2001.

Gondry, Michel. *Eternal Sunshine of the Spotless Mind*. United States: Focus Features, 2004.

Harron, Mary. *American Psycho*. United States and Canada: Am Psycho Productions, 1999.

Herzog, Werner. *Stroszek*. West Germany: Werner Herzog Filmproduktion, 1977.

Hitchcock, Alfred. *Psycho*. United States: Shamley Productions, 1960.

———. *Rear Window*. United States: Alfred J. Hitchcock Productions, 1955.

———. *Vertigo*. United States: Paramount Pictures, 1958.

Hopper, Dennis. *Easy Rider*. United States: Pando Company, Inc., 1969.

Iñárritu, Alejandro G. *The Revenant*. United States: Regency Enterprises, 2015.

Kieślowski, Krzysztof. *The Double Life of Veronique*. France and Poland: Sidéral Productions and Canal+, 1991.

Korine, Harmony. *Spring Breakers*. United States and France: Muse Productions and Division Films, 2012.

Kubrick, Stanley. *Eyes Wide Shut*. United Kingdom and United States: Warner Bros. 1999.

Malick, Terrence. *The Tree of Life*. United States: Cottonwood Pictures, 2011.

Mendes, Sam. *Spectre*. United Kingdom and United States: B24, Columbia Pictures, Metro-Goldwyn-Mayer, 2015.

Moretti, Nanni. *Habemus papam*. Italy and France: Sacher Film, Fandango and Le Pacte, 2011.

———. *Il caimano*. France and Italy: Sacher Film, Bac Films, Stéphan Films, 2006.

Murnau, F. W. *Nosferatu*. Germany: Jofa-Atelier Berlin-Johannisthal, Prana Film GmbH, 1922.

Nichetti, Maurizio. *Ladri di saponette*. Italy: Bambú Cinema e TV and Reteitalia, 1989.

Nichols, Mike. *The Graduate*. United States: Lawrence Turman Productions, 1967.

Pasolini, Pier Paolo. *The Gospel According to St. Matthew*. Italy and France: Arco Film, Lux Compagnie Cinematographique de France, 1964.

Rosi, Francesco. *Salvatore Giuliano*. Italy: Galatea Film, 1961.

Rossellini, Roberto. *Rome, città aperta*, Italy: Excelsa Film, 1946.

Schrader, Paul. *American Gigolo*. United States: Paramount Pictures, 1980.

Scola, Ettore. *La terrazza*. Italy and France: Dean Film, International Dean, Les Films Marceau-Cocinor, 1980.

Scorsese, Martin. *Goodfellas*. United States: Warner Bros., 1990.

———. *Taxi Driver*. United States: Columbia Pictures Corporation, 1976.

———. *The Wolf of Wall Street*. United States: Red Granite Pictures + Appian Way, 2013.

Scott, Ridley. *Blade Runner*. United States: The Ladd Company, 1982.

Sorrentino, Paolo. *The Dream* (short). 2014.

———. *Giovani talenti italiani* (video; segment: "Quando le cose vanno male"). 2004.

———. *Il divo*. Italy and France: Indigo Film, Lucky Red, Parco Film, 2008.

———. *In the Mirror* (short). 2011.

———. *Killer in Red* (short). 2017.

———. *L'amico di famiglia* (*The Family Friend*). Italy and France: Fandango, Indigo Film, Medusa Film, 2006.

———. *L'amore non ha confini* (short). 1998.

———. *La grande bellezza* (*The Great Beauty*). Italy and France: Indigo Film and Medusa Film, 2013.

———. *La notte lunga* (short). 2001.

———. *La partita lenta* (short). 2009.

———. *La primavera del 2002: L'Italia protesta, l'Italia si ferma* (video documentary). 2002.

———. *L'aquila 2009: Cinque registi tra le macerie* (video documentary short; segment: "L'assegnazione delle tende'). 2009.

———. *Le conseguenze dell'amore* (*The Consequences of Love*). Italy: Fandango, Indigo Film, Medusa Film, 2004.

———. *Le voci di dentro* (TV movie). 2014.

———. *Loro*. Italy: Indigo Film, Pathé, France 2 Cinéma, 2018.

——. *L'uomo in più* (*One Man Up*). Italy: Indigo Film and Key Films, 2001.

——. *Napoli 24* (short). 2010.

——. *The New Pope*. Italy, France, Spain, United Kingdom, and United States: Wildside, Haut et Court TV, Mediapro, Sky Italia, HBO, Canal+, 2019.

——. *Rio, I Love You* (segment: "La Fortuna"). Brazil, United States, and France: Conspiração Filmes, 2014.

——. *Sabato, domenica e lunedì* (TV movie). 2004.

——. *Sabbia* (short). 2014.

——. *This Must Be the Place*. Italy, France, and Ireland: Indigo Film, Lucky Red, Medusa Film, 2011.

——. *Un paradiso* (short). 1994.

——. *The Young Pope*. Italy, France, Spain, United Kingdom, and United States: Wildside, Haut et Court TV, Mediapro, Sky Italia, HBO, Canal+, 2016 (10 episodes).

——. *Youth*. Italy, France, United Kingdom, and Switzerland: Indigo Films, Barbary Films, Pathé, 2015.

Stone, Oliver. *JFK*. United States: Warner Bros., Canal+, Regency Enterprises, 1991.

Tarantino, Quentin. *The Hateful Eight*. United States: Visiona Romantica, 2015.

——. *Pulp Fiction*. United States: Miramax, A Band Apart Films, and Jersey Films, 1994.

——. *Reservoir Dogs*. United States: Live Entertainment and Dog Eat Dog Productions, 1992.

Tarkovsky, Andrei. *Mirror*. Soviet Union: Mosfilm, 1974.

Von Trier, Lars. *Breaking the Waves*. Denmark, Sweden, and France: Argus Film Produktie, Arte, Canal+, 1996.

——. *Melancholia*. Denmark, Sweden, France, and Germany: Zentropa Entertainments, 2011.

Visconti, Luchino. *Death in Venice*. Italy, France, and United States: Alfa Cinematografica, Warner Bros., PECF, 1971.

——. *La terra trema*. Italy: AR.TE.AS Film and Universalia Film, 1948.

——. *Ossessione*. Italy: Industrie Cinematografiche Italiane, 1943.

——. *Rocco and His Brothers*. Italy and France: Titanus and Les Films Marceau, 1960.

Wenders, Wim. *Alice in the Cities*. West Germany: Westdeutscher Rundfunk, 1974.

——. *Kings of the Road*. West Germany: Westdeutscher Rundfunk, 1976.

——. *Paris, Texas*. West Germany, France, and United States: Road Movies Filmproduktion, 1984.

——. *Wings of Desire*. West Germany and France: Road Movies Filmproduktion, 1987.

Wertmüller, Lina. *Love and Anarchy*. Italy and France: Euro International Film, 1974.

——. *The Seduction of Mimi*. Italy: Euro International Film, 1973.

Zanardo, Lorella. *Il corpo delle donne*. Italy: Rosso Film 2009.

BOOKS, ARTICLES, AND OTHER SOURCES

Aktsoglou, Babis. "Wim Wenders, A Filmmaker on the Road." In *Wim Wenders*, ed. Jason Wood and Ian Haydn Smith, 29–49. London: Wallflower, 2009.

Agamben, Giorgio. *Homo Sacer: Sovereign Power and Bare Life*. Trans. Daniel Heller Roazen. Stanford, CA: Stanford University Press, 1998.

Alvaray, Luisela. "National, Regional and Global: New Waves of Latin American Cinema." *Cinema Journal* 47, no. 3 (2008): 48–65.

Andrew, Dudley. Foreword to *Global Art Cinema: New Theories and Histories*, ed. Rosalind Galt and Karl Schoonover, v–xi. Oxford: Oxford University Press, 2010.

——. "The Unauthorized Auteur Today." In *Film Theory: An Anthology*, ed. Robert Stam and Toby Miller, 20–29. Oxford: Blackwell, 2000.

Antonello, Pierpaolo. "The Ambiguity of Realism and its Posts: A Response to Millicent Marcus." *The Italianist* 30 (2010): 258–62.

——. "*Il Divo*: Paolo Sorrentino's Spectacle of Politics." In *Italian Political Cinema: Public Life, Imaginary, and Identity in Contemporary Italian Film*, ed. Giancarlo Lombardi and Christian Uva, 291–306. Oxford: Peter Lang, 2016.

Antonello, Pierpaolo, and Florian Mussgnug, eds. *Postmodern Impegno: Ethics and Commitment in Contemporary Italian Culture*. Oxford: Peter Lang, 2009.

Augé, Marc. *Non-Places: Introduction to an Anthropology of Supermodernity*. Trans. John Howe. London: Verso, 1995.

Barthes, Roland. "The Death of the Author." In *Theories of Authorship: A Reader*, ed. John Caughie, 208–213. London: Routledge, 2001.

Baudrillard, Jean. "The Precession of Simulacra." In *Simulacra and Simulation*, 1–42. Ann Arbor: University of Michigan Press, 1994.

Bayman, Louis, and Sergio Rigoletto. "The Fair and the Museum: Framing the Popular." In *Popular Italian Cinema*, 1–28. New York: Palgrave Macmillan, 2013.

——. "Melodrama as Seriousness." In *Popular Italian Cinema*, 82–97. New York: Palgrave Macmillan, 2013.

Bazin, André. "Cinematic Realism and the Italian School of the Liberation." In *What Is Cinema?*, trans. Timothy Barnard, 215–50. Montreal: Caboose, 2009.

Benjamin, Walter. "Paris, the Capital of the 19th Century." In *Selected Writings*, vol. 3, *1935–1938*, ed. Howard Eiland and Michael W. Jennings, trans. Edmund Jephcott et al., 32–49. Cambridge, Mass.: Harvard University Press, 2002.

Bergfelder, Tim. "Love Beyond the Nation: Cosmopolitanism and Transnational Desire in Cinema." In *Europe and Love in Cinema*, ed. Luisa Passerini, Jo Labanyi, and Karen Diehl, 59–86. Bristol, UK: Intellect, 2012.

"Berlusconi Cuddles Lambs in Vegetarian Easter Campaign." *Guardian*, April 10, 2017. https://www.theguardian.com/world/2017/apr/10/silvio-berlusconi-vegetarian-easter-lambs-italian.

Bisoni, Claudio. "Paolo Sorrentino: Between Engagement and *Savoir Faire*." In *Italian Political Cinema: Public Life, Imaginary, and Identity in Contemporary Italian Film*, ed. Giancarlo Lombardi and Christian Uva, 251–64. Oxford: Peter Lang, 2016.

Bolter, Jay, and Richard Grusin. *Remediation: Understanding New Media*. Cambridge, MA: MIT Press, 1999.

Bondanella, Peter. *The Films of Federico Fellini*. Cambridge: Cambridge University Press, 2002.

——. *The History of Italian Cinema*. 3rd ed. New York: Continuum, 2009.

Bonsaver, Guido. "Dall'uomo al Divo: Un'intervista con Paolo Sorrentino." *The Italianist* 29 (2009): 325–37.

——. "The Family Friend." *Sight and Sound* 17, no. 4 (2007): 1–6.

——. "Prince of Darkness" (Interview). *Sight and Sound* 19, no. 4 (2009): 42–44.

Bordo, Susan. "Beauty (Re) Discovers the Male Body." In *Beauty Matters*, ed. Peggy Brand, 112–54. Bloomington: Indiana University Press, 2000.

Bordwell, David. "Explanation of Style, Styles of Explanation." Keynote address at the Classical Hollywood Conference, Wilfrid Laurier University, May 2018.

——. "Intensified Continuity: Visual Style in Contemporary American Film." *Film Quarterly* 55, no. 3 (2002): 16–28.

——. *The Way Hollywood Tells It: Story and Style in Modern Movies*. Berkeley: University of California Press, 2006.

Boym, Svetlana. *The Future of Nostalgia*. New York: Basic Books, 2001.

Bradatan, Costica, and Camil Ungureanu, eds. *Religion in European Cinema: The Postsecular Constellation*. New York: Routledge, 2014.

Bradshaw, Peter. "*The Family Friend*" (rev.). *The Guardian Online*, March 16, 2007. https://www.theguardian.com/film/2007/mar/16/worldcinema.drama.

——. "*La grande bellezza* (*The Great Beauty*)" (rev.). *The Guardian Online*, September 5, 2013. http://www.theguardian.com/film/2013/sep/05/le-grande-bellezza-great-beauty-review.

Branigan, Edward. *Point of View in the Cinema: A Theory of Narration and Subjectivity in Classical Film*. Berlin, Germany: Mouton, 1984.

Brecht, Bertolt. "A Short Organum for the Theatre" (1948) *Brecht on Theatre*, trans. John Willet, 179–208. New York: Hill and Wang, 1977.

Breton, Andre. *Nadja* (1928). Trans. Richard Howard. New York: Grove Press, 1960.

Breuer, Thomas. "From Maradona to Jude Law: Sport in Paolo Sorrentino's Movies." *Studies in European Cinema* (2018). DOI: 10.1080/17411548.2018.1554776.

Brook, Clodagh. "Postsecular Identity in Contemporary Italian Cinema: Catholic 'Cement,' the Suppression of History and the Lost Islamic Other." *Modern Italy* 22, no. 2 (2017): 197–211.

Brunetta, Gian Piero. *The History of Italian Cinema*. Princeton, NJ: Princeton University Press, 2003.

Buonarroti, Michelangelo. *Pietá*. 1498–1499. Marble, 174 × 195 cm. St. Peter's Basilica, Vatican City.

Burke, Frank, ed. *A Companion to Italian Cinema*. Hoboken, NJ: Wiley-Blackwell, 2017.

——. *Fellini's Films*. Woodbridge, CT: Twayne Publishers, 1996.

Buscombe, Edward. "Ideas of Authorship." In *Theories of Authorship: A Reader* (1981), ed. John Caughie, 22–34. London: Routledge, 2001.

Cartwright, Lisa, and Marita Sturken. (2001). "Spectatorship, Power, and Knowledge." In *Practices of Looking: An Introduction to Visual Culture*, ed. Marita Sturken and Lisa Cartwright, 72–93. Oxford: Oxford University Press.

Caruana, John, and Mark Cauchi, eds. *Immanent Frames: Postsecular Cinema between* The Tree of Life *and* Melancholia. Albany: State University of New York Press, 2018.

Casarino, Cesare. "Images for Housework: Expression, Representation, and the Time of Domestic Labor in Gilles Deleuze's Study of the Cinema." Keynote address at *Thinking Through Deleuze: Nomadic Subjects, Global Citizenship, and Posthumanism* conference, Brock University, St. Catherine's, Ontario, Canada, February 6, 2015.

Cattelan, Maurizio. *La Nona Ora (The Ninth Hour)*. 1999. Polyester resin, natural hairs, accessories, stone, and carpet, dimensions variable. Galerie Emmanuel Perrotin, Paris.

Caughie, John, ed. *Theories of Authorship: A Reader*. London: Routledge, 2001.

Céline, Louis-Ferdinand. *Journey to the End of Night* (1932; 1952). Trans. Ralph Manheim (1983). New York: New Directions, 2006.

Celli, Carlo, and Marga Cottino-Jones. *A New Guide to Italian Cinema*. New York: Palgrave Macmillan, 2007.

Cheu, Johnson. "Seeing Blindness On-Screen: The Blind, Female Gaze." In *The Problem Body: Projecting Disability on Film*, ed. Sally Chivers and Nicole Markotić, 67–82. Columbus: Ohio State University Press, 2010.

Clarke, R. "Review: The Great Beauty." *Sight and Sound* 23, no. 8 (August 2013). http://www.bfi.org.uk /news-opinion/sight-sound-magazine/reviews-recommendations/great-beauty.

Coates, Paul. "The Evidence of Things Not Seen: Sound and the Neighbour in Kieślowski, Haneke, Martel." In *Religion in Contemporary European Cinema: The Postsecular Constellation*, ed. Costica Bradatan and Camil Ungureanu, 91–109. New York: Routledge, 2014.

Corrigan, Timothy. "The Commerce of Auteurism." In *Critical Visions in Film Theory: Classic and Contemporary Readings*, ed. Timothy Corrigan, Patricia White, and Meta Mazaj, 416–29. Boston: Bedford/St. Martin's, 2011.

Crowdus, Gary. "Exposing the Dark Secrets of Italian Political History: An Interview with Paolo Sorrentino." *Cineaste* 34, no. 3 (Summer 2009): 32–37.

——. "In Search of *The Great Beauty*: An Interview with Paolo Sorrentino." *Cineaste* 39, no. 2 (Spring 2014): 8–13.

Cucco, Marco. "Che cosa è un film? *La grande bellezza* in una prospettiva di economia e politica dei media." In *La trama dei media. Stato, imprese, pubblico nella società dell'informazione*, ed. Marco Cucco, 101–19. Rome: Carocci, 2014.

Dalle Vacche, Angela. Review of Millicent Marcus, *Italian Film in the Light of Neorealism*. *SubStance* 19, no. 1 (Issue 61): 120–22.

Dante, Alighieri. *Inferno*. Trans. Allen Mandelbaum. Toronto: Bantam, 1992.

——. *Paradiso*. Trans. Allen Mandelbaum. Toronto: Bantam, 1992.

——. *Purgatorio*. Trans. Allen Mandelbaum. Toronto: Bantam, 1992.

Davis, Lennard J. "Introduction: Disability, Normality, and Power." In *The Disability Studies Reader*, 5th ed., ed. Lennard J. Davis, 1–16. London: Routledge, 2017.

De Santis, Pierpaolo, Domenica Monetti, and Luca P. Pallanch. *Divi e Antidivi: Il Cinema di Paolo Sorrentino*. Rome: Laboratorio Gutenberg, 2010.

Deleuze, Gilles. *Cinema 1: The Movement Image*. Trans. Hugh Tomlinson and Barbara Habberjam. Minneapolis: University of Minnesota Press, 1986.

——. *Cinema 2: The Time Image*. Trans. Hugh Tomlinson and Robert Galeta. Minneapolis: University of Minnesota Press, 1989.

Di Martino, Loredana, and Pasquale Verdicchio, eds. *Encounters with the Real in Contemporary Italian Literature and Cinema*. Newcastle-Upon-Tyne, UK: Cambridge Scholars Press, 2017.

Doane, Mary Ann. "Film and the Masquerade: Theorizing the Female Spectator." In *Film Theory: An Anthology*, ed. Robert Stam and Toby Miller, 495–509. Oxford: Blackwell, 2000.

Dostoevsky, Fyodor. *The Brothers Karamazov*. Trans. Richard Pevear and Larissa Volokhonsky. New York: Vintage, 1991.

Dotto, Silvia. "Paolo Sorrentino: L'arte nell'immagine cinematografica." Tesi di Laurea [Bachelor of Arts thesis], Università Ca' Foscari, Venezia, 2016.

Easthope, Anthony. "Cinécities in the Sixties." In *The Cinematic City*, ed. David B. Clarke, 129–39. London: Routledge, 1997.

Elkann, Alain. "Alain Elkann Interviews Italian Director and Screenwriter Paolo Sorrentino." Alain Elkann Interviews (website), March 5, 2017. http://www.alainelkanninterviews.com/paolo-sorrentino/.

Elsaesser, Thomas. "Bertolt Brecht and Contemporary Film." In *Reinterpreting Brecht: His Influence on Contemporary Drama and Film*, ed. Pia Kleber and Colin Visser, 170–85. Cambridge: Cambridge University Press, 1990.

Erll, Astrid. *Memory in Culture*. Trans. S. B. Young, New York: Palgrave Macmillan, 2011.

Ezra, Elizabeth, and Terry Rowden. "General Introduction: What Is Transnational Cinema?" In *Transnational Cinema: The Film Reader*, 1–11. New York: Routledge, 2006.

Ferrari, Antonio. "Perché Aldo Moro è il Kennedy italiano." *Corriere della Sera*, March 12, 2018. https://www.corriere.it/extra-per-voi/2018/03/06/perche-aldo-moro-kennedy-italiano-a09644bc-2153-11e8-a661-74ccbd41f00f.shtml.

Ferrero-Regis, Tiziana. *Recent Italian Cinema: Spaces, Contexts, Experiences*. Leicester, UK: Troubador, 2009.

Flaubert, Gustave. *Bouvard and Pécuchet* (1881). Trans. A. J. Krailsheimer. London: Penguin Classics, 1976.

——. *Madame Bovary* (1857). Trans. Lowell Blair. New York: Random House, 2005.

Forgacs, David D., and Robert R. Lumley, eds. *Italian Cultural Studies: An Introduction*. Oxford: Oxford University Press, 1996.

Foucault, Michel. *This Is Not a Pipe*. Trans and ed. James Harkness. Berkeley: University of California Press, 1982.

——. "What Is an Author?" In *Theories of Authorship: A Reader*, ed. John Caughie, 282–91. London: Routledge, 2001.

French, Philip. "*The Family Friend*." *Guardian*, March 18, 2007. https://www.theguardian.com/film/2007/mar/18/worldcinema.thriller.

Friedberg, Anne. *Window Shopping: Cinema and the Postmodern*. Berkeley: University of California Press, 1994.

Fumarola, Silvia. " 'The New Pope': John Malkovich entra nel cast accanto al 'giovane' Jude Law." *Repubblica*, July 2, 2018. http://www.repubblica.it/spettacoli/tv-radio/2018/07/02/news/_the_new_pope_-200628620/?ref=search&refresh_ce.

Fuqua, Joy Van. " 'Can You Feel It, Joe?' Male Melodrama and the Feeling Man." *The Velvet Light Trap* 38 (Fall 1996): 28–38.

Fusco, Coco. "Angels, History and Poetic Fantasy: An Interview With Wim Wenders." *Cineaste* 16, no. 4 (1988): 14–17.

Gabardi, Chiara Isabella Spagnoli. "*Loro* Is Sorrentino's New Cinematic Diptych." *Gainsayer*, May 1, 2018. http://www.gainsayer.me/loro-is-sorrentinos-new-cinematic-diptych/.

——. "*Loro Part 2*: Sorrentino Finishes Off Silvio Berlusconi." *Gainsayer*, May 4, 2018. http://www.gainsayer.me/loro-part-2-paolo-sorrentino-finishes-off-silvio-berlusconi/.

Galt, Rosalind. "The Prettiness of Italian Cinema." In *Popular Italian Cinema*, ed. Louis Bayman and Sergio Rigoletto, 52–68. New York: Palgrave Macmillan, 2013.

Galt, Rosalind, and Karl Schoonover. "Introduction: The Impurity of Art Cinema." In *Global Art Cinema: New Theories and Histories*, 3–30. Oxford: Oxford University Press, 2010.

Garland-Thomson, Rosemarie. *Staring: How We Look*. Oxford: Oxford University Press, 2009.

Gates, Philippa. "The Man's Film: Woo and the Pleasure of Male Melodrama." *Journal of Popular Culture* 35, no. 1 (2001): 59–79.

Gennari, Daniela Treveri. *Post-War Italian Cinema: American Intervention, Vatican Interests*. New York: Routledge, 2009.

Gilman, Sander. *The Jew's Body*. New York: Routledge, 1991.

Giuffrida, Angela. "Berlusconi Biopic *Loro* Is 'a Tender Look at the Weaknesses of an Old Man.' " *Guardian*, May 3, 2018.

Gledhill, Christine. "Melodrama and Cinema: The Critical Problem." In *Home Is Where the Heart Is*, 5–13. London: BFI, 2002.

Godard, Jean-Luc. *Godard on Godard*. Ed. Jean Narboni and Tom Milne. New York: Viking Press, 1972.

Goethe, Johan Wolfgang von. *Faust, A Tragedy*. Trans. Walter Arndt. Ed. Cyrus Hamlin. New York: Norton, 1976.

"*La grande bellezza*." The Internet Movie Database. Accessed November 4, 2019. http://www.imdb.com /title/tt2358891/trivia.

Grant, Barry Keith. *Auteurs and Authorship: A Film Reader*. Oxford: Blackwell, 2008.

Grey, Thomas, ed. *Richard Wagner: Der fliegende Holländer*. Cambridge: Cambridge University Press, 2000.

Gross, Kenneth. *Shylock Is Shakespeare*. Chicago: University of Chicago Press, 2006.

Grusin, Richard, ed. *The Nonhuman Turn*. Minneapolis: University of Minnesota Press, 2015.

——. *Premediation: Affect and Mediality After 9/11*. London: Palgrave Macmillan, 2010.

Gunning, Tom. "The Cinema of Attractions: Early Film, its Spectator, and the Avant Garde." In *Early Cinema: Space, Frame, Narrative*, ed. Tom Gunning, Thomas Elsaesser, and Adam Barker, 56–62. London: BFI, 1990.

Guerrini, Riccardo, Giacomo Tagliani, and Francesca Zucconi. "Introduzione." In *Lo spazio del reale nel cinema italiano contemporaneo*, 9–15. Genoa, Italy: Le Mani, 2009.

Habermas, Jürgen. "Notes on a Post-Secular Society." *New Perspectives Quarterly* 25, no. 4 (2008): 17–29.

Hansen, Miriam. "The Mass Production of the Senses: Classical Cinema as Vernacular Modernism." *Modernism/Modernity* 6, no. 2 (April 1999): 59–77.

Haskell, Molly. *Reverence to Rape: The Treatment of Woman in the Movies*. Chicago: Chicago University Press, 1974.

Hasted, Nick. "Maestros and Mobsters." *Sight and Sound* 20, no. 5 (2010): 24–27.

Hennessy, Brendan. "Reel Simulations: CGI and Special Effects in Two Films by Paolo Sorrentino." *The Italianist* 37, no. 3 (2017): 449–63. DOI: 10.1080/02614340.2017.1409582 2017.

Hill, Lee. "Paris, Texas." *Cinémathèque Annotations on Film* 72 (October 2014): 1–5.

Hilsabeck, Burke. "The 'Is' in What Is Cinema? On André Bazin and Stanley Cavell." *Cinema Journal* 55, no. 2 (2016): 25–42.

Hipkins, Danielle. "The Showgirl Effect: Ageing Between Great Beauties and 'Veline di turno.' " *Cinepanettone-Academia: ReadingItaly*, December 11, 2013. https://wp.me/p2iDSt-bW.

——. "Why Italian Film Studies Needs a Second Take on Gender." *Italian Studies* 63, no. 2 (2008): 213–34. DOI: 10.1179/007516308X344360.

Hirsch, Marianne. *Family Frames: Photography, Narrative and Postmemory*. Cambridge, MA: Harvard University Press, 1997.

Holtsmark, Erling B. "The *Katabasis* Theme in Modern Cinema." In *Classical Myth and Culture in the Cinema*, ed. Martin M. Winkler, 23–50. New York: Oxford University Press, 2001.

Homer. *The Odyssey*. Trans. Robert Fagles. New York: Penguin, 1996.

Hope, William, ed. *Italian Film Directors in the New Millennium*. Newcastle upon Tyne, UK: Cambridge Scholars, 2010.

Hutcheon, Linda. *A Theory of Adaptation*. 2nd ed. New York: Routledge, 2012.

Hutcheon, Linda, and Michael Hutcheon. *Bodily Charm: Living Opera*. Lincoln: University of Nebraska Press, 2000.

Iannone, Pasquale. "Journey to the End of the Night." *Sight and Sound* 23, no. 10 (2013): 38–41.

Jameson, Fredric. *Postmodernism, or The Cultural Logic of Late Capitalism*. Durham, NC: Duke University Press, 1999.

Johnston, Trevor. "This Must Be the Place." *Sight and Sound* 22, no. 4 (April 2012): 78–79.

Jones, Stan. "Wenders' *Paris, Texas* and the 'European Way of Seeing.' " In *European Identity in Cinema*, ed. Wendy Everett. Bristol, UK: Intellect, 1996.

Kafka, Franz. *Letter to His Father/Briefe an den Vater*. Trans. Ernst Kaiser and Eithne Wilkins. New York: Schocken, 1966.

Kaplan, E. Ann. "Is the Gaze Male?" In *Feminism and Film*, ed. E. Ann Kaplan, 119–38. Oxford: Oxford University Press, 2000.

Kilbourn, Russell J. A. "Adapting Venice: Intermedial Relations in Visconti, Sebald, and Kafka." "lifedeath": *Mosaic* special issue 48, no. 3 (Sept. 2015): 57–74.

——. "American Frankenstein: Modernity's Monstrous Progeny." *Mosaic* 38, no. 3 (2005): 167–83.

——. *Cinema, Memory, Modernity: The Representation of Memory from the Art Film to Transnational Cinema*. New York: Routledge, 2010.

——. "The 'Primal Scene': Memory, Redemption, and 'Woman' in the Films of Paolo Sorrentino." Special issue, *Journal of Italian Cinema and Media Studies* 7, no. 3 (2019): 377–94.

Kliemann, Carlotta Fonzi. "Cultural and Political Exhaustion in Paolo Sorrentino's *The Great Beauty*." *Senses of Cinema* 70 (March 2014). http://sensesofcinema.com/2014/feature-articles/cultural-and-political-exhaustion-in-paolo-sorrentinos-the-great-beauty/.

Knausgaard, Karl Ove. *My Struggle*. Books 1–6. New York: Vintage, 2013–2018.

Kodak Corporation. "Vision3 500T Colour Negative Film 5219/7219." Accessed October 30, 2019. https://www.kodak.com/vn/en/motion/Products/Production/5219/default.htm.

Kolker, Robert. "Image and Reality." In *Film, Form, and Culture*, 3rd ed., 10–29. New York: McGraw-Hill, 2006.

Kornhaber, Spencer. "What *The Young Pope* Preached About Love." *The Atlantic*, February 14, 2017. https://www.theatlantic.com/entertainment/archive/2017/02/the-young-pope-season-one-finale-hbo/516600/.

Kovács, András Bálint. *Screening Modernism: European Art Cinema, 1950–1980*. Chicago: University of Chicago Press, 2007.

Kracauer, Siegfried. *Theory of Film: The Redemption of Physical Reality*. Princeton, NJ: Princeton University Press, 1997.

Kraemer, Joseph A. "Trauma and Representation in the Animated Documentary." *Journal of Film and Video* 67, no. 3–4 (2015): 57–68.

La Capria, Rafaelle. *Ferito a Morte* (1961). Milano: Oscar Mondadori, 2014.

Landsberg, Alison. "Prosthetic Memory: The Ethics and Politics of Memory in an Age of Mass Culture." In *Memory and Popular Film*, ed. Paul Grainge, 144–61. New York: Manchester University Press, 2003.

LaPlace, Maria. "Producing and Consuming the Woman's Film: Discursive Struggle in *Now, Voyager*." In *Home Is Where the Heart Is: Studies in Melodrama and the Woman's Film*, ed. Christine Gledhill, 138–66. London: BFI, 2002.

Leopardi, Giacomo. *Canti*. Trans. Jonathan Galassi. New York: Farrar Straus Giroux, 2010.

Leotta, Alfio. "Do Not Underestimate the Consequences of Love: The Representation of the New Mafia in Contemporary Italian Cinema." *Italica* 88, no. 2 (Summer 2011): 286–96.

Levi, Primo. *If This Is a Man* and *The Truce*. Trans. Stuart Woolf. Bungay, Suffolk, UK: Sphere, 1988.

Levy, Shawn. *Dolce Vita Confidential: Fellini, Loren, Pucci, Paparazzi and the Swinging High Life of 1950s Rome*. New York: Norton, 2016.

Leys, Ruth. "Trauma and the Turn to Affect." In *Trauma, Memory, and Narrative in the Contemporary South African Novel: Essays*, ed. Ewald Mengel and Michaela Borzaga, 3–28. Amsterdam: Rodopi, 2012.

Lombardi, Giancarlo and Christian Uva. *Italian Political Cinema: Public Life, Imaginary, and Identity in Contemporary Italian Film*. Oxford: Peter Lang, 2016.

Luchetti, Lia, and Anna Lisa Tota. "The Period of the 'Strategy of Tension' in Italy (1969–1993) and the Piazza Fontana Bombing in Milan." In *Routledge International Handbook of Memory Studies*, ed. Anna Lisa Tota and Tever Hagen, 382–87. New York: Routledge, 2015.

Lyotard, Jean-Francois. *The Postmodern Condition: A Report on Knowledge*. Trans. Geoffrey Bennington and Brian Massumi. Minneapolis: University of Minnesota Press, 1984.

Magritte, Rene. *The Treachery of Images*. 1929. Oil on canvas. 60.33 cm x 81.12 cm. Los Angeles County Museum of Art.

Manganelli, Giorgio. *Pinocchio: Un Libro Parallelo*. Milan: Adelphi, 2002.

Mann, Thomas. *Death in Venice* (1913). Oxford: Oxford University Press, 1971.

Marcus, Millicent. *After Fellini: National Cinema in the Postmodern Age*. Baltimore, MD: Johns Hopkins University Press, 2002.

——. "Fellini's *Amarcord*: Film as Memory." *Quarterly Review of Film & Video* 2, no. 4 (1977): 418–25. DOI: 10.1080/10509207709391365.

——. "The Ironist and the Auteur: Post-Realism in Paolo Sorrentino's *Il Divo*." *The Italianist* 30 (2010): 245–57.

——. *Italian Film In the Light of Neorealism*. Princeton, NJ: Princeton University Press, 1986.

Mariani, Annachiara. "The Empty Heterotopic (Non-)Space of Sorrentino's Female Characters in *The Great Beauty* and *The Consequences of Love*." In *Female Identity and Its Representations in the Arts and Humanities*, ed. Silvia Giovanardi Byer and Fabiana Cecchini, 168–84. Newcastle, UK: Cambridge Scholars Publishing, 2017.

——. "Megalomaniac: The Obsession with Power in Sorrentino's Diptych *Loro*." Paper presented at JICMS Second International Conference: Global Intersections and Artistic Connections: Italian Cinema and Media Across Times and Spaces, American University of Rome, June 2019.

Marini-Maio, Nicoletta. "A Spectre is Haunting Italy: The Double Emplotment of the Moro Affair." In *Terrorism, Italian Style: The Representation of Terrorism and Political Violence in Contemporary Italian Cinema*, ed. Ruth Glynn, Giancarlo Lombardi, and Alan O'Leary, 157–174. London: IGRS, 2012.

——. *A Very Seductive Body Politic: Silvio Berlusconi in the Cinema*. Milan, Italy: Mimesis International, 2015.

——. "'È solo l'alito di un vecchio': Corpi di donne, mascolinità senile e maschere dell'impotenza in *Loro* (2018) di Paolo Sorrentino" (forthcoming in *L'Avventura*).

Mariniello, Silvestra, and James Cisternos. "Experience and Memory in the Films of Wim Wenders." *SubStance* 34, no. 1 (2005): 159–79.

Marlow-Mann, Alex. "Beyond Post-Realism: A Response to Millicent Marcus." *The Italianist* 30 (2010): 263–71.

——. "Character Engagement and Alienation in the Cinema of Paolo Sorrentino." In *Italian Film Directors in the New Millennium*, ed. William Hope, 161–74. Newcastle: Cambridge Scholars Press, 2010.

——. *The New Neapolitan Cinema*. Edinburgh: Edinburgh University Press, 2011.

Matsumoto, Neil. "Time and Age." *American Cinematographer* (January 2016): 20–26.

Mayersberg, Paul. "Naked Masks." *Sight and Sound* 22, no. 4 (April 2012): 20–21.

McFarland, Melanie. "HBO's 'The Young Pope' Makes High Art for TV, but the Result is Less Than Divine." Salon.com, January 14, 2017: 1–8.

McGowan, Todd. *The Real Gaze: Film Theory After Lacan*. New York: State University of New York Press, 2007.

Mecchia, Giuseppina. "Birds in the Roman Sky: Shooting for the Sublime in *La grande bellezza*." *Forum Italicum* 50, no. 1 (2016): 183–93.

Menarini, Roy. "Generi nascosti ed espliciti nel recente cinema italiano." In *Lo spazio del reale nel cinema italiano contemporaneo*, ed. Riccardo Guerrini, Giacomo Tagliani, and Francesca Zucconi, 42–40. Genoa, Italy: Le Mani 2009.

Michalczyk, John J. *The Italian Political Filmmakers*. London: Associated University Presses, 1986.

Millington, Barry, ed. *The New Grove Guide to Wagner and His Operas*. Oxford: Oxford University Press, 2006.

Minuz, Andrea. "Com'è fosco il potere raccontato dal cinema italiano." *Il Foglio*, February 5, 2018. https://www.ilfoglio.it/cinema/2018/02/05/news/cinema-sono-tornato-sorrentino-fosco-potere-176959/.

——. *Political Fellini: Journey to the End of Italy*. Trans. Marcus Perryman. New York: Berghahn, 2015.

Modleski, Tania. "Clint Eastwoood and Male Weepies." *American Literary History* 22, no. 1 (November 2009): 136–58.

Moliterno, Gino. *The A to Z of Italian Cinema*. Lanham, MD: Scarecrow Press, 2009.

Morgan, Daniel. "Rethinking Bazin: Ontology and Realist Aesthetics." *Critical Inquiry* 32, no. 3 (Spring 2006): 443–81.

Mulvey, Laura. "Visual Pleasure and Narrative Cinema." In *Film Theory: An Anthology*, ed. Robert Stam and Toby Miller, 483–94. Oxford: Blackwell, 2000.

Neale, Steve. "Art Cinema as Institution." *Screen* 22, no. 1 (May 1981): 11–40.

Nietzsche, Friedrich. *The Birth of Tragedy and The Case of Wagner*. Trans. Walter Kaufmann. Toronto: Random House, 1967.

——. *The Gay Science*. Trans. Walter Kaufmann. New York: Vintage, 1974.

Nixon, Sean. "Exhibiting Masculinity." In *Representation: Cultural Representations and Signifying Practices*, ed. Stuart Hall, 293–330. London: Sage, 1997.

Novalis, "Longing for Death." *Hymns to the Night*. Trans. Justin E. H. Smith. Justin E. H. Smith (website). Accessed October 31 2019. http://www.jehsmith.com/1/2013/09/novalis-longing-for-death.html.

Nowell-Smith, Geoffrey. Foreword to *Italian Film Directors in the New Millennium*, ed. William Hope, ix–x. Newcastle, UK: Cambridge Scholars Press, 2010.

O'Leary, Alan. "Locations of Moro: The Kidnap in the Cinema." In *Remembering Aldo Moro*, ed. Ruth Glynn and Giancarlo Lombardi, 151–70. Oxford: Legenda, 2012.

——. "Marco Tullio Giordana, or The Persistence of Impegno." In *Postmodern Impegno: Ethics and Commitment in Contemporary Italian Culture*, ed. Pierpaolo Antonello and Florian Mussgnug, 213–31. Oxford: Peter Lang, 2009.

——. "Political/Popular Cinema." In *Italian Political Cinema: Public Life, Imaginary, and Identity in Contemporary Italian Film*, ed. Giancarlo Lombardi and Christian Uva, 107–117. Oxford: Peter Lang, 2016.

——. "Towards World Heritage Cinema." In *Screening European Heritage: Creating and Consuming History on Film*, ed. Paul Cooke and Rob Stone, 63–84. London: Palgrave Macmillan, 2016.

O'Leary, Alan, and Catherine O'Rawe. "Against Realism: On a 'Certain Tendency' in Italian Film Criticism." *Journal of Modern Italian Studies* 16, no. 1 (2011): 107–128.

"*One Man Up*." The Internet Movie Database. Accessed November 10, 2019. https://www.imdb.com/title/tt0295671/trivia?ref_=tt_trv_trv.

O'Rawe, Catherine. "Brothers in Arms: Middlebrow *Impegno* and Homosocial Relations in the Cinema of Petraglia and Rulli." In *Intellectual Communities and Partnerships in Italy and Europe*, ed. Danielle Hipkins, 149–67. Oxford: Peter Lang, 2012.

——. " 'I Padri e maestri': Genre, Auteurs, and Absences in Italian Film Studies." *Italian Studies* 63, no. 2 (Autumn 2008): 173–94.

——. *Stars and Masculinities in Contemporary Italian Cinema*. New York: Palgrave Macmillan, 2014.

Pasolini, Pier Paolo. "What Is This Coup d'État? Io So." Trans. Giovanni Tiso. *Overland*. March 28, 2012. https://overland.org.au/2012/03/what-is-this-coup-detat-i-know/.

Paulicelli, Eugenia. *Italian Style: Fashion and Film from Early Cinema to the Digital Age*. New York: Bloomsbury Academic, 2016.

Pence, Jeffrey. "Cinema of the Sublime: Theorizing the Ineffable." *Poetics Today* 25, no. 1 (Spring 2004): 29–66.

Plantinga, Carl. *Moving Viewers: American Film and the Spectator's Experience*. Berkeley: University of California Press, 2009.

Prince, Stephen. "The Discourse of Pictures: Iconicity and Film Studies." In *Film Theory and Criticism*, 6th ed., ed. Leo Braudy and Marshall Cohen, 87–105. New York: Oxford University Press, 2004.

Proust, Marcel. *In Search of Lost Time, Vol. 1: Swann's Way*. Trans. C. K. Scott Moncrieff. London: Vintage, 1996.

Pulver, Andrew. "Paolo Sorrentino: 'I Never Use a Crude Approach to Showing the Naked Bodies of Older People.' " *Guardian*, January 15, 2016. https://www.theguardian.com/film/2016/jan/15/paolo-sorrentino-michael-caine-youth-oscar-great-beauty.

Rancière, Jacques. *The Emancipated Spectator*. Trans. Gregory Elliott. London: Verso, 2009.

Reed, Christopher Llewellyn. "*Loro*: Bad Behaviour." *Hammer to Nail*, October 22, 2018. www.hammer-tonail.com/film-festivals/loro-review/.

Renga, Dana. "The Mafia Noir: Paolo Sorrentino's *Le conseguenze dell'amore*." In *Unfinished Business: Screening the Italian Mafia in the New Millenium*, 65–79. Toronto: University of Toronto Press, 2013.

———. "*Romanzo criminale* as Male Melodrama: 'It Is in Reality *Always* Too Late.'" In *Italian Political Cinema: Public Life, Imaginary, and Identity in Contemporary Italian Film*, ed. Giancarlo Lombardi and Christian Uva, 373–88. Oxford: Peter Lang, 2016.

Restivo, Angelo. *The Cinema of Economic Miracles: Visuality and Modernization in the Italian Art Film*. Durham, NC: Duke University Press, 2002.

Robertini, Giovanni. "*Loro 1*, Sorrentino ci prende tutti per il culo." *Rolling Stone Italia*, April 23, 2018. https://www.rollingstone.it/cinema/news-cinema/loro-1-sorrentino-ci-prende-tutti-per-il-culo/409529/.

Rodowick, D. N. *The Virtual Life of Film*. Cambridge, MA: Harvard University Press, 2007.

Romney, Jonathan. "On the Road Again." *Sight and Sound* 22, no. 4 (April 2012): 16–20.

———. "Tragedies of Ridiculous Men." *Sight and Sound* 17, no. 4 (April 2007): 40–42.

Rorty, Richard. *Contingency, Irony, and Solidarity*. Cambridge: Cambridge University Press, 1989.

Rosen, Philip. "Belief in Bazin." In *Opening Bazin: Postwar Film Theory and Its Afterlife*, ed. Dudley Andrew with Hervé Joubert-Laurencin, 107–18. Oxford: Oxford University Press, 2011.

Roth, Philip. *Operation Shylock: A Confession*. New York: Vintage, 1993.

Rushton, Richard. *The Reality of Film: Theories of Filmic Reality*. Manchester, UK: Manchester University Press, 2011.

Salvestroni, Simonetta. *La grande bellezza e il cinema di Paolo Sorrentino*. Bologna, Italy: Archetipo Libri, 2017.

Sarris, Andrew. "Notes on the Auteur Theory in 1962." In *Film Theory and Criticism*, 6th ed., ed. Leo Braudy and Marshall Cohen, 561–64. New York: Oxford University Press, 2004.

Schiesari, Juliana. *The Gendering of Melancholia: Feminism, Psychoanalysis, and the Symbolics of Loss in Renaissance Literature*. Ithaca, NY: Cornell University Press, 1992.

Sconce, Jeffrey. "Irony, Nihilism, and the New American 'Smart' Film." *Screen* 43, no. 4 (2002): 349–69.

Scorsese, Martin. "Standing Up for Cinema." *Times Literary Supplement*, May 31, 2017. http://www.the-tls.co.uk/articles/public/film-making-martin-scorsese/.

Seraillon (blog). "The Great Lost Moment: Rafaelle La Capria's *The Mortal Wound*." November 25, 2015. http://seraillon.blogspot.com/2015/11/the-great-lost-moment-raffaele-la.html.

Shakespeare, William. *Macbeth*. London: Penguin, 2005.

Shakespeare, William, and Tom Lockwood. *The Merchant of Venice* (1605). Ed. M. M. Mahood. 3rd ed. The New Cambridge Shakespeare. New York: Cambridge University Press, 2018.

Shohat, Ella, and Robert Stam, eds. *Multiculturalism, Post-Coloniality and Transnational Media*. New Brunswick, NJ: Rutgers, 2003.

Sicinski, Michael. "Paolo Sorrentino: A Medium Talent." *Cinemascope* (2017): 17–21.

Silverman, Kaja. "Suture [Excerpts]." In *Narrative, Apparatus, Ideology: A Film Theory Reader*, ed. Philip Rosen, 219–34. New York: Columbia University Press, 1986.

Simor, Eszter, and D. David Sorfa. "Irony, Sexism and Magic in Paolo Sorrentino's Films." *Studies in European Cinema* 14, no. 3 (2017): 1–16. DOI: 10.1080/17411548.2017.1386368.

Sinnerbrink, Robert. "Postsecular Ethics: The Case of Iñárritu's *Biutiful*." In *Religion in European Cinema: The Postsecular Constellation*, ed. Costica Bradatan and Camil Ungureanu, 166–85. New York: Routledge, 2014.

Smith, Murray. *Engaging Characters: Fiction, Emotion, and the Cinema*. Oxford: Clarendon Press, 1995.

Sontag, Susan. "Bergman's *Persona*." In *Ingmar Bergman's* Persona, ed. L. Michaels, 62–85. Cambridge: Cambridge University Press, 2000.

Sorrentino, Paolo. *Everybody's Right*. Trans. Anthony Shugaar. New York: Europa Editions, 2011.

———. *Gli aspetti irrilevanti*. Milan, Italy: Mondadori, 2016.

———. *Hanno tutti ragione*. Milan, Italy: Feltrinelli, 2010.

———. *Il peso di Dio: Il vangelo di Lenny Belardo*. Turin: Einaudi, 2017.

———. "Interview with Antonio Monda." *La grande bellezza*. DVD. Directed by Paolo Sorrentino. New York: Criterion, 2013.

———. *Tony Pagoda e i suoi amici*. Milan, Italy: Feltrinelli Milano, 2014.

———. *Youth*. Trans. N. S. Thompson. London: MacLehose Press, 2015.

Spadafora, Alberto, ed. *The Great Beauty: Told by Director of Photography Luca Bigazzi*. Self-published, CreateSpace Independent Publishing Platform, 2014.

Spagnoletti, Giovanni, and Roy Menarini. "Istruzioni per l'uso: Forme della politica nel cinema italiano contemporanea." *Close-up* 23 (2007–2008): 3–8.

Spoladori, Simone. *Paolo Sorrentino: Le conseguenze di un autore*. N.p.: Le Mani Microart S, 2014.

Stanska, Zuzanna. "*The Young Pope*: All 10 Paintings From the Opening Explained." *Daily Art Magazine*, December 5, 2016. http://www.dailyartmagazine.com/young-pope-paintings-opening-explained/.

Sturken, Marita, and Lisa Cartwright. *Practices of Looking: An Introduction to Visual Culture*. Oxford: Oxford University Press, 2001.

Sturton, Kevin. "One Man Up (Paolo Sorrentino)." *Cinemashame* (blog), May 30, 2017. https://cinemashame .wordpress.com/2017/05/30/one-man-up-2001-paolo-sorrentino/;

Tagliani, Giacomo. "Depicting Life, Analyzing the Power: The 'Actuality' of Italian Cinema." *Journal of Italian Cinema and Media Studies* 2, no. 2 (2014): 199–214.

———. "Le conseguenze del vissuto." In *Lo spazio del reale nel cinema italiano contemporaneo*, ed. Riccardo Guerrini, Giacomo Tagliani, and Francesca Zucconi, 91–103. Genoa, Italy: Le Mani, 2009.

Taylor, Charles. *A Secular Age*. Cambridge, MA: Belknap Press of Harvard University, 2007.

Tenaglia, Allesandro. *"L'aldilà è un soppalco": Uno sguardo teleologico—e non solo—sull'opera di Paolo Sorrentino fino a* The Young Pope. N.p.: Tana dell'Orso, 2019.

Tennyson, Lord Alfred. "Ulysses." In *Alfred Tennyson: The Major Works*, ed. Adam Roberts, 80. Oxford: Oxford University Press, 2000.

Thomson, Patricia. "A New Pope." *American Cinematographer* (May 2017): 24–28.

Thompson, Kristin, and David Bordwell. *Film History: An Introduction*. 3rd ed. Boston: McGraw Hill, 2009.

Toumarkine, Doris. "La Dolce Bellezza." *Film Journal International* 116, no. 12 (2013): 28–30.

Tunefind (website). "The Young Pope Soundtrack." November 18, 2016. https://www.tunefind.com/show /the-young-pope/season-1/38422.

Tremblay, Odile. "Les revanches de Sorrentino." *Le Devoir*, December 15, 2015. https://www.ledevoir.com /culture/cinema/458180/les-revanches-de-sorrentino.

Uva, Christian. "The New Cinema of Political Engagement." In *Italian Political Cinema: Public Life, Imaginary, and Identity in Contemporary Italian Film*, ed. Giancarlo Lombardi and Christian Uva, 31–42. Oxford: Peter Lang, 2016.

Van Dijck. José. *Mediated Memories in the Digital Age*. Stanford, CA: Stanford University Press, 2007.

Vermes, Timur. *Er ist Wieder Da*. Köln: Bastei Lübbe Taschenbuch, 2012.

Vigni, Franco. *La maschera, il potere, la solitudine: Il cinema di Paolo Sorrentino*. Florence, Italy: Aska Edizioni, 2017.

Vivarelli, Nick. "Paolo Sorrentino on Why Maradona Has a Special Place in His Heart." *Variety*, December 13, 2015. https://variety.com/2015/film/global/paolo-sorrentino-on-making-youth-and -why-maradona-has-a-special-place-in-his-heart-1201660014/.

Weissberg, Jay. "Film Review: Paolo Sorrenino's *Loro 1*." *Variety*, May 8, 2018, 1–4.

Wheatley, Catherine. *Michael Haneke's Cinema: The Ethic of the Image*. New York: Berghahn, 2009.

Wikipedia, s.v. "Pinocchio." Last edited on September 25, 2019, 18:09. https://en.wikipedia.org/wiki /Pinocchio.

Wikipedia, s.v. "Song for Athene." Last edited on May 31, 2019 16:36. https://en.wikipedia.org/wiki /Song_for_Athene.

Williams, Linda. "The American Melodramatic Mode." In *Playing the Race Card: Melodramas of Black and White from Uncle Tom's Cabin to O.J. Simpson*, 10–44. Princeton, NJ: Princeton University Press, 2001.

Wollen, Peter. "The Auteur Theory" (1969). In *Film Theory and Criticism*, 6th ed., ed. Leo Braudy and Marshall Cohen, 565–77. New York: Oxford University Press, 2004.

———. "The Auteur Theory" (1972). In *Theories of Authorship: A Reader*, ed. John Caughie, 146–51. London: Routledge, 2001.

Wood, Mary. *Italian Cinema*. Oxford: Berg, 2005.

——. "Italian Film Noir." In *European Film Noir*, ed. Andrew Spicer, 236–72. Manchester, UK: Manchester University Press, 2007.

——. "Lipstick and Chocolate: Paolo Sorrentino's the *Consequences of Love*." In *Mafia Movies: A Reader*, 2nd ed., ed. Dana Renga, 277–82. Toronto: University of Toronto Press, 2019.

"*Youth*." The Internet Movie Database. Accessed November 15, 2019. https://www.imdb.com/title/tt3312830/trivia?ref_=tt_trv_trv.

Zaccagnini, Edoardo, and Giovanni Spagnoletti. "Intervista a Paolo Sorrentino." *Close-up* 23 (2007): 109–116.

Zagarrio, Vito. "The 'Great Beauty,' or Form Is Politics." In *Italian Political Cinema: Public Life, Imaginary, and Identity in Contemporary Italian Film*, ed. Giancarlo Lombardi and Christian Uva, 119–32. Oxford: Peter Lang, 2016.

Zanetti, Alberto. "La doppia vita di Antonio." *Cineforum* 409 (November 2001): 63–65.

INDEX

Page numbers in *italics* refer to figures.

directorial intentionality, xxii

disability studies, 121, 190n8

disorientation, 35–36, *36*

Divo, Il, xv, 157; *American Psycho* and, 134, 154–55; auteurism in, 158; as biopic, 45; at Cannes Film Festival, xi; confessionals in, 58–66, *59–60, 62, 64*; *The Consequences of Love* and, 139; content in, xxiii; *The Family Friend and*, 152; family in, 111; *The Great Beauty* and, 156; Hennessey on, xvi–xvii; impegno in, 53–58, *54*; male body in, 129; nostalgia in, 176–77; as political art film, xxvi, 46–53, *48–50*; politics in, 151–52; postrealism in, xxvii, 93, 123–24; Sorrentino on, 181n37; success of, xxi; tracking shots in, 26; voiceovers in, 77; *The Young Pope* and, 34, 192n8

Doane, Mary-Anne, 100

documentary style, 51

Dolce Vita, La, 35, 88, 91, 94–95, 140; homage to, 105–6, 109; reputation of, 107, 171–72, *172*; women in, 159–60

Do the Right Thing, 49, *50*

Double Life of Veronique, The, 3, 5, 11

"Down On the Street," 206n11

dream scenes, 129–30, 202n25; in *One Man Up*, 7–9, *8–9*; in *The Young Pope*, 42, 137–41, *138–41*

Easy Rider, 73

ecclise, L', 62–63

editing, 16, 26, 40, 90; for disorientation, 35–36, *36*; narratives and, 107; shot-reverse shots, 167–69, *168*; for temporality shifts, 29–30; by Travaglioi, 136–37

EDM. *See* Electronic Dance Music

8 1/2, 57, 88, 98, 198n8; homage to, 117; *Youth* and, 106

Electronic Dance Music (EDM), 129, 138

elegiac nostalgia, 104

Elkann, Alain, xi

elliptical editing, 16

Ellis, Bret Easton, 62

Elsaesser, Thomas, 53

engagement, *33*, 33–34, 38–39

epistemology, 148–49

Erll, Astrid, 56

escapism, xxiii–xxiv

Esmeralda, Santa, 5–6

Eternal Sunshine of the Spotless Mind, 101

ethics, 2–3, 51; cinematic, xiii–xvii, 41–42, 101; gravitas and, 72–73; of identity, 177; of religion, 135; in *This Must Be the Place*, 80–84, *83*

ethnic identity, xxii

Europe, 43, 125, 127

European gaze, 73

evangelization, 131

Everybody's Right, xviii, 70, 188n6, 200n47; characters in, 3

existential ennui, 20, 129, 132–33

existentialism, 62–63

extradiegetic flashbacks, 24–25

Eyes Wide Shut, 109

family, 111, 129–30, 132–33

Family Friend, The: aesthetics of repugnancy in, 41–45, *42*; as art film, 35–41, *36–37, 39–40*; cinematography in, 2, 191n20; comedy in, 68, 111; dialogue in, 106; *Il Divo* and, 152; ideology in, 153; Jews in, 68; lighting in, 46–47, 93; non-normative identities in, *33*, 33–35; style of, 13; themes in, 31–33

fantasy, 29–30

fascism, xxv, 32, 206n20

Fassbinder, Rainer Werner, xxii–xxiii

fatherhood, 111–12, *112*

Faust (Goethe), 101

feelings, 99

Fellini, Federico, 88; comedy of, 51; influence of, 34–35, 91, 105, 106, 139–40, 171–72, *172*, 202n23; reputation of, 90, 93, 194n43, 201n5. *See also Amarcord*; *Dolce Vita, La*; *8 1/2*; *I Vitelloni*; *Roma*

female gaze, 107, 136–37

feminist theory, xii, xvii–xviii, 200n49; Sorrentinian subject and, 109, 115; viewers in, 159–60; women in, 165

Ferrero-Regis, Tiziana, xvi

De Filippo, Eduardo, xv–xvi

film: capitalism and, 95; comedy in, 51; digital, xvi–xvii; escapism in, xxiii–xxiv; during fascism, 32; filmmakers, xix, 175; fourth wall in, 58; in France, 35; history of, xii, xviii–xix, xxii; Hitler in, *112–13*, 112–15; ideology in, 152–53; for Italy, xxi–xxii; mnemic reveries in, 99–100; music in, xxii–xxiii; narration in, xxvii–xxviii; philosophy in, 46–47; political film, 47–53; popular cinema, xxv–xxvi; scholarship on, xvi, 207n1; social critiques in, 174, 180n12; stereotypes in, xviii; symbolism in, 10–11; technology in, xxvi–xxvii; television compared to, 124; theory, xi–xii, 92, 180n10; transnationalism for, xi, xiv, xxiv–xxv; vignettes in, 47–48; voyeurism in, 107–8, *107–8*. *See also specific topics*

poststructuralist theory, xii, xix
postwar art film, 14
prestige television, 123–24
privileged experiences, 96
promotions, 204n26
protagonists. *See specific films*
prototransnational film, 73–80, *74–75, 77–79*
psychoanalytical theory, xii–xiii, 110
Puna, Lali, 17
Putin, Vladimir, 68

Reagan, Ronald, 63
realism, xiii–xvii, 101. *See also* neorealism;
    postrealism
Red Brigades, The, 47, 57–58
redemption, 165
reflective nostalgia, 86–94, *87–89, 91*
relationships, 4–5, 39, 43, 111, 119–20
religion: in comedy, 203n29; in culture,
    80–82, 172; ethics of, 135; evangelization,
    131; globalization of, 124; God in, 148;
    humiliation and, 44; in narratives, 121–22;
    philosophy of, 75–76; politics of, 131–34, *133*;
    saintliness, 141–44, *144*; secularism, 125
remediation, 182n38
"Remegio," 20
Reservoir Dogs, 51–53, *54*, 56
Reverence to Rape (Haskell), xvii
Roma, 88, 105, 139–40
Roma, città aperta, 134, *134*
Rosi, Francesco, xv, 51
"Rossetto e cioccolatto," 27
Roth, Philip, 44–45, 195n68

Sabato (De Filippo), xv–xvi
Said, Edward, 98
saintliness, 141–44, *144*
Salinger, J. D., 132
Sarris, Andrew, xxi
satire, 89, 106, 182n51
satirical postrealism, 68
Scarface, 55–56
Scary World Theory, 17
scene framing, 9
scholarship, xvi, xxv–xxviii, 53, 120–21, 207n1
Schoonover, Karl, xiii
Schrader, Paul, 127, 204n12
Scola, Ettore, 101–2
scopophilic objectification, *108*, 108–9
Scorsese, Martin, xv, 51, 55, 156, 160–61, 197n26
screenplays, 69, 179n2, 186n10
secularism, 125
Seduction of Mimi, The, 140

self-discovery, 76–77, 124
sentimental politics, 136
Servillo, Toni, xxii, 3, 13–14
sexism, 100, 116. *See also* male gaze
Shakespeare, William, 41, 43, 61–62
Shining, The, 205n36
shot-reverse shots, 167–69, *168*
Sky TV, 126, 150
slow motion, 48–49, 86–87, 192n12, 207n23
slow motion footage, 37
Smith, Robert, 68
social critiques, 44; of art, 115–16; of
    communism, 89–90; in film, 174, 180n12;
    in *The Great Beauty*, 125; of history, 112; of
    Italy, 156–57; in *Loro*, 150–51; in *The Young
    Pope*, 172
socialism, 89–90
"Song for Athene," 129
Sontag, Susan, 180n12
Sorrentinian subject, the, 180n8, 182n47, 195n75;
    age for, *119*, 119–20; feminist theory and,
    109, 115; film theory and, xi–xii; in *The Great
    Beauty*, 101–5, *102–4*; identity of, xvii–xviii,
    122, 200n61; in illusionism, xiv–xv; in *Loro*,
    151–52; masculinity in, 2–3, 32–33; in *One
    Man Up*, 2–3; spectatorial identification of,
    xiii; in *This Must Be the Place*, 31–32
Sorrentino, Paolo, 13, 86, 106, 199n31; art film
    by, 15, 35–41, *36–37, 39–40*, 70; Bigazzi and,
    26, 37, 142, 186n6; on career, xi, xxiii–xxiv;
    casting by, 137; cinematic ethics of, 41–42;
    close ups by, 98–99; coincidences for, 12;
    for critics, 183n60, 183n63, 185n116; culture
    for, xv–xvi; on *Il Divo*, 181n37; female gaze
    for, 107; filmography of, xxi; homage by,
    41; imagery for, 182n59; intensified style of,
    xxvi–xxviii, 17–18; Marlow-Mann on, xiii,
    37; masculinity for, 109–10; melodrama
    for, xxii–xxiii; modernism for, 20; music
    for, 5–6; point of view for, 26–27; politics
    for, xxiii, xxviii; postmodernism for, 56; on
    promotions, 204n26; reputation of, xv, 52;
    scholarship on, xxv–xxvi; screenplays, 69;
    self-awareness of, 115–16; social critiques by,
    44; style of, 174–78; stylistic approach of, 100;
    transnational intermediality for, xxi–xxiii;
    transnationalism for, xxvii, 65–66; viewers for,
    185n109; women for, 201n6, 203n31. *See also
    specific films*; specific topics
spectacular death, 24–30, *27–29*
Spectacular Life of Giulio Andreotti, The, 52
spectatorial identification, xiii
Spinazzola, Vittorio, xxv

Directors' Cuts